CliffsTestPrep®

Praxis II®: Special Education
(0351, 0352, 0690, 0371, 0381, 0321)

by

Judy L. Paris, M.Ed.

WILEY

Wiley Publishing, Inc.

About the Author

For more than 35 years, Judy Paris has been professionally involved in the field of education as a teacher, a special education director, a superintendent, a consultant, an author, and a mentor and currently serves as adjunct faculty at several universities. She holds degrees/certifications in special education, early childhood education, elementary education, and educational leadership/administration. It is because of her desire for all children to be allowed to learn through discovery, to be offered a variety of educational opportunities, and to experience the world around that has led to her newest endeavor of developing a children's museum for her community.

Author's Acknowledgments

The development of this book was touched by many people, and it is because of their support and love that it is now completed. Thanks to my husband, John, my parents, Shirley and Ellsworth, and my children, Jocelyn and Justin, for their encouragement to continue my beloved work. Gratitude to my dear friends, Dale, Cindy, Maggie, and Paula, who listened and laughed when deadlines approached. A special acknowledgment to my daughter-in-law, Andrea, for her critique and tech edit support. Thanks also to Kelly Henthorne, for her detailed review and guide preparation, and to Greg Tubach, for his belief in me and his support of this project. You all enrich my life's journey!

Publisher's Acknowledgments

Editorial

Project Editor: Kelly D. Henthorne

Acquisitions Editor: Greg Tubach

Composition

Proofreader: Lisa Stiers

Wiley Publishing, Inc. Composition Services

CliffsTestPrep® Praxis II®: Special Education (0351, 0352, 0690, 0371, 0381, 0321)

Published by:
Wiley Publishing, Inc.
111 River Street
Hoboken, NJ 07030-5774
www.wiley.com

Copyright © 2008 Wiley, Hoboken, NJ

Published by Wiley, Hoboken, NJ
Published simultaneously in Canada

Library of Congress Cataloging-in-Publication data is available upon request.

ISBN: 978-0-470-23842-4

WILEY

Teaching Students with Behavioral Disorders/Emotional Disturbance (0371)

PART II: PRACTICE TESTS WITH ANSWER EXPLANATIONS

Introduction

Welcome! You are in the final chapter of an exciting career adventure. Entering the field of education as a professional, who works with students with special needs, is both satisfying and gratifying. It takes a tremendous amount of energy and a great amount of knowledge about special education to be the very best teacher for your students.

Every child you meet will truly be an individual with unique needs and personal desires. Remember to address each child with respect, integrity, and kindness, as no child with a disability chooses this particular life path. When a child enters school for the very first time or even attends on the first school day of each successive year, she may appear with both apprehension and excitement. It will be because of you that the child becomes comfortable in her environment, absorbs the concepts of the curriculum, and is eager to continue learning.

If you are a lifelong learner, your joy of gained knowledge will be reflected on your students. You should continue to learn all you can about the on-going changes in education, particularly special education and your specialty area. You may be an agent of change for your students as you apply knowledge of these areas to classroom management, behavior interventions, curriculum design, and learning strategies. Join professional organizations, read the research studies, take additional courses, attend professional workshops, and subscribe to professional journals. Find a trusted mentor who may help guide you and remain a constant contact in your professional life. All of these strategies will give you the motivation and desire to continue to be an effective educator for your students.

Good luck on the Praxis II exam(s) and best wishes for a fabulous journey in education!

Getting Started

The time has arrived to show what you know! The work you have done in your teacher preparation program culminates in taking an exam in your specialty area and perhaps a core knowledge exam. It may be that you have been teaching and are now moving to another state, so the background and experience you have gained will be most useful in studying for the exam. Whether you are a recent college graduate or an experienced teacher, you are now faced with taking the Praxis II exam and passing it.

This guide will help you. Use the study information and the practice exams provided to help check your knowledge level of the subject areas. You should also count on using your college texts, Internet research and websites, the library, and your school resources. You should become well prepared to pass the exam(s) you need and be on your way to finalizing the certification or licensure for your state.

The practice exams should give you an idea of what to expect when you take one of the Praxis II exams. Notice the format and the types of questions, as well as the speed with which you answer each question. This will help you plan pacing for the actual exam. (However, remember that the content and the questions of the practice exam and the actual exam may differ in complexity.) After you complete the practice exam, check your score and use the explanations of the answers for further study on the specific topics.

A second Praxis II exam, titled Education of Exceptional Students: Core Content Knowledge (0353), is also available and required for certification in some states. The study guide information for that exam may be found in another book developed by the same author and published by Wiley called *CliffsTestPrep Praxis II: Exceptional Students (0353, 0382, 0542, 0544)*.

Note: There is limited information included in this study guide about students who are identified as deaf or blind since those types of disabilities are generally serviced by specialized professionals, and these are not topics included on the exam. Some information is included as background information since all special education professionals are in contact with students who have these conditions and may need to serve students with multiple disabilities.

Format of the Exam

Each Praxis II exam identified in this guide is constructed to assess your general knowledge base regarding special education and some specialty area in the special education field. You may be required to take more than one Special Education Praxis II exam, depending on the requirements for certification or licensure in your state. Your ability to pass these exams is based on the wisdom you have gained in your coursework and from the experience obtained from teaching, student teaching, or internships.

Each of the special education exams selected for study in this guide differs slightly in composition. Each exam is comprised of a set of multiple-choice questions; however, the number of questions varies. Some of the exams include multiple-choice questions that refer to a case study. All of the questions in the exams are based on a teaching situation, a definition, or a concept that relates to special education or a specialty area.

There are six special education topics included in this study guide, each with an accompanying practice exam. The specific code and title for each exam are listed here.

#0351	Special Education: Knowledge-Based Core Principles	
#0352	Special Education: Application of Core Principles across Categories of Disability	
#0690	Special Education: Preschool/Early Childhood	
#0371	Special Education: Teaching Students with Behavioral Disorders/Emotional Disturbance	
#0381	Special Education: Teaching Students with Learning Disabilities	
#0321	Special Education: Teaching Students with Mental Retardation	

Multiple-Choice Questions

These questions include a statement (*stem*) and four answer choices. The stem may be in a *question*, a *fill-in the blank*, or a *complete the statement* format. The four answer choices are identified by using the "A," "B," "C," "D" selections with only one choice being the correct answer (*key*). The other three possibilities (*distractors*) may be closely related to the correct answer, but you must be prepared to select the best possible answer. The questions are not designed to trick you, but instead to test your true knowledge of the subject. The questions are factually written with all four choices most likely connected in some way to the stem. So, think carefully when you make your final answer selections.

There are also five sample multiple choice questions at the beginning of each special education topic section in this guide. These sample questions are provided as an introduction to the topic area and as a preview of your knowledge of each topic. Choose the most reasonable, but not necessarily the most obvious, answer. Remember that some answers may fit in certain situations but only one reveals the right answer.

Although many philosophical views exist in the field of special education, the facts remain the same, as based on federal laws, developmental stages, and best practices. Remember that the exam questions will be focused on both fact and the most appropriate practices. Understand that the exam questions may not reflect your personal philosophy so contemplate the best selection that reflects national standards.

When in doubt, ask yourself:

- How would the educators I know answer these questions having been in the field?
- What have I gained from my studies to help me logically come to a conclusion?
- Is this answer what I think it should be or what is required and recommended?

Multiple-Choice Strategy

The discrete multiple choice questions that are included on these exams require that you have strong reading skills and that you are knowledgeable about the content areas being tested. These questions reflect the *best practices* and *best answers* to educational situations.

When you are ready to take an exam, read each of the multiple-choice questions more than once to better examine the primary idea. Read the four choices and think about each of those possible answers. You know that only one of the choices is correct based on the information given, but each of the other possibilities may have relevance. After reading the question and considering the four possible answers, choose the most appropriate answer.

The several types of multiple-choice formats are explained more fully here.

- **Complete the Statement:** This type will offer information and a partial sentence that must be finished using one of the presented options. Select the one that best completes the sentence using the facts and data you know about special education.

- **Which of the Following:** This type asks a short question that must be answered by selecting one of the four options. It is a frequently used question type on multiple-choice exams. Read the question carefully and think about all of the options, choosing the one that BEST suits the question posed.

- **Least/Not/Except:** This type of question often requires that you select an answer that is not correct, or less likely to be correct. These questions place a negative slant on the outcome of your answer, so beware of selecting the appropriate response. You may need to rephrase the question in a positive way in order to correctly select the answer. An example may read: "Which of the following is NOT included on a transition plan for older students?" This type of question is included in the Praxis exams, but is not included here on the practice exams, for fear that you may study incorrect information in preparing for the actual exam.

- **Case Histories:** In the practice test and on the actual exam, some of the multiple-choice questions are based on a 500 word (or more) case history that presents an actual teaching situation. Think about how you would answer these questions based on the case and what you would do in that circumstance. Read each case carefully and consider all of the information when you answer the related questions.

Time Frame

The amount of time allowed for each Praxis II exam is based on the specific format of the test. In the six exams listed in this book, you are allotted 1 hour to answer between 50 and 60 multiple-choice questions and 2 hours to answer 110 multiple-choice questions.

You will need to pace yourself on the actual exam, so remember to think about your time as you work on the sample questions and take the practice exams. When you finally take the actual Praxis II exams, you will need time to read each question, to consider each answer, and then to review all of the final answers before submitting the test for a score.

Even if you are unsure of the correct response for a multiple choice question, answer every one on the exam. No penalty is assessed for guessing an answer on the exam. Think about all the possibilities and do your best to select the most appropriate response.

The specific exams, the number of questions, and the time limits are listed here.

Knowledge-Based Core Principles	60 Questions	1 hour
Application of Core Principles across Categories of Disabilities	50 Questions	1 hour
Preschool/Early Childhood	110 Questions	2 hours
Teaching Students with Behavioral Disorders/Emotional Disturbance	50 Questions	1 hour
Teaching Students with Learning Disabilities	50 Questions	1 hour
Teaching Students with Mental Retardation	50 Questions	1 hour

Content of the Exam

Each of the specific subject area tests in this guide is comprised of *content categories*. The actual Praxis II exams assess your understanding of the concepts related to these content areas.

Review the general list here for each test that includes each of the broad topics, the number of questions, and the percentage of your score for the exam(s) you will be taking.

- Special Education: Knowledge-Based Core Principles
  - Understanding Exceptionalities   15   25%
  - Legal and Societal Issues   8   13%
  - Delivery of Services to Students with Disabilities   37   62%

- Special Education: Application of Core Principles across Categories of Disability
  - Curriculum   10   20%
  - Instruction   10   20%
  - Assessment   10   20%
  - Managing the Learning Environment   10   20%
  - Professional Roles/Issues/Literature   10   20%

Note: This exam may include questions related to case studies.

- Special Education: Preschool/Early Childhood
  - Human Growth and Development   16   15%
  - Knowledge of Disabling Conditions   12   11%
  - Evaluation, Assessment, Eligibility Criteria   16   15%
  - Planning and Service Delivery   17   15%
  - Family and Community Aspects   21   19%
  - Professional Practice   28   25%

- Special Education: Teaching Students with Behavioral Disorders/Emotional Disturbance
  - Factors Other than Direct Instruction that Influence the Education
    of Students with BD/ED   10   20%
  - Delivery of Services to Students with BD/ED   40   80%

Note: This exam may include questions related to case studies.

- Special Education: Teaching Students with Learning Disabilities
  - Factors Other than Direct Instruction that Influence the Education
    of Students with LD   10   20%
  - Delivery of Services   15   30%
  - Curriculum and Instruction   25   50%

Note: This exam may include questions related to case studies.

- Special Education: Teaching Students with Mental Retardation
  - Factors Other than Direct Instruction that Influence the Education
    of Students with MR   11   23%
  - Delivery of Services to Students with MR   39   77%

Note: This exam may include questions related to case studies.

Frequently Asked Questions

There are usually questions that examinees wish to ask prior to taking a Praxis II exam. Hopefully, the most pressing questions are answered here. If assistance is needed, contact the Educational Testing Services at www.ets.org/praxis or call 800-772-9476.

Q: What is a Praxis II exam for Special Education?

A: The Praxis II exam(s) has been developed by the Educational Testing Service (ETS) to measure an individual's knowledge in specific special education subjects and in general teaching practices that relate specifically to children with disabilities. Many states require these examinations as part of the certification or licensure process. Some professional organizations also require the completion of a Praxis exam for membership.

Q: How should I register for the exam(s)?

A: Most people find that registering online is quick and easy. Contact the Educational Testing Services on the website or at the telephone number listed previously. Registration may be completed at any time prior to taking the test. It is recommended that registration be completed 1–3 months ahead of the testing date.

Q: What if I miss the registration for the test date I want?

A: Late registration is allowed, but hurry to get the correct information and a place at the test location. A fee may be assessed for late registrations. Find out the specifics about late registrations on the ETS website.

Q: Can the registration date be changed if needed?

A: It has been allowed in the past through ETS, but be sure to contact them as soon as you think you have a conflict or problem. They should be able to help you with scheduling issues or changes to your registration. A fee may be charged for any changes.

Q: Which states require the various special education Praxis II exams for certification?

A: Some states use their own certification tests created in the state or by a test development company and do not require the use of the Praxis II exams. You will need to contact your specific state department of education to find out which exams are required in your state or the state to which you are moving. You should also ask about the passing score, as the acceptable scores differ in each state. If you have already taken the exam in one state and you are moving to another, ask whether your score will be accepted. Most states will allow the transfer of a score as long as you meet the passing score in each state and did not take the exam too many years ago.

On the ETS website, (www.ets.org/praxis/states) you can access each state's requirements by clicking on the name of the state. However, it is highly recommended that you speak with someone at your state department of education, since regulations change sometimes before websites do.

Q: Which exam(s) should I plan to take?

A: Each state that mandates the completion and passing score on Praxis II exams for special education certification or licensure differs in the particular test that is required. You should research the test requirements for teacher certification/licensure by contacting the department of education in your state. The teacher certification office should have the information you need to select the correct exam or a combination of exams.

Q: What is considered a passing score for teacher certification?

A: The teacher certification office at the department of education in your state should provide you with the score(s) considered as acceptable for teacher certification. Contact this office in your state to find out which score you should aim for.

Q: When can I expect to receive my score?

A: The ETS attempts a quick return of your score(s), so you may expect your score to be delivered in four to six weeks, pending no major holidays. A list of dates is available on the ETS website, as well as an informational guide to interpret your score.

Q: Are accommodations permissible for an individual with a disability?

A: Yes. Individuals may apply for accommodations if they have a disability or if the primary language is not English. Information on accommodations is available in the Praxis II test registration booklet or on the website.

Q: What should I plan to bring to the exam site on the date of the test?

A: You will need to consider the following items:

- Identification that includes your name, a photo, and signature
- An alternative identification that includes the same (optional but recommended)
- Admission ticket (proof of registration)
- Several pencils (#2) and an eraser
- Watch (optional but recommended)
- Extra clothing (optional but recommended, as the temperature in the rooms varies)

Q: How can I best prepare to take the Praxis II exam(s)?

A: The use of this study guide is a great way to improve your chances of passing the Praxis II exam(s). Understanding the test format, taking the practice exams, and reviewing the contents of the study guide should reinforce your knowledge base. Use the websites in the Resource sections to seek additional study information in those areas where you need to gain further guidance.

Suggestions for Using This Study Guide

Cliffs TestPrep Praxis II: Special Education includes several test preparation supports to guide you through your study period.

1. **Specific Special Education Topic Sections**
   A. **Introduction Sections:** Included for each special education topic exam are general broadly stated questions about the subject and samples of test questions. Some may include a case history and associated *multiple-choice questions* or *constructed-response questions.*
   B. **Content Area Information:** This is a comprehensive section to be used for study purposes according to the content categories described on the exam. The headings should guide you in selecting topics needing review or additional study.
2. **Final Thoughts and Tips:** Test-taking strategies and techniques are provided on how to answer the various types of questions that may include multiple-choice and constructed-response questions. Tips for test preparation to achieve exam success are also available.
3. **Practice Exams:** A sample full-length test is provided for each of the six separate special education topics. These tests are a sample of the content and format of the actual Praxis II exam questions.
4. **Sample Test Answers:** Not only are answers clearly stated, but an explanation is provided to each of the questions to help you in your further studies.
5. **Resources:** A list of specific websites, categorized by subject areas, is found in an appendix at the end of this book and includes information pertinent to all six exams.

PART I

REVIEW OF SPECIFIC SPECIAL EDUCATION TEST SECTIONS

Knowledge-Based Core Principles (0351)

Application of Core Principles Across Categories of Disability (0352)

Preschool/Early Childhood (0690)

Teaching Students with Behavioral Disorders/Emotional Disturbance (0371)

Teaching Students with Learning Disabilities (0381)

Teaching Students with Mental Retardation (0321)

Introduction

Throughout the history of the special education movement, educational professionals have observed a multitude of changes due to political influences, societal attitudes, medical technologies and advancements, instructional design improvements, and changes in students themselves. The laws and litigation have shaped how services are delivered to students with disabilities. According to the current federal special education laws, school programs must be provided to accommodate the individual needs of students from ages 3 through 21 while younger children (0–3 years) may receive services through state programs.

Some historical cases in the special education movement that affected the services for students with disabilities and were turning points for the creation of federal laws are listed here. Some cases are explained in more detail along with additional cases in the "Legal and Societal Issues" section.

1896	Plessy v. Ferguson	Separate-but-equal legal segregation
1954	Brown v. Board of Education KS	Integration of students required; Segregated schools are unequal
1972	PARC v. Commonwealth of Penn.	FAPE (Free Appropriate Public Education) is required
1972	Mills v. Board of Education	Must provide services regardless of district's ability to pay
1989	Danny R v. State Board of Ed	LRE-FAPE Right to inclusion to maximum extent possible

Professionals believe the primary focus for persons with disabilities is to reach attainable, realistic, and individualized goals to become successful and productive citizens. Many individuals with disabilities endure complications and barriers, but educators must support their efforts and guide them toward successful accomplishments. Take part in the efforts of your school, community, and state to enhance the education and productivity of individuals with disabilities.

During your university studies and work in this field, you may have discovered that information about individuals with disabilities is enormously complex. You may be aware of the various influences of all disabilities, the varieties of conceptual approaches, and the variations in curriculum design and instructional strategies that focus on these students. This very general information about special education is covered under the federal law IDEIA (Individuals with Disabilities Education Improvement Act–2004, formerly IDEA). These are also the areas that are critical for your preparation to complete the Special Education Praxis II exam.

Prior to taking the exam, you should review the basic concepts about disabilities: the characteristics, the causes, the prevalence, the various definitions, the facts about assessments, the placement steps, and the program issues, as well as curriculum and instruction information. As you peruse the study guide materials, notice they are not comprehensive but rather presented in summation format. If you need information not available in this guide, refer to your college texts, search the Internet, or speak with practicing educators. Websites related to special education are provided in the "Resources" section.

This Special Education Knowledge-Based Core Principles Praxis II exam (0351) is a knowledge-based assessment prepared for individuals who plan to teach students with disabilities in grades preschool though 12. There are 60 multiple-choice questions included, and the time allowed for examinees is one hour. The four content categories acknowledged in this assessment include Understanding Exceptionalities (15 questions, 25%), Legal and Societal Issues (8 questions, 13%), and Delivery of Services to Students with Disabilities (37 questions, 62%).

Your role as a special education professional and your participation in special education programs will involve collaborations with other professionals, support to families, implementation of student programs, being a student advocate, and participation in professional development activities. This is a serious but enjoyable career choice that may offer you many moments of pleasure as you observe and support students with disabilities.

Content Clusters

As you prepare for the Praxis II exam on Special Education Knowledge-Based Core Principles, use the following questions to determine the areas you may need to study further. Although these questions do not reflect the type found on the actual exam, they provide the opportunity to examine your overall broad knowledge of the subject. Read each question and compose an answer that covers the important information. Write these answers on a separate sheet to use during your studies. If you read a question you are unsure of, identify that topic as an area for more intense study.

These questions are based on the content categories and should help you prepare to take the exam.

1. Identify the components of at least four theories related to the principles of human development and learning.

2. List the categories of disabilities under special education according to the federal law and explain the basic premises of each disability's identifying definition.

3. Explain the basic principles of each of the following federal laws: IDEA-2004 (IDEIA), Section 504, ADA (Americans with Disabilities Act), NCLB (No Child Left Behind), and FERPA (Family Education Rights and Privacy Act).

4. Define the conceptual approaches that pertain to the delivery of services for students with disabilities that may include: psychodynamic, behavioral, cognitive, sociological, and others important to special education services.

5. State the steps in the assessment process, identify some of the methods, and list common measurement tools used for students with disabilities.

6. Describe the issues related to families of children with disabilities that include advocacy, program participation, transition services, and support systems.

7. Provide examples of various behavioral interventions used with students who are identified in each of the disability categories.

8. Analyze the various aspects (steps) in the placement process, including a description of the continuum of services.

9. Clarify the diverse benefits of early intervention and early childhood programs for children with disabilities and the differences between Part B and Part C of the general special education law (IDEA-2004 or IDEIA).

10. Reveal the various teaching strategies, methods, and activities best suited for the different disability groups.

Preview Questions

This section provides you with five multiple-choice questions that pertain to many areas of special education. Use this section to self-assess your recall of knowledge and to envision the types of questions that are included on this Praxis II exam. The answers to these questions will be found interspersed in the study guide materials that follow.

The questions and answers have been developed based on federal law and professional practices for students with disabilities in school settings. Some practices are different across the states, so do consider the answers you select based on the terminology, policies, best practices, and the law according to IDEIA.

1. The influential case of *Brown v. Board of Education* ended the practices of

   A. residential institutions.
   B. separate but equal schools.
   C. expulsions related to discipline.
   D. accommodations on assessments.

2. An organization that is highly recommended for practicing educators in the field of special education is

   A. APA.
   B. CEC.
   C. ASHA.
   D. AAMR.

3. All children with disabilities are entitled to _____ according to federal law.

   A. related services
   B. clinical therapy
   C. private school tutoring
   D. nutritional interventions

4. When team members conduct separate assessments and share results through communication and collaboration, and then develop a plan for interventions, this is called a(an) _____ team.

   A. intradisciplinary team
   B. interdisciplinary team
   C. transdisciplinary team
   D. multidisciplinary team

5. The first model to consider in the *least restrictive environment* provision is

   A. some therapy.
   B. the resource room.
   C. the residential facility.
   D. the general education class.

The correct answers are

1. **B.** The *Brown v. Board of Education* case occurred during the civil rights movement and caused schools to integrate children rather than separate them.

2. **B.** The (CEC) Council for Exceptional Children is a national organization for professionals that provides information and support regarding children with disabilities.

3. **A.** Related services is one of the components allowed on an IEP for children with disabilities.

4. **B.** An interdisciplinary team promotes sharing information about children with disabilities so team members may collaborate and develop a student education plan together.

5. **D.** The general education class is considered the first in a list of least restrictive environments under federal law and promoted for inclusion.

Study Information

The topic of *special education* is broad and comprehensive. Prior to taking the exam, it is important to review the general principles, theories, guidelines, and practices that pertain to the core knowledge of all disabilities as the programs and services for students with disabilities are mandated under federal law, IDEIA. In addition, the information included in this study guide in the "Preschool/Early Childhood" and "Application of Core Principles across Categories of Disability" sections will aid in your studies for the core knowledge exam.

Special Education is a constantly changing field of professional practices, trends, issues, and research. Studying these topics for the core knowledge exam will help you get started in the continuous study of the field. Even though current and contemporary practices are defined here, those may change in a couple of years; this should not diminish your interest and dedication to the students who will benefit from your support and your perseverance.

The population of students with disabilities is ever changing. Due to the number of birth defects, genetic complications, and childhood accidents, exactly how many students with disabilities are served varies from year to year. All of the categories of special education show increases and varying numbers from time to time. Some of the issues related to the increased numbers include the identification definition for students, the range of culturally and linguistically diverse students, the movement of students across districts, and the manner in which states promote their programming.

Thirteen unique categories of special education are recognized under federal law; however, individual states may label students differently. When you are ready to teach in your state, check with your school district or state department of education on the proper terminology used for students with specific disabilities, remembering that for this exam you will need to follow the required federal terms.

Be aware of the characteristics of various disabilities and the problems that individuals face. Learn the strategies and methods that are research-based and proven effective as you seek to understand the interventions that support academic achievement. An enormous variety of programs are offered for students with disabilities across the states, but all students with disabilities need the individualized instruction and interventions that will support them throughout their lifetimes.

As you enter this field, be aware of the professional status you bring to teaching. You have arrived at this point due to your interest, your commitment, your special training, and your studies. Continue to work toward competence in the field and strive to be more effective in your career each day.

Understanding Exceptionalities

Educators working with students who have disabilities should be very familiar with the typical patterns of development in all domains of learning, as well as the various kinds of disabling conditions. Learning about the typical stages of growth and development will help you understand the delays that children with disabilities exhibit. Knowing more about the different disabilities will support you when dealing with student issues in the classroom. Download a copy of a growth and development chart from the Internet or obtain one at the local health department.

Theories and Principles of Human Development and Learning

Theories about how people develop and learn abound, and you probably studied this information in your university courses. You may still have textbooks that reflect the detailed information you may want to study. Check the Internet for additional articles, theories, and developmental charts.

Following is a brief description of each area of development; however, for further information, turn to the Human Development Section of the "Preschool/Early Childhood" portion of this study guide.

Social-Emotional Development

The social-emotional area of development is key for students to gain a sense of self. They can build upon their self-concept, self-esteem, self-confidence, and self-competence if they have strong skills in this area. A child's environment has great impact on this area of development, and parents, gender, siblings, and a child's temperament are all factors in how a student will develop in this domain. Communication, language, and cognition are also important to the proper growth of this area. Social-emotional development has been influenced by the work of Maslow, Skinner, Erikson, Gardner, and Freud.

Language Development

Communication, language, speech, and literacy are all prime components for success in academic areas. Children must not only learn the words, structures, and patterns of language, but make the connections, use the gestures, observe the body movements, and figure out the facial expressions that are critical to understanding. Language affects reading, listening, writing, all academic areas, and social relationships. Bilingual and second language learners have other issues that cause lags in this developmental area.

Cognitive Development

Several theories of cognition have influenced thoughts about human development of this domain: Behavioral, cognitive, socio-cultural, and the constructionist theories all have early beginnings in education. The names Piaget, Skinner, Vygotsky, and Gardner are well-known as people who have studied and presented ideas about how people learn.

The cognitive area is the most important area of development as it impacts all domains. This area of mental skill development focuses on thinking and reasoning with specific clusters of mental skills that are important to learning.

Physical Development

Physical development is the first area of growth and learning that a child experiences. It includes skills related to gross motor, fine motor, sensory-integration, and perceptual motor development. The theories that impact this area are those of Gesell, Piaget, Ayres, and Kephart.

Characteristics of Students with Disabilities

This section briefly explains the basic and stereotypical characteristics of each disability category. Know that students labeled in these categories exhibit their own very special qualities and unique characteristics.

- **Medical/Physical:** Includes problems related to diseases, illnesses, trauma, genetics, fine and gross motor, sensory input, and sensory perception.
- **Educational:** Includes cognitive and metacognitive deficits, low academic achievement, poor memory, attention problems, hyperactivity, and perceptual disorders.
- **Social:** Includes affective behaviors, poor social skills, poor self-concept, poor motivation, and debilitating mood states.
- **Psychological:** Includes various behaviors, adaptive behavior deficits, disruptive behaviors, and withdrawal issues.

Types of Disabilities

The following is a list of the major disability categories:

Autism: Communication and language deficits, impaired social relationships, exhibiting difficult behaviors, and possible demonstration of limited intellectual functioning with atypical reactions to sensory stimuli

Behavioral Disorders/Emotional Disturbance: Exhibit inappropriate internalizing and externalizing behaviors, atypical emotions, disruptive behaviors, and lack skills for developing positive relationships

Hearing Impairment: Difficulties processing linguistic information and using spoken language to communicate, problems with social relationships, deficits in emotional maturity, and delays in academics

Mental Retardation: Deficits in adaptive behaviors, problems with learning, difficulties with memory, issues with problem solving, and delays in social skills

Orthopedic Impairment: Physical problems such as cerebral palsy, muscular dystrophy, and spina bifida, possibly requiring adaptations with devices and equipment

Other Health Impairment: Limited strength, vitality, and alertness with medical problems such as diabetes, epilepsy, attention deficits, and disease

Specific Learning Disability: Demonstrate difficulties with listening, reasoning, memory, attention, social skills, perception, and processing information and may emerge with problems in reading, written language, math, and behavior (Achievement is not commensurate with their abilities.)

Speech/Language Impairment: Difficulty using expressive and receptive language; delays in pragmatics; and problems with fluency, voice, and articulation

Traumatic Brain Injury: Difficulties in the areas of cognition, memory, attention, judgment, and problem solving, as well as physical and sensory changes, social, behavioral, or emotional problems

Visual Impairment: Problems with developing language concepts, impaired motor development and mobility, and lack of social adjustment skills and relationship interactions

Basic Concepts

Children who differ from the norm, physically, intellectually, or behaviorally, may be eligible for services under a category identified in special education. Although some professionals believe that labeling a child is not generally a positive act, it becomes a necessary task in order for the student to obtain the appropriate services and for funding to flow into the schools supporting the special education programs.

Children identified collectively in a category share certain characteristics, patterns in learning, and types of behavior. Children are considered disabled and eligible for services only if the exhibited problem(s) have a major impact on learning, and special education is necessary to benefit from an education. Each category under federal law is accompanied by a definition to more clearly describe the children who may be identified.

Definitions and Categories

In spite of the debates about labels or categories for children, it is the comprehensive assessment process that determines the label and eligibility for services. Although the federal special education law creates the general categories, each state may develop its own labels to suit the definitions of the disabilities.

The 13 specific federal categories for students ages 3 through 21 years to receive special education services are

- Autism
- Deaf-Blindness
- Developmental Delay
- Behavioral Disorders/Emotional Disturbance
- Hearing Impairment
- Mental Retardation
- Multiple Disabilities
- Orthopedic Impairment
- Other Health Impairment
- Specific Learning Disability
- Speech/Language Impairment
- Traumatic Brain Injury
- Visual Impairment

The definitions for each category found in federal law are summarized here.

Autism: A syndrome related to neurological function that appears through deficits in social interactions, communications, and patterns of behavior. Autism is one of the disorders associated with pervasive developmental disorder (PDD), now more currently referred to as autism spectrum disorders (ASD). The various disorders in this group are differentiated by the age of onset and severity of symptoms.

Behavioral Disorders/Emotional Disturbance: Conditions that exhibit two or more of the following: an inability to learn, an inability to maintain relationships, inappropriate behaviors, pervasive moods, or a tendency to develop physical symptoms or fears.

Deaf-Blindness: The combination of both auditory and visual disabilities that cause severe communication and other developmental and learning needs such that the individual cannot be appropriately educated in special education programs solely for children with hearing impairments, visual impairments, or severe disabilities without supplementary assistance.

Developmental Delay: Indicates a lack of age-appropriate skills in one or more of the following domains: cognitive, language, motor, self-help adaptive, and social-emotional. This category is generally used for children ages 3 through 5, but is allowed under federal law for students up to age 8.

Hearing Impairment: Suggests a hearing loss that adversely affects the educational performance and makes the child eligible for special education (includes deaf and hard of hearing).

Mental Retardation: Significantly subaverage general intellectual functioning that exists concurrently with deficits in adaptive behavior and manifests itself in the developmental period that adversely affects a child's educational performance.

Multiple Disabilities: A combination of concomitant impairments (mental retardation–vision impairment, mental retardation–physical impairment, and so on) that causes severe educational conditions that cannot be accommodated in special education programs for only one disability.

Orthopedic Impairment: A physical impairment that adversely affects educational performance. These impairments may be caused by genetic anomalies, disease, or other causes.

Other Health Impairment: Health impairments may be related to diseases or health conditions that prevent a child from participating in educational activities. If a child is found to have limited strength, vitality, or alertness due to a chronic or acute health problem, which adversely affects the child's educational performance, then the child is considered OHI. Some states provide services to students with ADD or ADHD under this category.

Specific Learning Disability: A disorder in one or more of the basic psychological processes involved in understanding or in using language and may manifest itself in an imperfect ability to listen, think, speak, read, write, spell, or do math.

Speech/Language Impairment: Communication disorders that affect educational performance in an adverse manner that may include stuttering, impaired articulation, language impairments, or voice impairments.

Traumatic Brain Injury: This category includes children who have an acquired injury to the brain caused by external physical force that results in total or partial functional disability or psychosocial impairments and adversely affects the child's educational performance. It does not include brain injuries that are congenital, generative, or birth induced.

Visual Impairment: This category includes any impairment of vision that even with correction adversely affects a child's educational performance. This includes a wide range of vision impairments: totally blind, functionally blind, and low vision issues.

Causation and Prevention

Although there are literally thousands of known causes for disability-related conditions, sometimes for a specific child the cause can be considered *unknown*. Among the known causes for disabilities, some may influence the development of several different types of disabilities, such as an illness that can create problems with hearing, seeing, thinking, and walking. Due to the significant number of causes, a summary of the more commonly known causes related to each specific disability is provided.

Autism: Not a specific known cause, but believed to be related to neurobiological conditions, abnormal brain development, genetics, multiple biological causes, and environmental factors.

Behavioral Disorders/Emotional Disturbance: Two major areas may contribute to these disorders: biological factors (brain disorders, genetics, temperament) and environmental factors (home, community, school).

Hearing Impairment: Many causes that include genetic factors, illness, prematurity, diseases, and noise-induced complications.

Mental Retardation: Many causes are related to this condition, and they are classified as either biomedical, environmental, or unknown. These causes result from factors that occur in one of three stages: prenatal, perinatal, or postnatal.

Orthopedic Impairment: Primarily related to illness, disease, trauma, accident, or injury.

Other Health Impairment: Primarily related to illness, disease, trauma, accident, or injury.

Specific Learning Disability: Many times, the cause is unknown; however, the four most prevalent known causes are brain damage, heredity, biochemical imbalance, and environmental.

Speech/Language Impairment: Many possible causes, most likely attributed to damage, or dysfunction of a specific part of the body, environmental factors, cognitive impairments, hearing loss, brain injury, or diseases.

Traumatic Brain Injury: Primarily related to illness, disease, trauma, accident, or injury.

Visual Impairment: Damage or changes in the optical, muscular, or nervous system that may be from diseases, trauma, malnutrition, or genetics.

Although some disabilities appear from unknown causes and some are lifelong problems, some of the disabilities inflicted upon children could be prevented by proper and early medical care, prenatal care, appropriate mother and child nutrition, genetic counseling, PKU (phenylketonuria) testing, amniocentesis, limit toxic exposure, environmental improvements, early intervention programs, parent training, and vaccinations and immunizations.

Behaviors

The behaviors children exhibit are unlimited, and the methods used to manage them can be complex. The types of behaviors demonstrated might be related to a specific disability, and methods common to that group of children may be helpful.

Helpful terms:

- **duration:** a measure of the length of time a student engages in a particular behavior
- **degree of severity:** a measure of how problematic or complicated a particular behavior is
- **extinction:** when a reinforcement for a previously reinforced behavior is withheld, so the behavior will decrease until it no longer exists
- **frequency:** the amount of time (how often) that a behavior reoccurs
- **intensity:** the degree to which a behavior is repeated
- **maintenance:** the extent that a previously learned behavior continues once the intervention to support it has been ended

Legal and Societal Issues

Great influences on the programs for students with disabilities come from federal and state laws as well as litigation on behalf of individuals with disabilities. Laws and regulations may be changed when decisions are handed down from these legal cases. It is the responsibility of educators to be knowledgeable about the changes made to improve situations and programs for those with disabilities.

Federal Laws

The impetus for the creation of special education laws that protect individuals with disabilities began during the civil rights movement of the 1960s. In 1954, the *Brown v. Board of Education* case based on the segregation of students according to race went before the Supreme Court, who ordered that education must be on equal terms for all children.

The result of this decision caused a movement in the education field that has been unequaled, and eventually children with disabilities gained the right to a free and appropriate public education.

Historically, many believe that the passage of the special education law, The Education for All Handicapped Children Act (EAHCA, also EHA), in 1975 (PL94–142) is "landmark legislation" and marked a tremendous change in how the needs of students with disabilities were addressed across the country. Since this date, the law has been amended and reauthorized five times.

1. 1983–Amendments to the Education of the Handicapped Act
2. 1986–Education for the Handicapped Act Amendments
3. 1990–Individuals with Disabilities Education Act Amendments (PL101–476)
4. 1997–Individuals with Disabilities Education Act (IDEA) (PL105–17)
5. 2004–Individuals with Disabilities Education Improvement Act (IDEIA), known as IDEA–2004 (PL108–446)

These changes did not come easily but were based on the collaborative efforts of professionals, parents, politicians, and community members. The federal special education law provided educational rights to children with disabilities and their parents in accessing services in schools across the country. States still individually interpret the law, but must comply with the basic provisions.

IDEIA

The purpose of IDEIA (formerly IDEA) is identified in four key statements:

1. To ensure all children with disabilities are guaranteed a free and appropriate public education (FAPE)
2. To assist States in establishing early intervention services for infants and toddlers with disabilities
3. To ensure that educators and parents have the necessary tools to improve the education for children with disabilities
4. To assess the effectiveness of the education for children with disabilities

IDEIA extends the right to an education for all students with disabilities in the public school system. There are six major principles:

1. Zero reject (Child Find system): No child with a disability may be excluded from a public education.
2. Protection in the evaluation process: Nondiscriminatory identification and evaluation must be conducted, which includes the procedures and the tools.
3. Free Appropriate Public Education (FAPE): Education of students with disabilities must be at the public expense based on the development of an IEP (Individualized Education Program) to include related services.
4. Least Restrictive Environment (LRE): Children with disabilities must be educated with nondisabled children to the maximum extent appropriate, and a continuum of placement services must be imposed.
5. Due Process Procedures (Procedural Safeguards): Required parent and student rights regarding assessment, placement, and service implementation of education program.
6. Parent and Student Participation and Shared Decision-Making: Parents and students (as appropriate) must be included in the special education process.

Other provisions stressed for students with disabilities include the following:

- Extension of services to children age 5 and under
- Access and participation in the general education curriculum
- Participation in and accommodations for district and statewide high stakes tests
- Related services and Assistive Technology (AT) required to access and benefit from special education
- Federal funding of special education provides funds to states to support programs
- Tuition reimbursement costs for private school placement is available

When IDEA–1997 was reauthorized to IDEIA (IDEA–2004), all of the major provisions and components remained, but changes mounted and the impact they may have on special education programs remains to be seen. These were some of the changes proposed.

- Paperwork reduction
- Short-term objectives and benchmarks eliminated from IEPs
- Implementation of comprehensive and multiyear (3-year) IEPs
- Focus on highly qualified teachers to align IDEIA with NCLB

Specific within the federal special education law are two main provisions for students with disabilities that schools and communities use in guiding delivery of the most appropriate services to all students with disabilities. They have some similarities and some differences, which are outlined here:

IDEIA-Part B:

- Students with disabilities ages 3 through age 21
- Educational programs in public school settings
- Educators, staff, and other school professionals provide services
- Yearly evaluations and annual review of program
- Participation in transition from Part C
- IEP describes the individual student's needs

IDEIA-Part C:

- Students with disabilities ages birth to three years
- Family and child services in natural environments, particularly the home
- Service or case manager coordinates the necessary services
- Evaluations two times per year and regular reviews
- Participation in the transition services to Part B
- IFSP describes the child and family needs

Other Federal Laws

Section 504 (Rehabilitation Act of 1973): Extends civil rights to individuals with disabilities, prohibiting discrimination in education, employment, and other community settings. It requires compliance by any recipient of federal funds; however, the requirements are not supported by federal funding.

ADA (Americans with Disabilities Act–1990): Based on Section 504, it extends civil rights to individuals with disabilities to private sector employment, public services, public accommodations, transportation, and telecommunications.

NCLB (No Child Left Behind–2001, the Reauthorization of the Elementary and Secondary Education Act): The primary goal is that all children will be proficient in all subject matter by 2014, and it imposes a requirement that all teachers must be "highly qualified." There are four key principles:

- Stronger accountability through district and state testing
- Increased flexibility for use of federal funds
- Additional options for parents
- Focus on curriculum and instructional methods with proven effects

FERPA (Family Educational Rights and Privacy Act): Although not a specific special education law, it affects education programs and those professionals associated with students who have disabilities. This federal law protects the privacy of all students' education records and is applicable to all schools receiving federal funds.

Legal Cases

Court decisions have proven to be a critical indicator of the interpretations and changes in the special education law over the years. It seems to be the nature of special education that parents, schools, and advocates challenge the law and the decisions made about students. Because of the numbers of due process hearings and the amount of court cases, professionals and parents must take a strong look at the programs and services that students with disabilities receive. Although the law does not clearly define many of the provisions and requirements, schools should strive to avoid the confrontational proceedings, as they are costly and time-consuming.

One of the most difficult rulings for schools is the requirement to provide health-related services for medically fragile students, which could include a one-on-one nurse and medical equipment imposing a financial burden.

1972—*Mills v. Board of Education*: Determined that financial problems cannot be a reason for the lack of appropriate programs to children with disabilities.

1972—*Pennsylvania Association for Retarded Citizens v. the Commonwealth of Pennsylvania*: Established the right for all children with mental retardation to a free public education.

1979—*Armstrong v. Kline*: Ordered schools to provide extended school year services for students with disabilities who may regress over long periods without school.

1982—*Board of Education of the Hudson School District v. Rowley*: Upheld that each child with a disability has the right to an individualized program and supportive services deemed appropriate and necessary.

1984—*Department of Education v. Katherine D.*: Ruled homebound instruction for a student with multiple health problems did not comply with the LRE and required the student to be placed in a class with nondisabled children with related medical services.

1984—*Irving Independent School District v. Tatro*: Forced the school to provide nonphysician required medical services to allow a physically impaired student to attend school.

1988—*Honig v. Doe*: Ruled that students with disabilities may not be excluded for misbehavior that is disability-related, but services could cease if the behavior was not related to the disability.

1989—*Timothy v. Rochester School District*: Upheld that all children with disabilities must be provided a free, appropriate, public education without exception.

1993—*Zobrest v. Catalina School District*: Determined that a student in a parochial school should be provided the assistance of a related service due to the disability and that these findings did not violate the constitution of the separation of church and state.

1999—*Cedar Rapids v. Garrett F.*: Ruled that medical services necessary to a student with a disability to access and benefit from special education must be provided by the school as long as the service does not require a physician.

Issues of Family, School, and Community

Family members and the community have an impact on students with disabilities. Involvement in the educational programs of students with disabilities aids in successful student achievement and positive outcomes. They may share in advocacy efforts to help individuals with disabilities gain the support they need throughout their lifetime.

Advocacy

Advocacy can have a tremendous effect on the outcomes for persons with disabilities. It seems that many of the changes in the laws, services, and program delivery over the past several decades have been because of the on-going and consistent efforts of individuals with disabilities, parents, educators, and communities. When groups of people with the same mission attempt to clarify or improve something for individuals who need the support, changes occur.

Whether those changes happen because of amended laws, court cases, or awareness rallies, the influence on those with disabilities can be staggering.

It seems that the biggest problem for individuals with disabilities is how they are treated by others. It is important to not just accept that individuals with disabilities are in the schools and communities, but that they are capable of productivity and a quality of life much like other people.

Advocacy instruction must be a part of the educational program for children with disabilities so they may understand their rights and come to know their own capabilities. Through instruction on advocacy issues and self-advocacy actions, individuals with disabilities will begin to make a difference for themselves. It is an especially important component of the transition plans that are developed and implemented for students age 16 and older.

Advocacy groups have been established for persons with disabilities in order to help them protect their rights, gain information, maintain their dignity, meet others under the same circumstances, and join in the efforts to sustain positive outcomes. Joining an advocacy group, and being a self-advocate requires that the person be self-determined.

Family Participation

Under federal law, educators and professionals working in school programs are encouraged to include parents and families of children with disabilities in the special education process and the implementation of special education programs. For all practical purposes, the parents and family members are to be considered partners in the education of the child with a disability that is based on respect and dignity.

Research has shown that parents can be a positive influence in their child's education, as the effectiveness of the student's program seems to improve, and the child performs at a more successful level. Involving parents is a meaningful activity as they may aid in developing proper IEP goals; they can deliver consistency for the child; they may be able to access additional resources; and they may provide opportunities for additional learning situations.

Several of the most common methods of providing home-school communication to effectively involve parents on a regular basis include parent-teacher conferences, telephone calls or e-mails on daily progress, written messages, class newsletters or websites, parent group meetings, parent classroom volunteers, family homework activities, and class activities with family spectators.

Attitudes Toward Individuals with Disabilities

Students with disabilities face problems with discrimination, sympathetic people, the ignorance of others, teasing, and cruelty. These actions do not generally stop when a student becomes an adult. Even adults with disabilities find themselves in problematic situations. How others react to individuals with disabilities affects their lives in school and as adults.

Very often people without disabilities are uncomfortable in the presence of someone with a disability. Many people assume that children with disabilities are different than their peers, when in fact, they are more alike. It is how people respond to their unique differences that will impact the child's school achievement and future success.

There have been increased efforts on behalf of individuals with disabilities over the past several years, as educators have found that individuals with disabilities blend better into society and enjoy the same privileges as those individuals without disabilities. When educators effectively guide and support children with disabilities to use their realistic potential, reach reasonable academic and behavioral performance, improve their self-esteem, and develop independence, these professionals do much to enhance the individual's ability to participate in community life.

Terms related to disability constantly change (disability, handicap, impairment, and so on), and many of these terms conjure up the idea of individuals who are unable to do things. Due to the negative image, the preferred terms are those that impose the **person-first** concept for individuals with disabilities. Person-first terms are a more respectful way of speaking and writing about students who have disabilities, as the child is always mentioned before the disability. Those who favor and promote these terms believe that children are children first, whether they have a disability or not, and should not be denigrated because of the impairment. Using the person-first language is a critical step toward including these individuals in society and enhancing their lives.

Following are examples of person-first language:

- the young boy with cerebral palsy as compared to the young cerebral palsied boy
- the child with mental retardation as compared to the mentally retarded child
- the girl with a physical disability as compared to the physically disabled girl

Public attitudes toward persons with disabilities have changed greatly in recent years. People are more accepting, more tolerant, more respectful, and far less negative. These changes will not erase the disability, but they will pave the way for more appropriate responses and a smoother journey within communities.

Cultural and Community Influences

Communities and the various cultures within have great influences on the development and progress of individuals with disabilities. Society establishes rules about how people should function and in the past, individuals with disabilities were not completely approved as members of the greater society or local communities. Now, with changed attitudes, more individuals with disabilities are considered viable contributors to the everyday function of their communities.

When a person with a disability is allowed to participate in daily activities and given the freedom to join in the regular routines of life, her skills and abilities seem to improve. When society's attitudes are more accepting, communities are more likely to embrace the membership of individuals with disabilities in work environments, local businesses, and neighborhood living situations. By treating people with disabilities as individuals and accepting their differences, we move closer to more unified communities who treat all productive citizens equally.

Delivery of Services

The realm of special education is diverse and constantly changing, just as the students are unique and evolving. The delivery of services to students with disabilities must be clearly individualized and provided in compliance with the laws, policies, and best practices. It is mandated that children with disabilities access their programs according to a free and appropriate public education in the least restrictive environment.

In pursuing the appropriate delivery of services for students with disabilities, consider several essential elements: the student's disability and assessed needs, the environment, the strategies used, the professionals involved, and the partnerships with parents. A team of professionals must implement the delivery of services also based on the assessment process, the curriculum and instruction components, the strategies and methods of instruction, and the management of the environment.

Research has proven that children with disabilities and those without disabilities benefit academically and socially when they are educated together in the same setting. Therefore, the inclusion movement offers a realistic placement for students with disabilities and the delivery of services should be carefully contemplated by the IEP team. This is critical to the student's academic achievement and success.

The number of students with disabilities has grown over the years, and they are significantly dispersed within the general population. As an educator, find the most appropriate ways to guide and support all students so they may lead productive and independent lives.

Conceptual Approaches

The theories related to how students learn are important guidelines for educators in knowing how to instruct students with disabilities. Not every theory works for every child or every situation so educators also need to know what their own personal philosophy is about how children with disabilities learn.

Students have constantly emerging needs, and since they are uniquely individual, the approaches used to support their needs must be based on research and theoretical topics that include information, interventions, and strategies. As an educator, continue to search for quality information that will help students reach their fullest potential and go on to lead productive lives.

This section discusses six of the learning theories related to academic achievement of children with special needs: medical, psychodynamic, behavioral, cognitive, sociological, and eclectic.

Medical

Many disabilities are the product of medically related issues, whether resulting from genetic causes, diseases, illnesses, accidents, or unknown etiologies. The medical field can provide information about the diagnosis, treatment, and prognosis as well as how to service those issues for children with disabilities. This field focuses on clinical therapy, but can also support programs through medical practitioners, physicians, public health professionals, and mental health professionals who follow a child's condition, prescribe medications, and make adjustments throughout the child's early life. Medical theory does not apply to the school programs, but has a place in the development of a child's education program.

Psychodynamic

The names of Brucke, Jung, and Freud may be familiar as they are the drivers of the psychodynamic theory, which is the study of human behavior based on motivation and drives, and the functional significance of emotions. It is believed that an individual's personality and reactions are the result of interactions in an individual's mind, genetic constitution, emotions, and the environment. These emotional and motivational interactions affect behavior and a person's mental state. Additionally, internal forces affect a person's behavior. This approach is based on the premise that human behavior and relationships are shaped by conscious and unconscious influences.

Behavioral

The behavioral learning theory emphasizes a systematic approach to learning and instruction. This theory is based on the work of Skinner and incorporates the ABC model to instruction (A = antecedent or stimulus, B = target behavior or target response, C = consequences or reinforcement). Examples of this theory in the field of special education include the development of an IEP and the use of Functional Behavior Assessments and Plans, as they demonstrate measurable learning behaviors that can be observed and documented.

Since Skinner believed that learning is a function of the changes in behaviors and the responses to these events, the key components of this theory emphasizes the effectiveness of **explicit teaching** and **direct instruction.** This type of instruction focuses on the tasks to be learned, the skills to be developed, and the established environmental setting. Educators assess a student's learning by examining the presented task and observing how well the student performs to the response (known as *operant conditioning*).

Cognitive

Based on Gestalt psychology and the work of Piaget, the cognitive theory examines the internal mental processes that include problem solving, memory, and language. This theory is most concerned with how people understand, analyze, and solve problems. Theorists believe that the student constructs the acquisition of new information and skills based on prior knowledge.

Instruction under this theory must be delivered at the student's particular level or stage of development while managing the environment and allowing the student to develop necessary and generalized skills. Motivational activities should be utilized to enhance and encourage learning. The instructional application of the cognitive theory includes the styles of learning, metacognition, learning strategies, peer tutoring, scaffolded instruction, behavioral temperaments, and the social context of learning.

Sociological

The social learning theory is based on observation. Bandura discovered that children learn through their observations of others. This concept focuses on providing modeling and demonstrations so children may observe what they need to learn.

Eclectic

Since special education stresses the use of an individualized educational program for every child with a disability, some professionals choose to select certain components of several different theoretical approaches when constructing a student's instruction. The eclectic approach utilizes a combination of practices to best suit the student's individual special needs. Certain approaches work best for certain types of disabilities and certain characteristics in individual students. The teacher should base selection on the comprehensive assessment conducted on the student.

Professional Roles and Responsibilities

As a professional responsible for the education of students with disabilities, clearly understand the educator's role in this process. Maintaining professional competence includes acknowledging the role educators play in supporting students and families as well as pursuing continued education and gaining further information to improve professional skills and abilities.

Reveal your professionalism to the families you serve, your teaching peers, and the community in several ways. Show your dedication to the education of children, use appropriate individualized procedures, and demonstrate your knowledge of the scope of the position and expose your competencies regarding required policies. Read professional journals, stay abreast on rising issues, enroll in training workshops, join professional organizations, and attend conferences. Utilize instructional practices and strategies that are research-based as these will acknowledge your further effectiveness as a professional.

Collaboration

Teachers in special education and general education must work together to enhance the individual educational programs by sharing their expertise and demonstrating appropriate communication practices, especially for students placed in inclusive settings. It is a valuable practice when students with disabilities are receiving more of their specialized individual programs in the general education program.

This method is called **collaborative teaming** and usually focuses on the successful programs of inclusion. It is recommended to develop an effective team, the members should determine their shared goals, apply voluntary participation procedures, use proper on-going communications, practice team decision making, share the responsibilities, schedule planning time together, and pool resources. Team members may work together, collaboratively, in three different ways: coordination, consultation, and teaming.

Coordination is a very simple form of collaboration and includes communication and cooperation so the services to students with disabilities are ensured delivery. Professionals do not necessarily share their expertise, their information, or ideas with one another about individual students, but rather may provide updates on how well the implementations are going.

During the **consultation** process, professionals work with one another to meet the needs of students with disabilities by communicating and sharing expertise to improve the services to students. It is the responsibility of the special education teacher to manage the student's program and provide support to the general education teacher and the student so the individualized program proceeds adequately and appropriately. Teachers share strategies and methods that will help students access their educational programs.

Another important professional practice in special education programs, effective for inclusion settings, is the use of **co-teaching.** When two or more teachers work together to plan lessons, deliver instruction, and assess students, it provides the additional supports to students with disabilities that improves student performance and achievement.

Teaming

Three types of teams utilized in schools and critical to the effectiveness and implementation of the special education process are described here.

Multidisciplinary teams are described as professionals with defined roles, who work independently of one another. This is not an encouraged practice in the schools, as it promotes more fragmentation of student programs. If a student is seen as a whole person, then the services should be delivered to the student as a whole and not separately as this type of team implies. Because this kind of team often conducts separate assessments, delivers services independent of other providers, and works with the families separate of other professionals, this kind of teamwork shows a lack of communication and a lack of understanding about student needs.

Although the **Interdisciplinary team** has members who conduct independent assessments, unlike the multidisciplinary team, this group promotes communication and collaboration. An interdisciplinary team uses more formal communication efforts by meeting together to share the gained information and develop a plan for interventions and strategies that will enhance the student's educational success. Then team members implement their separate portion of the program, while remaining in contact with other team members.

The **Transdisciplinary team** is the more preferred type, as it demonstrates a high level of coordination and involvement; however, due to schedules and the numbers of professionals involved, it may be the most difficult to achieve. This team tries to deliver services in an integrated approach across disciplines, which includes assessment, information, program development, and interventions, while including the family in all stages. Team members usually work together by sharing roles, and the responsibility for assessment and interventions, unlike multidisciplinary and interdisciplinary teams that work in isolation.

Assessments

Assessments are required under the law for students to be placed and receive services in special education no matter which disability category is identified. The process can be lengthy and at times debatable among professionals, but without the proper assessment and application of student information, it will be very difficult to develop and implement an appropriate program for a student with a disability. The assessment process may depend on a variety of measurements in order to gather the best information needed: observation, interventions, case history, and informal and formal tests.

The purposes of an assessment include

- To determine the nature of the problem
- To decide the eligibility for special education and related services
- To discover the present levels of performance and areas of need
- To target skills or identify content areas
- To ascertain which factors support learning
- To plan student instruction and types of interventions
- To manage the data related to instruction

Over the years, this sensitive area of special education has produced numerous due process claims and created many legal cases across the country. Some of the supported changes made to the law provide more proper assessment processes, techniques, and tools for students with disabilities were due to certain cases. Three such cases stand out: *Hobson v. Hansen,* 1967; *Larry P. v. Riles,* 1972–1984; *Diana v. State Board of Education,* 1970. These cases collectively indicated that IQ tests may not be the primary means for placement in special education, and the assessment methods and procedures for certain individuals must be changed according to the individual's needs, including the use of nonbiased tests.

Following are the steps in the assessment process:

Pre-referral: This is the initial step of the entire special education process and begins with the assessment procedures. When a teacher suspects that a student may be having problems in the general education classroom, interventions are imposed to determine whether the student may benefit from them. This is an informal process and should be a problem-solving procedure for the teacher and student. The student's difficulties may be brought to the attention of the school assistance team for further discussion and support. If the student is not making the expected progress, the second step is followed; however, if the student does make adequate progress, the referral for special education support ends.

Screening: In this step, professionals provide a quick assessment that covers basic skills and information to detect individuals who may require more comprehensive evaluation and may need the support of special education services.

Referral: In this step, professionals use information from a variety of sources (parents, teachers, others) and conduct observations to identify classroom performance and behaviors. In particular, the concerns of the general education teacher are reviewed, and the professional watches for those problem areas as the student is observed.

Evaluation and identification: This step necessitates a comprehensive evaluation by all related professionals to determine a student's eligibility for special education services and to identify the special education category. This process has imposed timelines and requirements under federal law for the types of measurement tools to be used. Specifically, a **multifactored assessment** conducted by a multidisciplinary evaluation team, using a variety of test instruments and procedures as required under IDEIA, determines the educational placement for special education services.

Instructional program planning: The use of assessment information to create goals, determine placement, and make plans for instructional delivery is essential to assist in the program development for a student with a disability. The team meets to discuss the results of the evaluations and to make critical decisions about the student while identifying the services that are necessary.

Placement: At the team meeting, after the instructional program is designed, the team makes decisions about the LRE and how and when the services will begin. The IEP is then implemented.

Review and evaluation: Monitoring the progress of a student, as it pertains to the IEP, is the final step in the process and required in order to develop regular progress reports and adjust the IEP if necessary. A review of the student's progress may be conducted using various approaches and may include formal, informal, or alternate measurements.

Utilizing Appropriate Assessment Procedures

Appropriate assessment procedures are a requirement under the law and must be implemented for every student for each evaluation. A variety of assessment tools and strategies must be administered in the child's primary language and be free from racial or cultural bias, since they are used with diverse groups of students. The assessment tools used should be appropriate for the particular student in order to gather relevant functional, developmental, and academic information while providing the relevant information to help a team determine the educational needs of the student.

Several types of measurement tools may be used throughout the special education process, whether during a comprehensive evaluation or for evaluation of on-going student progress. Following are some of the assessments that may be utilized.

- **Achievement test:** A formal tool used to measure student knowledge or proficiency in a subject or topic area that has been learned.

- **Active student response:** A frequency-based measure used to determine a student's participation rate during an instructional period.

- **Anecdotal record:** An informal measurement of teacher notes based on observation of student work and performance and often used for parent conferences.

- **Aptitude test:** A formal measure of standardized or norm-referenced tests that evaluate a student's ability to acquire skills or gain knowledge.

- **Authentic assessments:** An informal method of determining a student's actual understanding and performance on a skill, particularly used in classroom assessments of specific criteria.

- **Behavior assessments:** A variety of behavior evaluation tools are available to track student behaviors and to document progress on a behavior intervention plan or the use of self-management techniques.

- **Criterion-referenced test:** A formal measure that evaluates a student on specific information, most often used to check a student's knowledge of subject areas by answering specific questions, and does not compare one student to another.

- **Curriculum-based measure:** This evaluation of a student's progress and performance of skills is based on the curriculum and lessons presented, which helps teachers determine how to assist the student and is used in parent conferences.

- **Ecological-based assessment:** This involves the use of an informal observation of the child interacting with the natural environment during a regular schedule.

- **Functional Behavior Assessment (FBA):** The process of gathering information about problem behaviors on an individual student and used to evaluate the student's need for intervention in the behavior area or to create a behavior intervention plan.

- **Intelligence test (IQ test):** A norm-referenced test used to assess a student's learning abilities or intellectual capacity as it measures cognitive behaviors.

- **Norm-referenced test:** These formal tools are also referred to as standardized tests and are used when attempting to compare a student to peers in the same age group, primarily helpful in developing curriculum options and identifying interventions.

- **Observation:** Teachers or professionals watch a student in several settings and make notes regarding performance and behaviors, particularly helpful in developing behavior plans and required as a component of a comprehensive special education assessment.

- **Performance assessment:** An informal measure used by teachers to assess a student's ability to complete a task specific to a topic or subject area, such as a mathematic equation, an oral report, or an art project.

- **Portfolio assessment:** An informal method of gathering information based on the student's completed products (art work, compositions) over a period of time; particularly helpful for evaluating progress and sharing information with parents.

- **Standards-based assessment:** This more formal evaluation can be either a criterion-referenced or norm-referenced test and measures a student's progress toward meeting goals or standards as previously established by district, or state.

- **Summative evaluation:** This informal procedure is a method used to check student achievement and teacher instruction.

Interpretation of Results

The results of a comprehensive evaluation are used to develop a student's individual education program (IEP). Generally there are several professionals (teacher, psychologist, speech pathologist, other therapists) who have worked with the student, conducting an evaluation, and who have information to share on evaluation outcomes. Each professional is an expert in the assessment area for which she has gathered the results.

Under IDEIA, the examiner who has conducted the evaluations of a student, or at the very least a person who is qualified to interpret the results of the evaluation, is to be present at the team meeting. Prior to creating an IEP, the assessment results are presented and discussed with other team members, which include the parents. The results should be considered valid if proper selection of the evaluation tools and consideration of bias on the assessment were made prior to the testing.

During the meeting, the team members should take turns at providing background information about the assessment that was conducted. A review of the testing instruments, the setting of the evaluation, information about the student's testing abilities, and the procedures used all give valuable insight into the assessment process and the student's learning style. As the members contribute the scores and results, they should be translated into educational terms and present levels of educational performance. Members then work together to develop the goals for the student's educational program and identify the materials, methods, and strategies best suited to the student's needs.

Use of Results for Various Purposes

A comprehensive evaluation is necessary in order to evaluate all aspects of the student's growth and development. The results can then be used to help the team make quality decisions about the student's educational program.

The primary purpose of an assessment is to determine the specific needs of the student as well as to identify the instructional strategies and methods most beneficial to the academic achievement of the student. The assessment results will guide the development of the IEP, in which the present levels of performance determine the goals, interventions, accommodations, and related services. The evaluation results will also help the team make a decision regarding the least restrictive environment and the method for monitoring student progress.

Certain assessments pertain to instruction and should be considered by teachers for gathering information to prepare periodic progress reports, to discuss with parents at conferences, and to make decisions at IEP annual reviews. The options include systematic observations, formal assessments, criterion-referenced tests, rating scales, interviews, charting, and alternative assessments (direct assessment, outcome-based assessment, portfolio assessment, performance assessment).

Development of Reports and Communication of Findings

Report writing is a skill, and most professionals in the field of special education who are examiners have developed this skill. There are certain requirements of report writing and specific criteria to include in the final report. A written report must indicate a statement of the disability, identify the specific characteristics of the student's disability, explain how the disability affects learning, and suggest methods and interventions for instruction. The types of assessments conducted and the related scores should be described and explained, and a review of the student's past performance, health and developmental history, behaviors, and family influences are important pieces of report information.

The **communication of findings** (results of the evaluation) should be provided at a team meeting. The examiner (or a person qualified) should review the scores and data and interpret the results, sharing the most pertinent information with the other members. If more than one evaluation was conducted through other examiners, they should give the information that will aid the team in making appropriate educational decisions.

Placement and Program Issues

Children with disabilities should be placed, according to the law, in the environment where the child's needs may best be met, with an emphasis on being placed with nondisabled peers to the greatest extent possible. This decision should be made by the team according to a comprehensive assessment and the selection should be the primary placement for all service delivery.

Previously, children with exceptional needs were placed in special segregated classes unless they had mild disabilities. More and more schools, because of the emphasis on the law and preferences of parents, are creating general education classes as inclusive settings for students with disabilities. These inclusive programs allow students a more natural environment for their education services and prepare them for community settings as adults.

Continuum of Services

Under IDEIA, a provision related to placement is called the **continuum of alternative** (educational) **placements.** It specifies that there must be options for the implementation of the educational program in order for students with disabilities to receive their special education services and the necessary related services, and to access the general education curriculum.

This **continuum of placement options** must be discussed when an IEP team convenes to discuss the student's program and related services. The general education setting is the first recommended placement to consider and the **least restrictive environment** for all students with disabilities. Many students with disabilities are successful when appropriate services, accommodations, and supports are implemented. It can be challenging for the IEP team to make a decision about placement, but the student's social and educational needs must be assessed prior to making the final decision.

Inclusion

The basic concept of *inclusion* is that students with disabilities and students who are nondisabled should be placed in classes together so those with special needs will receive instruction in the general education curriculum with either pull-out therapies or reach-in therapies, as needed. Around the 1990s, inclusion became the recommended practice so students with disabilities could obtain the support needed in the general education classrooms with their same age peers in neighborhood schools. The hope was that students with disabilities would avoid placement in segregated settings.

Placing students with disabilities in general education programs can be a daunting task for regular education teachers. Students with varying disabilities are diverse learners and often require adaptations, modifications, and accommodations to be successful. Each student with a disability has different characteristics and a range of needs. The methods and strategies they need require special attention and time to implement, which causes difficulty for the regular education teachers. It is important for the special education teachers to support and assist the general education teachers in order to enhance students' education programs and encourage successful inclusion.

Mainstreaming

This term pertains to the practice of implementing educational services in such a way that students with disabilities are placed in special education programs part of the day and regular education programs part of the day. This type of placement has been promoted since 1975 as a way to provide services to students with disabilities in the least restrictive environment. This process has been used mostly for students with mild to moderate disabilities where they remain in the general education program as much as possible. A popular delivery of services system, it is used in combination with a resource room delivery model, promoting more collaborative efforts between general education and special education personnel.

Least Restrictive Environment

Children with disabilities should learn to function in a variety of environments and interact with typical peers. The least restrictive environment (LRE) is a provision of the federal special education law that pertains to the educational placement of children with disabilities, in which the setting of service delivery closely resembles a regular school program while meeting the child's special needs. It must be considered by the IEP team for every child with an IEP, but only after the student's educational needs are determined and special education goals and related services are outlined. This requirement was established so IEP teams will consider the setting in which a student's special education services may be best delivered. Each district must be prepared to offer the continuum of placement options and service alternatives.

The least restrictive environments options for students with disabilities include general education classroom (inclusive model), general education classroom (consultative model), co-teaching setting (collaborative model), resource room (pull-in model), self-contained program (separate, segregated model), separate school (private setting), a residential facility, homebound placement, and hospital setting.

Every child with a disability has the right to be educated with nondisabled peers to the maximum extent appropriate. Special classes, segregated programs, and separate schools are to be the placement of choice only when the severity of the disability prohibits the education of a student with a disability in a more typical setting. A natural environment (especially in early childhood programming) is recommended under the law.

Related Services

Another requirement under IDEIA is that children with disabilities must be provided those additional services such as transportation, speech therapy, physical therapy, occupational therapy, counseling, behavior coach, paraprofessional, and so on, if necessary, in order to access and benefit from special education. These services, called **related services,** are added to the IEP according to the decisions of the team, based on the comprehensive assessments of the student's needs and the goals set to meet those needs. How these services are provided and where they are conducted is at the discretion of the professionals who implement the services.

Early Intervention

Under Part B (3–5 years) and Part C (0–3 years) of IDEIA, young children are entitled to individualized programs that address their special needs. Early childhood education is at the forefront of the special education movement, as research on the brain and human development has given this area of education the credibility it deserves.

Children placed in preschool programs or early intervention programs are identified under categories other than the regular school age special education labels. Each state creates its own category headings, but for the younger children a less descript label of *developmental delay* is often used.

Refer to the "Legal and Societal Issues" section earlier and check the "Preschool/Early Childhood" section later in this study guide for more information on this topic.

Transitions

Over the years, research has shown that adults with disabilities face barriers in their daily lives that prevent them from feeling independent and being successful. Because of issues determined through research studies, the federal government has implemented requirements in the special education law to help students with disabilities prepare for their futures. The studies found that adults with disabilities are challenged with underemployment, job dissatisfaction, dependent living arrangements, social skills difficulties, poor work habits, and job selection problems.

Transition, under federal law, must begin at age 16 for children with disabilities. It is not only a plan for services, but a recommended statement of the responsibilities of the student, the parents, the school, and the interagencies who will provide the resources to the student. Special education law requires that school personnel assist students in planning their post-school activities so they may be more successful as adults. This program must be based on the student's individual needs and include the student's interests and preferences. The areas to be incorporated are postsecondary education, integrated or supported employment, vocational training, continuing and adult education, adult services, independent living, community participation, and recreation and leisure activities.

The transition plan for a high school student must outline the activities and resources that will support the student's movement from school, usually upon graduation, to adulthood. The student should be involved in the creation and development of this plan, as capable, as consideration of the student's ideas, interests, and preferences is important to the outcomes. The team consists of school personnel, the student, community and agency personnel, and parents, as appropriate.

Another formal transition mentioned in the law may occur when a child is moving from Part C services (early intervention) to the Part B services (school age). An IEP should be created based on the services that were implemented just prior to the child's third birthday. The Part C personnel, the Part B professionals, and the parents should convene to evaluate the student's present needs and create an appropriate program.

Assistive Technology

Another requirement of IDEIA is the provision of assistive technology for those students with disabilities in order to access and benefit from special education. Assistive technology includes devices and services, such as augmentative communication tools, specialized equipment for computer use, visual aids, and other low- and high-tech devices or services. The use of the devices and services are based on an assessment of the student with the disability, and decisions are made by the IEP team as to the need for and type of assistive technology provided.

Curriculum and Instruction

The curriculum design used for students with disabilities may be the single most important factor in their education. What is selected for instruction is important to their ability to achieve academic standards. The use of special materials, methods, adaptations, modifications, and accommodations of the general curriculum all add to the success of their program. Students with disabilities have diverse needs and span all levels of abilities, so choosing a curriculum means that the educator knows each student well.

Many children with disabilities need systematic instruction for skills that are easily acquired by their nondisabled peers without instruction. Some require intense and specialized instructional periods or tutoring to gain skills and knowledge. Curriculum choices are not easy, and must be made with the unique characteristics of the students in mind. The general education curriculum may be appropriate for some students with disabilities, while others need a more specialized program.

Different curriculum types are available for students with disabilities.

- **Behavioral-based curriculum:** Demonstrates student interactions in the environment in order to instruct students in functional and age appropriate skills.
- **Cognitive-developmental curriculum:** Provides age appropriate activities that are discovery-based and interactive, such as DAP.
- **Life skills curriculum:** Used in functional skills training for supporting the transition into the community.
- **Social skills curriculum:** Used to improve social skills, aid with interactions, following directions, handling various situations, increasing self-competence, and utilizing appropriate behaviors across settings.
- **Functional curriculum:** Helps develop knowledge and skills to support independence in school, community, work, personal, social, and daily living situations.

Instructional variables related to learning and student achievement can make all the difference in the success of the program and the outcomes for the student. When preparing for instruction, teachers should focus on learning time, ensure high rates of success for students, provide easy access to materials and supplies, impart a quality educational environment, plan and maintain motivation, and participate in teacher training programs.

IEP Process

Students with disabilities from ages 3 through 21 are entitled to the creation of an IEP (Individualized Education Program) based on their disability and their needs, which are determined through a non-discriminatory assessment. The development of an IEP follows a systematic process and should establish a realistic and appropriate program. After an IEP has been finalized, it must be implemented by specific personnel and follow these seven steps: pre-referral, referral, evaluation, eligibility, development of the IEP, implementation of the IEP, and annual review.

After a student with an identified disability is assessed, an IEP team collaboratively prepares to develop the individualized plan. Seven components focused on the individual student with the disability must be included in this plan.

1. Present levels of academic performance
2. Statement of measurable annual goals, including objectives as needed
3. Description of the method to measure progress
4. Statement of related services, supplementary aids, and services
5. Explanation of the extent of involvement in general education programs
6. Statement of accommodations and participation in state and district testing
7. Description of the date, frequency, location, and duration of services

As the IEP is prepared, the team must ensure that the program is appropriate to the needs of the student and that it is not based solely on the disability or the current, available school programs. The least restrictive environment must be considered, and the scope and sequence of the curriculum with methods and strategies for instruction discussed in relation to the goals set. The IEP will guide instruction for the student with a disability and will reflect a measure of accountability of the student's program and the staff involved.

Instructional Implementation

Instruction for students with disabilities is not much different than that for other students, except that it must be more individualized. Because of the diversity of learners in special education, instruction must include activities, curricular materials, resources, equipment, specific classroom personnel, tutoring, and the use of technology. Integrating all of these features into a general education classroom can be overwhelming for regular education teachers, so the special education team needs to be available to the general education teachers as they attempt to meet the needs of all children, including those with disabilities.

Enrichment and remediation are important for special needs learners. **Enrichment** extends the lesson for those capable of more, which may help students with learning disabilities, autism, deafness, blindness, orthopedic impairments, and emotional disabilities. **Remediation** is important as it is the use of various strategies to teach and reinforce skills for those needing more practice. Although this technique may apply to all students, it is particularly helpful to those with mental retardation, deafness, speech-language problems, other health impaired, and traumatic brain injury.

The following are essential elements of instruction: present anticipatory set, explain objective and purpose, provide input (step by step instruction), model task, check for understanding, allow guided practice, give closure, and allow independent practice.

Reading is an area in which many students with special needs must have a variety of programs and strategies available. Through the assessment process, the team should be able to identify the approach that will offer the student the most success. Reading instruction approaches found to be beneficial to students with disabilities include basal reading approach, literature based reading approach, phonics approach, linguistic approach, whole language approach, language experience approach, and individual reading approach.

Writing is another academic area that can be challenging to students with disabilities. The various components that are covered in the writing process are fluency and syntax development, vocabulary development, structural development, and content development.

Mathematics is a difficult subject area that must include instruction that focuses on problem solving, mathematical concepts, mathematical reasoning, application of daily math, estimation, computation, and measurement.

Strategies and Methods

Again, it cannot be stressed enough that the instruction for students with disabilities is based on an individualized program, with specific strategies and methods. The strategies must support the learner and encourage independence. Instructional strategies must focus on the strengths and needs of each student while teaching the generalization of skills. The methods must be age appropriate, engage an active learner, and emphasize motivation. Instructional methods are generally an outcome of empirical research.

There are two very distinct methods for providing instruction and these are used for various disability groups depending on the functioning level and the subject area:

> **Explicit instruction:** The teacher provides the knowledge and supports the learning process.

> **Implicit instruction:** The focus is on the students as active and involved learners who construct knowledge by using previously learned knowledge.

Following are some of the terms related to instructional strategies and methods:

- **Adaptations:** Changes made to the environment or curriculum
- **Accommodations:** An adjustment that enables a student to participate in educational activities
- **Active student response*:** Engagement of the learner in tasks and activities
- **Content enhancements:** Techniques used to enhance the organization and delivery of curriculum (guided notes, graphic organizers, mnemonics, and visual displays)
- **Cues and prompts:** Provides assistance to ensure adequate support of instruction
- **Diagnostic-prescriptive method:** Individualizing instruction to develop strengths and remediate weaknesses
- **Direct instruction:** Synonymous with explicit instruction
- **Direct measurement*:** Frequently checking on student performance
- **Fluency building:** Practice to gain smooth skill use
- **Generalization*:** Using skills learned across various settings
- **Mediated scaffolding:** Providing cues and gradually removing them so students can perform and respond independently
- **Modeling tasks:** Acting out sequences while students observe and then having students imitate the task to learn it; it helps make connections between the material to be learned and the process to learn it

- **Modifications:** Changing the content, materials, or delivery of instruction
- **Naturalistic teaching procedures:** Involves activities interesting to students and naturally occurring consequences
- **Peer tutoring:** Assistance of nondisabled student to enhance learning
- **Precision teaching:** Direct daily measure of student performance
- **Repetition:** Helps build rote memory skills
- **Response cards:** Signs, cards, or items held up by students in class to demonstrate responses
- **Strategic instruction:** Planned and sequential instruction to show similarities and differences between old and new knowledge
- **Systematic feedback*:** Providing positive reinforcement and confirmation to improve learning
- **Task analysis*:** Reducing complex skills into smaller sequential tasks
- **Transfer of stimulus control*:** Providing instructional prompts to aid in correct responses

*Examples of explicit, systemic instruction.

Instructional Formats

Instructional formats are designed for different subject areas and a variety of lesson activities. Certain formats are more beneficial for particular students, and the purpose of the instruction must be chosen in congruence with the student's unique needs. Examples include individualized instruction, small and large group instruction, modeling, and drill and practice.

Areas of Instruction

The school program developed for individuals with disabilities should not be limited to academic instruction. Students with disabilities need instruction in other areas to best absorb the information. Depending on the type of disability and the severity, different students will need different areas of instruction and various levels of instruction and methods added to the IEP. The primary areas that must be considered are academics, study skills, social skills, self-care skills, vocational skills, and behavioral skills. Students should be assessed in these areas when a comprehensive evaluation is conducted by the team members, and decisions should occur with the entire team.

Academics

Because every child with a disability is an individual and the disability influences the child's development and academic achievement in ways different than others with the same disability, remember that what works for one child may not work for another child. A child's academic achievement is based on the areas of need that are identified, the goals developed in the IEP, the interventions provided, the professionals who guide the child, the setting, and the accommodations. No one can predict the success of a child, but every IEP team can prepare for the best program based on the comprehensive evaluation results to support the child.

This section briefly identifies some of the academic areas that are of particular importance for students with specific disabilities, but this information is provided in a general sense and should not be interpreted as the only way to work with these children.

- **Autism:** Varies depending on the functioning level, and uneven skill development is common.
- **Emotional disturbance:** Behaviors and social interactions interfere with academics and most score in the low average range on IQ tests.
- **Hearing disability:** Difficulty with all academic areas, especially reading and math.
- **Learning disabilities:** Problems with reading, written expression, math, and inappropriate behaviors, and lack of social skills that interfere with learning.

- **Mental retardation:** Learning rate below average and most have problems in all academic areas, especially with generalizing skills.
- **Vision impairments:** May need specialized services in all academic areas.

Study Skills

Research has shown that the use of appropriate study skills promotes student achievement, so students with disabilities need extensive instruction in this area. Students should be assessed in study skill areas so an appropriate program may be developed and strategies for study skills instruction implemented. Topics of study skill instruction include reading, listening, note taking, outlining, report writing, oral presentation, graphic aids, test taking, library use, time management, and behavior self-management.

Social Skills

Although social skills instruction is helpful to children in all categories of disabilities, social skills development is an area of instruction that is critical for some children with particular disability types. Children with disabilities who specifically lack social skills noticed in the general characteristics of the disability include autism, emotional disabilities, hearing and vision impairments, learning disabilities, and mental retardation.

All students with a disability should be evaluated in the social skills area during the evaluation process. Following are some of the social issues related to specific disability types.

Autism: Isolated due to communication issues and lack of social competence, avoids people and forming relationships, not able to express or understand emotions, or social gestures, lacks pragmatic language skills.

Emotional Disturbance: Difficulties forming relationships, low levels of empathy, and lacks the ability to interpret social gestures.

Hearing Impairment: Due to communication barriers and the imposed isolation, may lack the ability to make friends and be accepted socially; have behavior problems and difficulty in social situations; and are often withdrawn, inattentive, and distractible, causing disruptive behaviors.

Learning Disabilities: Generally have poor relationships, a lack of self-esteem, difficulty perceiving the emotions of others, problems with attention and behaviors, hyperactivity, and compulsive.

Mental Retardation: Due to limited cognitive processing skills, lack of strong language development and inappropriate behaviors. Social situations are a challenge, and they do not have many appropriate personal relationships with peers or others, so instructing in the social skill area is extremely important to these students.

Vision Impairment: Often delayed in the social area, as interact less often with peers and others in the environment, are socially isolated, and are not able to respond to visible social cues, gestures, and body language, so must develop social competence.

Self-Care Skills

Self-care skills or daily living skills have been found to be an area of weakness for many adults with disabilities. It is for this reason that this area should be included in the educational program designed for students with disabilities, and these students should be given every opportunity to practice these skills prior to their transition from school into the community as adults. Instructing students with disabilities in the areas of personal hygiene, housekeeping, social skills, daily tasks, and social communications will help them to become better prepared to function appropriately in their community. Students who learn can practice these skills early in their school program and can become more independent as they begin to generalize these skills across settings.

This area of self-care is of critical importance to students with mental retardation as they generally lack the adaptive skills necessary for appropriate performance. Without instruction to improve these skills, they face a limited adult life. Direct instruction and environmental cues, such as using a routine schedule, aid them in learning these skills.

Vocational Skills

Vocational skills instruction is an area supported under federal law, as it follows the provision to include transition services and plans on the IEP once a student with a disability reaches the age of 16. The selection of vocational skills training to be imposed depends on the characteristics of the individual student's disability and a thorough assessment of abilities and vocational needs. Contact between educators and outside agencies will enhance the support of a student's on-going program.

To aid students with disabilities in learning these vocational skills, they often require structured learning experiences in integrated settings. Students with disabilities need to gain the proper functional skills so they may participate in a productive life of independent living, access and maintenance of employment, enjoy leisure activities, utilize routine living skills, and join community events. **Community-based instruction** is one highly recommended method (based on extensive research) that includes hands-on, interactive opportunities in vocational and life skills training. **Supported employment** is another recommended method that is primarily used for students with more severe disabilities.

Studies have shown that for a person with a disability, being employed seems to be one of the most valuable components of adult life. Adaptations to the environment may be necessary for students with physical disabilities or vision impairments, and assistive technology may be a critical component added to student programs. Educators must be in contact with vocational teachers as well as vocational rehabilitation counselors in community agencies to select the proper skills and career track for each student with a disability.

Management of the Learning Environment

Research suggests that effective instruction is the foundation for classroom management. Establishing a positive environment is known to increase the appropriate and desired behaviors for students, increase positive student-teacher interactions, and reinforce the individual learning programs. Educators must self-evaluate their teaching skills and maintain effective strategies for students with disabilities. Management of the environment takes skill and time, but the primary purpose is to build upon academic success.

Behavior Management

Assessments of social-emotional and behavior development are often needed for students with certain types of disabilities and characteristics. Social-emotional development yields valuable information about how a student may perform with peers in social settings. Common methods of assessment are conducted through student observation and interview, as well as rating scales from the parent, student, teachers, and other adults. The information collected should include the type of behaviors, the frequency, the intensity, and the duration.

Other tools used in social-emotional and behavior development assessments include observer-rater scales, measures of adaptive behavior, self-report instruments, Sociometric techniques, and Naturalistic observation.

In order to maintain classroom management, student behaviors must be under control, whether imposed by the teacher or self-regulated by the student. Educators must understand how behaviors impact learning and the influences that the classroom environment have on positive behavior management.

Behavior analysis can be a step forward in developing a Behavior Intervention Plan (BIP) for a student with a disability. The process steps are record and track systematic behaviors, use contingency contracting, focus on target behaviors and use of reinforcements or consequences, and use token reinforcement system.

Behavior modification techniques include using extrinsic motivators to reinforce appropriate behavior, moving toward intrinsic motivators, using reinforcement techniques immediately for appropriate behavior, using reinforcements continuously, using shaping for target behaviors, and avoiding the use of punishments.

Manifestation determination, a team review of the relationship between a student's inappropriate behavior and the disability is required under IDEIA when a student violates a code of conduct. It includes a Functional Behavior Assessment (FBA) and results in a Behavior Intervention Plan (BIP) with a possible alternative placement for those students with disabilities who violate discipline codes. The IEP team should also conduct a review of the IEP and continue the implementation after final changes have been made.

Classroom Organization

Students with special education needs are a diverse population, and management requires that teachers examine the physical space, classroom tone, rules, expectations, class procedures, active engagement of the learners, schedule, sequence of lessons and activities, access to materials, and types of praise and positive reinforcements used. Research suggests an enriching environment that is comfortable, positive, and safe for all students is of great value in learning. Just as important as the environment is the educator's ability to organize and manage it. Every child's needs must be accounted for with accommodations and interventions implemented appropriately.

Documentation

Records management can be a daunting task, as special education has requirements for the completion of specific paperwork. It is most reasonable to ask for information from your school district and special education office regarding the specific guidelines for safekeeping student documents, and you must understand the rights of parents to access their child's files. Remember that access to student information is protected, under IDEIA and FERPA, so proper storage of student documents and records is critical.

Organization is the key to maintaining the proper files and documents pertaining to each student's program. It is important to keep valuable, accurately written information about each student since teachers must be prepared for meetings, progress reports, and annual reviews, in addition to the daily records. Teachers have the right to access files, which may include medical records, assessment results, psychological information, behavioral information, therapy summaries, progress notes, letters, and parent information.

The IEP and the BIP are the most often used documents for classroom teachers, so easy access to these two documents will save time. The IEP goals and the BIP interventions should be reviewed regularly and additional documentation added.

Introduction

The history of special education is both informative and colorful. Many changes have occurred over the years in the laws, policies, and procedures. School programs have changed from primarily segregated settings to more inclusive models. Therapists are moving services into classrooms and more natural environments. Teachers are more open to trying new strategies and methods and collaborating with other professionals. It is a great time to be in special education!

Federal laws impose the mandates that public schools must follow, and students with disabilities are currently entitled to programming beginning as early as age 3 and as early as birth in many states through special statewide programs. Research, interventions, and attitudes have come a long way for individuals with disabilities.

Prior to taking the exam, you should review the basic concepts about all disabilities: the information about the characteristics, the causes, the prevalence, the various definitions, the facts about assessments, the placement steps, and the program issues, as well as curriculum and instruction information. Peruse the entire study guide and the various materials in specific disability categories. If you need additional information, not available in this guide, refer to your college texts, search the Internet, or speak with practicing educators. Websites related to disabilities and special education are provided in the "Resources" section at the end of the book.

This Praxis II exam, 0352, is a knowledge-based assessment prepared for individuals who plan to teach in special education programs for students with disabilities in grades preschool though 12. There are 50 multiple-choice questions and a case study, which are pertinent to the content categories of the application of core knowledge principles, and the time allowed for examinees is one hour. The content categories acknowledged include Curriculum (10 questions, 20%), Instruction (10 questions, 20%), Assessment (10 questions, 20%) Managing the Learning Environment (10 questions, 20%), and Professional Roles/Issues/Literature (10 questions, 20%).

Content Clusters

You probably have studied the Praxis II exam on Knowledge-Based Core Principles (0351) and are now preparing for the Praxis II Application of Core Principles across Categories of Disability. It is wise to have read and studied the core information first, as this exam focuses on the application of that knowledge. Use these 10 essay questions to determine the areas you may need to study further as they are based on the five content categories covered in the exam. These questions do not reflect the type found on the actual exam, which are multiple choice, but they do allow you an opportunity to examine your overall broad knowledge of the application of core knowledge related to special education. Read each question and think carefully about your answer.

1. Define the terms **accommodation, modification,** and **adaptation** and identify some of the various examples used with students who have disabilities.

2. Explain how to address diversity in the classroom with all children, including those with disabilities.

3. Define **assistive technology,** give examples, and explain how it would benefit certain children with disabilities.

4. Describe the assessment approaches that pertain to students with disabilities and identify several measurement tools.

5. State the steps in the assessment process regarding students with disabilities.

6. Describe the steps in the IEP process and the ITP process for students with disabilities.

7. Provide examples of various behavior management interventions used with students who are identified in each of the disability categories.

8. Analyze the impact of classroom organization for students with disabilities and explain some of the ways to manage a classroom.

9. Clarify the diverse roles and responsibilities of special education teachers and the general education teacher with regard to students with disabilities.

10. Explain how to utilize paraprofessionals and identify the roles they play in the education of students with special needs.

Preview Questions

These five multiple-choice questions pertain to the testing categories explained previously. Self-assess your knowledge to determine the areas you need to study.

The questions and answers have been developed based on federal law and professional practices for students with disabilities in school settings. Some practices are different across the states, so select your answers based on the terminology, policies, best practices, and the laws.

1. When an assessment has been completed and the results are to be shared, who should interpret the results for the team?

    A.   the counselor
    B.   the special education teacher
    C.   the examiner or a person qualified
    D.   the principal or special education director

2. When an IEP is to be implemented, what is the MOST essential item the general educator needs to know?

    A.   the agencies involved
    B.   the types of related services
    C.   the format of instruction allowed
    D.   the types of accommodations required

3. If a student with a vision impairment is placed in a language arts class, what is one of the critical accommodations that should be discussed?

    A.   special furniture
    B.   graphic organizer
    C.   computer technology
    D.   homework exemptions

4. When team members work independently of one another on implementing student programs, we call this a(an) _____ team.

    A.   intradisciplinary team
    B.   interdisciplinary team
    C.   transdisciplinary team
    D.   multidisciplinary team

5. When a student has a behavior that repeats beyond an end point, and the student has problems changing tasks, this is called:

    A. target

    B. antecedent

    C. discrete trial

    D. perseveration

The correct answers are

    1. C. The person who conducted the evaluation or a person qualified should interpret the results of an assessment on a student. The team can use this information to develop an educational program.

    2. D. It is the role of the general educator to implement the appropriate accommodations for a student with a disability when the student is included in the general education program. These accommodations are based on the IEP decisions made by the team.

    3. C. A student with a vision impairment would need accommodations to access computer programs. There are many available computer programs to support students with vision impairments.

    4. D. A transdisciplinary team is comprised of professionals who work independently of one another to assess and implement a program for a student with a disability.

    5. D. Perseveration is the continual repetition of a behavior by a student who is most likely not able to stop this behavior or make any change of the task without an intervention.

Case Study Information

The Application of Core Principles across Categories of Disability (0352) exam may contain a case study about a student or situation in special education with related multiple-choice questions included. When you answer the questions related to the case study, you are demonstrating your application of core knowledge. Your answers should reflect what you will do as a competent and qualified teacher who works with students who have disabilities.

Read the case study carefully and put yourself into the situation. Ask yourself: What does the law mandate about this topic? What would my professor tell me to do? What did I learn about this topic that will support my answer? What should I do to ensure the free and appropriate public education that students with disabilities are entitled to? Draw your conclusions based only on the information given and not what you think should be included. Read the case several times to be sure you understand the problem and what you are being asked to do. Then carefully and thoughtfully answer the multiple-choice questions that are included. Another case study is included in the practice exam for this section.

Study Information

The information in this study guide reflects your application of core knowledge principles. It is based on all that you have studied in school, and at work. Review the different topics of special education throughout this book and think about how you would use this information in a real setting with actual students as that is how you will be tested on the exam. You have learned the information and must then demonstrate competency.

Curriculum

Curriculum and instruction are important areas to address when developing and implementing programs for students with disabilities. Many types of curriculum and various kinds of instruction are effective with certain learners. Know the students and the availability of curriculum. Be prepared to accommodate, modify, and adapt.

Modifications and Adaptations

Accommodations, modifications, and adaptations are all terms that have been used in special education interchangeably in reference to placing supports in a student's program for instruction, the educational environment, and the curriculum. Before explaining how to use these with students, read the definition and examples. Remember that these definitions reflect the opinion and experience of the author, and some professionals may have a different definition for these terms. Some professionals use these terms to mean the same thing and make no distinction between them.

Accommodations: The instructional supports or services needed by the student with the disability to access the instruction or learning environment and to demonstrate his knowledge. These supports or services must not change the curriculum or the subject covered. They are provided to reduce the barriers caused by a deficit or disability and, therefore, provide an "equal opportunity" to the student with the disability.

Examples of accommodations include oral reports, amplification system, Braille writer, preferential seating, additional time, books on tape, and a note taker.

Modifications: These are changes made to the curriculum, the environment, or the expectations in order to meet the individual student's needs. These changes may be imposed if the work or task is above the student's ability. They are provided to reduce the expectations or content because of the severity or type of disability so the student may have some success.

Examples of modifications include limiting number of math problems, completing half of the spelling words, and exemption from certain tasks.

Adaptations: These are more widely used in reference to facilities and equipment and may also be reflected under the requirements of Section 504. These supports may make changes in how the student accesses the environment or instruction and may be confused with accommodations and modifications.

Examples of adaptations include wheelchair accessibility, head gear on computers, special furniture, providing frequent breaks, and posting a daily picture chart.

There are literally hundreds, perhaps thousands, of accommodations, modifications, and adaptations for students with disabilities. Some work best with certain types of disabilities and some are particularly beneficial for certain students. When using accommodations or modifications, be sure that all staff who are working with the student are well informed about which to use and how the accommodations or modifications should be applied and used regularly to support the student's program.

Any accommodation that is utilized during the regular school day is also allowed in a testing situation; however, modifications are different in that respect and cannot be allowed if they alter the validity and reliability of the exam. Check with the testing coordinator or schedule a team meeting to discuss the specific types of accommodations that will be used and any modifications that may be allowed for testing, especially for the state standard exams.

Accommodations and modifications are particularly useful in an inclusion model as they help to address the student's needs more specifically than just placing the student in the general education program. It may be wise to train general education staff in how and why you need to use accommodations and modifications and to explain that using these does not show favoritism. Fair is not always equal.

Accommodations and modifications may be used in a broad range of situations, including accessing the general education curriculum, conducting instruction and activities, during peer tutoring or therapy, and at extracurricular activities or sporting events.

The primary questions to ask when approaching a team decision regarding the use of accommodations, modifications, or adaptations are

1. How can we help this student participate in the lesson, in the classroom, or in the activity in the same way as all the other nondisabled students?
2. What can we do to support this student so she may have full access and as much benefit as possible in the educational program?

Additional Common Accommodations

Accommodations should be helpful to students so they are able to retain and repeat the information and concepts learned without the barriers of a disability. They do not change the concept, lesson, or environment.

- Use of daily schedule
- Tape recordings of lectures
- Word processor for written assignments
- Peer tutoring
- Open book tests

- Calculator
- Graphic organizers
- Large print books
- Visual aids
- Assistive computer technology

Additional Common Modifications

Modifications may change the actual content, lesson, or environment. Some modifications implemented may be to

- Reduce the amount of work
- Change the task
- Eliminate homework
- Allow more time on class test

If you are unsure of the types of accommodations, modification, or adaptations to use, refer to national professional organizations or go online for the specific disability types to peruse lists of options. The best method is to discuss the student's problem or concerns with the team and brainstorm how you can support the student.

Specialized Programs and Materials

Special education professionals are bound by the premise that assessments provide a realistic view of a student's present levels of educational performance and deliver a comprehensive look at the student's abilities, strengths, and weaknesses. The needs outlined from the assessment drive instruction for the student. Therefore, the selection of programs and materials should be based on the individual instructional needs.

Teachers must be able to use a multitude of different instructional programs and materials due to the diversity of the learners. Many curricula options are on the market, and so many programs have been created for special learners. Beware that these programs are not appropriate for all students. Students are diverse in a multitude of ways, so purchasing one program or one shelf of materials will not go far in addressing individual learners in your program.

Knowing the types of programs available and how they affect students educationally is very important. Understanding students, their characteristics, and how the disability impacts their learning and their interests, will aid in choosing the programs and materials.

The following terms are related to curriculum and instruction used with students who have disabilities.

Authentic learning: Teaching that uses real-world projects and activities to allow students to discover and explore in the manner that is relevant to them.

Differentiated instruction: To address the different abilities, strengths, and needs of various learners and their style of learning. The keys of differentiated instruction include choice of learning activity, tasks that suit the learning style, student groupings, authentic lessons, and problem-based learning.

Direct instruction: When the teacher very specifically provides additional support for curricular topics to individual students (may be used with large groups for initial concept delivery).

Multiple intelligence strategies: The nine areas of learning to be addressed in classrooms, identified by Howard Gardner, are linguistic, logical-mathematical, spatial, bodily-kinesthetic, musical, interpersonal, intrapersonal, naturalistic, and existential.

Peer tutoring: Under the guidance of a teacher, a peer with competencies in a particular area helps a student with a disability who needs assistance with this area of study.

Universal design: The concept that everything in the environment, in learning and in products, should be accessible to everyone.

Addressing Diversity

The state of this country is changing, and it is predicted that in the next 10 years, children will come from more culturally diverse homes, speak primary languages other than English, and live in higher rates of poverty than ever before in history. These population changes impact the composition of U.S. schools, and it is expected that more children will be placed in special education due to the problems they will have with learning.

Special education researchers are now examining the areas that affect learning in children of ethnic origins: low socioeconomic status, culture, and race. They are determined to study the definitions and cultural impact and find unbiased methods and procedures for assessing and teaching these students. These studies may influence future special education policies and practices in relation to the increasing numbers of non Anglo-Saxon children and how to best meet their various needs.

Establishing environments conducive to learning for all students will help in the diversity movement. Environment places a major role in the development of young children. When young children live and develop in poverty stricken homes, lack the language of the schools, and are of a minority race, research shows that they will be more at-risk for placement in special education programs. Keeping literacy materials accessible, that include learning options, providing activities that are interesting and sensitive to all children, supporting all learning styles, and providing technology resources will enhance learning for students with disabilities.

Prevention is one possibility if diversity factors are addressed, although it takes money that does not yet exist. Investing in groups of children who are at-risk for disabilities at a young age may certainly reduce the cost of remediation and special education programs in the future. As academic standards are increased and additional accountability is placed upon the schools, children of diverse cultures and backgrounds may begin to slip through the cracks unless support is provided swiftly and early.

Another form of diversity in special education falls within the actual categories listed in federal law. There are 13 suggested under IDEIA, yet within each of the categories is a multitude of characteristics with no two children acting or learning in the same way. Educators have a diverse set of learning needs to support. This causes a tremendous strain on the educators, the schools, and the programs to meet each and every child's unique needs.

Whether addressing cultural diversity or categorical diversity, writing an IEP or an ITP, implementing interventions, or conducting an assessment, educators need to reflect on their personal opinions and perspectives so they may better understand and serve all children in this changing society.

Using Technology

Federal regulations state that assistive technology is any item, piece of equipment, or product system, whether acquired commercially off the shelf, modified, or customized, that is used to increase, maintain, or improve the functional capabilities of children with disabilities. Students should be assessed in the area of assistive technology in order for the proper program and device to be selected. Training is often a necessity for the student, parents, and staff.

Assistive technology may be high- or low-tech devices that are used to remove barriers or to help solve everyday problems for individuals with disabilities. For example, these devices may be environmental controls, or voice activated or switch controlled augmentative communication systems. They may include simple tools such as a reaching device, or more complicated tools like taped instruction. They are available to assist individuals with disabilities to complete tasks and can aid with writing, reading, communicating, listening, doing math, organizing, and remembering.

Following are examples of technology-based applications for special education:

Augmentative technology: Supports students with disabilities who have oral language problems.

Assistive technology: For use with students with all types of disabilities, but especially helpful for those with physical disabilities, hearing impairments, and visual impairments.

Instructional technology: Provides drills and practice for students who have problems in the basic skill areas and with motivation issues.

Oral reading software: For students with reading problems (learning disabilities, autism, mental retardation, and so on).

Word processing software: To support students with written expression deficits.

Instruction

The key to instruction is individualization. We can discuss and explain the enormous quantities of information on the varieties of strategies, formats, and methods available, but nothing will compare to your ability to establish and implement an individualized plan for each of your students with disabilities. You need the background information, but it will only be useful if you can apply it to your individual students based on the special education knowledge you have gained.

Implementing the IEP

After the IEP has been developed by the IEP team, it is the responsibility of the special education teacher (or speech therapist if the student only qualifies under speech language impairment) to implement the services and manage the team of professionals who will carry out the plan (although some schools use case managers). This act of implementation includes being in contact with related services providers of the supplementary aids and services, as well as pursuing program accommodations and modifications found in the IEP. The implementation review should prepare the team for the student's involvement with nondisabled peers and other school activities.

In most states the implementation begins immediately upon the writing of the plan and in some states, there may be an allowance to begin the IEP within 14 days of the day it was written. It is the responsibility of the team to ensure that services begin and that copies of the IEP are provided to all professionals who will be a part of the educational program staff, including general education teacher(s). Each member of the team should be fully aware and understand the responsibility of involvement as the success of any IEP implementation depends on teamwork.

In order to implement the IEP, several steps must be taken, and review should occur at the conclusion of the IEP meeting.

- Identify all team members and their roles.
- Describe the related services, providers, and resources.
- Determine where services will occur and the need for changes to routine day.
- Discuss any accommodations or adaptations to materials, environment, and so on.
- Identify any need for assistive technology and how that will be handled.
- Explain the testing formats that will be used and any accommodations.
- Decide whether there is need for agency involvement and how that will occur.
- Prepare for progress updates.

Selecting and Using Appropriate Strategies and Methods

In selecting strategies and methods for the instruction of students with disabilities, use the approach of individualization. Some strategies work with certain groups of students with disabilities, and some are beneficial to particular subject areas. But as a teacher, you must first know your student and his needs. Following are some terms related to strategies and methods that will help you with your studies.

Strategies: The skills or techniques that may be used to assist a student in learning the curriculum. For special education, these must be individualized based on the IEP goals and the student's abilities and level. Examples may include: color coding words, visual cues, flip charts, or highlighting sections of print.

Chained response: The break down of a task into component parts. The student is required to finish the task by starting with the first step in the sequence and performing each component progressively in the sequence until the task is completed.

Chunking: A strategy that allows students to remember and organize large amounts of information.

Contingent teaching: A strategy that supports a student as she needs help and eventually fades out the support as she gains mastery.

Learning strategy approach: Teaching students how to learn instead of teaching the particular content.

Prompting: A technique where a visual, auditory, or tactile cue is presented to facilitate the completion of a task or to perform a behavior.

Response generalization: The application of a learned behavior or skill to another setting.

Scaffolding: Applying stages to learning content and tasks, by first observing the student to see what he can do and then helping the student so he understands the how and why until he can perform himself (direct instruction, tutoring, modeling, independence).

Task analysis: A strategy in which the goals are broken into smaller steps and sequenced while keeping the learner's pace in focus.

Managing the Learning Environment

There are standard practices recommended for use in managing learning environments in education; however, there are different types of environments and learners. This section reviews some basic information on classroom management and an overview of how behaviors play a part in the management of students with disabilities.

Behavior Management

Behavior management has much to do with the individual student and the environment. Examine the student's disability and the impact it has on the student's skills and abilities. Observe the behavior choices the student makes in multiple settings. Talk with others who work with the student and converse regularly with the family so consistency is a strong component of the student's program. You may need assistance from a professional in behavior interventions, such as a behavior specialist, a psychologist, or psychiatrist. It is difficult to provide all of the information about behaviors in this study guide, as it is a complicated and highly individualized area of a student's educational program.

Think about establishing guidelines for students about acceptable behaviors, which is a proactive approach to managing the classroom and helping students learn self-management. This helps them follow rules and abide by expectations, which is a future skill needed in the adult world.

This section provides you with general strategies and defines the terms to help you move toward individualizing your behavior management techniques for students.

- Make the environment comfortable and safe.
- Involve students in creating rules.
- Avoid power struggles and confrontations.
- Implement and track behavior plans.
- Develop expectations for appropriate behaviors that are realistic for all learners.
- Use immediate, honest, and consistent feedback and reinforcements.
- Individualize instruction and give time to each student each day.

Students aim to please. They want to do what is right, but sometimes they do not know what is proper. And sometimes something is not quite right with their lives that causes them to misbehave. Remember that inappropriate behavior is usually the result of something gone awry and not a personal vendetta against the educational staff.

Implement a standard of behavior in the classroom and then impose a system of rewards and consequences for those who are able to manage themselves. For those who cannot manage, other strategies may be necessary, which are discussed later. A motivator that produces improved behaviors in students is *incentives*. These can be any positive reward for doing the right thing. An incentive can be used as an unexpected reward (like a sticker), or a known goal to reach (like free time). Make a list in the classroom of options students may select from (let them help create it), use a chart system of tracking behaviors, and then enjoy the reward yourself of motivated, active, and engaged learners. Examples of incentives may include the following:

- Work on an art project of your choice.
- Be the line leader.
- Read a favorite book.
- Work on the computer.
- Read to another class.
- Get additional school supplies.

- Listen to music.
- Have lunch with an adult.
- Play a game.
- Choose from the treasure box.
- Get a free homework pass.
- Get a bookmark.

With regard to students in special education, there are certain mandates for behavior under federal law that must be followed. The following are both comprehensive procedures that may fluctuate in steps and processes depending on your state or district, but are required.

- Functional Behavior Assessment
- Behavior Intervention Plan

The following terms will be helpful in your study of behavior interventions and management with students who exhibit disabilities. Be sure to read the information about behavior in the Knowledge-Based Core Principles section of this book.

- **Acting out behavior:** The inappropriate (aggressive or disruptive) behavior considered more damaging and serious than other behaviors.
- **Applied Behavior Analysis (ABA):** A method of behavior analysis to determine how and why the student responds to certain events, situations, or the environment the way he does. It allows for a training component of rewards and reinforcements to help the student learn the target behavior.
- **Alternative school placement:** A public school placement option that may be utilized when a student cannot function in the traditional form of a public school system due to uncontrolled behaviors or due to a disruption that caused a suspension or expulsion and, therefore, a temporary placement.
- **Antecedent:** A stimulus used in behavior management and behavior modification that occurs prior to the behavior and establishes the reason for the behavior. Part of the ABC assessment.
- **Behavioral intervention:** Strategies or actions used to extinguish, change, or redirect an inappropriate behavior; three types are positive reinforcement, negative reinforcement, aversive intervention.
- **Behavioral rating scales:** An evaluation tool that lists specific observable behaviors to assess the severity, frequency, and type of exhibited behaviors that is completed by staff, parents, or student.
- **Consequences:** The stimulus that follows a behavioral action used in behavior management or behavior modification to increase or decrease the behavior.
- **Contingency contract:** A written agreement between the student and the teacher that outlines the student's expected performance and the consequences or reinforcers used.
- **Discrete trial training:** A strategy in which the function or task is broken down into steps that are rewarded immediately in a trial by trial basis.
- **Modeling:** The use of imitation by a student to set in place the desired behaviors.
- **Negative reinforcement:** Utilized in behavior modification in which the student is motivated to use a desired behavior in order to avoid a negative consequence (like taking away privileges).

- **Perseveration:** When a behavior continues repeatedly beyond the typical endpoint, and the student demonstrates difficulty switching tasks (such as self-stimulating behaviors).

- **Positive reinforcement:** Utilized in behavior modification in which the student is motivated to use a desired behavior because of the reward that can be obtained.

- **Target behavior:** The behavior selected for intervention. Most often in **behavior modification,** it is an undesirable behavior that should be extinguished or changed. In **behavior management,** it may be a positive behavior that the team wants the student to continue to use in school situations.

Classroom Organization and Management

Classroom management is absolutely essential when functioning in an inclusion model, as there may be many types of learners, whether placed in special education or not. Of the special education learners, there may be many varieties of disabilities and within those disabilities, many characteristics. Managing and organizing a classroom for diverse learners is a tremendous task, but because a special education teacher is creative and flexible, the mission becomes less overwhelming.

Be sure you understand the essential ingredients of managing a classroom. Procedures are a key component, not only for you, but for the students. They need to know the rules and expectations in order to make learning their focus. After these are established and the students clearly understand, you will notice a reduction in disruptive and inappropriate behaviors. Here are some of the procedures to consider instituting:

- Classroom rules
- Attention-getting techniques
- Homework process
- Activity transitions

- Discipline techniques
- Project and activity details
- Completed work guidelines
- Dismissal procedures

Particularly helpful in classrooms for special needs students is the implementation of effective learning strategies so every member of the class is learning at his rate and level. Use a multimodal approach that involves the use of teaching methods and strategies that are visual, auditory, tactile, and kinesthetic. Addressing all styles of learning will encourage and motivate your learners.

Here are some of the strategies to implement to be sure the classroom environment meets the needs of students:

- Remove distractions, both visual and auditory.
- Eliminate unnecessary materials and keep areas tidy.
- Help students organize work and personal area.
- Keep extra supplies for projects and forgetful students.

- Implement a break time between activities.
- Maintain equipment in working order.
- Set up displays and special areas for enrichment.

Strategies to improve student work include the following:

- Allow enough time for assignments.
- Move about the room to help all students.
- Give directions in clear, easy, and repetitive ways.
- Modify, adapt, and accommodate for certain students.
- Use modeling and demonstration for new tasks and activities.
- Explain the "why" when students make mistakes.

- Implement instructional strategies based on learner needs.
- Provide supplementary aids such as notes and graphs.
- Deliver feedback and reinforcement for desired behaviors.

Professional Roles/Issues and Literature

Teachers wear many hats in many places. Special education teachers have similar hats and their responsibilities range across a very broad expanse. The primary goal of special education for teachers is effective teamwork so student programs will be enhanced and they may become more successful.

Working in inclusive settings offers a wide variety of tasks to be addressed with huge variations in implementation and interventions. Services to students grow and become more refined when teachers and other professionals share their expertise. Both the special education teacher and the general education teacher have important team roles in the delivery of services.

Teacher's Role

The basic role of the general education teacher is to instruct students in the general education curriculum according to district standards and state requirements, while implementing accommodations, modifications, or adaptations for students with disabilities.

The basic role of the special education teacher is to manage the IEP team, implement the IEP, provide accommodations through the general education staff, and support the student in the general education settings.

Specific duties of a special education teacher include the following:

- Conduct assessments.
- Plan for learning time and a variety of learning styles.
- Plan for specifically designed instruction.
- Implement instruction and accommodations.
- Monitor progress.
- Collaborate, consult, and confer with team members.
- Schedule and run IEP meetings.
- Conduct transition assessments and create ITP.

- Train staff and students in advocacy.
- Communicate with parents.
- Facilitate programs and activities.
- Supervise paraprofessionals.
- Manage behavior assessments and plans.
- Participate in staff development and workshops.
- Join professional organizations and attend conferences.
- Read research and journals about current trends.

Whether you work in a segregated setting, a resource room, or an inclusive model, your duties are much the same, and the load can be heavy. Schedule yourself and stay organized. Use resources and helpers to meet all your deadlines and complete tasks. Keep your students as your main focus and work with others in a pleasant and professional manner. Check your district policies and meet with your special education director and principal to be sure you know the expectations for your position.

Consultations and Collaboration with Others

It is recommended that you read the Core Knowledge portion of this study guide regarding "Collaboration and Teaming" for additional information. It includes more detailed descriptions of collaborative teaming, coordination, consultation, co-teaching, and the three primary types of teams used in public school programs: **multidisciplinary, interdisciplinary,** and **transdisciplinary.**

Collaboration: Professionals work together and use the expertise of one other to provide more appropriate direct services to students with disabilities.

Coordination: Includes communication and cooperation so the services to students with disabilities are ensured delivery.

Consultation: Professionals work alongside one another to share methods and strategies that will meet the needs of students with disabilities.

Co-teaching: Two or more teachers work together to plan, deliver instruction, and assess students.

Multidisciplinary team: Professionals with defined roles, who work independently of one another.

Interdisciplinary team: Members who conduct independent assessments but promote communication and collaboration.

Transdisciplinary team: Demonstrates a high level of coordination and involvement by team members through integrated approach across disciplines.

Throughout history, teachers have worked in isolation, delivering instruction to their students and managing their own classrooms. But in the past decade, educators have found that one of their very best resources for ideas and support was in the classroom next door. Before the 1970s students in special education were kept apart of the mainstream of the school population, and services were delivered in separate rooms. In the 1990s, the movement of inclusion changed how services were implemented and, therefore, changed how educators interact. They can now share their expertise, their skills, their perspectives, and their ideas, which enriches the field of education.

Paraprofessionals

The addition of paraprofessionals in special education programs has become an essential staff position that spans a wide range of duties and responsibilities. Under the tutelage and supervision of a special education teacher (or other special education professional), a paraprofessional can help the teacher by providing more direct special education services and additional instructional opportunities or activities on a consistent and regular basis to students with disabilities.

As case loads soar and the numbers of identified students increases, the expansion of programs and services are possible with these assistants in special education classes, as well as in general education rooms and for individual instruction. A particularly positive aspect of utilizing paraprofessionals is the flexibility of their role, as they may work with a wide variety of students, many types of disabilities, and in various settings. They actually extend the special education teacher to more places and more children by being a part of the educational team.

Although the special education teacher or professional is ultimately responsible for every student's program, the paraprofessional, who is a member of the education team (not the IEP team), can help with a multitude of tasks. The list is endless, yet the paraprofessional may not conduct some duties that are solely the responsibility of a certified person and those are realistically identified in each state or in each school district.

Paraprofessionals may help by performing some of the following tasks:

- Prepare paperwork.
- Set up the classroom.
- Utilize, modify, and care for materials.
- Provide personal care assistance.
- Provide guidance on instructional work.
- Monitor independent work of students.
- Assist teacher in gathering data.
- Chart behavior actions.
- Help in behavior management.
- Aid in classroom and instructional preparation.
- Attend workshops and trainings.
- Maintain confidentiality about students and families.

It is critical that the supervisory professionals establish clear guidelines and outline the roles and responsibilities of and for the paraprofessional. These practices will ensure a more successful working relationship and the positive delivery of services to students. The traits most often observed in successful paraprofessionals include being flexible, dependable, motivated, tolerant, patient, cooperative, resourceful, and positive.

Other terms synonymous with paraprofessional are paraeducator, educational aide, instructional aide, teacher aide, classroom assistant, and classroom aide.

Transition Planning

The development of an Individual Transition Plan (ITP) is a requirement under the federal special education law to assist students in preparing for their futures. Students who are reaching the age of 16 should participate with the team in beginning the transition process. A plan must be set in place by the 16th birthday (IDEA required age 14) and it becomes a part of the formal IEP.

Considering the future for a student with a disability can be a complicated process, but one that will aid the student in pursuing her interests and living as productively as possible. It may be difficult for students with disabilities at age 16 to think about the future with such things as housing, employment, and recreation, but a team of people can guide the student through the process and prepare the student for the future.

Both the student and the parent are important members of the ITP team, as this plan is about planning for the student's future, when IEP services will no longer be an option. The students with disabilities age out of high school programs at age 22. The ITP will help the student prepare for this termination of special education services.

Other members of the team are professionals from the school: therapists, teachers, and so on, as well as community members or agency staff. Involving the interagencies who will provide the adult services are as important as the student in this process. The interagencies will be knowledgeable about the services available in the community for adults and help to transition the student upon graduation. Effective transitions are essential for students, and these are enhanced when teams work collaboratively.

The four key areas to discuss and develop in a transition plan include the following:

- Post-secondary education/vocational training
- Employment
- Independent living
- Community involvement

The transition plan must include a coordinated set of activities that are based on the student's needs, interests, and preferences. The actual transition services may include additional instruction, self-advocacy training, functional and life skills development, instruction on social skills, employment opportunities, and community experiences. For most students with disabilities it is necessary to conduct a vocational assessment to determine the skills, interests, and abilities of the individual student.

Note: The age of majority is a procedure that should be reviewed and finalized with parents and the student. In the law, when students become of majority age (differs in each state), they become an adult. The student has the right to make educational decisions without notification or consent of their parent, unless they choose to involve the parent. This majority age generally occurs for students with disabilities before they leave high school, so this is a component of the IEP that must be addressed. Each state and each district will have policies and procedures to follow for the transfer of rights and for the option regarding incompetent students.

Professional Literature and Research

Educators use little of the professional literature or journals that are published to seek new information. Not all educators join organizations or read the research on specific disabilities or issues. But these two practices do not coincide with the fast pace of changes in special education. Professional literature, resources, and organizations are essential to teachers so they may gain the best information in their practice.

In this age of technology there is incredible access to the millions of articles, thousands of journals, and hundreds of professional organizations that support a quest to improve programs for students and to gain information that will enrich your career. Do not underestimate the resources that are available, as they will save you time in the long run. Conducting your search for information may take time, but you will learn the ease of finding information by becoming familiar with the texts, sites, or other sources.

When you are seeking information about instruction, strategies, or methods, look for empirical research or studies that are conducted based on the realistic situations of real students with disabilities. These scientifically based studies will provide you with information about students that are similar to those in your situation.

Introduction

Most likely you have studied the field of early childhood education for a number of years in your formal training. You may be a recent college graduate and getting ready to take this exam for your certification; you may have taken additional courses to add this specialty field to your existing certifications; or you may have worked in an early childhood setting and need to take the exam for certification in another state. Whichever description fits, you were probably exposed to a significant amount of early childhood information, practices, and applications. However, not knowing the expectations of the Praxis exam may pose several questions for you as you study and prepare.

The Special Education Preschool/Early Childhood Praxis II exam is a knowledge-based exam that covers the principles and practices of teachers in preschool through grade 1 settings. This information is based on the theories, the laws, the specialized instruction, and the application of practices in school environments for children ages 3 to 6 and the early intervention services for children birth through 2.

The exam, for which you are allotted two hours, has approximately 110 multiple-choice questions that range between six main content categories. These include Human Growth and Development (15 percent, 16 questions); Knowledge of Disabling Conditions (11 percent, 12 questions); Evaluation, Assessment, Eligibility Criteria (15 percent, 16 questions); Planning and Delivery of Services (15 percent, 17 questions); Family and Community Aspects (19 percent, 21 questions); and Professional Practice (25 percent, 28 questions).

This study guide summarizes the information so you may focus your studies prior to taking the Praxis II exam (0690). Websites are available in the "Resources" section of this book, so you may search for additional information.

Content Clusters

Before reading this entire section, try to answer each of the following questions. These questions should provide a review of your individual knowledge base for each broad topic. Although these questions are not multiple choice, they span all the content categories represented in the Praxis II Preschool/Early Childhood exam which should help you in your studies.

1. Describe these various assessment terms: criterion-referenced test, norm-referenced test, portfolio assessment, standards-based assessment, ecological assessment, authentic assessment, play-based assessment, curriculum-based assessment, dynamic assessment, family-based assessment, running record, event sampling, and anecdotal record.

2. What goals, interventions, and activities would be beneficial to a child who exhibits a delay, a disability, or is at-risk in each of the following domains of learning: language, motor, cognitive, self-help/adaptive, and social-emotional?

3. Explain how the value of play and the environment, both indoors and outdoors, will support and promote appropriate skill development in all learning domains.

4. What is the difference between these terms: communication, language, speech, and literacy? What do these words mean: semantics, pragmatics, syntax, phonology, morphology, expressive, and receptive?

5. Identify the most prevalent issues related to each of the following:

   a. cultural and linguistic diversity in young children
   b. early childhood programs
   c. assessments

6. What skills are considered cognitive functions and what activities or strategies will promote cognitive development in young children?

7. What is the role of the family unit in a child's education and what are three ways that an early childhood educator might encourage a family to participate in their young child's educational program?

8. What is the difference between a syndrome and a disease, and what are the various characteristics or disabilities that are manifested in children with genetic syndromes?

9. How does the current brain research explain a child's developmental stages as they pertain to the five domains of learning and how do each of these domains affect the education of children with disabilities?

10. What educational theories are related to human growth and development, and how do they impact our perspective of children in an educational setting?

You have now completed the first step to assessing your knowledge. How did you do? How well did you recall the information? The next few pages provide definitions, theories, and early childhood information that recap the more important concepts in this area of special education. If you had some difficulties with the answers to the 10 preceding questions, you should read over the materials in this section and then ask yourself the questions again.

Preview Questions

The following multiple-choice questions are provided as a preview of the types of questions that will be on the Praxis II exam. This demonstrates what you may need to study and how you should attack the early childhood/preschool questions on this exam.

Regardless of your personal philosophy, remember that the exam questions are focused on the most appropriate answers as demonstrated in federal law, the developmental stages and domains, and the professional best practices.

---

1. Which of the following is considered a current trend that *strongly* affects early childhood programs?

   A. transition services
   B. community projects
   C. assistive technology
   D. administration views

---

2. The Behavioral Approach Theory that focuses on both utilizing direct instruction and teaching specific skills was developed by

   A. Jean Piaget.
   B. B.F. Skinner.
   C. John Dewey.
   D. Frederich Froebel.

---

3. The type of measurement that is MOST often used to identify the skills a young child has mastered is the

   A. behavior assessment.
   B. alternative assessment.
   C. norm-referenced assessment.
   D. criterion-referenced assessment.

---

4. When a child has difficulty with _____ she will most likely exhibit social-emotional problems, and the team should develop goals and interventions to address this area.

    A. talking

    B. sleeping

    C. bonding

    D. listening

5. A strong predictor of success and positive outcomes for a young child with a disability is

    A. program efficacy.

    B. educator involvement.

    C. parent responsiveness.

    D. therapeutic consistency.

The correct answers are

1. C. Assistive technology is required under the special education law and it involves aspects that are both philosophically based and economically difficult for schools. It is an on-going issue that must be addressed.

2. B. Skinner was a behavioral psychologist who believed that imitation and reinforcement are key to learning.

3. D. A criterion-referenced test is used to evaluate a child's mastery of skills that have already been learned, identifying those that may need instruction, and does not compare the child's score with a normed group.

4. C. The bonding and attachment formed in a parent-child relationship affects all future relationships. A child who demonstrates difficulty in this area will need support through goals and interventions.

5. C. Research shows that when parents and family are involved in a child's educational program, the child is more successful in school.

Study Information

Early childhood education services and early intervention services are mandated and defined under the same federal law, IDEIA, that special education programs are required to follow and therefore reflect many of the same practices used in all special education processes programs.

Early childhood education has only come to the forefront in recent years, and it is currently a focus for many educational institutions. Following are the three main reasons that young children are now receiving the attention and services they need.

- Added brain and development research support
- Changed social policies and pertinent legislation
- Improved and increased effective programs for young children

The research that has been conducted over the past decade adamantly supports programs for young children, prior to the regular school age attendance. Brain research shows that learning occurs beginning at birth and by age 8 children have developed a powerful foundation for future learning. Certainly, the relationships a child experiences and the environment the child is in make all the difference. From research on social issues for young children (poverty, nutrition, and abuse), it is evident that early intervention works for young children who are faced with these constraints. Finally, medical research has documented infants who have lived through compelling medical circumstances, only to need special services to access their education and daily activities. All these research topics point to the encouraging and successful effects of early childhood interventions and programs.

The recent legislation and social policies have taken a commanding stance on providing services to very young children. Gone is the day when a child enrolls in school for the very first time in the first grade. There was once a time that even kindergarten was not required. Lawmakers are taking a different perspective on the value of the young mind and beginning to support and even initiate programs that fulfill the needs of the youngest society members.

The research conducted and the laws established have paved the way for early childhood and preschool programs to evolve. More and more intervention and education programs are available to young children, and these programs are improving each day, which is due in part to universities that now offer courses and the states that now require certification in this field. Educators must continue to advocate for young children, as they cannot do it themselves.

Early childhood education, spans ages birth to 8 years; however, the Praxis exam you are studying covers ages birth to 6 years. More and more educators are seeking certification in this field, in addition to holding an elementary or a special education certification. This is a wise choice with the variations in the programs and the numbers of young children requiring services. This knowledge will assist any elementary teacher or special education teacher who works with very young children preschool through second grade.

This guide is not comprehensive of all the information available about early childhood programs and services, but it does help the examinee select the specific topics to study prior to taking the exam.

Human Growth and Development

Children bring into the classrooms of America some genuine qualities. They are natural, honest, curious, innocent, and dependent. They have a desire to please, a need to belong, a wish to be liked, and a yearning to be believed. Educators must help them look forward to each day and satisfy their hunger for life's knowledge.

Every child must be provided the opportunity to learn and develop skills to the best of her ability. Children should be allowed to be children. They should be provided with a spectrum of experiences, a chance to meet daily challenges, and an opportunity to grow educationally, emotionally, and physically. They should be allowed to be themselves, to be heard, and to be happy. Whatever the age of the students, they should be nurtured, guided, and cared for unconditionally. It is the educator's responsibility to see that children's diverse needs are met.

Adults think, observe, act, and play differently than children. When you enter the world of early childhood to work with young children, remember that adults do not perceive the world in the same way that children do. You should observe children to determine how they think and notice what they do. Educators want young children to grow up to be the best adults they can be. Your support and understanding will guide them to learn about the world, becoming lifelong learners.

Aspects of Development

You have most likely studied human growth and development in your formal training. In this section you will find abbreviated information about the growth and development of young children. The key to understanding the theories and the developmental stages is in knowing how these factors affect the children in your program. This section should provide the framework for your further study on this topic.

Knowing and understanding the aspects of development are key elements for an early childhood educator. In serving young children with special needs, an educator must be aware of the typical development of young children and what may cause proper development to go awry. As a teacher creates an educational program for a young child with special needs, the five domains of learning and developmental milestones must be considered.

Following are the general learning milestones that children make between birth and 8 years of age:

- Personality is set by age 3.
- Behavior patterns are fixed by age 5.
- Language patterns are established prior to age 7.

- Learning styles and brain patterns are identified by age 8.
- Learning from play will be imprinted for the rest of a child's life.

Genetics and Medical Anomalies

Varied reasons and different events cause the development of a fetus to be adversely affected. These conditions can occur as early as cell division, and the loss or addition of a chromosome can result in significant alterations for hundreds of genes. Single gene defects appear to play a primary role in more than 7000 known disorders. The greatest risk for developing a severe disability occurs during the period between conception and birth with the more common types of disabilities being mental retardation and various other congenital defects.

The factors that affect the growth and development of a fetus include environmental, genetic, and medical influences. The primary categories include the following:

- Nutrition (of the mother and later the infant)
- Exposure (to chemicals, medications, drugs, other teratogens)
- Infections (STDs, herpes, rubella)
- Illnesses (chronic conditions: thyroid disorder, diabetes, autoimmune issues)
- Diseases (HIV, AIDS, FAS)
- Syndromes (Down, Williams, Fragile X)

A child may be born with a syndrome condition that causes a disability. A syndrome is usually a stable, but persistent condition, and neurological regression is very uncommon. A syndrome may be caused by a chromosomal change or by teratogens. Some syndromes are very rare and others are more common. Children with the same syndrome may exhibit different characteristics of it. Early childhood educators should be familiar with syndrome conditions and the impact certain syndromes have on a child's growth, development, and education.

Although the percentage of children born with problems is small, it is many of these children who need special services and individual programs to properly access their education. Learn more about their specific conditions so you may support them in their growth, development, and learning.

Ages and Stages

Review the stages of typical development in children ages birth to 8 years. It is critical for early childhood educators to understand these stages so they may apply this knowledge to their work with children who demonstrate disabilities. If you are not familiar with the developmental stages in young children, you are urged to review some of the available developmental charts found at the library, or on the Internet on such sites as The U.S. Department of Health and Human Services. (Refer to the "Resources" section at the end of this book.)

As you review these charts, notice the natural developmental progression of the mind and body of a typical child. These are the general expectations for most young children, and knowing these will help when you are working with a child who has a delay. Sometimes, children grow more rapidly in one domain while lagging briefly in another. A typical child often catches up with the ages and stages expectations defined on these charts while a child with a delay may not.

Be cognizant of the fact that a child with a disability might fall behind in one or more domains, and it may be problematic for the child to progress to the expected age norms. Sometimes it is hard for parents or professionals to notice that a child is not at a certain level, as one cannot separate a child into different sections to examine his growth in separate areas. Educators tend to look at the whole child and notice the overall progress and gains.

The skills developed in each domain blend with other domains. Most closely related to the cognitive domain are the skills associated with the language and motor domains. It would be impossible to separate cognitive development from language and motor development as they are all affected by one another as a child grows and learns.

Brain Research

In recent years, there has been increased research on the brain, and professionals now know more about the human brain, growth and development, and early learning than ever before. Scientists, physicians, psychologists, and psychiatrists have studied the areas of development and found that the early years from birth to age 8 offer the greatest opportunity to instill and enhance quality learning in young children.

Intelligence is not fixed at birth. The early experiences promote growth and development and dictate the child's path to learning for the rest of his life. You have probably heard about the **windows of opportunity,** the critical period of development between the ages of birth and 6 years. This is the time when children learn the easiest and the fastest. It is because of this phenomenon that early childhood teachers should be aware and clearly understand the function of the brain. They can offer support to parents, and prepare their programs to suit the needs of all children.

A child's early relationships and a child's participation in the environment play incredibly complex roles in early development. Studies have shown that if a child forms secure attachments and bonds with the primary caregivers, the child will demonstrate positive growth and development. Just the same, if the environment is stimulating, and a child is exposed to a variety of enriching experiences, the brain cells will experience positive neural connections that affect the child's intelligence and abilities.

Domains of Learning

A **learning domain** is a specific area of development; there are five early domains to learning in which children continue to grow and develop during the early years. A program established to incorporate instruction in the domains provides a child with a strong educational foundation. Related activities should be created so they cross all domains and blend with the curriculum. Children with disabilities may experience a delay in one or more of these areas.

The five domains are

- Social-Emotional
- Self-Help/Adaptive
- Cognitive
- Language/Communication
- Physical

The five learning domains are each summarized here and additional information that pertains to delays and disabilities related to these domains are found in the section "Knowledge of Disabling Conditions."

Cognitive Domain

Cognition is the most important domain of learning, and its development begins very early. Children are born with the full capacity to learn. Mental skills are important to the development of all other domains and affect all areas of learning throughout children's lives. Cognition can be described as intellect, information processing, mental skills, or thinking abilities. Each of these descriptors refers to the knowledge that human beings may utilize in daily life.

The cognitive domain involves the development of a child's mental skills, which focus on thinking and reasoning, and these specific clusters include the following:

- Remembering
- Using abstractions
- Paying attention
- Problem-solving
- Making decisions
- Labeling and naming
- Organizing ideas
- Developing concepts
- Using verbal and figural analogies
- Developing rules and generalizations
- Reflecting on judgments and evaluations
- Forming knowledge and recognition skills
- Understanding cause-and-effect relationships
- Drawing inferences and understanding perceptions

Cognitive skills transform through consistent sequences based on a child's maturity level. Children learn the skills, and then through practice and aging, the skills become more refined and useful.

In early childhood education, educators must emphasize the importance of the cognitive domain on early learning, with parents, and preschool staff. As an early childhood educator, your knowledge of typical development, particularly related to the cognitive domain, will be vastly important. This information better equips you to understand and provide for the needs of every child, whether delayed, disabled, or typical.

For further study of the cognitive domain, investigate the following:

- Watson/Skinner-Behavioral Learning Theory
- Piaget-Cognitive Development Theory
- Vygotsky-Socio-Cultural Theory
- Constructive Learning Theory

Physical-Motor Domain

The motor domain holds the first learning that a child experiences. Children are born with the capacity and motivation to move, and they can gather massive amounts of data through the motor domain, storing the information in their brains. Their early experiences begin in the womb and involve physical contact, such as sucking and rocking. After birth, they experience more motor-related experiences such as eating, grabbing, and bathing. And later, as they begin to notice themselves, they touch their feet, mouth things, and crawl. As children interact with their environment, they do little speaking, but are much more active, experiencing their world in a very physical manner.

Children pass through many important developmental stages to reach critical milestones, such as crawling, walking, or holding objects. An early childhood educator must study the specific areas of typical motor skill acquisition to better serve those children who exhibit a delay, as they require additional support.

The motor domain includes

- **Gross motor:** Use of large muscles such as those in the torso, neck, arms, and legs
- **Fine motor:** Use of small muscles of the hands, fingers, feet, toes, and face
- **Sensory-integration (sensori-motor):** Use of sensory information to include tactile, sense, vestibular sense, and the proprioceptive sense
- **Perceptual motor:** How the muscles coordinate their movements with the information that is received through the environment by the senses

The most basic premise of motor development results from the various theories formed by Gesell, Piaget, Ayres, and Kephart and can be studied in more detail to fully understand how they apply to young children.

Social-Emotional Domain

Humans are programmed to be social; yet, for a child to become a **social being** she requires a set of learned skills. Infants depend on parents and caregivers to ensure their basic needs will be met, and this creates a bond and strengthens trust. Through this early relationship, young children begin their social lives, and as they grow they socialize with siblings, neighbors, and eventually their peers. Young children gain social skills as the result of many interactive experiences, especially those where they engage in relationships with others.

Emotions are an expression of feelings that reflect needs and desires. When a child is born, he experiences the feelings of hunger and sleep, but by the time the child reaches age two, he experiences expanded emotions that include happiness, sadness, anger, and fear. They continue to learn more complex emotions throughout the preschool years.

Not all children develop their social-emotional skills in the same way, but during the development of social-emotional skills, a child should build upon self-esteem, self-confidence, and self-competence. Several factors affect a child's social-emotional development: parent interactions, parenting styles, gender, communication, siblings, and temperament to name a few.

The **parent interactions** have a stunning affect on a child's social-emotional development. The bonding and attachment that is formed in this relationship influences all other relationships the child will experience, significantly affecting a child's development in this domain. Parents can provide the child with many social opportunities and may even teach the child certain social skills pertinent to their family culture. Even the **parenting style** (authoritative, authoritarian, permissive) impacts a child's social-emotional development.

Over the years, **gender** influences have determined that boys exhibit more aggression (verbal and physical) and competition than girls do, although girls demonstrate more relationship issues as they mature. Boys may experience more rejection from peers due to the aggression, and this may cause an impact on social-emotional development.

Communication impacts a child's ability to function with her peers and affects the child's social-emotional status. When a child develops typically in the cognitive and language domains she begins to understand and develop emotional competence, expanding on social skill development. If a child has positive social interactions and uses effective communication skills she will exhibit appropriate social behaviors.

A child's social interactions often reflect those used in **sibling** relationships. Having a sibling provides a child with more chances to practice learned social skills and to observe new skills. When children play with siblings, they learn appropriate and acceptable behavior skills such as sharing, resolving conflicts, and communicating.

A child's **temperament** affects how and when the child internalizes certain social skills and emotional abilities. These attributes of temperament (easy, difficult, slow-to-warm-up) demonstrate how a child will respond to a situation and to other people. Social competence is especially critical since it indicates the ability to interact appropriately with others.

Enrollment in a preschool program is an important step for a child's development in the social-emotional domain, as it offers opportunities to interact with other children at the same age level. Through play with peers, a child learns more about the social function of his behavior and how to use it with others. Establishing an environment that supports and encourages healthy social-emotional development and reflects developmentally appropriate play activities is critical for all children, but it is an essential component to the development of children with disabilities.

For more information about the social-emotional domain, research the following:

- Maslow-Humanism Theory
- Skinner-Behaviorism Theory
- Erikson- Psychosocial Theory
- Bandura-Social Learning Theory
- Kohlberg-Moral Reasoning Theory
- Gardner-Multiple Intelligence Theory

Self-Help/Adaptive Behavior Domain

Adaptive behaviors are a composite of abilities based on a child's age and the cultural mores of the family. Adaptive behaviors include self-help skills, the most important of which are feeding, dressing, and toileting. A child who can master these competencies will build upon her self-esteem and develop a sense of independence.

Adaptive behaviors are normally acquired during daily routines and activities in the early years. These are skills necessary throughout a lifetime. Children who acquire appropriate adaptive behaviors and self-help skills will function independently, leading to more social acceptance by their peers. For any age and ability of a child, this provides a strong sense of accomplishment.

Support for the acquisition of adaptive behavior skills in young children often depends on the family. However, families have certain expectations for their children, and teachers must be cognizant of their preferences, beliefs, and values. It also requires that educators are culturally aware and informed.

Educators must understand how these skills develop and are acquired in typical children so the lack of these skills in children with delays will be more obvious. If a child demonstrates a self-help/adaptive behavior delay, the educator should focus on teaching the skills in natural situations on a daily basis and inspire the family to replicate the program at home.

Language, Communication, Literacy Domain

Communication and language are of great importance and it is through everyday experiences that language becomes meaningful. But, more than 70 percent of communication is nonverbal. Even though children are bombarded daily with new words, language structures, and pattern combinations, they must also be able to learn the gestures, body movements, and facial expressions that portray communication. At birth, children know no certain language, cannot communicate well, and have a guttural oral presentation. By age 1, a child can recognize her name, say several words, imitate familiar words, follow directions, and recognize words as symbols. You can see the value of human language is the communicative power it provides!

Scientists continue to study the hows and whys of language acquisition related to young children and their abilities to learn and master the complex structures of language. They have determined that a child, at about 18 months old, shows a sudden expansion in vocabulary and the grasp of language, but scientists do not know why. One thought is that children may begin storing sounds and meanings of words while infants and that they are able to make those connections of the words to the meanings later. Learning words requires the storage of both sounds and meanings.

Some of the other studies conducted have found that

- When infants are listening to people talk or to adults who read stories, they are storing the information about sound patterns that frequently occur.
- Babies as young as 6 months learn to recognize a word that follows the infant's own name, and this type of segmentation is believed to be a critical step in language acquisition.
- Children as young as 3 years old possess a remarkable knowledge of language structure and syntax.
- Words in isolation are easier for children to grasp, even though children are programmed to segment long sentences.

Language acquisition requires a brain, and it takes both sides of the brain to work the system of language and communication. Brain damage or trauma, even if it is only on one side, can affect some part of the language, speech, and communication areas.

The language domain is the most critical of all for educators to understand. An educator should stay abreast of the changes in this field, work closely with a speech/language pathologist, utilize the interventions that work, and try new strategies that aid children in their development of this significant domain.

Early literacy begins future academic skill building for children, their first introduction to reading and writing. Children need to prepare for writing skills by developing fine motor control, posture, an interest in the process, and an ability to express themselves with the language. They need to prepare for reading by enjoying words in different activities and gaining strong listening skills. They need developmentally appropriate activities to stimulate oral language and promote listening skills.

Children from homes where another language is spoken are called **second language learners.** When working with these children, educators should be culturally aware of the home environment, and the language and customs of the family. Children who are bilingual will not have perfect transitions from one language to another, but these are normal and necessary until the child becomes familiar and comfortable with the newer language.

Knowing these terms may be especially helpful.

- **Language:** The systematic use of sounds, signs, or written symbols for the purpose of communication or expression.
- **Receptive language:** Ability to understand and comprehend information that is presented.
- **Expressive language:** Ability to communicate thoughts, feelings, and ideas through words, gestures, sign systems, assistive devices, and so on.
- **Articulation:** Using movements of the mouth area to make speech sounds.

- **Phonological awareness:** The sound system of language, including rules for structure and the sequence of speech sounds into words.
- **Pragmatics:** Knowledge of successful and appropriate language rules in social and conversational situations.
- **Semantics:** Pertains to the meaning that language communicates; governs vocabulary development.
- **Syntax:** A system of combining words into sentences with rules that govern how words work together in phrases, clauses, and sentences.
- **Speech-language pathologist:** A professional who provides interventions to children who exhibit delays in the speech, language, or communication areas.

Perceptual Development

This area is a component of the motor domain and refers to how the muscles coordinate movements with the information that is received through the senses. The development of the perceptual-motor area begins shortly after conception, and at birth, children have immediate access to sensory possibilities as well as the abilities to interpret information provided through sensory stimuli. Perceptual-motor skills are evident in the first few weeks of life, and these skills will continue to improve as the child matures. When the child is older, these perceptual-motor skills become more sophisticated into higher levels of the thought processes.

Some professionals refer to perceptual-motor development as **body awareness** and **spatial awareness.** Body awareness explains how children learn about where their body is in relation to objects or other people. Spatial awareness enables children to understand the position of their bodies as they are engaged in motor activities and to coordinate their muscles. **Temporal awareness** is also in motion as the children learn to sense time and sequential events.

Perceptual-motor skills are a combination of what children perceive through their senses and their body movements. The perceptual skills include the broad categories of: visual, auditory, tactile, olfactory, and gustatory. These skills provide an outlet for children to use their senses and motor skills to access, explore, and involve themselves in their environment.

When early childhood educators gain knowledge about early perceptual-motor skill development, they can use these facts to create an environment for children to enhance learning. Occupational therapists are excellent resources in learning more about this area and in setting up centers and activities to enrich the development of these skills.

Perceptual abilities also support the intellectual or cognitive development of a child. However, a child must learn to organize and orient one's self into the world around before the child can perform the academic skills.

Play and Development

Play has tremendous value to young children. It is the most spontaneous, creative, and natural activity that young children engage in and an excellent vehicle for educators to promote and enhance learning. Play is what children do; it is what they want to do; and it is what they need to do.

It is children who define play, and they change it as they play. They learn best through play because they select their own activities, objects, and materials and interact with others at the levels they desire. It is believed that play is the major activity for 2–6 year olds, and it is expected that between the ages of 5–8, it reaches its highest point of influence over all areas of development. It is from these positive and motivational play experiences that children build the foundations for school success and their futures. It is through active, child-directed play that children learn.

The importance of play and its role in a child's education is boundless, and early childhood educators must continue to investigate and research the concepts of play. Since it is a critical component in children's learning, it must be an essential ingredient in an early childhood curriculum, and a primary focus in the structure of any early childhood program.

When play is integrated into an early childhood curriculum, teachers must remember several important factors. They must provide indoor and outdoor activities, in large and small spaces, as well as quiet and loud areas. The play must utilize the philosophy of developmentally appropriate practices by selecting proper settings, materials, and activities. Teachers should provide for the diversity of the children and include cultural influences.

Observing children at play provides insight into their behaviors, their development, and their needs. As with the five domains of learning, developmental stages occur at different ages when you examine the topic of play. More can be found in the developmental charts.

There are various stages of social play, and once internalized, children may enter and exit these stages at any age, depending on the play circumstance. These are Exploratory (birth to 12 months), Pretend Play (9 to 18 months), Solitary Play (18 to 24 months), Parallel Play (24 to 36 months), Associative Play (36 to 48 months), and Cooperative Play (48 to 60 months).

There are also particular types of play that demonstrate the growth process of children and their interest levels. At certain ages, children should be participating in specific stages of play as well as particular types of play. Following are the cognitive play types:

- **Exploratory** (Functional): Explore, discover, examine, organize
- **Manipulative** (Constructive): Develop hand-eye coordination and concept development
- **Imaginative or Symbolic** (Dramatic): Improve social skills, increase language concepts
- **Games with Rules** (Structured): Follows rules, shares, cooperates, and reasons

An appropriate early childhood environment is a critical element in promoting brain development and enhancing learning. When you create an environment for young children, remember that play must be central, cross all domains of learning, and may be organized through the use of centers, with materials and equipment developmentally appropriate and workable. The environment must be accessible to all children and allow for freedom of movement. Centers provide you with the opportunity to informally assess children's progress as they play independently. Centers can be expanded into several areas, such as art, blocks, motor, science, music, drama, and so on.

Children with disabilities may demonstrate difficulty in this area of play and depending on the disability, they may need some level of support to participate in play activities. They may need instruction, modeling, and guidance on how to play and interact in a play environment with toys, materials, and other children.

Knowledge of Disabling Conditions

Children with disabilities are identified under the federal law, IDEIA. As explained earlier in this chapter, this law has been in effect, albeit, amended over the years, to assist in creating the appropriate interventions for young children (ages 0–6). Children with disabilities in the areas of cognitive, language, self-help/adaptive, social-emotional, and motor domains are guaranteed early intervention services and special education services under this special education law. These children are assessed to determine the area of the disability, and an individualized program (through an IFSP or an IEP) is created to support the child in the educational system.

There are specific areas of exceptionality in reference to the school age special education population and different areas of special education categories in early childhood education. The more specific categories for school age children relate directly to those identified under state and federal laws. (See "Knowledge-Based Core Principles" for further information.)

Causes of Disabling Conditions

As you read in the section "Genetics and Medical Anomalies," genetics and medical issues play an important role as causes for disabilities in young children, and certainly, there are environmental factors that also contribute to these problems.

Medical problems can affect certain domains and may place children at-risk for disabilities, while some have more serious long-term and permanent effects. Some of the medical problems occur during pregnancy, due to teratogens and poor prenatal care, while others occur at birth. Medical issues may also be influenced by illnesses and diseases of either the child or the mother (HIV, AIDS, FAS, diabetes, and so on).

A child affected by genetic mutations, diseases, traumas, and parent-influenced effects, may demonstrate delays across the five learning domains. The child may show a delay in cognitive functioning, language acquisition, speech production, motor abilities, self-help/adaptive skills, or social-emotional growth. A child may also be affected in more than one domain, with more severe conditions crossing all domains.

Characteristics of Various Learners

Recall from earlier in this chapter that there are five domains of learning recognized in early childhood education. Together, these domains comprise a whole child, and each domain must develop independently as well as dependently of one another. It is within these domains that you may discover children with delays that result in a disabling condition. If one domain is delayed, it is possible that another domain also will be delayed. The characteristics of these developmental delays are distinguished by the child's inability to perform at the same level in a particular domain as typically developing peers.

Cognitive

Many types of cognitive disabilities exist, and children may be affected in a wide variety of ways as they access their environments at home, in school, and throughout the community. Children who exhibit cognitive delays function at a lower intellectual level and the simplest task may be overwhelming.

Children who exhibit delays or disabilities in cognition are often affected in the language, self-help adaptive, and the social domains. They may have problems using mental skills and processing information or they may have varying difficulties with thinking skills such as remembering, problem-solving, organizing ideas, and developing concepts. They may display problems with perceptual skills, making comparisons, classifying, categorizing, learning vocabulary, sequencing, reasoning, or making judgments. They may reveal delays in learning concepts such as colors, shapes, numbers, or remebering the names and uses of objects in their environment. Because children may have reduced mental capacities, from mild to severe, the interventions for these children are different.

Teachers with special education training are those most likely to provide interventions and implement strategies for children with cognitive impairments. Additionally, they may require assistance for certain children from a psychologist or neurologist in order to determine the type of disorder, and the characteristics of the child's problem.

Language

When children have a delay in the language domain, they may demonstrate problems with language, speech, or communication. They may be unable to produce words; they may not understand how to form sentences; they may not be able to make correct speech sounds; and they may have trouble conversing and sharing ideas. Communication, or the use of pragmatic skills, may also be inhibited in certain language-disabling conditions, such as autism or mental retardation.

Children who have a lack of stimulating experiences may have depressed speech and language development. Difficulty learning language is the most common problem in young children. It is often the very first problem that is recognized by adults in children who are determined to be at-risk or disabled. Children with language disabilities should be placed with peers who do not have these disabilities. They will then hear the normal, spontaneous language and speech of typical children, build upon their vocabulary, develop appropriate listening skills, and practice their pragmatic skills.

Several areas of language may be inhibited when a child demonstrates a disability in this domain. The two broad language areas are receptive (receive) language and expressive (transmit) language, and children must be observed, supported, and monitored in these areas. A speech disorder may include articulation, voice, and fluency problems. The other more specific areas of language affected by a delay or disability include phonological problems, sematic issues, syntax complexities, and pragmatic delays.

Children with delays in language and speech need an environment that provides intellectual and verbal simulation. Research indicates that the environment and daily activities promote appropriate language development and improve speech skills. Children need extensive language interaction with peers, which develops experiences and provides modeling of language and speech. Children who are second language learners need a teacher who understands the linguistic and cultural differences of the family and it is important to know whether the use of primary language is appropriate for the age.

Because children with delays in language can also be negatively impacted in their social, motor, and cognitive development, early childhood educators should work closely with a **Speech-Language Pathologist** (SLP) to gain further insight on how to handle children with language delays. An SLP is the person who provides services to children with speech and language disabilities in the areas of communication, articulation, stuttering, and voice disorders as well as supports programs focused on prevention, identification, and interventions related to speech and language problems.

Motor-Physical

The motor domain includes functions in the physical aspects of the body. These delays may be evident in a child's large motor skills (difficulty crawling, walking, sitting or standing, not being able to hold large objects, or move independently), and some are evident in the fine motor areas (problems grasping or reaching for small items, crossing midline, moving head and face, and eye-hand coordination). They may demonstrate abnormal muscle tone and poor posture, inadequate balance, or be identified with sensory processing disorders or oral-motor problems.

Children who exhibit delays in the motor area often demonstrate delays in other areas as well. The motor domain affects their perceptual skills and social skills. Children's motor delays may range from mild to severe impairments and can be difficult to notice. Parents are often not aware of the fine and gross motor expectations for certain ages and may not distinguish how well a child is doing in these areas. The more severe motor difficulties, however, can be discovered and diagnosed early.

It is ultimately important that motor delays be identified by a team of professionals. The interventionists who could provide expert guidance are an occupational therapist (OT) or a physical therapist (PT). They can direct an assessment, the development of a program, and on-going care and interventions. For children who need additional assistance in the classroom or therapeutic measures, these two professionals specialize in motor delays and support children, teachers, and the families.

An **occupational therapist** is the person who provides services to children with motor disabilities in the area of fine motor and sensory integration. The OT also works on balance, self-help skills, and body awareness to improve function when it is impaired through an injury or illness. A **physical therapist** is the person who provides services to children with motor disabilities in the area of gross motor, abnormal muscle tone, and abnormal movements. The PT also works on gait and mobility problems and tends to restore, prevent, or alleviate a problem due to dysfunction.

Social-Emotional

Children have a desire to be a part of the social world, to feel competent and independent with a sense of autonomy. This area is relatively new to early childhood education, as it was previously only identified if the child had a disability or delay in another domain as well. With the changes across society and the impact of various factors on young children, this category can now stand alone regarding eligibility and diagnosis. Although difficult to determine a very young child's need to be identified under this category, there are professionals who can aid the team in making those determinations. These include the social worker, a psychologist, a behavior specialist, or a psychiatrist.

Children who exhibit social-emotional needs may exhibit their delays through an inability to build satisfactory relationships, using inappropriate behaviors, and demonstrating fluctuations in temperament. A delay in a young child is particularly evident when the child attempts to interact with another person, whether it is a parent, a peer, or a sibling. However, children with social and emotional difficulties often go unnoticed, as people believe they may just be going through "a stage." Some children delayed in this area may be diagnosed with attention deficit hyperactivity disorder (ADHD) and might exhibit aggressive or withdrawn behaviors or socialization problems.

Delays in this area can be difficult to treat and making changes to learned behaviors often requires on-going and consistent interventions throughout each day in every environment. It requires not only the school intervention team's direct attention, but that of the family and other caretakers. A functional behavior assessment and specific program goals for changing the behaviors are often required.

Self-Help/Adaptive

Self-help/adaptive skills pertain to daily routines and independent functioning to meet one's own needs. For a young child these skills are in the areas of feeding, toileting, dressing, and grooming. Since these skills require sequential processes, children must learn the steps and then be able to generalize the skills at other times of the day.

Self-help/adaptive skills are somewhat difficult to assess and recognize as being delayed in the very early years. Unless the child has a significant disability evident in another domain, these skills may go unnoticed. Sometimes the primary caregiver completes tasks for the child, and when adults fulfill the child's needs by performing these independent personal tasks, children may not learn these skills. In this area, it is important to determine whether the child has not yet learned the skill, because of the lack of opportunity or whether the child was not able to internalize the skill no matter how many times it was presented.

The team members most likely to provide the interventions in this area include the teachers and the parents, with support from the occupational therapist and perhaps a speech and language therapist.

Vision

Children who are blind or partially sighted demonstrate difficulties in many areas of development due to their limited experiences. In the early years, they have problems with concept development since they lack the visual sensory experiences that are needed to accompany the conceptual skill development. They also lack the opportunities to learn pragmatic skills, and therefore, their vocabulary is somewhat stilted, resulting in language delays. They exhibit problems with social-emotional development as they are more isolated than most other children, and they show delays in self-help/adaptive skills as they cannot imitate the aspects of daily routines by watching others.

Hearing

Children who are identified as deaf or hard of hearing are those children who are unable to hear properly, even though some may be assisted with hearing devices. These children exhibit difficulties learning speech and language as they have not been able to imitate speech sounds and do not receive the auditory feedback of those with normal hearing. These children demonstrate delays in language, in following directions, developing vocabulary, and creating proper sentence structures and may also have difficulty with articulation. These children demonstrate significant communication impairments throughout their lives and have problems with cognitive and social development.

Types of Disabilities

Significant research and ongoing observation of children provides evidence of the effectiveness of early intervention and early childhood services for children and their families. These have been found to have a dramatic affect on the improvement of a child's performance. When children are provided with services, parent participation, and community resources, the benefits can be overwhelming. Professionals in the field know that the most critical period is during infancy and the toddler-preschool years, the best time for children to participate in programs suited for interventions and support.

It is to assist children with disabling conditions that an IFSP or an IEP should be created. By meeting their on-going needs, establishing goals in the delayed areas, and implementing supports to more easily access their education, the child will demonstrate progress. Providing intervention at an early age for children identified at-risk or for those who exhibit disabilities will make a huge impact on the child's future success.

There are 13 federal categories found in IDEIA for students eligible for special education and used for children over the age of 5. Children with special needs below the age of 5 years, who are identified with disabilities, generally fall into certain categories broadly defined as physical, language, cognitive, behavioral, or learning. Specific categories are regularly used to identify the type of disability a child exhibits. Early childhood terms may be more generic than those labels used in K–12 special education programs, as the early childhood categories vary from state to state. These terms are less restrictive and may simply identify a child with a **developmental disability** until age 8, which is allowed under the law. The majority of children identified and placed in early childhood settings for special education services are those with speech-language delays.

There are some regular special education terms that may be used in preschool and early childhood education, as these conditions are considered more permanent for a child and, therefore, can be diagnosed at an early age. These may include, but are not limited to the following:

- Cognitive Disabilities
  - Mental Retardation
  - Autism
  - Traumatic Brain Injury
- Motor Disabilities
  - Cerebral Palsy
  - Spina Bifida
  - Muscular Dystrophy
- Sensory Impairments
  - Deafness
  - Blindness
- Language Disorders
  - Autism
  - Ataxia
  - Pervasive Disorders

Biological, Environmental, and Nutritional Factors

Children with special needs exist at all levels of the education system. Since these children are at-risk for school failure, they often require appropriate assessments, additional services, special programming, and curriculum modifications to succeed in the schools. Children with disabilities and those identified at-risk have conditions that are often the result of a biological, environmental, or nutritional factor. These are children whose problems began at birth or in the early years of development. These are children who need constant intellectual stimulation in a caring and appropriate environment, along with specific interventions to address the areas of delay. Children who are at-risk will continue to perform poorly in school if they do not receive the proper supports.

The very early years are critical to a child's growth and development. Children who are considered at-risk may demonstrate conditions associated with biological factors (medical issues, illness, disease, trauma, drug exposure), environmental factors (abuse, neglect, foster care, low-income, or homeless families), or nutritional factors (lack of prenatal care, low birth weight, lead poisoning, and so on). Although these children exhibit delays in learning and need additional services, some of them will not qualify for services according to special education law. With the proper interventions, these children may catch-up to typically developing peers in their age group while others will be eligible for services under a disability category in special education.

Evaluation, Assessment, and Eligibility Criteria

Assessment is a critical stage in the overall special education process, whether working with very young children or school age children. There are six steps to the assessment process. The process outlined here is not specific to early childhood education, so further information may be found in the sections, "Knowledge-Based Core Principles" and "Application of Core Principles across Categories of Disabilities." This section outlines the process of assessment, which ultimately leads to placement, and the implementation of services with an emphasis on the aspects of assessment that **do** focus on early childhood education. Following are the six steps of the assessment process:

1. Child find
2. Developmental screening
3. Diagnosis

4. Development of an IEP and interventions
5. Performance monitoring
6. Program evaluation

Steps 1–3 are explained in more detail in this section, and steps 4–6 are detailed later in this guide.

Child Find

The federal special education legislation mandates that comprehensive activities be conducted within communities to identify children as early as possible who may have delays. These activities are supposed to be coordinated among the various agencies and schools to search for children and refer them for screening and possible evaluation. The goal of **child find** is for individuals to refer children who are suspected to need intervention services. Each community will generate a plan to identify the children to be screened. They may vary the target groups and conduct specific screenings.

Child find is the initial step in the assessment process. It is the method utilized to provide community awareness of the services and programs available to children. Sometimes parents are unaware of their child's development, or they may be tentative about admitting any problems the child may be experiencing. Some parents may not be aware of the programs they may access for their child. Therefore, child find provides a service to children initially through their families.

It is important for a community to organize the child find efforts and include

- Awareness (importance of early intervention and available services)
- A referral system
- Publicity to reach families (radio, television, newspapers, Internet)
- Contacts at schools and agencies
- A tracking system to follow the children

Screening

The next step in the assessment process, **screening**, is one step closer to a more formal assessment. The primary purpose of a screening is to determine the need for further evaluation, possible interventions, and/or support services. If a child appears to have difficulty with the screening, services may be provided, or a referral for a comprehensive evaluation will be made to the appropriate agency.

When conducting a screening on a child, an early childhood educator or other professional is required to obtain information from multiple sources. The family is an essential part of this process as they may know information about the child's early development, the typical milestones, and childhood health issues.

A screening covers one or more of the five learning domains in order to determine a child's level of functioning. Often a screening includes a vision and hearing check. By evaluating these seven areas, an educator should be able to identify any present risks associated with learning for each child.

There are specified instruments used for screening, and although some assessment tools may overlap in purpose, they should not be used for dual purposes. The tests should be standardized, but quick and easy to administer. Some screening procedures check large groups of children in short periods of time and are very quickly administered. Some screening tools do not require that a child participate. Sometimes an observation, a checklist, or a parent completed rating scale may be used. Both the test and the method of administration must be nondiscriminatory, reliable, and valid with objective scoring. Personnel conducting the screening should receive comprehensive training to ensure accurate overall presentation of materials.

After a screening is conducted on a child, the results should be shared with parents in a brief conference format. Many parents are eager to know how well their child performed. Not every child will have positive results, so it is the responsibility of the early childhood educator to present the information in a pleasant and easy to understand manner. If the child exhibited difficulty, the parents may share concerns and have questions about the results. This may be the first time they have heard that their child is not performing at typical levels and needs further evaluation.

Referral

A referral is the process of identifying a child for further evaluation due to the suspicion of a delay or disability. It may be conducted either by an individual or through a screening process. A referral may be made by parents, neighbors, physicians, teachers, therapists, or other people involved in the care of the child. It is often done by making a telephone call, completing a form, or submitting a report to an agency.

When a referral is received by the agency or school, professionals may still conduct a screening to verify the suspicion of a delay and to determine the specific areas that may need further evaluation. In some cases, interventions may begin prior to the evaluation, especially for children covered under the Part C portion of the federal law.

Parents should be involved in this step of the assessment process. They can offer valuable information about their child and the home environment. Professionals working with parents during this step instill trust and build rapport for the future, through the evaluation stage and throughout program development and implementation stages.

Diagnostic Evaluation

From the referral stage, the team can proceed with a comprehensive evaluation on a child. Parent permission and parent participation are requirements under the law for any child who is to be evaluated for special education services.

The purpose of a diagnostic evaluation is to answer questions about a child's problems and identify the types of interventions that should be prescribed. The diagnosis determines the nature and severity of the child's problems and this information is the basis for determining eligibility in special education. Overall, there are three primary reasons that an assessment needs to be conducted.

1. To gather information about young children with special needs
2. To determine eligibility for special education services
3. To create an appropriate individualized program

Several points must be considered prior to conducting an assessment:

- Identify why the assessment is needed.
- Choose the proper method for the situation.
- Keep the evaluation free from bias.
- Make sure the testing tool is reliable and valid.
- Test all learning domains to cover integrated skills.
- Gather pertinent information about the child's performance.
- Use medical and family information as data.
- Plan the IFSP or IEP based on the assessment results.

Instrumentation and Procedures

Federal law mandates that the assessment of young children be conducted using a team approach. The assessment must be comprehensive, include the domains of learning, and provide enough information so decisions about the child and her program can be made by the team. IDEIA further requires that the assessment include family strengths and needs and be nondiscriminatory of culture, linguistics, gender, ethnic origin, socioeconomics, and religion.

Many types of assessment instruments and different methods are used to evaluate young children. Assessments fall into two main categories: formal and informal. A **formal assessment** collects the primary data via standardized tests that have an identified special purpose. An **informal assessment** uses a variety of methods to gather data but may also determine the need for a more formal assessment after the data is reviewed.

Standardized tests generally are used for screenings, formal or informal assessments. However, in an early childhood setting, there are concerns about certain types of standardized assessments as some professionals believe they use isolated facts and impose a controlled setting to evaluate young children, and the children do not always perform well on **controlled evaluations.** It is recommended that early childhood professionals use the **naturalistic assessments** (in which the child is observed in a natural setting, accessing and utilizing the materials for his specific age and directs self), rather than **controlled assessments** (in which the setting is more sterile, the testing is predetermined, and the child is directed to perform).

Methods of Assessment

The following assessment types lists are not inclusive, but rather offer the more common selections used with young children.

Authentic-based assessment: Similar to the performance-based method, but the task is observed when it is naturally occurring.

Curriculum-based assessment: A type of criterion-referenced test used to evaluate a child's skills according to the curriculum presented.

Dynamic assessment: An ecological approach that identifies a child's ability to learn during an instruction period (teacher-directed) and actively involves the child.

Ecological assessment: Gathering information about the child's performance and interaction in the typical environment.

Family-based assessment: Used for **family-focused approach** programs to identify family strengths and concerns for the benefit of setting up a plan, interventions, and resources for the child and the family.

Judgment-based assessment: A clinically-based approach to collect information from multiple sources to evaluate the child.

Performance-based assessment: Requires multiple observations of the same task to reflect on the child's learning process.

Play-based assessment: Useful, natural method for children with disabilities ages 6 months to 6 years, in which the child performs in the natural environment with materials of the child's choice. Scored when child performs alone and then when a peer is included (Linder Approach).

Observation Types of Assessment

Anecdotal record: Short written narrative description of a child's behaviors taken any time during the day for any activity.

Checklist observations: Predetermined category and certain times to record behaviors.

Event sampling: Observation focused on predetermined event or behavior for one or more children that includes frequency, duration, causality, and severity.

Rating scales: Used to record efficient information on a variety of preselected behaviors.

Running record: Naturalistic approach in observation format for special period of time. The observer records exactly what is said and done.

Time sampling: Documentation that focuses on units of time for special behaviors or events.

Alternative Types of Assessment

Authentic assessment: Focuses on performance of skills in an appropriate child environment and includes observations, assessment, and portfolios.

Case studies: Profiles of an individual or a family, developed by gathering information via different sources and instruments that are used to address particular problems.

Developmentally appropriate assessment: Conducted as a child initiates her own activities and allows the child to perform in an appropriate setting.

Portfolio: Collections of information over a period of time that includes health records, work samples, test results, projects, products, and so on used to follow a child's progress.

Work sampling system: Classroom assessment that documents skills, behaviors, and other accommodations in various areas for a specified period of time.

Eligibility Criteria

The assessment process is the basis for determining eligibility for special education and related services. The interdisciplinary team gathers the information and presents the results at a team review. They decide whether the child will qualify for special education based on the disability and the needs. Under the law, a child is eligible if the disability is a barrier for the child to access his education.

There are essentially two groups of children who would qualify for services in early childhood special education: those with a disability and those considered at-risk for school failure. Under IDEIA, Part C, very young children (ages 0–2) are identified under the category of **developmental delay** in the area of _____ (domain). Under IDEIA, Part B, children (ages 3–5) may be identified using a categorical label. There are two ways this may occur:

1. A child may be identified under any of the other 12 federal categories of Part B or an amended category chosen in each state.
2. A child may be identified as delayed in a particular domain or any other specific term created by individual states. States may choose a category in early childhood so as not to label a child too young.

The categories formed in each state for early childhood special education programs are usually changed once the child turns 5 years old, unless one of the 12 federal categories was used. A team would reassess any child transitioning out of a preschool program to decide whether the services should be dismissed or to determine the need for continued services, and which of the 12 categories to use. A similar process occurs when a child moves from early intervention services (Part C) to early childhood services (Part B). The label may change depending on the program and the state.

Family Contributions

The assessment phase of special education can be a difficult time for parents of young children as it may be the first time anyone has suggested that there is a problem with their child's performance and development. They may feel insecure, afraid, guilty, and upset, so explaining the steps to them along the way, being available to support them, and answering their questions will help in building this long-term relationship.

Parents play a vital role in the assessment process as they can gather and share important information about the child's early medical and developmental history, about other family members, the home environment, and characteristics of their child's current condition. When parents are involved in the assessment process, they may better understand their child's problems and be prepared to join the team in creating and implementing an appropriate program.

To help parents feel more comfortable with the testing procedures, professionals should explain the process, the purpose for the assessments, the types of assessments, and tools used, the environment where the evaluation will occur, and when and how the results will be shared. Showing parents the evaluation materials, allowing them to observe a portion of the assessment, and answering their questions may help relieve their fears about the overall process.

Upon completion of the assessment, the entire team meets to discuss test results and determine the next steps for the child and the family. It may lead to the development of a program under the guidance of an IFSP or IEP (see "Planning and Service Delivery").

It is best for you to become familiar with the assessment requirements in your area. Although the mandates are clear in the law, states have discretion about whether they create their own assessment model for young children, and the interpretations of the law may be different across the country. This is also true of the categorical names used in all states. Check on the tools and practices used by educators and other service providers to assess and identify young children. It may be beneficial for you to spend time observing an evaluation in an early intervention or early childhood program and seek information about the assessment tools, and methods used, and the eligibility criteria.

Planning and Service Delivery

Special education planning and service delivery varies depending on the age and disability of the children. The main focus, however, is to meet the individual needs of each child. This section pertains to the early childhood components. For further study, see "Knowledged-Based Core Principles."

Individual Family Service Plan (IFSP)

An **IFSP** is a legal document required under IDEIA as a provision of Part C for infants and toddlers, birth through 2 years. It is written to support families of infants with developmental delays and outlines the services the family and child will receive.

In an IFSP, the needs of the family are the central focus. The family role is emphasized since parents or the primary caregiver are allowed to be part of the IFSP team. The family members are included not only as recipients of services, but they may provide input about the child's development, reveal their concerns, help identify an appropriate environment for services, and share ideas and goals to support the child's progress.

The components of an IFSP are very much like an IEP. (Similarities and differences are explained later.) The family's resources, concerns, and needs are evaluated by team members in order to create a plan that details outcomes for the child and family. This information is written into the statement of present levels of functioning.

The family is the primary service provider for the child, and a service coordinator may be selected from the early intervention agency to assist and support the family through the IFSP process and through the implementation of the IFSP services. Each 6 months, the family has the option to accept or decline continued services.

Individualized Education Program (IEP)

Each child with an identified disability must be provided with an **IEP** under the law (IDEIA). As a provision of IDEIA-Part B, an IEP is a legal, program-specific document, for preschool aged children (3–5) and older students up through age 21. An IEP is written to support the educational needs of a child with a disability or a developmental delay and outlines the services the child will receive.

Some children may enroll in an early childhood program with an existing IEP from another public school program, if the child is 3 years old or older. Some children may come with an existing IFSP. Transition services (more on transitions later in this chapter) are required under both an IFSP and an IEP. When a child transitions into a public preschool program, he may be re-evaluated, the IFSP reviewed, and an IEP created to align with the child's current educational needs. The law does allow for an IFSP to be used for preschool aged children and an IEP for children age 2 who will transition in one year to a preschool program. However, this is not a common practice.

The purpose of an IEP is to ensure that proper educational services are delivered to children with special needs. An IEP is constructed for a child, after a comprehensive evaluation is conducted and the child's eligibility determined, by a team of professionals (therapists, teachers, specialist, and parents). Parents must be involved as team members throughout the special education process and in developing the IEP for their child. As partners, parents help make decisions about the goals, the services, and the child's placement. It is often the early childhood teacher who manages the team and the process.

Some of the required areas covered under an IEP include the present levels of educational performance (based on the child's strengths and weaknesses), the specific annual goals, the certain services (based on the child's needs), and the environment in which the program will be provided.

The forms used for both IEPs and IFSPs are very different, depending on the state, and the local schools and agencies with which you may work. You might be interested in seeing a copy of an IEP form from a local school district, or an IFSP from a Part C local agency to help you more fully understand the components. An added source for perusing these forms is the Department of Education in your state, as they should have a generic form that outlines all of the state and federal requirements. Also check websites by searching for IFSP or IEP to find relevant information about these documents for further study.

Similarities in an IFSP and an IEP

Both are mandated as legal documents to be written within 45 days of the child's referral for special needs services. These documents are to be compiled in a collaborative fashion with professionals and parents to meet the identified needs of the child. Both an IFSP and an IEP include information about the child's disability, the present levels of functioning, a set of goals, information about interventions and services, and the selected environment for the services. Both include a component for transition services into the next program level.

Differences in an IFSP and an IEP

Although both an IFSP and an IEP require a present level of the child's functioning, there are specific differences in these two statements. An IFSP provides an overall statement of functioning across all developmental abilities, and the IEP must focus on the present levels of educational performance as it pertains to the specific disability. An IFSP is to be reviewed by the team every 6 months, and an IEP has an annual review with regular progress reports throughout the year (most often quarterly). Both require goals to be written, but the differences are in the focus of these goals. The IFSP produces general goals that are primary to the family needs along with the child's needs. The IEP focuses on more detailed goals as they relate to the child's specific educational needs and the specific area of disability.

Interdisciplinary Process

There are three types of teams utilized in the special education process. Refer to "Application of Core Principles across Categories of Disabilities (0352)" to read about the definitions of a **multidisciplinary team** and a **transdisciplinary team**.

An **interdisciplinary team** is a group of professionals with defined roles and includes the parent(s). These team members work closely together for each individual child they serve. They utilize ongoing communications and often evaluate children together, conferring often to share results and child progress. Their focus is to develop an integrated plan of services for the child and family, so fragmentation or duplication of services does not occur. This type of teamwork is very effective in early childhood settings.

Service Delivery Systems

Under IDEIA, children with disabilities are provided their education to the maximum extent possible with nondisabled peers. It further promotes that special classes and special schools must be considered only when the nature and severity of the disability prohibits the child from receiving an education in a more typical setting. To comply with this mandate, many schools have created a variety of programs for children with special needs. This section focuses on those that pertain to early childhood education.

The environment from which a young child receives special services is very important to his development and success. Under the law, teams are required to assess the child's needs, determine the appropriate services, and then decide which environment is most suitable to meet the needs of the child. Different environments are possible through the schools. There are many philosophies, too, that surround best placements for young children. Remember that the child should always be at the forefront in these discussions on making placement decisions and service delivery must be based on individual needs following the guidelines of the law.

Research shows and the laws promote that children should be allowed to access their education in a **natural environment.** This is the setting that the child would participate in if the child did not have a delay or disability. The natural environment is considered by many professionals in the field to be an effective and developmentally appropriate approach to providing interventions to young children with disabilities. That may be the child's home, a school, or a community environment.

Two generic terms define the service delivery systems available for early childhood settings: the **home-based program** and the **center-based program.** The home-based services are most typical of early intervention programs under Part C of IDEIA, and the center-based typify early childhood programs under Part B of IDEIA.

The *home-based* program services are delivered to the child in the natural setting of the home. Therapists and interventionists provide direct services to a child with consultation and training given to the family, particularly the parents.

Parents learn to accept more responsibility for the child's skill attainment on a daily basis when the professionals cannot be present. These services tend to be individualized yet isolated, since there are usually no other children participating.

In *center-based* programs, children receive services in an educational environment, typically a school, rather than the home. These comprehensive services focus on the child's needs and are provided by many specialists and many constructs of program design.

Program Models and Environments

Federal mandates define the requirements for providing services to children with special education needs in the early childhood population. One of the components of IDEIA requires that states ensure, to the maximum extent appropriate, early intervention services to infants and toddlers under 3 years old in natural environments and recommends the same for children 3 to 5 years. This provision for addressing the placement of the child for services is called the least restrictive environment (LRE). (See the "Professional Practice" section.)

Children have a wide range of developmental, educational, and therapeutic needs, and the activities provided to address these needs enhance a child's overall development and her relationship with the family. There are several considerations to make for placement. In an early childhood LRE, the choices narrow, but nevertheless still follow the provisions of the law. When the team decides a child's placement, it must consider the program that will not only best meet the child's needs, but that which has the most contact with same aged peers without disabilities. These may be

- Typical integrated preschool classroom for children of any ability
- Reverse mainstream classroom with peers for a period of time
- Separate self-contained classroom for children with disabilities
- Separate school such as a school for the deaf or school for the blind
- Residential facility mostly for mental health and behavioral issues
- Homebound/hospital for children with illnesses and diseases

Program models are identified based on a particular educational theory. Several are listed here.

- **Academic-based model:** Traditional teaching of pre-academic skills in which children are engaged in teacher directed activities.
- **Activity-based approach:** Stresses instruction for a child's individual goals through child-initiated activities.
- **Contextual model:** The role of the environment is key to enhancing the child's development (also ecological, functional, and transactional).
- **Language-based model:** Focuses on the development of language through techniques, activities, and materials.
- **Naturalistic approach:** Instructional method emphasizes teaching in context of the child's daily routines.
- **Play-based approach:** Promotes learning and skill building through natural child-selected and directed activities using age-appropriate materials.
- **Psycho-social approach:** Emphasizes psychological and social development.

Professional Service Providers

Team members participate in the program models created by the school or agency. Some of the special area professionals who may comprise a child's team in or out of school may include

- **Audiologist:** Assesses the child to determine the level or loss of hearing and provides direct or consultative services related to hearing losses and equipment.
- **Early childhood specialist or early interventionist:** Delivers essential instruction to the child, monitors the child's progress, manages the classroom, travels to the home, and may organize the team.
- **Occupational therapist:** Evaluates and provides treatment for skills that focus on the development of readiness abilities, fine motor skills, and functional skills.
- **Physical therapist:** Evaluates and provides treatment for gross motor control, basic mobility, and balance.

- **School psychologist:** Administers evaluations, interprets results, and may counsel families.
- **Service coordinator:** Helps to coordinate the professionals and agencies who work with the child in early intervention models.
- **Speech/language pathologist:** Evaluates and implements services to children who qualify in the areas of language, articulation, speech, fluency, and other communication disorders.

Other members of a child's team may include those professionals with medical or mental health backgrounds, such as a school nurse, a social worker, a neurologist, an ophthalmologist, an otologist, and a general physician. It is the role of the service coordinator and the responsibility of an early childhood professional to communicate and organize these professionals as the child's plan is developed and services implemented.

Program Efficacy

The research is clear on the benefits of children receiving early intervention services as well as attending quality preschool programs. When children participate in appropriate programs, they demonstrate higher academic achievement in later years and most likely will NOT drop out of school. When children with special needs are enrolled in preschool programs, their need for special education services in later years minimizes. Early childhood programs are so valued that the cost of serving young children reduces the need for social services as adults almost tenfold.

To ensure that a program is of the same quality as these studies, it is recommended that programs go through a self-study and eventually an accreditation process. Many directors perform informal assessments and on-going evaluations of their programs and staff. Many programs, however, prefer to obtain accreditation through the National Association for the Education of Young Children (NAEYC) or another accrediting entity, as it shows parents and community members that this is a high-quality program in which young children flourish.

There is a comprehensive process for accreditation, and even a director's informal evaluation can be time-consuming and very thorough. Programs should consider evaluation for many reasons. Program improvement, research, and accountability are excellent reasons to review practices and services. Factors that appear to significantly contribute to the quality of a program include class size, adult-child ratio and interactions, developmentally appropriate integrated curriculum, child-focused and family services, policies and procedures, and staff training.

Case Management and Interagency Collaboration

The term **case management** has been recently revised to **service coordination.** Service coordination is mandated for children who receive services under Part C (ages 0–3), but not for those receiving services under Part B (ages 3–5). Most often under Part B services, it is the teacher, professionals, and parents, who provide these services in an informal manner.

Service coordination is established to assist families in accessing early intervention and related services according to the IFSP. Coordination with other relevant agencies is essential in maintaining a consistent program for the child and supporting the family. The service coordinator, who is often a person most relevant to the current needs of the child, coordinates other professionals and agencies, which can be a complex task. This person must coordinate the evaluations, facilitate the team implementing the IFSP, identify providers, assist in accessing services, coordinate medical interventions/services, and organize the transition. The service coordinator may be a direct provider of specialized services or may function only in the coordinator role. Sometimes this coordinator is a social worker, an early childhood interventionist, or a therapist.

Collaboration (collaborative teaming) has been shown to increase the performance of children and enhance family and community involvement, as it is a means to meeting children's diverse needs. **Interagency collaboration** is a recommended procedure under Part C. This is the result of a variety of agencies set up to provide comprehensive and coordinated services to young children and their families. Now each agency can provide a specified function or special services, while sharing resources, expenses, and expertise to the family and child. This requires periodic planning and evaluation of the services.

Since there are a wide variety of state and private agencies that have been established to provide the early intervention services outlined under Part C, it is recommended that educators become familiar with those available in the local area, as the names and models may change, but the requirements for services remain the same under the law. You should become familiar with the agencies in your area, understand your role in the process, and become knowledgeable about the existing interagency agreements.

Some of the agencies available to children and families may include Head Start, state early intervention programs, schools for the deaf and/or blind, hospital settings, community nursery schools, residential schools, private childcare settings, in-home nannies, non-profit group interventions, private therapists, local government agencies, and play groups.

Family and Community Aspects

Much of a child's early learning is based on the time spent in the individual family unit. Families are the number one teacher in a child's life. Because children spend most of their time with their families, much of their learning is affected by the relationships they develop with family members, by the involvement they have in the family environment, and by the contact they have in the family culture and value system. No wonder children enter schools with a vast array of abilities and learning styles. It is the master teacher who knows how to accommodate and meet the many needs of children and families in a classroom. Communicate with families, involve them, and serve them for the sake of the child.

Family Systems Theory

Research has shown that when families/parents are involved in their child's education, the children are more successful in school. It is of great value for the early childhood educator to build a strong home-school relationship with each family. Families are often much more involved when a child is young, so for the benefit of the child, early childhood educators should encourage families to continue to be involved as the years pass.

IDEIA promotes that early intervention services and early childhood programs become more family-centered. This is based on the premise that families may be viewed as a system, and although each member functions independently, they all affect one another. It is believed that family members exert strong influences upon one another and when something happens to one, it happens to the entire family system.

Most home-based programs are parent oriented, as they provide professionals in the home to train the parent to work with the child. Currently, more programs are focusing on the combination of a child-centered, family-centered approach in which the entire family system is provided intervention services. An educator should spend some extended informal time with a family, prior to requesting participation or making suggestions for interventions.

Family Structures

In recent years, the family structure has greatly changed. These structures demonstrate a rich family diversity as well as show how families interact with their children in the various ways. There are different types of families, and children grow and learn in these varied family settings. Examples of these family structures include multicultural, multigenerational, blended, separated, divorced, single, adoptive, and foster. Some families live in large cities, and others in small communities. Some families live in houses, some in apartments, and some in their cars. There are families of great wealth and prosperity, while others are affected by poverty and suffer abuse. Because of these variations, early childhood educators must demonstrate trust and build rapport with each family.

Children gain their learning styles and develop certain abilities from their families. The family, particularly a parent, is known as the **first teacher.** It is important for a parent to provide a child's basic needs (food, shelter, safety) and be a positive role model. Children have a basic need to feel loved and feel like they belong and when they do, they develop self-esteem and a can-do attitude. Under Maslow's theory on belonging, he believed that children require that their basic needs be met, at a minimum level. But, he also found that the more a child is supported, the greater the benefit.

Parents gain parenting skills from their early role models, and this style is carried forward into the next generation. For parents who are having problems, support and guidance may be necessary. Educators should not judge a parent, but rather obtain services for the parent who is in need.

In many homes, grandparents and other relatives step into the role of primary caregivers, acting as parents, for children whose parents cannot or will not care for them. Some of the family situations include substance abuse, illness, child abuse/neglect, economic hardship, incarceration, divorce, violence, and death. Due to these situations, grandparents often fill in as the sole guardian of the children.

Family Issues

Families of children with disabilities may have other stressors in their lives. Understanding the disability and how the child fits into the family unit may cause concern for parents. Early childhood educators must understand the challenges that families face and respect their values and culture. Educators should be quick to recognize families in crisis and assist them with accessing community resources.

Stages of Grief

Ken Moses identified that parents of special needs children display and must work through grief while Elisabeth Kuebler-Ross developed a theory about the various stages of grief. Several theories deal with the grief of parents and a family whose child is identified with a disability. Families pass through these stages and may revert back to other stages before they resolve their feelings. These stages may include shock, disbelief, denial, anger, bargaining, depression, and acceptance. A key to understanding parents and families is recognizing these stages of grief as the adults pass through them. However, educators should realize they are not trained to help every parent. An outside community resource might be necessary for a family in crisis, and educators must be able to identify these resources and assist parents in accessing them.

Abuse/Neglect

The effects of abuse on children are far-reaching. Abuse can damage a child's outlook on life and cause developmental delays in several domains of learning. Children with parents who are having difficulties or children in families that have many stressors often fall victim to abuse and neglect. Early childhood educators must be able to recognize the signs and symptoms of neglect and abuse. The reporting of child abuse and neglect is mandated in every state. Educators should review policies and procedures in their state, their county, and their schools to be sure they understand the guidelines, and their responsibility to protect children.

Stress

In a family with a child who has special needs, stress may be heightened. Not only is it difficult for parents to continue to be the primary caregiver, but also caring for the siblings, maintaining a marriage, addressing the disability issues, working, focusing on culture, accessing religion, and finding family time all contribute to stress on a family unit. Some families will benefit from additional community support and services, which the early childhood educator or the service coordinator should help them locate.

Communication

In general, parents are very interested in knowing about their child's development, the program, the interventions, and the progress. Many families want to be involved in their child's education, and many parents need to be welcomed into the program.

The educator's role in communicating with the family/parents is critical. It is important that when educators communicate with parents they acknowledge feelings, support ideas, listen to statements, reflect on concerns, and comment on their actions. Parents need to be respected for their points of view and their participation.

Educators may need to further train themselves on the many ways they can communicate with parents and families to improve the home-school relationships. It should be an easy task for educators to utilize informal communications each day with parents. This includes using eye contact, a variety of facial expressions, and gestures. When parents are speaking, educators should utilize active listening, and for written information, it should be delivered in the parents' primary language. An educator should prepare for formal meetings with parents to ensure effective and successful communication. If the parents use another language, oral communications may require a translator.

Support Systems/Community Resources

The current changes in world economics, the advances in technology, the distances between family members, and the social status of parents affect families in different ways. Some create stressors that require additional professional attention. Because of the increased mobility of society, parents must rely on support services and community resources to assist them when dealing with these issues and with their children who have disabilities.

Under the law, educators are encouraged to include families in program development, intervention services, and assessments on their child. The programs must reach out to families and help them understand their child's education needs, encouraging participation in the overall program. Sometimes parents need more support, and this can be found in support systems and community resources.

In order for the educator to help the parents to access community resources, a family assessment should be conducted. Together the family and educator can set family goals, detail the outcomes, and identify the resources needed to achieve success. Part of the assessment is in knowing what community resources are available and how to obtain them. There are many varieties of community agencies and resources: medical providers, health professionals, therapists, mental health centers, respite care, employment centers, counselors, and so on.

Sometimes a family needs an active support system. Research shows that a child's progress is enhanced when the family's needs are met. Families may find support from others who can give emotional support, explain disability issues, and share life experiences. Families may need to rely on extended family members for practical help in caring for their child so these family members could be included in program development, as they may have a unique perspective on the child's abilities and the family's needs. There are also **natural supports** that a family can draw upon in the community. These include those people within the family's environment, such as friends, fellow workers, religious group members, civic organizations, and neighbors. Educators need to be sure that families do not feel alone in their quest to improve the life of their child.

Family Involvement

Being a family is hard work, and many families are stretched beyond their limits. Being a family with a child who has special needs is something very different and can be very difficult. Treating parents respectfully, and creating a program that focuses on the family and their involvement, is a major step toward improving the educational programs for the young child.

Through the mandates of IDEIA, schools are encouraged to include families in early childhood programs and the process of special education. Educators should promote parent involvement through strategies that include: suggesting classroom visits, providing information about the child's disability and interventions, writing notes, making telephone contacts, asking for volunteers at classroom activities, inviting to parent meetings, and treating one another like team members.

When families are accepted and they participate as a resource in their child's program, the benefits affect the entire family unit. In child-centered and family-centered programs, the team can work together to develop a shared vision for the child and family; facilitate collaboration with all team members; respect the family culture, values, and choices; help link families to the resources they need; and model good communication skills.

Family Training

A central feature of involving family/parents is the training component. Educators should empower families and parents by providing information on family issues, by showing them how to guide their child's activities and skill development, and by encouraging them to be effective advocates in managing their child's care and program.

Professional Practice

Early childhood education for the exceptional child is an exciting, but relatively new field in our nation. Although theories and ideas about the education of the young child began in the 1700s, it has been a slow-growing field. The education of youngsters with disabilities gained momentum from the early education theories and programs for children without disabilities. The growth and awareness that have been generated over the past decade in this field is extraordinary. Educators are now more convinced of the value of early intervention for young children with special needs, as many of the former study subjects have grown up and are showing the positive aspects of having received assistance and support at a very early age. Early intervention and early childhood education promote substantial gains in all areas of a child's development and contribute to future learning.

In this section, you explore the historical perspectives, the legislation, the philosophies of various people, curriculum, and the current trends and issues that have brought about the quality programs and services for young children with special needs. The knowledge gained from this inquiry will provide the early childhood educator with a strong foundation of understanding and provide further study review. For additional information on these topics, websites are listed in the "Resources" section of this book.

Education History

Early childhood education and early intervention services for children with exceptional needs are included in the laws that govern special education for all children. Programs for young children with special needs are now mandatory in every state beginning at birth. Special education laws requiring specific services for children arose from the civil rights actions of the 1950s and 1960s. Early childhood programs got their beginnings from the influences of Lyndon Johnson's War on Poverty, which established Head Start and the many early theorists (see later discussion) who understood and believed that young children were ready and able to learn.

In addition, the research that has been conducted on the brain and early learning supports the efforts of early childhood education. At no other time in the history of education has there been more positive commitments shared by federal and state governments, agencies, universities, colleges, public and private schools, and local communities to enhance the education of young children through programs staffed with trained personnel.

Legislation

Beginning in 1975, PL94-142 mandated that services for children with disabilities be provided to children ages 5–21. With regard to early childhood education for younger children, public laws began to specifically address the education of these children under the age of 5 years in 1985 (PL98-199) and in 1986 (PL105-17), The Education of the Handicapped Children's Act amendments. This law extended services to 3–5 year olds. In 1991, PL102-119 added amendments to include infants and toddlers and created the Part B and Part C (formerly Part H) to support young children and their families.

Other influences to current special education legislation for young children was the passing of Project Head Start (Johnson's War on Poverty) in 1965, which provided early education programs for 4-year-old children from economically disadvantaged homes. The Handicapped Children's Early Education Act (PL89-750) of 1966 allowed funding for experimental and model programs for early education. Current laws (IDEA and IDEIA) continue to mandate services for the 0–5 age group and include changes that benefit the children.

Specifically for early childhood, Part B and Part C of IDEIA support programs and interventions for very young children. Part B provides for the education and special services of young children ages 3–5. Part C provides for the early intervention services for families and young children ages birth through 2. The Part C programs are primarily provided as home-based services, and the Part B services are most often provided as center-based programs in schools.

Philosophy and Ethical Issues

Young children are treated with more respect for their abilities and with more value for their minds than they were once credited prior to 1990. A component that influenced the growing field of early childhood education is the major contributions by a number of renowned researchers, educators, and philosophers who studied young children and who theorized about the functions of the brain and general child development.

There are many theories, and each of these theories has significant value, as they provide the foundations for early childhood education and encourage educators to build successful programs for young children. Theorists such as Piaget, Skinner, and Vygotsky are key supporters of early development, but in varying ways. Each theory has its place in this field, and sometimes ideas are merged together to form a strong union in early childhood programs. Some theories are based on developmental stages and others include cognitive, social, behavioral, and family focuses. Each educator must form an opinion about which theory or combinations of theories are congruent to his own views. This will aid the early childhood educator in creating an appropriate environment for children of varying levels and abilities.

The following people have contributed a great deal to the world of education for young children. They have aided the educators of today in defining teaching styles, exploring different methods, and establishing environments that are appropriate for young children. Knowing how each of them has provided to the education of young children is important, as it gives a sense of the evolution to the programs of today.

They include

- Johann Pestalozzi, Whole Child Theory
- Jean-Jacques Rousseau, Environment Focus
- Fredrich Froebel, Father of Kindergarten
- Rudolf Steiner, Waldorf Philosophy
- Maria Montessori, Montessori Programs
- Arnold Gesell, Maturation Theory
- Lev Vygotsky, Sociocultural Theory
- Jean Piaget, Cognitive Development Stages Theory
- B.F. Skinner, Behavioral Approach Theory
- Howard Gardner, Multiple Intelligences Theory

Sometimes you remember only those theories you believe are appropriate for children, as it is generally based on your own philosophies and preferences. Find a way to remember the concepts related to each theory and think about how they affect children and early childhood programs.

Early childhood educators will become advocates for young children and should promote early childhood education for ALL children so each has a chance in our ever-changing world to become successful. There will be problems, issues, and barriers along the way. Be knowledgeable about the impact of these issues and be prepared to address them.

Four main areas will continue to have implications for programs that serve young children. These issues are technology, natural environments, parent-family services, and cultural diversity.

Technology plays an essential role in programs for young children. Children of the future must be prepared to live successfully with technology tools. For programs to remain current on the newest tools and materials may be difficult. Research recognizes the benefits of technology use with children. But in addition to the typical technology that all children will learn, children with disabilities are provided the use of technology under the law. Both through IDEIA and the Technology Act of 1994, children with disabilities are allowed to access and use technology devices to overcome barriers to learning. This type of technology is called **assistive technology** and must also be considered, discussed, and addressed on an IEP or IFSP. Accessing, maintaining, and managing the varying needs for technology stress even the finest programs.

Natural environments are recommended under the law. The law emphasizes that children with disabilities must be educated to the maximum extent possible with children who do not have disabilities. These natural environments are placements for children that would be the choice setting if the child did not have a disability. For very young children, under the age of 3, these natural environments include the home, a family member's home, a child care center, or a therapeutic setting. For children 3 and older, those settings may continue to be used, along with schools, and other therapeutic settings. The concept of natural environments is logical, but the implementation can be difficult. It is the philosophy of the natural environments that must be clearly understood, accepted, and valued by all adults working with children who have disabilities for it to be a successful setting.

Parent-family partnerships is another area that is supported under the law but still not being adequately promoted in early childhood programs. When families are involved in their child's education program and the family needs are also met, children thrive and achieve goals, making their programs very successful. This is a major goal for early intervention and early childhood program models, yet the time, resources, family diversity, and staff numbers make it sometimes unreasonable to reach the proper status. This may continue to be an ongoing issue for early childhood educators, as society evolves, family units change, and resources dwindle.

Cultural diversity, awareness, and sensitivity must all be recognized and dealt with in early intervention and early childhood programs. Early childhood educators should be first aware of their own cultural values and then understand the diversity of the family cultures. Knowing more about the perspectives that families have about disabilities, young children, therapy, and education will help the educator propose more appropriate programming for children, so it is not resisted. Communication efforts may also be affected by cultural differences. As society continues to change, educators will need to know more and more about various cultures.

Records Management

To become less overwhelmed by the abundance of paperwork in special education, and reduce the time spent on making a paper trail, a teacher should be knowledgeable about the requirements for records management. A teacher should develop a simplified system for filing records with an emphasis on easy access, especially for the following documents: a child's IEP or IFSP, the functional behavior plan, and any anecdotal records that support goal attainment. The teacher must also know the requirements for parent access to files under the procedural safeguards portion of the law.

Research

Research is endless, and the results of these studies focus on the issues and methods that relate to special education and the way you work with children. Research data can provide special educators and early childhood educators with important findings that expand their knowledge base, broaden their understandings, and inspire new and different ways of implementing services in their classrooms and programs.

There are many credible sources for obtaining information: research journals, professional associations, and educator organizations. Some of the more common topics of interest to early childhood educators include learning abilities, types of disabilities, early intervention methods, assessments, families, natural environments, and brain research. Using solid information helps educators to make decisions about children and improve outcomes.

Curriculum Considerations

A curriculum is considered a plan through which a child learns. It includes goals and outcomes with resources, the environment, teacher training, funding, and evaluation all being components of an effective curriculum. Generally a curriculum is based on an educational philosophy. The primary models of curricula include developmental, cognitive, constructivist, behavioral, ecological/functional, psychosocial, and developmentally appropriate.

The following definition of **curriculum** is taken from the NAEYC:

> "Curriculum is more than a collection of enjoyable activities. Curriculum is a complex idea containing multiple components, such as goals, content, pedagogy, or instructional practices. Curriculum is influenced by many factors including society's values, content standards, accountability systems, research findings, community expectations, culture and language, and individual children's characteristics."

A key recommendation from the NAEYC with regards to curriculum is to "implement curriculum that is thoughtfully planned, challenging and engaging, developmentally appropriate, culturally and linguistically responsive, comprehensive, and likely to promote positive outcomes for all young children."

Curriculum drives an early childhood program. The NAEYC suggests that there are several indicators of effectiveness in a comprehensive curriculum. Some of the factors to search for in a quality curriculum are clear shared goals, the curriculum is evidence based, and it builds on prior learning and experiences, allowing for children to be engaged. Professionals recommend that educators implement curriculum that is planned, coherent, and well-implemented, while being based on evidence and evaluated for effectiveness.

Most states have created and adopted standards for preschool programs in public school settings. **Standards** vary from state to state, but most states do require them, and they must be followed in an early childhood program with regard to both the curriculum implemented and the IEPs that are written. States and districts require that early childhood curricula be aligned with the state standards. State websites of each Department of Education should identify the ECE standards. If a state does not have prepared standards, there are guidelines on the website for NAEYC.

Developmentally Appropriate Practices (DAP) are key to implementing a curriculum for young children. In creating an environment that is suitable for the learning processes of young children, it is recommended that these practices be followed to ensure that the curriculum will be matched to each child's level of mental ability. The experiences provided to all children should correspond to their individual intellect and abilities, while challenging their individual interest levels. When utilizing DAP in a preschool program, teachers must be aware of any state requirements or standards for early childhood education. These practices and standards must not only be incorporated into the daily activities, but also addressed in student IFSPs and IEPs. A developmentally appropriate curriculum uses the daily routines of children for teaching skills. Play, the environment, the materials, and the activities are all important components of this type of curricula.

Because children with disabilities vary greatly in the needs to be addressed, an appropriate curriculum with emphasis on an adequate learning environment and developmental learning activities promotes progress in each of the five learning domains. It is for this reason that looking at all elements of a curriculum will aid the early childhood educator in selecting an appropriate tool to accommodate and meet each child's individual needs.

Transitions

Transition is the period during which a child is transferred from one type of program to another (most often from Part C services to Part B services) which changes the service model, the delivery of services, the interventions, and the family role. Early childhood educators often take a lead role in managing the transition services and must know the various agencies that provide services, the models that support those services, and the different professionals who might be involved with the child and the program. Early childhood educators must be sensitive to family needs and be prepared to guide, support, and inform the family members as the transition steps proceed.

Although transition planning and services differ among states and community locales, it is required in order to receive federal funds under Part B and Part C. Family involvement is mandated under the law so the team needs to be aware of the impact and work closely with the family to ease the child into a new setting.

Least Restrictive Environment (LRE)

Federal law is clear about the requirements that interventions be provided in the least restrictive environment. The speech therapist, the occupational therapist, and the physical therapist should all work in a general education classroom with young children. The advantages are based on the fact that therapy is part of the child's regular routine, so the skills are addressed in a more functional nature, and therefore, the child is more likely to use the skills in everyday life.

Natural environments are a key topic of the federal law for early childhood environments. It is a recommended practice and research validates it as a critical component of a quality early childhood program. Educators should embrace this philosophy for early childhood services.

Although some schools still practice a segregated special needs only program, most early childhood programs embrace either a reverse mainstream model or an integrated setting for inclusion. A reverse mainstream model is a class in which children with disabilities may be enrolled for certain periods of time with children who do not exhibited disabilities. Although it may not provide full-time interaction with nondisabled peers, it is more closely related to a natural environment than a segregated setting. An integrated or inclusive setting does provide for full-time involvement and is a most appropriate setting for young children.

Inclusion is a philosophy, not a place. Inclusion is an attitude, not a program. The purpose of an inclusion program is to expose children with disabilities to typical settings, activities, and peers. It allows typically developing children to interact with and learn from their peers who have disabilities, building upon their character in a positive way. Significant advantages for children who are placed in inclusive settings includes opportunities for social interactions, access to the general education curriculum, noted academic improvement, acceptance of diversity, and positive behavioral outcomes. The whole premise of inclusion is to educate children together so all will receive equal opportunities.

Research has shown that young children with disabilities who are placed in inclusive settings learn as well as or better than they would in segregated settings, while also participating in opportunities that promote social peer interactions not available in segregated settings. Inclusion must be utilized during the early years as it provides benefits to the children with disabilities and those without disabilities.

Community Resources

In this period of history, there is far more information from and within communities available to families about and for their young children that address their special needs than in times before. Agencies, support groups, workshops, and literature are available in most cities and towns across America. There are books, videos, CDs, and DVDs for parents who want to learn more about their individual child and his condition.

During the past 10 years, more child-friendly places such as museums, sport events, programs, community parks, and events are geared to the young child than ever before. Each community establishes the supports based on the needs of the families who live there. Most families have access to health-related providers, mental health providers, and early intervention or childcare providers. Others include welfare agencies, abuse prevention groups, specialized state programs for the deaf or blind, various support groups, nutrition providers, child protective services, economic security divisions, social services agencies, public health groups, libraries, and play groups.

It is the responsibility of the early intervention team members to help parents and families access the resources they need to become healthy and informed. These resources are available to all families, but not always known to all families.

Placement

The laws that support young children being placed in environments that are natural and appropriate, maximizing the young child's education, are the special education mandates. A brief summary of each regarding placement follows.

1. **IDEIA:** To the maximum extent possible, children with disabilities must be educated with their nondisabled peers.
2. **PL99-457:** Policies and procedures established ensure that early intervention services are provided in a natural environment to the maximum extent appropriate.
3. **IDEA:** Specific wording formalizes a philosophy of inclusion with the active participation of young children with disabilities and typically developing children in the same classrooms and community settings. The law also promotes the principle of natural environments for young children.

A child should be placed in the environment in which the child's individual needs may best be met based on the team assessment and an individualized plan. Previously, children with special needs at the preschool level were placed in special education segregated settings. Many schools did not enroll children in this age group unless they had an identified disability. Now, more and more schools are creating general education classes or inclusion settings for young children utilizing peer role models. Therefore, inclusion settings allow children with disabilities to participate in more natural environments in the community.

Introduction

It is highly probable that you have studied the diverse nature of the special education category behavioral disorders and emotional disturbances (BD/ED), which is considered the fourth largest category in special education. You likely know the causes and the many varying definitions, the importance of assessment, the behavior management theories and plans, as well as instructional strategies. Your post-secondary courses most certainly reviewed much information about special education as it pertains to the federal law IDEIA, the Individuals with Disabilities Education Improvement Act, since BD/ED is one of several categories under law.

From studying the broad topic of special education and the important requisite to address individual student needs, you should understand that every child is unique and requires an appropriate program to succeed in school and in adult life. This concept has never been clearer than when you examine those who are diagnosed with a behavior disorder or an emotional disturbance. These disabilities place students at great disadvantage. Because the students present with such wide variations in behaviors and moods, they are not easy to assess or diagnose, and they are challenging to teach. The key, however, in placing a student with a condition that qualifies under BD/ED is that their behaviors must adversely affect their educational performance. These students require specific behavior management strategies and the collaboration of all those who come in contact with them.

Many students in the school population may have problems with changing moods, outbursts, and managing behaviors, but they may not receive services under special education because their school work may not be affected. It is estimated that about 33 percent of children experience behavior problems, displaying inappropriate behaviors in the classroom, and may need assistance on a short-term basis. Of this group, about 10 percent of school-age children may be eligible for services and need specific interventions or assistance from professionals.

Some research studies estimate that between 1 and 7 percent of school-age children may have chronic problems that require more intensive services. However, according to the U.S. Department of Education in 2004, only about 0.7 percent of the school-age population received special education services under the BD/ED category. Other research studies believe the most appropriate numbers are between 5 and 20 percent of school-age children who have mental disorders with about 1 percent served as emotionally disabled. However, not all mental disorders are emotional disabilities, and not all are eligible for or require special education services. Professionals think the differences in prevalence figures are due to several factors: societal attitudes/concerns about these conditions (social policies), the funding streams available (economic factors), the definitions, the difficulty of assessments, and on-going issues, such as the methodologies.

You have selected this material to aid in passing the Praxis II exam on Special Education: Teaching Students with Behavioral Disorders/Emotional Disturbance (0371). You will be examining the practice questions, reading summaries of information, and thinking about all that you have learned since your college graduation or from your previous teaching experiences. This section should serve as review for you prior to embarking on the quest for certification in your state.

As you may have noticed in the Table of Contents, many topics in this section are covered, but they are not explained in detail. If you believe you need further study of a particular topic, you may want to review your college texts, speak with someone in the field, or use the references and websites listed in "Resources" to search for more information. In further preparation for this exam, you should be familiar with the specifics about the following BD/ED topics: causes, characteristics and definitions, assessment, placement and individual programs, curriculum and instruction, as well as behavior management and the family unit.

This Praxis II exam, Special Education: Teaching Students with Behavioral Disorders/Emotional Disturbance (0371), is a knowledge-based exam of 50 multiple-choice questions with presented case studies and multiple-choice questions that follow. Examinees, who are individuals preparing to teach students with BD/ED conditions in preschool through grade 12, should plan on receiving 1 hour to finish the test. The content categories in this exam are similar to those in other special education exams: Factors Other than Direct Instruction that Influence the Education of Students with Behavior Disorders/Emotional Disturbance with 10 questions and Delivery of Services to Students with Behavior Disorders/Emotional Disturbance with 40 questions.

Content Clusters

Review these 10 questions. Although these are not formatted as multiple-choice questions like those in the exam, they will give you the opportunity to determine your knowledge about these general topics as they cover a broad exam content category. This should help you in analyzing the information you know and in thinking about which areas you want to focus your further studies.

1. Identify the five traits of an emotional disability that are found in federal law and list at least five behavioral/emotional disorders that are most often served in school settings.

2. Explain how behavior problems and academic performance are inter-related and identify what educators should watch for academically in students with BD/ED conditions.

3. Describe the characteristics of students with BD/ED conditions and explain the prevalence numbers and the factors related to those numbers.

4. Define the specific types of behavior problems that are related to each of the following ED/BD patterns: environmental issues, personal disturbances, relationship problems, and learning disorders.

5. Explain the process for conducting a functional behavior assessment and describe how to create a functional behavior plan for at least two BD/ED conditions.

6. Describe the four major model approaches (psychodynamic, sociological/ecological/values-based, behavioral, and cognitive) that are used with students receiving services under the category of BD/ED.

7. Illustrate the specific points related to classroom organization and management which benefits students with BD/ED (include all types of LRE settings).

8. Explain the areas that should be emphasized during a behavior analysis and detail why these areas are important for educators to review.

9. Identify the types of behavior interventions found to be effective and appropriate for the school-age population who are served under the BD/ED category.

10. Describe the various options for collaboration with professionals and community resources to support a student with a BD/ED condition in a school setting.

Preview Questions

A set of five multiple-choice questions and a case study with two multiple-choice questions are prepared in this section to let you test your memory and to preview what may be included on the Praxis II exam. The answers to these questions are provided at the end of the set; however, the details about the answers are found in the study section that follows.

1. When working with students who exhibit emotional and behavioral disabilities, the goal is to have the students learn to manage their behaviors. They can do so by using which of the following techniques?

   A. Self-control and self-expression
   B. Self-management and self-control
   C. Self-expression and self-reinforcement
   D. Self-reinforcement and self-management

2. Students with emotional and behavioral disorders may also be affected by cognitive deficits, and those may be addressed by using the techniques of

    A.   motivation and peer tutoring.

    B.   tokens and self-management.

    C.   modeling and problem solving.

    D.   reinforcements and observations.

3. Specific criterion outlined for the assessment of students with behavioral and emotional disorders is that the measurement should be

    A.   conducted in the presence of a parent.

    B.   free of cultural, racial, and language bias.

    C.   included in the medical evaluation on the student.

    D.   comprised of one standardized assessment per setting.

4. The three major categories that relate to the causes for the existence of an emotional disability or behavior disorder are those that stem from _____ factors.

    A.   medical, cognitive, and social

    B.   behavioral, learning, and emotional

    C.   health, relationship, and academic

    D.   biological, environmental, or at-risk

5. When a behavior is observed for assessment purposes, the examiner usually documents the stimuli that preceded the behavior, which is called the

    A.   function.

    B.   predictor.

    C.   antecedent.

    D.   consequence.

The correct answers are

1. B. Students learn to control their own behaviors through the use of self-management and self-control techniques and strategies.

2. C. Sometimes students with emotional or behavioral disorders also have cognitive deficits. They need the support of modeling techniques and should also learn to problem solve.

3. B. Like all assessments for students with special needs, the measurements should be free of cultural, racial, and language bias in order to be considered valid.

4. D. There are three major categories believed to be causes for an emotional disability or a behavior disorder and those include: biological, environmental, at-risk.

5. C. When referring to behaviors, the antecedent is the stimuli that preceded the behavior and may have influenced the behavior observed.

Sample Case Study Questions

Following is a case study about a student with an emotional disability in a school setting. Read the case study carefully. Answer the following questions based on the situational information.

A middle school student with an identified emotional disability has received services since third grade for problems with inappropriate behaviors. While in second grade, this student's father and grandfather were killed in a robbery. This student has a history of aggressive behaviors and the student's academic achievement was very low. However, an assessment determined that the student had above average potential in all academic areas. For several years, the student was using art and music as outlets for expression. But, by the time the student was in fourth grade, the art took on a gory and death-related focus. The staff was very concerned about the student and worried about the effect of this behavior on other students. The mother shared that at home, the student locks the door to the bedroom and listens to music that was not approved and sometimes uses vulgar language and throws things.

The student repeated fourth grade, since test scores revealed that the academics were below the third grade level and the behaviors were increasing. It was a very difficult year for the student and extremely challenging for staff and parent.

During fifth grade, the student received services in a residential treatment center (RTC). The IEP team reviewed all options, and since the behaviors were so out of control for the student, it would be nearly impossible for them to be managed in a school setting. The student had been very aggressive towards adults with academic work deteriorating, and the student started to exhibit self-destructive behaviors.

After fifth grade, the school IEP team met with the professionals at the residential center along with the parent. They reviewed the student's progress as well as the current academic achievement scores. The student could be placed in a sixth-grade class and was currently working at the fifth-grade level in math and reading. Other subjects were at the fourth-grade level, but with the positive results in reading and math, the team believed the student would be on target soon.

The student also demonstrated excellent gains in behavior management. Although outbursts are still common, the student is more aware of the triggers that cause behavior problems and learned coping skills to help calm down and regulate emotions and acquired self-management skills for specific behaviors. Overall, the student has made remarkable progress in one year and is now exhibiting positive academic achievement, strong athletic skills, and improvement on the behavior intervention plan. At the IEP team meeting, the members agreed that the student was prepared to re-enter school.

Answer each of the following questions.

1. Since the student is entering the middle school, the team believes the responsibility to monitor rewards for on-target behavior should be left to the student. What strategy works well with older students in managing the responsibility of the behaviors and rewards?

   A. A contract system
   B. A free time period
   C. A choice of games
   D. A list of incentives

2. The student has made remarkable progress and is very interested in trying out for a sports team. To be sure the student maintains positive academic achievement, maintains appropriate behaviors out of the classroom, and has access to extracurricular activities, what method should the team consider in order to support this student?

   A. Ask the coach to permit the student to be a junior assistant coach for the year.
   B. Tell the mother to enroll the child on a community sports team to meet the student's desire for athletics.
   C. Provide a paraprofessional to support the transition into extracurricular activities and help the student maintain behaviors.
   D. Inform the student that extracurricular activities are allowed only after all areas have improved and academics are on grade level.

Correct answers

1. **A.** A contract system that is established between the student and the teacher(s) is a positive way to give responsibility to the student for managing behaviors.

2. **C.** The use of a paraprofessional for the transition into extracurricular activities, even though it might be temporary, would seem to be the best choice for this student.

Study Information

The principles of serving children with disabilities did not evolve overnight. You can deduce from the various changes in the federal law that over many decades, definitions transformed and requirements were amended to meet the demands of society. Practices evolve and material usage must adjust to meet the needs of children. Students and young children with emotional and behavioral needs have been challenged over the years due to the changes in the laws, the definitions, and the strategies. This is a particular area of special education in which it pays to stay on top of the evolution of research, publications, and scientific studies.

This section of the book highlights the areas related to behavior disorders and emotional disturbances in the school-age population. In studying the information for the exam, since IDEIA impacts the services that are provided to students under the category of BD/ED, it may be helpful to also study the Praxis II information on the core knowledge and application exams. You will want to review the theories, interventions, practices, and assessments that are pertinent to children with BD/ED conditions. Should you need additional facts and content refer to the suggested list of websites in the "Resources" appendix.

Over the history of civilization, the education of children with emotional and behavioral conditions has been influenced by factors of religion, science, philosophy, politics, and laws. Research indicates that students with behavior disorders and emotional disturbances may be an underserved population. Studies point out that certain minority groups (in particular, African-Americans) may be over represented in this field, and it is documented that there are more males than females who need services for these conditions.

So, as far back as the 1800s, individuals with emotional and behavioral problems were noticed as needing specialized assistance, and many were served; however, the perceptions about this population were somewhat different than those of today. During the 20th century, scientists studied psychological development and realized that emotional problems could be associated with biological factors and some medical treatments were used. By the 1950–60s, research demonstrated an understanding for systematic procedures to identify and serve children with emotional and behavioral problems. The conceptual models emerged, and progress has been positive since that time.

Current issues exist in this field and are more philosophical in nature. They beg the questions: Where should these students be served and is this an underserved group?

Over the years, special education litigation has been numerous, and there has been some litigation related to children who exhibit emotional and behavioral problems. But even more than litigation, it was the establishment of agencies and organizations that advocated for services for this unique group of individuals and changed the attitudes and the types of services that are now provided.

Some of these groups include

- National Institute for Mental Health
- National Mental Health Association
- Council for Exceptional Children with Behavioral Disorders

The quality of services offered to children with behavioral and emotional conditions may fiercely influence the children's present and future achievements. Schools have improved the services and the number of programs offered to children with these disabilities. Changes in services have been tied to societal demands, such as cultural beliefs and changes in family units. These children are served to reduce the maladaptive behaviors that impair their education and to enhance their involvement with typical children, which encourages future success.

As you continue to peruse this study guide on behavioral and emotional disabilities, understand that this is just a summary of the information available on this significant area of special education. Research the websites and organizations listed in the "Resources" section for further information on the subject of behavioral disorders and emotional disturbances.

Factors That Influence Education

Students with behavioral disorders or emotional disturbances cause complex problems for public schools. These students vary tremendously in their behaviors and their needs, and a wide range of specially designed instructional services must be addressed in an IEP. It is not only the behaviors or the emotional components that professionals should concentrate on, but these students also may need interventions and support for academics, social skill development, communication, and family training. With proper treatments, many students with BD/ED problems will no longer present with those behaviors as adults, yet some will continue to exhibit maladaptive behaviors despite interventions.

One problem for schools is educators who are cautious about referring a child who exhibits inappropriate behaviors as they fear a label of BD/ED may remain with the child even after the school years. Many students act inappropriately at school, but distinguishing between acting out behavior and an actual disability is complicated. This decision should be guided by professionals who understand the differences and have expert knowledge about assessments. These professionals (a psychologist, a psychiatrist, or a medical practitioner) should continue to be members of the student's individual education plan team while the student receives interventions and services under special education.

Characteristics

Society establishes guidelines and sometimes rules for appropriate behaviors based on specific cultural and age groups. There are expectations for all individuals to function within families and the larger communities in proper and acceptable ways. When someone has problems managing his behavior or controlling his emotions, negative consequences are imposed. Without proper supports, these behaviors may increase, lengthening the time it takes to get them under control.

Some common symptoms adults notice when working with children who qualify for services include the following: an inability to learn, relationship problems, inappropriate behaviors, unhappiness or depression, and physical symptoms or fears.

When an individual's behavior falls significantly below expected societal norms, assistance may be warranted through access of medical help, school interventions, or community services. Individuals with BD/ED conditions often demonstrate delays in either internalizing or externalizing behaviors. Any patterns of abnormal behaviors may adversely affect the individual's academic achievement and social relationships.

Internalizing behaviors students exhibit are influenced by a lack of social development and appropriate interactions. These may include immature actions and withdrawal from others that affect further development. These children are more at risk, as they may not be identified immediately, since they do not act out. These children exhibit problems with mood and anxiety revealed through phobias, eating disorders, obsessive-compulsive disorder, depression, and bipolar disorder. If these emotional disorders are not treated and effective interventions not administered, these children may self-injure or attempt suicide.

Externalizing behaviors or antisocial behaviors are the most common of the disordered behaviors and generally involve aggressive behaviors such as fighting, stealing, destroying property, temper tantrums, and other noticeable noncompliant or inappropriate acts. Students with these problems have difficulty establishing positive relationships. Research studies indicate that when a child demonstrates a pattern of antisocial behavior early in life, it is probable that the child will become delinquent during adolescence with behaviors such as substance abuse, dropping out of school, and confrontations with the legal system.

Over the years, studies on behavior disorders and disturbances have defined five important patterns typical of individuals with these conditions. This information describes the characteristics of various problems, including emotional, behavioral, and cognitive characteristics. Many professionals refer to them as aggression, anxiety, depression, impulsiveness, and relationship problems. According to the Praxis II, you should study these four major topics: psychological, affective, adaptive/maladaptive behaviors, and behavior disorders/hyperactivity/impulsivity. Although research indicates five patterns for these behaviors, Praxis II has divided them into four broader categories. The five patterns familiar to most educators are indicated in bold.

Psychological

The psychological category of BD/ED includes neuroses, psychoses, **anxiety,** and **depression.** Students with these problems may be considered to have social phobias and mood disorders that also include panic disorders, bipolar disorder, obsessive-compulsive disorder, and posttraumatic stress disorder. Some of these disorders involve feelings, thoughts, or behaviors that are unpleasant or maladaptive. These students may feel scared, worried, guilty, or stressed and may think they are losing control, being criticized, or dying. It may cause problems with their ability to pay attention, remember, think clearly, or perform. They might have physical symptoms such as headaches, stomachaches, or muscle tension. These students usually have problems with peers as they are avoided and taunted by others.

Affective

Affective behaviors are those that pertain to social-emotional development, interpersonal skills, and **relationship problems.** Most people interact with others many times during the course of a day. It is important that children become adept at this healthy behavior. However, it requires varying skills and competencies in a few areas: communication, social development, and cognition. Children with socialization problems exhibit behaviors that may include being afraid, unhappy, lonely, rejected, or withdrawn. These problems may compound the issues of this condition as individuals must practice appropriate social behaviors to improve them. The affective components of these disorders may be co-morbid with depression, aggression, and anxiety disorders.

Adaptive/Maladaptive Behaviors

The adaptive and maladaptive behaviors formed may consist of self-injurious behaviors, eating disorders, substance abuse, **aggression**, social maladjustment, disruptive behavior disorders, and delinquency. Those most often observed behaviors in schools are related to aggression. Within this area you may hear the terms **conduct disorder** or **oppositional defiant disorder.** These aggressive behaviors are regularly imposed to inflict harm, injury, or pain toward others. Individuals with these disorders may demonstrate disobedience, disrespect, harassing behaviors, destruction of property, fighting, disruption, stealing, and bullying. A difficult aspect is that these students often demonstrate no guilt, nor do they take responsibility for their own behaviors.

Behavior Disorders/Emotional Disturbance: Distractibility, Hyperactivity, and Impulsivity

There is a relationship between behavior disorders/emotional disturbance and distractibility, hyperactivity, and **impulsivity**. These problems are most noticeable when students are in controlled settings where structure, prosocial behavior, and attention are required. Having these conditions can cause a student to be inattentive, to give inappropriate responses, and demonstrate over-activity. They may appear to be agitated and disorganized, while they ignore directions, are abrupt and rude, make poor choices, and are often disliked by peers. Because they may also have issues with defiance and opposition, and they involve themselves in risky situations, they resemble students with aggressive disorders.

Some states and professionals do qualify students with ADHD under the BD/ED category, while others qualify these students as having health problems that impair alertness and qualify them under the OHI (Other Health Impaired) category.

Causation and Prevention

Several theories are related to behavior disorders and emotional disturbances, which may explain how the cause can be interpreted into a plan for learning. Professionals have proposed conceptual models to help identify the types of behavior disorders and emotional problems that exist. Sometimes the cause is very difficult to analyze.

Most professionals believe that two main categories reflect the causes of emotional and behavioral disabilities: **environmental** and **biological.** When the cause of an individual's adverse behaviors has been determined, it is much easier for the team to create a proper program for success.

Environmental factors are associated with an individual's behavior in the family, at school, and in community settings. Research shows that conduct disorders and antisocial behaviors may emerge from deprivation during early experiences, aggressiveness in school, and rejection by peers.

The early environment is so important to the development of a child's brain and social relationships. The environment can be considered the home, the community, or the school. Strong, positive relationships built during the early period contribute to a child's development of appropriate societal behaviors. If the relationship with the primary caretakers is tainted with criticism, harshness, and hurt, a child may be adversely affected and begin using inappropriate behaviors, which become compounded over time.

After a child starts school, the behaviors may be increased if the setting and the teachers are not responsive to the child's needs. When a child already has problems, yet is not identified, the lack of rules and expectations, the need for accommodations, inconsistent discipline, and limited praise will all contribute to the antisocial behaviors and conduct disorders.

Biological factors may contribute to BD/ED include brain disorders (from abnormal development, trauma, or disease), genetic influences (mental illnesses), and temperament (how an individual responds to environmental stimuli).

Another area that contributes to the development of a BD/ED is the condition of being "at-risk." These at-risk children may experience a combination of problems, some of which may be associated with biological issues and others with environmental influences. These factors (poverty, parent criminality, abuse, media violence, and so on) place the child **at-risk** for school failure, future violence, and potential delinquency. The longer the child is exposed to these contributing risk factors, the greater the probability of a negative outcome.

Many professionals, if given the option to choose, would prefer prevention over intervention for individuals with BD/ED issues. Because these disabilities can adversely affect a person's entire life, it is wise to impose preventative measures whenever possible. Prevention may be delivered directly or indirectly to groups or individuals. Types of prevention include provide early identification and interventions, change learned behaviors in young children, teach competency skills (academic, social, and vocational), introduce medical interventions, increase public awareness, deliver parent training sessions, and request community support for young children and families.

Definitions

Creating a definition that is precise and covers all aspects of BD/ED conditions is difficult. However, definitions are important because they reflect how professionals and others in the field view individuals with these disorders. Definitions can provide a description of who might be eligible for services, as well as include research in the medical and scientific fields.

In the federal definition, emotional disturbance is the primary term used. However, some states may use terms such as severely emotionally disturbed, behaviorally disordered, emotional impairment, or emotional disability. The federal definition found under IDEIA includes

> "...a condition exhibiting one or more of the following characteristics over a long period of time and to a marked degree that adversely affects a child's educational performance:
>
> a. an inability to learn that cannot be explained by intellectual, sensory or health factors.
>
> b. an inability to build or maintain satisfactory interpersonal relationships with peers and teachers.
>
> c. inappropriate types of behavior or feelings under normal circumstances.
>
> d. a general pervasive mood of unhappiness or depression.
>
> e. a tendency to develop physical symptoms or fear associated with personal or school problems.
>
> The term may include schizophrenia, but does not apply to children who are socially maladjusted, unless it is determined that they have an emotional disturbance."

Some professional groups do not agree with the definition that has been used as a federal guideline to the states. These organizations have proposed other definitions and have advocated for the inclusion of other various conditions. One such organization is the National Mental Health and Special Education Coalition. They have created a preferred definition that they hope will be accepted in federal law one day. It is a comprehensive definition that they believe is more specific to children in school, and in part it begins,

> "Emotional or Behavioral Disorder (EBD) refers to a condition in which behavioral or emotional responses of an individual in school are so different from his/her generally accepted, age appropriate, ethnic or cultural norms that they adversely affect performance in such areas as self care, social relationships, personal adjustment, academic progress, classroom behavior, or work adjustment...."

For the full definition, see www.nasponline.org/about_nasp/pospaper_sebd.aspx.

According to the Council for Exceptional Children-Council for Children with Behavior Disorders (CEC-CCBD), they have also had difficulty accepting the federal definition. Overall, they state that the term **behaviorally disordered** is a more appropriate term that **emotionally disturbed** as it represents more children, does not focus on a particular theory or intervention, and does not have the attached stigma. They have further recommended changes to the federal definition and have combined efforts with the National Mental Health and Special Education Coalition to pursue changes in the federal definition through Congress. Their drafted proposal includes the following points and is in reference to the NMHSEC definition, as well.

- The disability must be related to behavior in school programs and compared to appropriate age and cultural norms, with response adversely affecting education performance on more than a temporary level, unresponsive to direct instruction, and exhibited in two settings.
- This condition may co-exist with other disability conditions.
- The term may include schizophrenic disorders, affective disorders, anxiety disorders, or other sustained disorder of conduct or adjustment.

The DSM-IV is a manual that offers definitions and outlines of eligibility for various conditions. However, the DSM-IV requires that a professional who uses these guidelines to make a diagnosis be either a clinical practitioner or a licensed professional. The conditions identified relate more to the mental health practitioners who provide services to individuals with behavior problems and emotional issues outside of schools, and they are not always related to special education, although there may be co-morbidity of problems in individual students. Some conditions, such as the disruptive behavior disorders like oppositional defiant disorder and conduct disorder, must be diagnosed clinically, yet if the student also has problems with social and academic functioning, may qualify for special education under the category of BD/ED.

Delivery of Services

Service delivery is a primary component in providing an educational program for students with disabilities. The service delivery models are based on education theory and involve a variety of professionals as well as the resolution of program issues to be beneficial to students.

Conceptual Approaches

A number of theories focus on the care for and services to individuals with behavioral and emotional disturbances. Some services are best provided in school settings, and others tend to be more appropriate to persons in segregated facilities, under clinical supervision. Some of these theoretical models include behavioral, psychoanalytic, ecological, sociological, cognitive, humanistic, biogenic, person-centered, reality-based, and social discipline. Remember that in the school system, many professionals use a more eclectic approach that combines several approaches based on different theories to adequately meet the demands of the school while also serving the needs of the children. When educators use this method of serving students, they must incorporate instruction and assessment techniques as they apply behavior management interventions, promote an appropriate environment, and manage the services to the student. The majority of the conceptual approaches are mentioned here, but additional information may be found on some of the websites listed in the "Resources" section in the appendix.

Psychodynamic Model

Psychodynamic Theory includes a spectrum of approaches that focus on the development of special types of mental activities and how these relate to emotions, thoughts, and behaviors, whether typical or not. Those are briefly mentioned here and include the possible interventions.

1. Psychoanalysis
2. Social discipline
3. Person-centered
4. Reality-based
5. Psychoeducational

Psychoanalysis is an approach to be used only by trained therapists. It is the beginning of the psychodynamic model and based on Sigmund Freud's work with individuals suffering from behavioral and emotional problems. This approach deals with personality and its development through various stages, and includes work focused on the three parts called **id, ego,** and **superego.** Therapists encourage their clients to free associate in an attempt to uncover how their minds function. Unresolved conflicts that are associated with personality development stages may cause anxiety disorders, phobias, neuroses, psychosis, and antisocial behaviors. Interventions under this approach (which most schools do not use unless they use a separate or residential care facility) involve group or individual therapy. Some students may receive psychotherapy through community-based agencies while they are also enrolled in special education programs. These therapy sessions may include conversations, music, art, or play.

Social discipline is an approach that schools rely on as they conduct functional behavior assessments. This theory is based on the premise that behaviors are goal-directed. Dreikurs established four goals that represent the purpose of students' behaviors, which are attention seeking, power, revenge, and helplessness. Interventions suggested for this approach include deciding the goal of the behavior, helping students learn appropriate behaviors, establishing logical consequences, developing adaptive behaviors, and providing encouragement for mastery.

The **person-centered approach** focuses on caring, cooperation, organization, community, and prevention. Students need to understand the problems that impede progress and learn to develop positive self regard. Included in this process is the method whereby students are presented with situations so their self-perceptions and their understanding of the events can be explored. The students learn to solve their own problems. If the students are not on track in these ways, they may feel rejected, become doubtful, and develop a poor self-concept. A child who is not allowed to make choices or control his future may develop a depressive disorder. Interventions supported through the work of Rogers, Gordon, and Frieburg recommend I-messages. Other interventions may include building upon trust and communications, using positive comments, allowing the student to explore self, establishing a loosely structured environment, and encouraging class cooperation and responsibility. These techniques must be internalized by the students and not directed by the adults.

Reality therapy, also called **choice therapy,** had its beginnings in the work of Glasser. The idea is to help students act rationally and improve through the four major needs: love, power, pleasure, and freedom. If these needs are not met, a child may feel like a failure. This theory proposes that the very tenants of education may cause children to develop inappropriate behaviors. Those who believe this point out that some educational practices develop attitudes of failure in students: grading, lectures, memorization, inappropriate learning materials, and irrelevant subjects and actions. Students with BD/ED need to learn how to behave and interact within the system to have their basic needs met, and they must be a part of the solution toward improvement. The proposed interventions are to

- Identify the behaviors
- Set expectations for success
- Make a plan
- Correct inappropriate behaviors
- Confront serious misbehaviors
- Enforce reasonable consequences

The **psychoeducational approach** is a combination of the psychoanalytic and psychodynamic models, based on the theory that behavior is the result of past experiences, current state of being, and environmental influences. If a child's biological needs and emotional needs are not balanced, personality disorders may emerge. At school if a student with these emerging conditions feels stressed, fearful, hostile, unhappy, aggressive, or negated, then behaviors will escalate. This is the approach that is most often used in schools as it reflects caring and discipline, while communicating expectations. The student must move from an external locus of control (the teacher) to an internal locus of control (self-control or self-management) of behaviors. This approach considers that behavior imitates the stress and the feelings related to the environment. It also emphasizes the proper student-adult relationships to build upon emotional stability. The teachers must be aware of their own reactions to maladaptive behaviors and inappropriate emotions when working with students under this model. The goal is to teach and model skills to help the student cope with stress-inducing situations. Some of the typical techniques used in classrooms are planned ignoring, interest boost, tension relievers, time-out periods, signal interference, proximity control, and value review.

Interventions designed under the **psychodynamic theory** are designed to help individuals with B/E disorders recognize their own inappropriate behaviors and develop coping mechanisms. This enables them to make positive choices and improve their mood, thereby alleviating problems with their education and social interactions.

Behavioral Model

The **behavioral model** is based on **operant conditioning** and the belief that behavior is related to the environmental stimuli either preceding or following it. School staff analyzes the student's behavior in order to pinpoint its function. Functional analysis helps identify the stimuli in the environment and can indicate ways to modify the target behaviors. This is most helpful when educators are conducting a Functional Behavioral Assessment.

In the behavioral model, it is evident that there are antecedents (before the behavior) and consequences (after the behavior). This idea resulted in the development of the ABC technique (antecedent-behavior-consequence), which is valuable when assessing a student and determining the behavior plan. The reinforcement of a behavior allows a teacher to strengthen the desired behavior and reduce the less desirable action.

Researchers use what is termed **applied behavior analysis,** while schools use behavior modification (operant conditioning) to improve behaviors. When behavior modification is effective it

- Increases the target behavior
- Decreases the inappropriate behavior
- Encourages cooperation with peers
- Analyzes antecedents appropriately
- Encourages self-management (self-control, self-reinforcement, self-monitoring)

Behavior modification programs do not articulate well into general education settings. The student often needs to learn self-management and generalization of behaviors to perform in the general education setting. Some of the known programs used for behavior modification in schools include

- CLASS program
- First Step to Success
- Home-based program
- Engineered classroom
- Franklin-Jefferson program

Some of the interventions that promote the behavioral approach include token economy, behavioral contracting, social skills training, self-management, time-out, group contingencies, and positive reinforcement.

Cognitive Model

The **cognitive model** is based on the social-cognitive theory by Albert Bandura (1960s), which relates to the process of modeling or imitating desired behaviors. This has been called the **cognitive-behavioral approach.** It is believed that cognition, behavior, and environmental stimuli are interactive and influence one another. These cognitive events may contribute to B/E disorders (misunderstandings of another's actions, worrying about events, aggressive responses, and so on).

The three influences on this social-cognitive theory are as follows:

- Individual's behavior (motor and verbal abilities, thoughts, and so on)
- Environmental events (physical and social prompts, modeling, and so on)
- Personal phenomena (beliefs, perceptions, and so on)

Four subprocesses are outlined in this theory: attention, retention, response reproduction, and motivation. The first three relate to learning the new behaviors, thoughts, or emotions (observational learning). The last defines how this is applied to what is learned and the performance of the behavior (vicarious effect).

Because this theory states that behaviors are related to environmental stimuli, it follows the premise of operant conditioning. However, it further states that the environment influences personal behavior changes indirectly, which explains why some children learn maladaptive behaviors from their caretakers and living situations. If children observe such things as impulsive actions, aggressive behaviors, drug/alcohol abuse, or bizarre or disordered behaviors, they may learn and internalize these through modeling and imitation. Some children have cognitive deficits, distortions, or social information processing problems that exacerbate the escalation of maladaptive behaviors.

Interventions suggested under the cognitive approach are primarily aimed at a specific pattern of behavior or a particular form of B/E disorders and may not be appropriate for every student with BD/ED problems. Recommended interventions are as follows:

- Implement modeling of appropriate behaviors.
- Support cognitive skill development to aid in self-instruction.
- Provide social problem-solving and decision-making situations.
- Employ an anger control program.
- Include skill-streaming instruction (of more than 50 social skills).
- Modify distortions of information processing, attributes, and beliefs.

Sociological Model

The **sociological model** addresses the social aspects and differences in individuals and subgroups according to the socioeconomic status, race/ethnicity, culture, and social causations (economic injustice, discrimination). Children are impacted by problems in the home and by caretaker models who demonstrate inappropriate behaviors.

Interventions may be selected on a case-by-case basis and be drawn from the various other models—cognitive, behavioral, and psychodynamic—according to the disability. Specific interventions related to this model are broadly stated and include

- Deliver services in culturally aware environments.
- Educate teachers and staff on cultural perspectives.
- Reduce bias in assessments.
- Advocate government and agencies to reduce undesirable circumstances in society.

Ecological Model

This model is concerned with smaller environments such as the classroom or a school. **Ecological theory** is based on the study of relationships in an ecosystem and how a student's behavior fits within the environment and is influenced by physical, social, and cognitive aspects.

Interventions include changes in a range of physical, social, behavioral, and psychological variables. Working collaboratively with all agencies involved in a student's program produces highly beneficial outcomes. There should be an assessment of the classroom and the school environment to determine whether they are appropriate for the individual or whether changes should be made. Educators must become advocates for the student as she moves along the ecosystem.

Values-Based/Spiritual Model

Professionals may disagree about this conceptual model as values and morals have different meanings to different people. It is very hard to agree on which values to teach students in schools. This theory, based on Kohlberg's theory of moral reasoning, is most often tied to mental health agencies and their services to students with BD/ED. However, many schools are including a character education curriculum as school-wide instruction to all students. It incorporates values into education, and students learn values and character traits that are acceptable in society. Educators model and teach strong, positive character. In community agencies, they often follow a 12-step program or religious and spiritual trainings or programs. Another program that may be used to support the values-based education is the **circle of courage** program that focuses on four basic needs: belonging, mastery, independence, and generosity. Schools must be cautious in implementing programs that are connected to values, religion, and spiritual ideas.

Implementing any of these theoretical models or conceptual approaches, or any that have not been mentioned, in general education settings may be very difficult. Due to the complexity of the individuals and their conditions, as well as the need for consistency in their programs, these practices may be better provided in residential settings, self-contained classrooms, or alternative school environments. The goal is to select the approach that matches the student's disability needs instead of using the same approach for all students.

Professional Roles/Issues/Literature/Research

Professionals who work with students who exhibit BD/ED conditions need to be knowledgeable about the theories, models, and strategies that serve this population. They must apply the appropriate interventions to each individual, as needs are so different. Educators should stay current on the research and seek journal literature about the most recent findings and studies. It is only through these educator practices that students with BD/ED problems will receive the education and support that they need.

Public Attitudes

As you read in the introduction section, public attitudes have changed tremendously over the past several centuries. Due to research of these conditions that began in the 1950s, progress was made in the identification and available services for children with behavioral and emotional disorders. With the surge of guidance clinics, the general public started to be more aware, and the professionals and the public more openly shared concerns about these children.

For some, it was the beginning of collaboration aimed at success for children with BD/ED issues. Many believed that services could be received in schools, the home, in clinics, and in the community. However, it was not certain that teachers were trained well enough to meet the needs of these diverse students.

Although attitudes have changed, there is still much that needs to be done to support children with BD/ED problems. In many schools, these children are not receiving services that meet their needs. This is not only the fault of the school, but the entire social system that should oversee proper care. Some communities have very limited resources for children, and the school may be the only hope for treatment.

Advocacy

Advocacy can take on several forms of support for students with behavioral and emotional disturbances. Advocacy is the collection of beliefs that may promote a condition or improve the rights of individuals. It is important for educators who specialize in this field to know the methods of advocacy they may pursue. Training students to be self-advocates is critical to their existence. Educators may advocate through professional organizations and may address public issues in their communities. This involvement may relate to policies, definitions, support services, work situations, and funding. Educators may want to share awareness with community members to alleviate discrimination and clarify perceptions.

Abuse/Neglect/Delinquency

Children may contract conditions of behavioral and emotional disturbance based on their early situations and experiences of abuse and neglect. The environment, nutrition, and care are so important to the life of a young child, but if those are askew, the child may develop significant problems. Here are only a few of the situations that may contribute to BD/ED issues:

- Drug/alcohol abuse by family members or the child
- Inappropriate and deviant sexual behaviors
- Neglect of care and affection as infants and toddlers
- Disregard for proper nutrition and medical attention
- Aggressive behaviors by family members in the home
- Criminal behavior by parents, siblings, or other caregivers
- Emotional, physical, or sexual abuse in childhood

These are the students who need positive role models the most. Many of them come from difficult home situations and families of low socioeconomic status. However, if the adults who work with them show they care, children will reap the benefits of these solid relationships. Research has proven that one positive adult relationship can increase the resiliency of at-risk children.

Improving Classroom Practices

One area that would help with overall classroom management and support to students who may have a BD/ED problem is to impose prereferral interventions prior to referring the student to special education. These practices are not as widely used as they should be. Many children with behavioral and emotional problems do respond to basic teacher-directed interventions. This practice alone may reduce the number of children being identified as BD/ED and, therefore, the resources may be used to support those who have more involved and serious conditions.

Expectations of Student Achievement and Behaviors

Expectations and standards for students with BD/ED conditions differ from teacher to teacher, setting to setting, day to day and children are sometimes caught unaware. Professionals must keep in mind that the children identified with BD/ED problems have gone through the scrutiny and testing of an entire team, and careful thought was placed on the decision to place the student in special education.

Two areas may cause educators to set unrealistic expectations on children with BD/ED. The first relates to intelligence. Many students with BD/ED problems score in the low average or mild mentally retarded range on an IQ test. It is difficult, however, to know whether the student is having trouble taking the test due to BD/ED problems or whether the student missed out on learning the previous information due to BD/ED problems. Students with BD/ED do perform about one or more years below their grade level in the classroom, and some demonstrate learning disabilities.

The second has to do with the actual disability and the demonstrated behaviors. Professionals may not be prepared to separate the child from the behaviors and may not understand that the child is already functioning below peers academically, so expectations should be set higher. The student may be expected to act like the others in the classroom, since related services and therapies are being provided. When the student acts according to the disability, some professionals become frustrated or even angry with the student and may impose unwarranted discipline.

Collaboration with Health and Social Service Providers

Collaboration with personnel outside of the school system is of high likelihood when working with students who have behavioral and emotional disturbances. Because of the varieties of services that students may need and may have access to, educators may be involved in meetings and discussions with the mental health system, juvenile justice system, medical/health care system, and family welfare system to enhance a student's program.

A student is placed in a program, according to the IEP and LRE. This placement may determine the additional services that are provided through the community system. Some of the specific mental health programs outside of the school environment include outpatient treatment centers, day treatment programs, and residential or psychiatric hospitals and settings. Students who are receiving services from the child and family welfare system may obtain respite services or foster care placement and therapy, and the school staff will be in contact with the case manager. Students who have contact with the juvenile justice system may be on probation or placed in detention centers, and the school will need to work with the probation officer. Other possibilities for students include specialized outdoor recreation services, vocational programs, and therapeutic measures that include a therapist and/or the clinical management of psychotropic drugs. Whichever program and whatever services the student encounters, the school is still responsible for the special education program, and follow-through is essential by school staff.

The coordination of these services is a form of intervention and referred to as the "system of care." These systems are developing at the state and local levels to guide and accommodate the needs of children and families faced with BD/ED problems. It is invaluable that students with BD/ED are supported by child service agencies that collaborate on service delivery, assessments, interventions, and care. Interagency collaboration provides a level of responsiveness to families and a commitment to the child, which enhances outcomes. Parental consent is critical when schools collaborate with outside service providers. A release of information signed by the parent or guardian is needed before any contact can be made.

Professional Organizations

Educators and other professionals should be involved with the professional organizations that support students with BD/ED conditions. These organizations offer membership, workshops, trainings, updated information, instructional strategies, and advocacy opportunities. Being involved as a professional enriches your career and enhances the education of the students you serve.

Some of the more well-known national groups include: National Mental Health Association, National Institute on Health, National Institute of Mental Health, Council for Exceptional Children with Behavior Disorders, and Federation of Families for Children's Mental Health. Other organizations that support individuals with behavioral and emotional difficulties are the local social services agencies and mental health agencies, as well as the state department agencies of behavioral, mental health, or social services.

Assessment

The purpose of the assessment process is to gather information about students to determine their strengths and needs. This particular section looks at identifying whether a student has a B/E disorder and what interventions would prove appropriate and successful. Most assessments for students with BD/ED measure both **reported functioning** and **actual functioning.** Assessment is mandated and guided under IDEIA, and assessment should be ongoing after a student is identified and being served. The key to an efficient assessment is to select the proper tools, conduct an appropriate evaluation, and use the results to develop a program.

Although assessments can be complex and are generally supervised or conducted by a psychometrist, a psychologist, or a psychiatrist, educators should know several points. Conducting an assessment and determining the scores allow the examiner to conclude the form and possible cause of the disorder, what educational strengths and areas of weakness exist, and the interventions or strategies that should be discussed. It is a recommended practice that educators keep specific measurement documentation of a student's actions relating to the B/E disorder. This may include the behaviors, academic achievement, physical indicators, and social aspects.

Reliability, validity, and norms are important terms in the assessment of a student who may have a B/E disorder. Further information on assessment may be found in the "Knowledge-Based Core Principles" section of this book.

Informal

Informal assessments may be used with students who demonstrate BD/ED; however, care must be taken regarding the interpretation of these sessions and whether the information is used to make major decisions about a student's program and services. Teachers often use informal formats for monitoring the behaviors in the classroom, observing the acquisition of skills, and meeting behavior goals. Informal measures for those purposes may be beneficial.

Formal

Assessment is critical for students with BD/ED problems and incorrect identification and placement can scar a child for the rest of his life. Assessments must be efficient, effective, and precise. Multiple measurement tools and methods, multiple settings, and various sources of information should be used. Physical, medical, academic, social, and environmental variables, as well as behavioral and emotional factors, are important pieces in an evaluation of a student who may be identified with BD/ED.

Formal assessment in special education follows a select set of guidelines. The following paragraphs offer insight into the specific types of measurements that may be used and how they are specific to the BD/ED population.

A **functional assessment** will support the development of a positive behavioral support system and plan by evaluating the problem behavior(s). It may include interviews with familiar adults, observations of the student, and an analysis of the variables regarding the problem behaviors. A functional assessment should be conducted in a student's natural environment, which may include the home, school, or community settings. After a functional analysis is completed, the most common types of interventions to be implemented are reinforcement-based.

A **Functional Behavior Assessment** (FBA) is a process whereby information is gathered so the IEP team may more fully understand the student's behaviors. The FBA measures the social and environmental variables surrounding a target behavior. These may be conducted using an interview process, an observation, or a combination of those and other methods. This information is often helpful when creating, revising, or implementing a behavioral intervention. An FBA is a requirement under IDEIA for all special education students if the behavior impedes the student's learning or that of others.

A **behavior rating scale** is a checklist or questionnaire with a standard list of items that describes certain characteristics of emotions and behaviors. The rater can be the student, a peer, a teacher, a parent, or another adult who is familiar with the student. Rating scales can be used to evaluate one characteristic or multiple characteristics and may be teacher created or published materials. These scales can help professionals determine areas of concern and help guide decision-making about those problems.

The **interview method** should be conducted by someone trained and skilled in the process. Several parties may be interviewed to gather valuable information: parents, the student, teachers, and other adults. The interviewer may collect facts about developmental milestones, early education and health, the family unit, problem areas, and activities out of school. There are **high-structured interviews** in which a standard set of questions are used and the responses are compared to norms. The **low-structured interviews** are completed using a more specific set of questions that pertain to the individual student's situation.

Personality measurements are usually conducted to analyze how an individual feels, thinks, and behaves in a variety of situations. These may be a standard measure or in interview format. This kind of measurement may also be used in connection with other assessments to gather pertinent information on the many aspects of a student's condition.

The **observation method** offers a clear view of the behaviors a student exhibits in the setting where they typically occur. There are various factors by which to measure a behavior such as frequency, duration, latency, magnitude, and topography. These factors may be recorded by observing in multiple settings such as the classroom, the cafeteria, the bus stop, another classroom, the hallway, or the playground. This approach allows the team to directly address the behaviors by taking action and then making changes in the plan if needed.

Additional assessments that are critical to the nature of a student's program include assessments conducted by medical practitioners, compiled psychiatric reports, related service providers' therapy reports, social worker evaluations, standardized academic tests, and curriculum-based measures. Professionals in the mental health sector often refer to the classifications and definitions found in the DSM-IV Manual (Diagnostic and Statistical Management of Mental Disorders).

Interpretation of Results

Being knowledgeable about assessment tools will aid the educator in understanding results interpretation. In most circumstances the comprehensive evaluation results are delivered by the examiner, who is an expert in the area. It may be a psychologist, social worker, or psychiatrist. Interpreting the results leads to program development and the design of instructional strategies and methods that address the student's behavioral or emotional problems.

Use of Results in Program Development

Using the results of assessment information is a primary piece to solve the puzzle about providing the appropriate delivery of services and implementing interventions for students with BD/ED disabilities. Assessments provide insight into a student's performance across many domains and settings. They offer information about the family and the health status of the student as well as results about academics, emotions, and behaviors. All of these components will help the team make conclusions about the student's needs and make decisions to create the most effective program possible.

The variety of tools that may be used to gather data about students is equally as important as using the results. Many types of measurement tools are available for assessing the various aspects of BD/ED problems. Here are just a few of the more commonly used in schools:

- Behavioral and Emotional Rating Scale (BERS)
- Behavior Assessment System for Children (BASC)
- Social Skills Rating Scale
- Behavior Evaluation Scale-2 (BES-2)

Preparation of Reports and Communication of Findings

Reports from the primary examiner are most helpful when discussing the results of a comprehensive assessment and may include the records and observations of other parties who work with or live with the student. Parents and siblings have critical information that may be collected on a student who exhibits behavioral and emotional concerns. Medical practitioners and outside agencies also may have information to add to a written report so the entire team understands the student's needs and can work together to enhance the student's program.

Two types of informational reports are used when sharing the evaluation results of students with behavior disorders and emotional disturbances. These are **reported function** and **actual function** reports. The reported function includes information gathered by the teacher or other professionals and includes the parents and the student. These findings may be reported either orally or in written form and may include school records, classroom testing, or assignments. The actual function reports include information gathered by observation method during classroom and school settings with comparison to behaviors and actions of typical students in the same circumstance.

Placement and Program Issues

The placement of students under the BD/ED category follows the special education process for assessment and eligibility. It requires careful review of the evaluation team to determine whether a student qualifies under the BD/ED category, requires services to benefit from an academic program, and what types of services to implement.

Continuum of Placements

LRE, the least restrictive environment, is one of the concepts mandated under the federal law. As for students with other types of disabilities, students with BD/ED are to be educated with their nondisabled peers to the maximum extent possible. However, for students with BD/ED, it becomes a debatable issue at IEP meetings and at professional trainings. Options in the continuum include general education, full inclusion classrooms, resource rooms, separate self-contained programs, special alternative schools, hospitals, or residential placements.

Many professionals, as well as parents, believe that these students are served better in segregated settings, which include alternative schools, private schools, and residential settings. Estimates are that about one-fifth of the BD/ED population are served in separate alternative settings. These settings often offer more intensive services, a structured environment, and comprehensive academic and behavioral instruction, and they may be better able to encompass the varying needs of individual students.

Due to the complexity and great variance of the disorders found under this category of special education, the individual needs are endless, and the outcomes may be more positive if students are managed with clinical care involvement and in less stressful regular education settings. As a primary point, it is critical for educators to advocate for the services each student needs to be successful in school and in the community.

Related Services

Related services are a component of the IEP and must be considered for any student in special education. Since students with BD/ED problems may also be diagnosed with other disabling conditions, such as learning disabilities (LD), deaf or hard of hearing (DHH), mental retardation (MR), and speech and language disabilities (SLP), they may require the support of other related services personnel. The related services personnel who may be involved are professionals who have expert knowledge of learning problems, hearing problems, and speech/language problems, such as teachers, audiologists, interpreters, and speech pathologists. Those professionals who work with the student for the recognized BD/ED problems include social workers, psychologists, behavior coaches, and paraprofessionals. Community personnel who may be included in the IEP process and provide services may be a psychiatrist, a mental health practitioner, a therapist, or a medical provider.

IEP/ITP Processes

A student in the BD/ED category required an IEP to establish the perimeters of the program. The IEP must focus on the unique needs of the emotional, behavioral, and academic skills of the individual and may include a behavior intervention plan. The process for developing an IEP is the same for BD/ED as for other special education categories.

Since the one area that is the most difficult for students with BD/ED problems is adjusting to life after they leave school, it is invaluable to them that the transition plan and services provide the exact support that they need now and will need in the future. The ITP for BD/ED students must include all the mandated requirements but must focus on the career interests and goals, vocational skills, and life skills components related to the student's preferences and abilities. Creating a proper plan will require the collaboration of many professionals in both the schools and the community.

Classroom Personnel and External Resources

Although each type of program has standards for staffing, the primary school programs will include educators, paraprofessionals, related services providers, and perhaps a behavior coach. These supports must be outlined on the student's IEP prior to beginning the interventions and behavior plan implementation.

Others who may be involved in the student's program include parents with whom the educator should develop rapport and establish a communication system. The school program and staff may need assistance from health care and mental health care providers to transfer interventions across settings. Some children live in foster homes, so foster parents and the foster care system staff may be helpful.

Alternative Methods of Instruction/Evaluation

Teams must review a student's strengths and weaknesses prior to determining a course of action and program placement. Several LRE options do incorporate alternative methods of instruction, evaluation, and alternate settings. Adaptations and accommodations suggest alternative methods as well.

Even within the general education setting, there are alternatives to providing services to students with BD/ED. Modifying the regular education format has proven effective for some students. Establishing a co-teaching situation with a general education teacher and a teacher who specializes in BD/ED would allow students to maintain general education structure and content work, while accessing a specialist for behavioral or emotional issues. The educators could consult and collaborate with one another and assist with various evaluations. Peer tutors, paraprofessionals, and related service providers are also included in this model to enhance student services through a natural setting.

Curriculum and Instruction

Some of the research on the impact of school programs and BD/ED factors implies that ineffective instruction may contribute to the lack of student success. Additionally, unclear rules, inappropriate expectations, inconsistent behavior practices, and the lack of praise and approval from adults hinder the progress of these students.

Schools must include curriculum and instruction in social skills training, classroom management skills, and self-management and group processing techniques to help these children throughout the school day as they also learn how to generalize these skills to other areas of their lives. Several different types of curricula are published for use with students who are identified as BD/ED. Since social skills are such an important component of a curriculum for students with these disorders, many are available from publishers. Some known to schools are the Psychodynamic Program and Curricula, the Self-Control Curriculum, or the Developmental Therapy Curriculum.

Levels of Performance

Most students with BD/ED have reduced academic achievement and are generally not on target academically with same aged peers. These students may perform one or two years below grade level with demonstrated difficulties in reading, writing, and math. Some have other disabilities such as speech/language deficits, mild mental retardation, or learning disabilities. These students seem to fail in all aspects of their daily life, and it has been reported that only about half complete high school.

Because the social, behavioral, or emotional deficits compound their ability to perform in school, working with students who are labeled as BD/ED can be a complicated and challenging task. They need successful events to overcome the feelings of failure, yet when their behaviors are out of sync with others and their academics are poor, they lack the motivation to learn.

Instructional Needs

Students with BD/ED issues face an array of factors related to their unique needs. Their instruction must be specialized to their behavioral and emotional conditions while incorporating the requirements of IDEIA. The primary focus of their learning must be on the appropriate and acceptable social behaviors they should utilize and the academic skills they need to improve.

These students thrive in classrooms when they are allowed to be active learners and not passive observers. Involving them in the instruction, the learning, and the development and creation of their program will help engage them in school. Instruction in content areas must be addressed, as they may be behind in concept development for these subjects. The special education teacher or the general education teacher may need to modify the lessons and present the information in creative ways.

Students with BD/ED need support for fundamental academic enrichment with techniques to enhance their study skills. Remediation in reading comprehension, vocabulary building and word attack skills, oral language, written language, and mathematics are key areas for guiding them towards progress in school. Learning effective study skills will help these students become more independent and give them the feeling of accomplishment. Study skill areas include time management, report writing, outlining, taking notes, completing homework, and studying for tests.

Instructional Activities and Materials

Engaging activities and innovative materials are the key to involving students with BD/ED in their education. Since these students are academically behind their peers, motivation is a barrier to overcome.

Many activities and materials are available to help educators enhance the educational experiences of students who suffer from behavioral and emotional difficulties. Many excellent materials can be purchased from education companies while others are teacher made and just as beneficial. Finding the right activities and materials to keep students interested and energized about learning is an important task.

Some basic instructional needs include a daily social skills curriculum, use of assistive technology devices such as computers and software programs, and simple teaching techniques such as response cards to increase academic participation and improve on-task behaviors.

Instructional Strategies and Teaching Methods

An effective and proven method for students with BD/ED is explicit, systematic instruction with proper classroom management. Instruction needs to be academically challenging and age appropriate. When handled properly, students benefit from cooperative learning situations in which peers may work as tutors and organized group project members.

Students with BD/ED can be provided with personal learning strategies that they can use independently in their classrooms to aid in their learning. The use of acronyms and paraphrasing provides students with cues to remember and to demonstrate their knowledge and behaviors. The use of these instructional strategies and the implementation of interventions improve independent learning and promote the acquisition of life skills.

Instructional strategies and methods used with students who are identified as BD/ED are

- Chart behaviors for analysis.
- Use intervention plans.
- Promote home communication.
- Utilize peer assistance or tutoring.
- Use consistent standards.
- Explore task analysis.

See the interventions and ideas in the "Conceptual Approaches" section.

Instructional Formats

Students with BD/ED may receive their educational program in a variety of settings (see the "Continuum of Placements" section). Within those environments, they need the subject information presented using an assortment of formats. Not every student learns in the same way at the same time, and the presentation makes a difference. The use of modeling and demonstration techniques, drill and practice methods, corrective feedback, and reinforcement all add to a student's inner motivation to learn. Instruction should be varied from individual sessions to small group to large group periods.

Managing the Learning Environment

There are different types of environments and learners, and there are general practices conducive to the management of classrooms and students. This section reviews some basic information on management and behaviors.

Behavior Management and Interventions

More schools are adopting **school-wide behavior support systems** that promote positive behavior for all children. The expectations are stated, social skills are explicitly taught, appropriate behaviors are reinforced, and the data is evaluated. Students learn from observing positive interactions, and students are not singled out as they learn. The positive aspects of using this school-wide system are that the peer group utilizes the preferred behaviors, cooperates with the program, and supports the effort.

Other specific methods that work to manage the behaviors of students with BD/ED are behavioral contracts, behavior intervention plans, positive reinforcements, behavior modification systems, group contingencies, token economy programs, and self-management programs.

Behavior Analysis

Documenting various behaviors in a practical and consistent manner generally makes sense to educators. They may use the method to support the on-going assessment of students and to make necessary changes in their programs. It is valuable to the professionals to identify and define the antecedents, the target behaviors, and the consequences. After conducting an analysis of a student's behaviors, the team may also record this baseline information and then periodically document the behavior and any changes, so the extent of the change may be calculated and used to drive further interventions. Measuring the target behaviors at set intervals will provide strong documentation on the effectiveness of the interventions and the progress of the student's program. Much research on behaviors and behavior modification programs has been conducted using the method of behavioral analysis.

Data Gathering and Procedures

Data collection is an integral part of program development and maintenance for students with BD/ED. Data can determine the student's functional abilities on a regular basis, as well as be useful in observing changes in behaviors in different environments. When collecting data on the actual functioning of a student, it should include target behavior recordings, a detailed description of the actions, and the actual performance in the real life situation. It can be challenging in a school setting to obtain regular concrete data regularly, and at times, it may require another person to observe and document.

Some methods of data collection include

- Teacher documentation of problems, interventions, progress, and changes
- Peer identification of positive and negative social interactions
- Rating scales (checklists, surveys, questions) by teachers, parents, and peers
- Self-ratings by the student on behavior contracting or progress of program
- Interviews by professionals
- Personality measurements

Classroom Organization and Management

Structure, organization, and consistency are effective tools, and an environment that increases positive interactions while reducing antisocial behaviors will benefit these students. Acknowledging expectations, establishing rules, and identifying consequences while allowing students to earn privileges and gain independence helps to improve control of inappropriate behaviors. The use of peer mediation and self-management skills also helps students stay on task and reduce targeted behaviors.

Many teachers of BD/ED students use proactive strategies (planned interventions) to manage the classroom. These strategies prevent an inappropriate behavior or occurrence before it starts (structure classroom, establish clear rules and expectations, schedule lessons, present engaging instruction, use social approval/praise). Other strategies that aid in classroom management are

- Shaping
- Contingency contracts
- Planned ignoring
- Reinforcements
- Overcorrection

A classroom that works well for students with BD/ED is one that incorporates the basic principles of structure, yet flexibility. Students must know the order and principles of the room, which include setting expectations, modelling demonstrations, providing guided practice, allowing independent practice, and setting time for generalization.

Teaching Students with Learning Disabilities (0381)

Introduction

Some famous people you may have heard of have something in common, other than fame. Leonardo da Vinci, Winston Churchill, John F. Kennedy, Walt Disney, Albert Einstein, and Thomas Edison were all impacted by having a specific learning disability. But as you know, this disability never stopped them from reaching goals and achieving a dream! They persevered in spite of the problems they faced. From their example, you know that individuals with learning disabilities are not affected by a lack of intellectual abilities, but rather in how they receive information.

The category of learning disabilities is the largest in population of all the categories of special education, and those numbers are increasing on a consistent basis. There appears to be a variety of reasons for this phenomenon, the most obvious being the possible misidentification of students, while another is the range of culturally and linguistically diverse students.

Because so many students are identified under this category and because each has specific characteristics and is impacted differently, there needs to be an array of services, a variety of methods, and explicit materials used with this population. Creating a plan for every student with a learning disability may be a challenge for even the most effective educator!

In your coursework, you probably studied the miscellany of information and the various influences that a learning disability has across an individual's life span. From your previous coursework, you may have gleaned an understanding of the many related factors, the assortment of conceptual approaches, and the types of curriculum and instruction that pertain to students with learning disabilities as well as general information about special education because this category of *learning disability* is covered under federal law IDEIA (Individuals with Disabilities Education Improvement Act-2004).

In preparation to take this exam, study the basic concepts about learning disabilities, information about the characteristics, and the causes; the various definitions; facts about assessments, placement steps, and program issues; as well as curriculum and instruction information. The following study guide materials may help determine which areas you need to review. If you need additional information, not available in this guide, refer to your school texts on those topics, search the Internet, or speak with practicing educators. Websites specific to learning disabilities and special education are provided in the "Resources" section. As you conduct your overall review of information, you will gain a better understanding of what you may expect on the Praxis II exam.

The Praxis II (0381), Special Education: Teaching Students with Learning Disabilities exam is a knowledge-based assessment that has been prepared to evaluate individuals who plan to teach students with learning disabilities in grades preschool through 12. This exam includes 50 multiple-choice questions covering various topics, and some of the questions are related to a detailed case study. The overall time allocation for this exam is one hour. The content categories recognized in this assessment are Factors Other than Direct Instruction that Influence the Education of Students with Learning Disabilities (20 percent, about 10 questions), Delivery of Services (30 percent, about 15 questions), and Curriculum and Instruction (50 percent, the remaining 25 questions).

Content Clusters

The following questions should assist you in assessing your basic knowledge related to the topic of learning disabilities. For those answers you are not sure about, it is recommended that you spend time studying that topic in order to prepare for the test. Although these 10 questions are written in a narrative format rather than the multiple-choice form, answering these questions should aid you in getting ready for the Special Education: Teaching Students with Learning Disabilities Praxis II (0381) exam. These questions are representative of the three content categories detailed in the test.

1. Describe the pros and cons of placing a student with learning disabilities, at any grade level, in a general education inclusive classroom.

2. Explain the critical steps in developing an Individualized Transition Plan (ITP) and point out the areas of transition most important for individuals with learning disabilities.

3. Define the various causes identified as contributing to the development of learning disabilities and reveal the different methods suggested for prevention.

4. Illustrate the various methods of managing a learning environment for students with learning disabilities.

5. List the various instructional formats, strategies, and methods proven effective for students with learning disabilities.

6. Document the conceptual approaches most often used when educators work with students who exhibit learning disabilities.

7. Identify the role of the educator for a student with a learning disability at each level of the education system.

8. Explain the basic concepts related to students with learning disabilities in the areas of cognition, language, academic skills (reading, writing, math) and social-emotional development.

9. Describe the methods of instruction that enhance student motivation for those with learning disabilities.

10. Clarify the assessment process and how to utilize the results of standardized and specialized assessments to develop an IEP and monitor instruction.

Preview Questions

In this section you will find five multiple choice questions and a case study with several multiple-choice questions. Use these to assess yourself and as a preview of the types of questions that are included on the Praxis II exam. If you are not clear about the answers to these questions, you will find further information in the study section or you may want to search the Internet as part of your studies.

1. Effective listening skills are critical for students with learning disabilities. Which of the following strategies would BEST support students in their development of listening skills?

   A. oral processing
   B. reading fluency
   C. auditory modeling
   D. phonological awareness

2. Students identified with learning disabilities quite often experience deficits in social skills. A characteristic that is common among those with a social disorder is the

   A. inability to organize a task.
   B. co-existence of a verbal disorder.
   C. lack of sensitivity toward others.
   D. process of recognizing concrete objects.

3. The purpose of the assessment process for a student with a possible learning disability is to

    A. make a referral and identify the needs.

    B. conduct an observation and speak with parents.

    C. discover medical history and obtain medications.

    D. provide modifications and appropriate related services.

4. When assessing a student for possible learning disabilities, an exclusionary clause must be considered by the team prior to qualifying the student for special education services under the category of *learning disability*. Which of the following types of disadvantages would exclude a student from being placed as a student with a learning disability?

    A. cultural

    B. physical

    C. economic

    D. educational

5. A factor of causation related to a child's potential to develop a learning disability is the family's

    A. medical history.

    B. economic status.

    C. genetic disposition.

    D. educational background.

The answers are

1. D. Phonological awareness is the understanding of the sounds of language and would promote effective listening skills.

2. C. Of the choices, the lack of sensitivity toward others is a form of a social disorder.

3. A. The assessment process includes the steps of screening, referral, and identifying needs.

4. D. An educational disadvantage would prevent a student from qualifying as a student with a learning disability, since it could not be determined whether the delay was caused by this disadvantage.

5. C. A family's genetic disposition can be an influencing factor in the development of a learning disability in a child. It has been determined that the tendency for learning disabilities is genetic.

Sample Case Study Question

Read the case study and then answer the multiple-choice questions that follow.

A second grade student who transferred from another elementary school mid-fall, due to a change in family status, entered the new classroom as a shy and somewhat withdrawn child. During the second semester, the student has exhibited difficulty in the classroom with certain academic tasks, and at times displays inappropriate social behaviors during unstructured times. The teacher has become concerned with the student's behaviors in the classroom, such as being easily distracted, not completing written tasks, and sometimes leaving the desk and wandering around the room. The student has also demonstrated difficulty on the playground with peers. Sometimes the student has outbursts that seem to develop quickly and then subside. Academically, the student seems to do well in math, but during spelling tests, the student may skip or even miss words. The written assignments are usually turned in late and only after coaxing from the general education teacher. No records from the previous school indicate the student has had problems in the past. The single parent reports that at home the child is not interested in playing with other children, procrastinates on doing homework, and gets upset easily. The student watches a lot of television and uses the family computer to play games, often turning the sound up on both of these electronic devices. When other family members call on the telephone, the child prefers not to speak with any of them. The teacher reports that the student is quiet in the classroom and avoids answering questions during the course of the day.

1. Which of the following would be the BEST choice of next steps for this general education teacher to take to support this student in the classroom?

   A. Change classroom settings.
   B. Set up a behavior contract system.
   C. Refer the student to the Child Study Team.
   D. Provide a paraeducator on the playground.

2. What is one area of development that should be immediately screened or evaluated on this student?

   A. motor
   B. vision
   C. hearing
   D. language

3. Based on the information provided, the academic task of _____ seems to be the most difficult for this child.

   A. writing
   B. science
   C. reading
   D. mathematics

1. **C.** The best choice is to refer this student to the Child Study Team. Since the problems span many areas and settings (academics, behavior, home, playground), it would be important to begin a series of interventions and get support for the child, the teacher, and the family.

2. **C.** The student's hearing may be a problem. The indicators are: being shy and withdrawn, sudden outbursts, missing spelling words on tests, turning up sound on electronic devices, not talking on the telephone or answering questions in class.

3. **A.** Writing seems to be the most difficult as the student does not complete written tasks, misses spelling words on tests, and turns in written assignments late.

Study Information

Since there exists two separate Praxis II exams for Learning Disabilities (0381 and 0382) additional information on the sections covered in 0382 may be found in another study guide, titled *CliffsTestPrep Praxis II: Education of Exceptional Students (0353, 0382, 0542, 0544)* by Wiley Publications, Inc.

The information found in this section is particular to the category of learning disabilities, although not comprehensive. Since this category is only one of the serviced areas in special education, it is important to review the general principles, theories, and guidelines of the Knowledge-Based Core Principles (0381) Praxis II in this guide. The programs and services available to students with learning disabilities are mandated under IDEIA just as other special education categories. Additionally, the services offered through early intervention programs and early childhood programs are an important asset in the education of individuals with learning disabilities so the examinee may want to review the Pre-School/Early Childhood Praxis II study section in this guide.

There has been an on-going debate regarding the definition of a **learning disability,** and this is due in part to the political involvement and to the philosophical differences that exist in the field. Definitions are found in the section "Factors that Influence Education." The definitions change regularly, and educators should be familiar with those laws and organizations that are involved in these amendments. The current primary identification factor is the discrepancy between ability and achievement.

Research and public attitudes toward learning disabilities have changed immensely in recent years. There has been an increase in the number of students with learning disabilities who are provided with educational services in school settings, and it may be due to the fact that people are more aware and knowledgeable about this condition. Most students with learning disabilities access their education through the general education programs. This means that all staff members in the schools should be made aware of the characteristics of learning disabilities and problems that students face. Staff should learn the strategies and methods that are proven effective and understand the implementation of the interventions to support academic achievement. There are, of course, a variety of programs that may be offered to students with learning disabilities, but all students with learning disabilities should receive instruction in specific learning strategies, which will support them throughout their lifetimes.

Students with learning disabilities do not learn in the same manner or at the same rate as peers without learning disabilities. Students with learning disabilities are quite different from one another, because their types of learning problems are so diverse. The most prevalent learning disability is in the area of reading, with mathematics, spelling, and social behaviors close behind. Students with learning disabilities need accommodations, modifications, and adaptations to the general education curriculum so they may be successful.

This study guide is divided into three sections that coincide with the Teaching Students with Learning Disabilities Praxis II exam. The information included in this guide is a brief description of the content available that pertains to individuals with learning disabilities, but it should provide you with some idea about what to study prior to taking your exam. Should you need additional information about individuals with learning disabilities, refer to the websites listed in the "Resources" section at the end of the book.

Factors that Influence Education

The category of learning disabilities is the most prevalent of the special education conditions in school-aged children. It was not truly noticed until the 1950s when parents began to seek help for their children who were not gaining in the academic world like other children of the same age. The children did not appear to be disabled, but something was causing them to be delayed in learning. Through this movement, terms emerged that are still used today to identify certain types of learning disabilities, and this area of special education is influenced by more disciplines than just education.

Many varieties and levels of learning disabilities exist, and some believe there could be as many as 500,000 different combinations of problems associated with learning and socio-emotional problems that emerge as learning disabilities. So for each child who is labeled as **learning disabled,** there is a unique set of characteristics and needs exhibited by the individual. Some children may possess a combination of many specific learning disabilities, and others demonstrate a single learning problem. These individuals are a highly diverse group. Although differing in characteristics and specific needs, most of these children experience rejection, isolation, frustration, and school failure. They have an invisible disability that causes problems throughout their lifetimes.

A learning disability is a complex neurological disorder that appears in school-age children as difficulty in reading, writing, spelling, reasoning, memory, and/or organizing information. It is important for both parents and professionals to encourage children with learning disabilities to acknowledge their strengths, accept their weaknesses, and obtain personal strategies for their individual difficulties. Learning disability conditions can exist throughout a lifetime and affect an adult in all areas.

Characteristics

Students with learning disabilities have significant perceptual and cognitive processing problems. They suffer difficulties in the areas of reasoning, memory, attention, listening, language, and the perception and processing of visual and auditory information. Due to these problems, they are faced with academic achievement issues related to reading, written language, and mathematics, as well as issues with social skills, attention deficits, and behavior problems.

Not all students with learning disabilities have the same characteristics or learning styles. They may have a disability in any one or more of the following areas: reading, written language, spelling, mathematics, and social skills. Many also display the characteristics of or may have a diagnosis of ADD or ADHD (attention deficit or attention deficit hyperactivity disorders).

Certain characteristics are descriptive of a student with a learning disability, although each student's disability affects her differently. The most common characteristics that may indicate a learning disability are

- Performs below expected academic achievement levels
- Possesses intelligence scores within the normal range
- Demonstrates language problems (listening and speaking)
- Learns differently and at a different pace than peers
- Exhibits disorders of attention and memory
- Has poor perceptual abilities
- Is disorganized and an inactive learner
- Has poor motor ability

- Has difficulty learning to read, underachieves in math, or has difficulty with written language
- Is deficient in using systematic approaches to new tasks
- Lacks emotional maturity
- Lacks motivation
- Has social skills deficits or poor peer relationships
- Has difficulty transferring and generalizing skills and knowledge to other settings or tasks
- Exhibits learned helplessness
- Exhibits behavior problems

Other characteristics may be more typical of some children but not of others and may include distractibility, hyperactivity, inattentiveness, poor problem-solving skills, and poor social skills.

Metacognition and Strategies

Research has shown that if professionals discover a child's learning disability early in life and then provide the proper supports, the child will gain a chance at developing those skills needed to lead a successful and productive life. Students with learning disabilities need to learn not only the information that is taught and retain the skills that are developed, but they must be able to decide how to use this information and which strategies to choose to help them apply the skills. They must have an awareness of their own learning and thinking processes, or **metacognition.** Because students with learning disabilities lack effective metacognitive strategies, they need to be exposed to strategy development instruction, which may then apply to various situations in their lives. Some specific strategies may include making lists, outlining materials, or rehearsing verbal passages. Researchers believe that the specific metacognitive strategies needed in school are **classification, checking, evaluation,** and **prediction.**

Language Skills

A strong relationship exists between poor language development and learning disabilities. Difficulties in the area of language can be of major significance to a child and more than half of the children identified with a learning disability have problems in this area. Language problems are the underlying basis for learning disabilities and reading problems in children, and these are generally diagnosed as oral language disorders.

Language problems in children with learning disabilities are most often identified in the particular areas of oral expression and listening comprehension. Oral language disorders include poor phonological awareness, delays in speech, disorders in grammar or syntax, deficiencies in learning vocabulary, or a poor understanding of general oral language. More specifically, children exhibit problems having a lack of word retrieval skills, slow response times, use of simple language structures, confusion with sequencing, and failure to follow directions.

As you may recall, four theories pertain to learning disabilities that may more precisely explain the acquisition of language skills.

- **Behavioral:** Language is learned through environmental influences, and language learning is shaped by behavioral principles.
- **Biological**: Language is innate, a biological function.

- **Cognitive:** Language is learned based on links between language, thinking, and experiences.
- **Social:** Language is based on the interpersonal contributions to language through the reciprocal relationships between children, parents, or other adults in their lives.

Educators must select a philosophical approach for children who exhibit learning disabilities. Carefully observe those children with limited English competency as they may have the potential for a learning disability that is not easily identified. Additionally, exposing very young children to early literacy skills will help in the early prevention and identification of learning problems.

Academic Skills

Children with learning disabilities generally have abilities similar to peers in most areas; however, their skills develop more slowly, and their rate of learning is different. In the early years of elementary school, it is the discrepancy between ability and achievement that is most noticeable in students with emerging learning disabilities. Academically, students with learning disabilities have problems in reading, written language, and mathematics. Reading is the most common and has the most devastating effect on children. If children have problems with reading, they may become less motivated, use inappropriate behaviors, and develop a lack of confidence. Reading problems may be related to comprehension, fluency, and vocabulary development. Mathematics is another critical area, and students may have specific problems with math calculations or math reasoning. Under the federal definition, seven key academic areas are identified as potentials for developing a learning disability.

Causation and Prevention

No one really knows or understands the specific causes of learning disabilities in children, except that they stem from complex neurological dysfunctions, simply stated as problems in the brain structure and function. This lack of knowledge about the causes is based on the fact that learning disabilities may appear in many different forms, and therefore, can be difficult to diagnose.

But in order to qualify the characteristics of a learning disability and to recognize the methods of prevention, professionals use four broad categories to identify the "causes" for learning disabilities in children and adults. These include environmental influences, genetics or heredity, neurological or brain dysfunction, and biochemical imbalances. Some cultural factors also may lead toward the development of a learning disability.

Prevention is thought to be possible when professionals and communities work together to acknowledge a problem and move toward a solution. With the reduced use of drugs and alcohol by pregnant women, the early identification of young children, and the cleansing of environmental causes, many learning disabilities will be eliminated and many reduced in severity. For example, if adults address the needs of young children through early intervention programs, in preschool programs, and in the early elementary grades through language development efforts and specialized instruction in phonemic awareness, these children will be better prepared to learn to read and write. If children are provided interventions before the learning disability is at its peak, the affects will be greatly reduced, and the need for further services limited.

Environmental

Studies have concluded that there is a correlation between a child's environmental conditions early in life to the achievement experienced after the child is placed in school. Because children with learning disabilities show a positive increase in school achievement when structured, systematic, and direct instruction is implemented, the environmental influence seems supported. The environment has been found to be of significance in the development of children. Children in nonstimulating environments that do not focus on their developmental needs may be prone to learning disabilities.

Learning disabilities may also be caused by other items in the environment. Traumas after birth, such as head injuries, malnutrition, fever, disease, stroke, lack of health care, and toxins, such as metals and pesticides, may disrupt the proper brain development in young children, affecting their learning. Neurologists are researching the effects of some metals on children's early development and brain function. Some scientists believe that learning problems can develop in youngsters who have been treated with chemotherapy or radiation for cancer, especially brain tumors.

Genetics/Heredity

Learning disabilities can exist in multiple family members, which may prove there is a genetic connection. Children whose family members have been diagnosed with learning problems have a higher likelihood of developing a learning problem. Family members may possess differences in their specific learning disabilities, such as a father who exhibits a reading problem, and a child who has difficulty with written language.

Scientists believe that inheritance in family members is actually the brain dysfunction or the structural brain differences that may lead to a learning disability. Others believe that the type of family environment may influence a child's development, and therefore, the child may appear to have a learning disability. Another genetic factor to be considered is chromosomal abnormality, and there are current studies focused on identifying a gene that is related to reading.

Neurological-Brain Dysfunction

The central nervous system, which is comprised of the brain and the spinal cord, has a relationship to learning, as the act of learning includes neurological processes that stem from the brain. If this area is impaired or damaged, the processes of learning will not function appropriately, either temporarily or permanently. Children who suffer from neurological deficits may emerge with permanent learning disabilities in some form, but not all children with brain damage have learning disabilities.

In the 1940s, scientists discovered that brain-injured children demonstrated difficulties with a variety of tasks. Because brain injuries may occur in the prenatal stage, during the birth, or in the post-natal stage, the impact can cover a range of problems and severity and is believed to impede development and affect learning.

Minimal brain dysfunction (MBD) is a term that emerged in the 1960s to describe children with mild neurological abnormalities that cause learning disabilities. These were children with average intellectual abilities, who exhibited behavioral and learning disorders.

Biochemical Imbalances

Some believe that chemical imbalances in the brain caused from either organic factors or imposed elements can affect learning. For mothers who ingest drugs, alcohol, or tobacco, the results may be damaging for a growing embryo. These toxins affect the health of the newborn, for weight, breathing, hyperactivity, physical defects, brain receptors, and neuron growth, thereby causing a learning disorder.

According to some researchers, other chemical influences may be found in the foods that children consume. These studies claim that food additives may influence the development of a learning disability in some children. Other studies have focused on the problems associated with a lack of vitamins in a child's system. However, neither of these studies has concluded any negative impact on a child's educational performance.

Another imbalance that may cause a learning disability is a complication between the mother's blood type and/or immune system. If these do not react to one another in the proper manner, the child's system may be attacked, and will affect the placement of the brain cells.

Cultural

Cultural influences are closely associated with the environmental situation and may be difficult to separate. The cultural factors that may affect learning and influence a disability appear to be related to the diversity of families and the types of involvement they have with their children.

Families of lower socio-economic status may lack proper parenting skills and, therefore, provide an environment that is inappropriate for young children. They may lack the ability to provide the basic needs and proper medical care, both of which may impact learning. These families also may not have available the materials that can enhance a child's early learning development. Families of ethnic origin who do not speak the language of the country may feel displaced and struggle themselves, thus causing a delay in the child's development.

Although the lack of appropriate developmental and educational opportunities are not to be considered a learning disability, the impact of a non-stimulating environment, lack of proper nutrition and care, and the possible hereditary tendency for learning problems can lead toward permanent learning deficits. These may result in an identified learning disability.

Definitions

The term *learning disability* was first coined in 1963 by Samuel Kirk. Over the years there has been a wide variety of definitions used to describe a person with a learning disability. Some of these definitions continue to be debated, as they represent various philosophical views. Those definitions that are used most often come from either IDEIA or from the National Joint Committee on Learning Disabilities (NJCLD).

Certain factors are related to the definitions that many professionals do agree upon:

- Difficulty with academics and learning tasks
- Discrepancy between potential and achievement
- Uneven growth patterns and psychological processing deficits
- Cause may be due to a central nervous system dysfunction
- Perceptual problems
- Possible minimal brain dysfunction or brain injury
- Problems exist across a person's life span
- Exclusionary of other causes

Federal

The definition of learning disabilities found in IDEIA is the root of various state definitions across the country. The definition has changed over the years, as the law was revised. The first definition emerged in 1975 when the first public law for special education was mandated (PL94-142-Education for All Handicapped Children). The definition was also found in the revisions and reauthorizations of this law: 1990–Individuals with Disabilities Education Act; 1997–Individuals with Disabilities Education Act; and the most recent in 2004–Individuals with Disabilities Education Improvement Act. As of 2004, a student can now be eligible without a severe discrepancy between achievement and ability. The following is the most current rendition:

> "...a disorder in one or more of the basic psychological processes involved in understanding or in using language, spoken or written, which disorder may manifest itself in imperfect ability to listen, think, speak, read, write, spell or to do mathematical calculations. ....includes such conditions as perceptual disabilities, brain injury, minimal brain dysfunction, dyslexia, and developmental aphasia. ...does not include a learning problem that is primarily the result of visual, hearing, or motor disabilities, of mental retardation, of emotional disturbance or of environmental, cultural or economic disadvantage."

The federal law includes an operational definition in the regulations for children with learning disabilities. This includes two main components to determine a student with a learning disability. The student

1. does not achieve at the proper age and ability levels in one or more specific areas when provided with appropriate learning experiences.
2. has a severe discrepancy between achievement and intellectual ability in one ore more of these seven areas (oral expression, listening comprehension, written expression, basic reading skills, reading comprehension, mathematics calculation, and mathematics reasoning).

Organizations

The NJCLD is an organization well known for its work in the field. It identifies that a learning disability is basically a discrepancy between a child's apparent capacity to learn and the child's level of achievement. It has defined *learning disability* as

"... a heterogeneous group of disorders manifested by significant difficulties in the acquisition and use of listening, speaking, reading, writing, reasoning or mathematical abilities. These disorders are intrinsic to the individual and presumed to be due to Central Nervous System Dysfunction. Even though a learning disability may occur concomitantly with other handicapping conditions (e.g. sensory impairment, mental retardation, social and emotional disturbance) or environmental influences (e.g. cultural differences, insufficient/inappropriate instruction, psychogenic factors) it is not the direct result of those conditions or influences."

The Interagency Committee on Learning Disabilities (ICLD) was commissioned by Congress to develop a definition for *learning disability*. This government committee developed a three-component definition that includes social skills deficits, which the federal definition does not include. The three elements include difficulties in listening, speaking, reading, writing, reasoning, mathematics, or social skills; occurring concomitantly with other conditions (socio-environmental influences and attention deficit disorders); and intrinsic to the individual, presumed to be caused by central nervous system dysfunction.

Definition Summary

The majority of states utilize some form of the federal definition when it applies to the education of students with learning disabilities. Many students in the general education population demonstrate learning problems. Schools must take great care in identifying those who truly qualify as students with a learning disability that requires services under the umbrella of special education.

Three criteria seem to be most reliable and most often used among states to determine a student has a learning disability:

- There must be a severe discrepancy between the student's intellectual ability and the student's academic achievement levels.
- The difficulties that the student is exhibiting may not be the result of other known learning problems, such as hearing problems, vision problems, educational disadvantage, among others listed in federal law.
- The student requires special education services directly related to the specific type of learning disability in order to access the general education programs and be successful in school.

In the new special education law of 2004 (IDEIA), a "response-to" model has been suggested for identification of students with learning disabilities. It states that

"when determining whether a child has a specific learning disability...a local educational agency shall not be required to take into consideration whether a child has a severe discrepancy between achievement and intellectual ability...(and) a local educational agency may use a process that determines if the child responds to scientific, research-based intervention as a part of the evaluation procedures."

Delivery of Services

The important elements in the delivery of services to students with learning disabilities are the educational environment, the collaboration of professionals, and the partnerships with parents/families. Most often, a student with a learning disability is placed in a general education classroom receiving related services as needed. These children benefit both academically and socially when they are educated alongside of their typically developing and performing peers.

With the emergence of the inclusion movement, the education of students with learning disabilities is occurring more often in general education classrooms and less often in other more restrictive settings. There has been a decline in the numbers of students with learning disabilities who are sent to resource rooms for services while missing the instruction that their peers receive. Some professionals still believe that students with learning disabilities need explicit, systematic, and intensive instruction from highly trained educators in order to succeed. No matter which philosophical view you may agree with, be sure that when you address the needs of a student with a learning disability, your decisions are made based on the individual.

As public laws are amended and trends in education change, you must consider that individuals with learning disabilities need clearer understanding from professionals and their communities. They are a large part of the general population and will go on to lead productive and contributing lives if their needs are met and they gain some independence.

Conceptual Approaches

Due to the broad range of learning disabilities and the interventions and methods that vary to meet the needs of all these individuals, educators should become familiar with not only how to teach these students, but educators should also understand the theories of learning. Three primary theories are discussed here: developmental psychology, behavioral psychology, and cognitive psychology.

Society and the students within are constantly changing, so the approaches used to address their needs must reflect new ideas, new information, and new strategies. Although several conceptual approaches are explained in this section, educators should continue to seek additional information about various learning approaches.

Developmental Psychology Theory

This theory emphasizes the natural progression of a child's growth and focuses on the sequential developmental stages of cognitive abilities. The concept that is key to learning is the child's maturity level or **readiness.** This theory emphasizes the fact that a child's ability to learn is based on his readiness level, which is based on the child's prior experiences.

Piaget was instrumental in designing a theory that focused on intellectual development occurring through stages. He believed that as children mature they naturally begin to learn. This may be the very reason that some children are diagnosed with learning disabilities; that the timing of their learning comes at a different rate than other children and, therefore, society is causing them to be labeled as *learning disabled.*

Vygotsky was another theorist who believed that if children are not functioning within their own level of learning, the learning will not occur (zone of proximal development-social influence of learning). Other educational philosophers believe that children must be allowed to pass through the stages of learning (exposure, grasping the knowledge, independence, and application) before they can grasp the entire concept, and teachers should instruct accordingly. For this very reason, students with learning disabilities need special instruction to strengthen their readiness abilities.

Behavioral Psychology Theory

The behavioral theory emphasizes a more systematic approach to learning and instruction. This theory is based on the ABC model (A=antecedent or stimulus, B=target behavior or response, C=consequences or reinforcement) and is related to the work of Skinner. This theory is closely connected to the development of the IEP and Functional Behavior Assessments and Plans where measurable learning behaviors can be observed and documented.

The key components of this theory emphasize the effectiveness of explicit teaching and direct instruction. This type of instruction focuses on the tasks to be learned, the skills to be developed, and the environmental setting. Educators can assess a student's learning by examining a task to determine the skills needed to achieve the task and how well the student is performing.

Cognitive Psychology Theory

In the theory of cognitive psychology, the mental skills necessary to learning are at the forefront. The student constructs the learning of new information based on prior knowledge. The instruction provided must be at the appropriate level for the student and include guidance in the social environment, and the development of automaticity of skills, while using motivational activities to enhance and encourage learning. The instructional application of the cognitive theory includes the consideration of cognitive styles of learning, metacognition, learning strategies, peer tutoring, scaffolded instruction, behavioral temperaments, and the social context of learning.

Psychological Processing

The theories that pertain to psychological processing deficits focus on how specific characteristics of an individual impacts his achievement level. Psychological processing suggests that the mental processes of memory, attention, or perception may be areas of concerns for students with learning disabilities. The perceptual disorders that have been evident in these students include visual, auditory, tactile, and kinesthetic deficits. When determining a student's needs, educators evaluate the deficits in skills, particularly those related to visual and auditory processing.

Assessments

Although parents and caregivers may suspect learning problems in a child before any assessment is conducted, the difficulties are more pronounced after the child is faced with academic situations in school. Even though learning disabilities may be present in toddlers, one of the first clear signs of a possible disability is when the child demonstrates complications with learning to read.

Learning disabilities must be identified through an assessment process, and a portion of that consists of an evaluation most likely conducted by a school psychologist. The assessment process includes gathering information from key people, such as the student, the teacher, the parents, and others who may work with the child. The actual evaluation consists of a battery of intelligence tests, academic achievement tests, school performance data, social interactions information, and an aptitude test.

There are two reasons to conduct the assessment on a student who is suspected of having a learning disability. The first is to determine the classification of eligibility based on the type of learning problems (see the definitions in another section of this guide), and the second is to plan the instruction and determine the interventions needed for the student. Both of these are critical to implementing an appropriate program for a child with a learning disability.

States often set their own criteria for the eligibility of students through their specific state departments of education according to the interpretation of the federal law, IDEIA. For the majority of students assessed for learning disabilities in the schools, discrepancy formulas are used for identification and for the development of an appropriate educational program. The discrepancy formulas are the unexpected differences (the disparity) between achievement and general ability. Many professionals believe that IQ tests are not always solely reliable in determining a learning disability, as they may be biased and unfair to certain groups of children. The results and process of an IQ test do not always determine the interventions or relate well to the actual classroom performance.

Other common areas of identification include students who exhibit an uneven growth pattern or have difficulty with academic and learning tasks. The most common method used is to compare the IQ score with the scores on standard achievement tests. However, a specific learning disability does not include academic learning problems that may be the result of mental retardation, emotional disabilities, sensory impairments, or the lack of opportunity to learn due to environmental, cultural, or economic conditions.

Other types of assessment to determine the exact areas of a specific learning disability may include perception, cognition, memory, attention, language abilities, and assistive technology. The resulting information is used to determine whether a child is achieving at her potential.

Response to Intervention (RTI)

Most schools use the Ability (IQ) and Achievement Discrepancy model to identify a learning disability in students. This discrepancy is the unexpected gap between potential and achievement; however, recent changes in the law and best practices are promoting the RTI method of assessment for learning disabilities. In the **Response to Intervention** method, students are provided interventions appropriate to their needs, but if they do not respond to the intensive interventions, they would be identified as disabled. They would not necessarily need to be evaluated according to the discrepancy in ability and achievement, as previously required.

The noted advantage to this approach is that students who may be determined learning disabled are identified sooner and provided with necessary interventions. This early identification is thought to allow students with learning disabilities more time to become successful rather than waiting to fail. This model is also considered a form of prevention for some students as they will obtain the assistance they need earlier and possibly not be labeled with a disability.

The model suggests a curriculum-based measure to identify any student whose performance is below that of peers. Then the student is provided with intensive interventions for about a 10- to 15-week period through individual or group supplemental tutoring and special assistance using a research-based program. If the student responds to this treatment, then the student is considered to be without a disability; however, if the student continues to fail, then a determination of learning disability and special education services is made. This model has also been referred to as **Response to Treatment (RT)** or **Response to Instruction (RTI).**

Informal

Informal assessments help professionals gather pertinent information about a student and the student's ability to perform within the natural environment. These informal measures may be used to support a more formal assessment as well as be used for continued and on-going progress checks. Some types include checklists, rating scales, and interviews. Informal assessments include anecdotal records, event samplings, running records, portfolio assessments, dynamic assessments, diagnostic teaching sessions, and other types of informal assessments.

- **Portfolio Assessment:** Samples of student work are collected for a specific period of time and are used to assess the student's achievement level and progress.
- **Dynamic Assessment:** A teacher determines a student's ability to learn in a particular situation rather than documenting what the student has learned.
- **Diagnostic Assessment:** A teacher continues to collect information about the student to use in assessment as the student is being taught.

Observation

Observations are required as a component of the more formal assessment, but are completed in a more informal manner. An observation is necessary in the assessment process for a student who is being evaluated for a possible learning disability, as well as for the re-evaluation of a student with a learning disability. The information gathered from the observation allows the evaluator to identify the learning behaviors of the student and how those behaviors affect the student's learning. During the observation, information is collected about the student's participation in class, on tasks completed, and in social interactions. Observations are also helpful when students are using inappropriate social behaviors so behavior management may be utilized.

Informal Reading Inventories

Reading is important for a student's overall program since all academic subjects require reading ability and skill. To determine a student's skills and to incorporate goals into an IEP, teachers are using informal assessments to better evaluate a student's abilities and to determine the areas and types of remediation to use.

Direct Daily Measurement

In a daily assessment, a student's performance on the skills that are taught each day is observed and recorded. This model documents a student's daily progress, and instruction for particular students may be modified as needed. This type of measurement is based on the behavioral approach and is being used more often in special education for progress reporting and individual program development.

Some teachers utilize **precision teaching** as an instructional approach component of **direct daily measurement.** Based on the information gained in the daily assessment, teachers make instructional decisions and adjustments to the student's work. The skills to be learned are identified; a measurement is performed; goals are set for improvement; progress is monitored and charted; and changes in the program are made if necessary.

Formal

Formal assessments are used to evaluate students on standardized instruments. These administrations are conducted in structured settings with certain requirements to follow for both the examiner and examinee. Formal assessments include standardized achievement tests, norm-referenced tests, curriculum-based assessments, and criterion-referenced assessments. Formal assessment provides a student's team with quality information to use in the development of an individualized program but should also include informal assessment results.

Standardized Tests

Intelligence and achievement tests that are standardized offer information about the discrepancy between intellectual ability and achievement, which is necessary when working with students who have learning disabilities. **Standardized tests** are norm referenced so the student's score may be compared to other students of the same age. Tests that are used to evaluate a student's overall academic achievement include Iowa Tests of Basic Skills, the Woodcock-Johnson Tests of Achievement, and the Wide Range Achievement Test-3.

Curriculum-Based Measurement

Recommended in the assessment of a student with a possible learning disability is the use of a **curriculum-based measurement tool** (CBM) as it is a more direct and regular assessment that addresses the student's learning patterns and growth, as well as providing information to educators, which is helpful in program development. A CBM is important as it can be used to frequently measure student performance, check student learning patterns and progress, and provide feedback to the teacher regarding effective instruction.

Interpretation of Results

According to IDEIA, the individual who conducts an evaluation of a student or the person who is qualified to interpret the results of the evaluation is to be present at the team meeting when the results are shared with other team members. If proper selection of evaluation tools and determination of assessment bias is made prior to testing, the team should consider the results valid.

Information about the student's testing abilities should be reviewed, as it gives the team members additional information about a student's learning style to be considered in the development of a student's educational program. Details about how the student approached the assessment and its related tasks will help in establishing student needs.

Use of Results in Program Development

It is essential for a comprehensive evaluation to be considered effective so the results may assist the team in making educational decisions about the student. The main purpose of an assessment for a student with a learning disability should be to determine the specific needs of the student while identifying the types of instructional strategies and methods for learning most beneficial to the success of the individual student. In creating the IEP based on the assessments, a student's present levels of performance will determine the proper goals, interventions, and accommodations. The assessment should also aid the team in making decisions about the educational setting and how to monitor student progress.

Development of Reports and Communication of Findings

The communication of findings should be conducted at a team meeting with a review of the scores and data gathered. The written report should reflect the statement of disability, the characteristics of the specific learning disability, how the disability affects the student's ability to learn, the best methods for the student to benefit from an education, the particular interventions that may support the student, the types of assessments conducted, and the related scores. Also needed in the report is a comprehensive look at the student's past performance, developmental milestones, medical information, behaviors across settings, and a description of the family.

Placement and Program Issues

Issues related to placement and programs for students with learning disabilities are being constantly addressed in schools across the nation. With the continued research and changes in strategies and methods, this is an evolving area of special education.

Professionals who work with students identified with learning disabilities primarily believe that these students should receive their education in the general education program and classrooms. Under the law, a continuum of service options is required for any student in special education and should certainly be considered for students with learning disabilities, based on the individual student's abilities and needs. It is the IEP team who will determine the placement of services.

Some service delivery models that are most commonly used with students who have learning disabilities include categorical classrooms (all are learning disabled), non-categorical (all with mild disabilities), inclusion (full-time general education), and resource room. As students age and enter the secondary level, vocational education programs and transition services are critical components to school success.

Consultative-Collaborative Models

Because high numbers of students with learning disabilities are placed in general education classes, it is a critical feature of their education for the professionals to work together to enhance the students' programs. In order to promote successful inclusion, the professionals must find ways to consult with one another and collaborate their efforts.

In a consultative model, professionals work with one another to meet the needs of students. The special education teacher manages the student's program and supports the general education teacher and the student in the general education classroom. The general education teacher can request information and use the guidance of the special education teacher to work with the individual students who have learning disabilities. The special education teacher would not necessarily provide direct services to the student, but rather work with the general education teacher to impart the student's education program.

In a collaborative model, the professionals work together using the expertise of each other in providing direct services to students. This method also focuses on a successful model of inclusion. The team members must have shared goals, equal voluntary participation, open and ongoing communication, practice team decision making, shared responsibility, scheduled planning time, and pooled resources in order for the model to be effective.

Continuum of Services-LRE Options

Under IDEIA, a provision related to the placement for services is called the **continuum of educational placement.** This provision specifies that there must be a variety of educational options available to students with disabilities in order for them to receive their special education services, the necessary related services, and to access the education provided through the general curriculum.

When an IEP team determines the best possible placement for a student with a learning disability, the continuum of educational options must be considered. Most students with learning disabilities do well when they are placed in the general education setting as long as proper services and supports are established and followed. Students with learning disabilities are capable of achieving in the general education curriculum with accommodations and modifications. It is important for the team to evaluate and address each student's social and educational needs prior to making the final decision for placement.

The challenge of the IEP team is to base the decision for services on the individual student. The least restrictive option is the general education classroom, while the most restrictive option is a homebound or hospital setting. As decisions are made, the team must remember that the ultimate goal for a student with a learning disability is to function appropriately in society. Therefore, the least restrictive environments for students with learning disabilities are the same as those for all children with disabilities. They include general education classrooms (inclusive model), resource rooms, self-contained programs (separate, segregated model), separate school (private setting), a residential facility, homebound placement, and hospital settings.

Inclusion has been a trend in the education field since the early 1990s. It was intended to reduce the number of placements of students with disabilities in restrictive and segregated settings while increasing placements for children with special needs in the general education programs. It is a preferred and highly recommended practice for students with learning disabilities since they have average to above average cognitive abilities. These students are capable of quality academic achievement with proper focus and attention on their strengths and abilities.

Placements of students with learning disabilities in the general education classroom can be very challenging for regular education teachers. These students are diverse learners, and may each have different needs. They require adaptations, modifications, and accommodations of the general education curriculum in order to be successful. They may also require drill, practice, feedback, and extra time, which may slow the pace of instruction. Special education teachers who are trained to work with individuals with learning disabilities can provide assistance to the general education teachers, which will enhance student education and their individualized programs.

Successful and effective inclusion for students with learning disabilities requires appropriate supports. Making decisions, providing instruction, and conducting assessments of students requires that teachers understand and agree to the goals of inclusion. They must be informed of the student's needs, be able to access supports and resources, and have professional development opportunities available.

Assistive Technology

The Assistive Technology Act was passed in 2004 to support students with disabilities who may need equipment or products to improve their overall daily function and to gain benefit from their education program. Assistive technology is a valuable component in the overall program for a student with a learning disability, and decisions about this area should be conducted by the IEP team through an assessment process.

Assistive technology (AT) consists of equipment or products that allow a student with a disability to overcome barriers caused by the disability and may include low- and high-tech devices. Assistive technology services are those that may assist a student with a disability in learning how to use the equipment or products.

The use of AT for students with learning disabilities augments their strengths and allows them to compensate for their disability. It may help them to access print, communication, and information in ways that better suit their specific disability by providing an alternative means to perform tasks and supplement instruction. AT also adds quality visual and auditory layouts that will enrich the traditional general education curriculum. Computer enhancements may help a student by providing a drill and practice of previously delivered concepts and help improve reading, writing, and mathematics. Students with problems reading may use taped books or voiced computer programs. For those with difficulty using written language, they may use word processing programs or spelling and grammar check programs.

IEP/ITP Process and Teams

Students with disabilities are provided individualized programs that are directly related to their specific type of disability and their needs as identified through comprehensive assessments. This process is mandated under the federal special education law and called an **individualized education program** (IEP). An **individualized transition plan** (ITP) is utilized for students with disabilities in addition to an IEP after the student is age 16.

IEP

The purpose of an IEP is to develop a written plan and manage the student's overall educational program. It is designed to address the student's very specific and individual needs through established goals and to implement services that are appropriate in meeting the needs. The significance of an IEP for a student with a learning disability is that for the majority, the educational services will be delivered in the general education environment with accommodations, so the general education teachers are highly valued service providers. They are responsible, along with the special education teacher, for the delivery of services, the implementation of accommodations, the monitoring of student progress, and the accountability for the educational program.

ITP

Students with learning disabilities seem to have the highest number of dropouts of all disability areas, even though the majority of them are capable of living and working independently given the proper supports. Those who are successful as adults possess compensation skills that help them in their lives. They are able to ask for assistance, monitor their work, and support their families. Students need assistance and training prior to graduation. Gaining skills in the areas of vocational education, study skills, learning strategies, and extracurricular opportunities will be important, and it is for these reasons that an individualized transition plan must be developed.

An individualized transition plan is a requirement of IDEIA for all students age 16 and over. A student's needs must be addressed through individualized non-bias instruments and procedures. The student, the parents, the teachers, and appropriate community agencies should be involved in the assessment process, the program development, and services implementation.

A transition plan must include all of the community functioning areas to prepare the student for the adult years. These include employment, continued education, daily living, health, leisure, communication, and self-determination/advocacy.

Teams

Participants in the development of the IEP and ITP are outlined under the law. The team must include the parents, a regular education teacher, a special education teacher, a school representative, the evaluator, the student (as appropriate), and others with knowledge or expertise pertaining to the student.

Related Services

A related service is a component of the IEP, and the decision to include these services in a student's program is made by the IEP team based on a comprehensive assessment of the student. These are support services that allow the student to gain benefit from the educational program. These may include speech-language pathologist, psychological services, physical or occupational therapists, social worker or counselor, and others who are identified as supports to the student based on the specific needs and the type of learning disability.

Family Participation and Support Services

In general, children with disabilities place stress on family members and impact the entire family unit. As school personnel work with families, these professionals must consider the interactions of those family members and the factors that cause difficulty for each individual as well as the entire family unit. Assessing the family unit, providing additional support to families, and connecting them with community resources is the role of the professionals and is encouraged under the special education law.

The **family system theory** is based on the premise that whatever affects one member affects all members. The members include all of the people living in the home with the child and all the people who are involved in the child's life as part of the family. Members who deal with a child with a learning disability can be impacted in many different ways throughout the child's lifetime. Adults may feel inadequate, frustrated, guilty, or embarrassed, while the children (including siblings) may feel angry, jealous, or ignored. Therefore, it is a valuable component in school programs to include treatments for the family, such as counseling, training, and support.

As with other children who have disabilities, parents of children with learning disabilities often pass through the **stages of acceptance** (grief), as the parents are experiencing a loss. Educators and professional staff should support the parents and family unit as they go through these stages. Family support groups are available in many school districts and through community agencies.

Parents are to be included in the assessment process and the stages of IEP development and implementation. They are afforded certain rights under the law called **procedural safeguards.** Parents may need instruction on the implementation of interventions, advocating for their child, ensuring the child's rights are met, and understanding their child's abilities. The school can offer ongoing training so parents become equal partners in the student's educational program.

Being in contact on a regular basis engages the family members in the student's overall program and should enhance any progress the student will make. Informal methods of communication may include notes, telephone calls, e-mail messages, or participation in classroom activities. More formal contacts include parent-teacher conferences, IEP meetings, and progress reporting.

Curriculum and Instruction

Remember that general education teachers, along with the special educators who attempt to select curriculum or to determine the proper instructional methods, must focus on the specific students with learning disabilities and not those students with learning differences, learning problems, or learning difficulties. These terms pertain to all students across the general population, and they do need some adaptations to the curriculum, but they are not included in the special education programming, and therefore, are not discussed in this guide. Learning disabilities pertains to a smaller group of the population, who have been identified for special education services due to their neurological disorders and need specific instructional methods and curriculum to be successful.

Students with learning disabilities demonstrate differences in how they collect and organize information, have limited background knowledge on academic topics, and are not efficient in dealing with learning activities. These students need proven procedures, direct instruction, and strategies that teach them to organize, comprehend, and remember information. Educators interested in selecting curriculum, instruction, and interventions can find research results through professional organizations that will aid in selecting scientifically validated materials.

Development of Instructional Materials and Activities

Students with learning disabilities are stereotyped as passive learners, with poor self-concepts, lack of motivation, and social behavior problems. Some of them exhibit attention deficits and may be hyperactive and impulsive. However, active and engaged learners are more successful in school, and cooperative learning and peer tutoring appear to increase achievement and motivation. For these reasons, it is imperative that students with learning disabilities in the elementary grades are provided with the learning strategy training they will need for the future.

The curriculum for students with learning disabilities has primarily been inclined to address academic topics in a remedial sense and has not emphasized the functional skills needed. The more current instructional focus for students with learning disabilities has changed from providing only these methods of remediation to delivering approaches of instruction that focus on the core curriculum used in general education programs and the functional skills needed for a lifetime. It is believed this realignment of instruction offers a more accurate academic focus for students with learning disabilities and may be monitored through data collection and created through data-based decision making.

Methods of Motivation

Students with learning disabilities often experience failure, frustration, doubt, and ridicule, while also suffering from the misunderstandings of others. These feelings and situations affect their overall emotional development in school and for the remainder of their lives. Educators should understand that every learning disability may impact students in every sector of their lives. Students who are identified with learning disabilities need support not only for academic success, but in building self-esteem and maintaining the motivation to learn.

Motivation is an essential ingredient for success as it is the main component that moves students to attain goals. Because the academics seem difficult for students with learning disabilities, they begin to doubt their own success and accomplishments. They begin to feel they do not have the intellectual abilities to complete their work and choose not to do work since they may fail. Students need the motivation to persevere and achieve.

There are several ways to assist students in being motivated to learn. Teachers should first develop a healthy relationship and trusting rapport with each student. Involving the students in their own program, to become active learners, who are responsible for their own achievements, can help students feel self worth. Establishing a structure for the student's program that includes interesting lessons, a variety of materials, and novel assignments, as well as consistent and honest praise and extrinsic rewards for success, will help to instill motivation and enthusiasm.

Specific strategies that aid in improving motivation are the use of charting or self-recording, tangible reinforcers, game time, verbal feedback, token economies, and contingency contracts with the last three proving to have the most benefit.

Alternative Methods of Assessment and Grading

Many types of assessment methods and tools are used for students with disabilities. The alternative methods of assessment offer more information of value to a classroom teacher. Because the teacher needs information pertinent to the student's performance in a natural environment, classroom observations, work samples, error analysis, curriculum-based assessments, or criterion reference assessments give good results.

In inclusive classrooms, progress monitoring is of great importance in examining a student's academic achievement. It allows the team to evaluate the effectiveness of the instruction, as well as the student's level of performance. This can be instrumental when determining the attainment of IEP goals. Progress monitoring allows the professionals an opportunity to change the instructional methods and to reconsider the set goals if necessary.

Grading is a practice used within the educational system. It allows educators to provide feedback to students and parents, while supporting future decisions about a student's progress and placement. Many methods are used for grading students, but the difficulty arises in considering the grading of students with learning disabilities in the general education classrooms. Because students with learning disabilities may exude difficulty in meeting the course standards, or they may meet them in diverse ways, some professionals believe that the grades should reflect those adaptations. The idea of selecting an appropriate grading system, however, is to prevent students from becoming disinterested, frustrated, or discouraged, which affects their motivation and self-esteem.

The equity in the grading systems currently used is often debated, and this debate may result in some schools promoting an alternative type of grading system that is more accommodating to those with disabilities. These alternatives may be pass/fail systems, IEP-based grades, contract grading, multiple grading, shared grading, and descriptive grading to mention a few.

Peer Tutoring

Peer tutoring is one method found to be effective for students with learning disabilities who are enrolled in regular general education classrooms. A teacher may organize pairs of students in which one student may assist the other in academic skill development and learning subject concepts. In general, the teacher establishes the relationship for the two students, decides upon the academic task, and provides the materials, so the students may work independently of others to complete the tutoring. The research on this method shows significant gains for the tutee and the tutor in both academic and social areas.

Technology

Technology has a significant effect on individuals with learning disabilities. Overall, the technological advancements have opened the world for persons with learning disabilities in the realm of school, business, communication, and knowledge. Not only do the available technologies aid students in the general education classrooms, but they will support them in their life transitions.

As more computer programs and systems are developed, students with learning disabilities are better able to access information and complete daily tasks. By using e-mail, the Internet, and CDs students may be more involved with their environment, find critical information, and communicate with others more easily. In addition, word processing programs, voice recognition devices, text readers, and other computer applications support those with learning disabilities in school, at work, and at home.

Diversity

When focusing on diversity, consider several factors: **cultural differences, linguistic development,** and **gender**.

Children with **cultural differences** include variances with language, customs, and values. They may already exhibit problems learning in school, but it could be nearly impossible to determine whether those problems are due to a learning disability or to a cultural difference. Teachers must be culturally sensitive and aware and understand the various aspects of a student's culture and language prior to making any determinations about a disability. Assessment procedures are critical when debating the educational needs of diverse students, and these procedures may need to be altered as the culture, language, and background of the child are considered.

The implementation of multicultural education is often more complex for those students who exhibit learning disabilities. If a student's proficiency in English is limited, he will experience more problems in school. For a student with an existing language disability or some other characteristic of a diagnosed learning disability, additional support may be needed to address the **linguistic development** of English competence even before the student may participate in learning activities or academic areas. Having a learning disability becomes a more complicated problem for the student if she is a member of another diverse group. Language differences make learning difficult just as a language disorder can, since most of the academic work done in schools uses standard English. For those students who already have problems with the language, the emerging concepts, ideas, and communication problems are multiplied.

Since different cultures possess a multiplicity of values, professionals who work with various cultural influences must be more aware of the impact of the values on the instruction and performance. Educators should respect each culture and be culturally sensitive when selecting the methods, materials, and activities for specific children. Collaborating with other professionals and communicating with families during the assessment process and the individual program development will aid in the appropriateness. Utilizing some form of differentiated instruction is a wise choice.

With regard to **gender,** there may be just as many girls with learning disabilities as boys, but girls are not always identified and may not receive proper services. Thus, the long-term affect may be significant. Evidence shows that girls may continue to have academic, social, and emotional problems long into adult life. The primary differences appear to be found in the types of learning disabilities that boys and girls actually have. It seems that boys tend to have visual-motor problems, spelling difficulty, and written language deficits while girls seem to have more cognitive, language, and social problems, with academic deficits in math and reading.

Teaching Strategies and Instructional Methods

Many proven instructional practices are effective with students who have learning disabilities, but those most commonly used will be described in this section. Educators should focus on the research-based methods that enhance the education of students with learning disabilities, while seeking information on those less traditional approaches to see which best suits their students. The focus of instruction for students with learning disabilities has recently been on language, social-emotional skills, and cognitive-metacognitive skills as the students proceed through the general education curriculum.

Just as there are many types of learning disabilities and a variety of characteristics in students with learning disabilities, so are there a multitude of instructional approaches. The principles to watch for when choosing a strategy include structured instruction, opportunities for practice, comprehensiveness, and whether it fosters independence.

Beneficial instructional methods from elementary through high school are listed here:

- Direct instruction
- Content enhancements
- Concrete examples
- Pictorial mnemonics
- Individual instruction
- Task analysis

- Scaffolded instruction
- Strategy training
- Phonics instruction
- Planned homework
- Peer assisted learning/tutoring
- Reciprocal teaching

Explicit Instruction

In this approach teachers use well developed and designed materials and activities that give students structure and support in the learning process with a focus on the academic tasks to be learned. **Explicit instruction** means that educators are very clear about the skills that must be attained, and each step is taught to the student. It includes the use of modeling, positive feedback, and practice opportunities (guided practice and independent practice). Explicit instruction is synonymous with **direct instruction.**

Direct instruction is based on the behavior theory and is generally recommended for students with learning disabilities, especially those with behavior issues. The environment should be easily accessible for learning and must be organized so the students may gain the identified learning skills. The teacher should be in control of the lessons, the environment, and the materials and allow proper time for instruction and student practice and performance. Students receive feedback and are expected to gain mastery before moving to the next skill level.

Through this approach, instruction proceeds in steps that accommodate the student's understanding of the materials with the primary outcome being the student's successful participation as an active learner. A review of previous concepts and the monitoring of student learning are important components in this approach.

Content Enhancements

This technique is most often used at middle and high school levels, as the academic content and instruction has become more complex. This approach allows teachers to use various techniques that enhance the information in the curriculum so students may remember and utilize it more efficiently. Several types of content enhancements include guided notes, graphic organizers, mnemonics, and learning strategies.

Learning Strategies Instruction

This is becoming a popular method of instruction for students with learning disabilities as it provides a more systematic and effective way to learn and remember. It focuses on how students learn instead of what students learn. Teaching learning strategies trains students to focus on how to learn and allows them to take responsibility for their own learning, as active participants. They become more independent by using this method and will become more efficient and competent in their work.

The model for teaching learning strategies was developed at the University of Kansas and may be used in all subject areas of the curriculum. It utilizes several steps to promote this instruction and include pretesting, describing the strategy, teaching modeling, practicing posttesting, and promoting generalization. The procedures that should be followed for implementing this model include

1. Providing explanations
2. Modeling the learning process
3. Delivering prompts to use the strategies
4. Engaging the learner
5. Asking questions

Task Analysis

The purpose of using this method is to help students move to the preferred level of skill achievement. This is accomplished by planning the sequential steps to learn the specific skill. Using task analysis breaks down an assignment or activity into sequential steps, and a student learns each step.

Scaffolded Instruction

This method sets in place the support of the teacher in the early stage of the student's learning of a task. When the student has reached a level of competency and can complete the task or activity more independently, the teacher's support is no longer necessary, and it is removed.

Reciprocal Teaching

This method is an example of scaffolded instruction and is considered the teaching side of dynamic assessment. Through dialogue between the teacher and student, learning is guided and internalized, and the teacher helps to shape learning opportunities and conducts ongoing assessments. Studies on using reciprocal teaching to teach reading comprehension strategies have found this type of teaching to be very effective in summarizing, asking questions, clarifying, and predicting.

Instructional Models

Educators should identify the model of instruction best suited to their teaching style and the students they serve. Some of the models most often used include

- **Co-teaching:** When general education and special education teachers actively share the teaching of all students.
- **Peer tutoring:** When educators use strategies that include same-age and cross-age peers to tutor students with disabilities.
- **Collaboration:** When teachers with diverse expertise work together to enhance the education of students with disabilities.
- **Cooperative learning:** When educators implement classroom situations that promote learning among students through cooperation not competition.

Use of Instructional Formats

Instructional formats, the manner of instructional delivery, vary according to the type and needs of students, the preferences of the teacher, and the subjects or content to be taught. These may include motivation, modeling, drill and practice, demonstration, corrective feedback, and reinforcements. These may be used with either individual students or small groups of students.

- **Motivation:** Explained in another section of this guide. (See "Methods of Motivation.")
- **Modeling:** The student observes the teacher giving information repeatedly without giving an immediate response.
- **Drill and practice:** The use of consistent repetition and rehearsal.
- **Demonstration:** The student observes the teacher or another student completing a task and then makes the attempt at task completion.
- **Corrective feedback:** The teacher makes comments that aid students in understanding correct and incorrect responses while informing them of their progress.
- **Reinforcements:** When a preferred response is made, the student receives a positive contact or object to reinforce that the student will make a similar response to a similar situation in the future.

Areas of Instruction

There are several areas of instruction, not including academic and learning strategy instruction, that are critical to the success of students with learning disabilities, and these areas should be incorporated into a student's individualized education plan based on the student's assessment results. Although these areas of instruction are not a formal part of the general education curriculum and may not be taught to all students, each area should be integrated into a daily routine or schedule. The instruction in these areas should be on-going through the transition from high school. Specific areas are self-care and daily living skills, social-leisure activities, study and organizational skills, functional skills, and vocational skills.

Management of the Learning Environment

In effectively managing the learning environment, educators can reduce the behavior problems and increase student achievement. This is an on-going activity for teachers as they must create an instructional program that suits the learners of the day and provide methods of instructional delivery that enhance those individual's learning needs. Educators should incorporate data on current research that is periodically conducted on the learning variables, such as the general environment, strategies, and materials.

Managing the environment for a diverse population of special learners takes skill and practice. It includes addressing the various components of classroom organization: classroom tone, classroom rules, engaging the learners, and addressing various accommodations. It also requires that educators are knowledgeable about the physical space, how it impacts learning and creates more responsive learners. Teachers must have plans for daily schedules, location of materials, homework guidelines, student motivation and engagement, and peer involvement. Educators need to understand how behaviors impact learning and the influences that the classroom environment have on positive behavior management. To successfully manage behaviors a behavior analysis (the identification and definition of antecedents, target behavior, consequent event) should be conducted.

Behavior Interventions

Students with learning disabilities not only exhibit academic or learning deficits but also those associated with inappropriate behaviors. Due to the frustrations they feel or the misunderstandings they experience, they begin to develop poor self-concept and lack self-esteem while using behaviors that are not appropriate for daily situations. Some students with learning disabilities demonstrate feelings of anxiety, depression, loneliness, and oversensitivity. Because of these emotional influences, these students begin to develop learned helplessness and lose the intrinsic motivation that is critical to learning.

Students with learning disabilities often demonstrate adaptive behavior deficits that impede academic learning and prevent positive social relationships from developing. When social skills are lacking or a student is frustrated about academic achievement, disruptive behaviors emerge. This promotes withdrawal, absenteeism, aggression, outbursts, swearing, and bullying. Students with these noted issues require interventions and effective preventative strategies.

Behavior management requires a systematic approach to behaviors that is observable and measurable. The following are all recommended methods: reinforcements, shaping behaviors, contingency contracts, token reinforcements, time-out, and home-school coordination.

Behavior Plans

The use of a **Functional Behavior Assessment** (FBA) and the development of a **Behavior Intervention Plan** (BIP) for a student with disabilities is a requirement under the special education law.

An FBA is based on the applied behavior analysis procedures, which are referred to as ABC (antecedent, behavior, consequence). It is a recommended practice under IDEIA and used when assessing a student's overall inappropriate behaviors or when a student is suspended or expelled.

A BIP is the set of goals created for a positive program of behavior management for an individual student.

Positive behavioral support is the application of positive interventions or systems to change socially important behaviors.

Classroom Organization

The management of a classroom for students with learning disabilities goes hand in hand with the management of student behaviors. If a teacher can address the instructional needs of the individual students and focus on the student achievement goals, which are realistic and clear, behavior problems will be minimal and easier to deal with.

Organizing a classroom includes several different areas. Involving the students in creating the specific guidelines may help them accept the standards, and perform appropriately in the environment. These areas include establishing a tone, developing classroom rules, engaging the learners, creating the physical space, and addressing the various accommodations.

The classroom tone reflects a teacher's attitudes about learning and about the learners. How the teacher behaves, attends to the environment, and supports students, as well as implements and follows through on expectations, will affect the learners. A teacher's behavior does impact a student's behavior. Teachers who are positive role models will establish a more affective classroom tone.

Instituting classroom rules and procedures is another structural component of effective classroom management and organization. Set rules will affect student behavior and will allow them to work more productively because they understand what is expected in the learning environment. Since rules and guidelines are important in society, students need to follow rules in the classroom, and teachers must be consistent in the reinforcement of the rule-related behaviors. In developing rules, attend to the number of the rules imposed, the positive manner of stating rules, the consistent consequences for behaviors, and creating classroom routines to engage students.

Additionally, the physical space is of great value in promoting learning, especially for students with learning disabilities. It should reflect the teaching style of the educator while addressing students' educational needs and be appropriate for the subject or topics to be delivered. Studies have shown that the arrangement of a classroom (students and materials) influences how much time students will spend as active learners. In general, a suitable classroom is one in which the students and teacher may move around easily, access materials without barriers, and work in groups (large instruction periods, lectures, experiments, games) or as individuals (centers, projects, tutoring) without problems.

Transitions between Activities

There is some discrepancy about the time of day that students with learning disabilities may be most alert and better motivated, which are important factors when preparing academic schedules and delivering academic information. Some researchers believe that students with learning disabilities differ from the general population of students in their alert times and motivational periods from morning to afternoon. Because students with learning disabilities vary tremendously among one another, planning some periods of academic activities during the morning and some in the afternoon may be the best choice.

Students with learning disabilities need a variety of activities as well as the structure of a daily schedule and school routine in order to benefit from their learning and remain motivated to learn. They may be more active in accessing their education if they are involved in creating the learning activities and participating in the schedule planning. Making swift changes between activities may cause problems for children who exhibit learning problems, so carefully planned transitions between activities, lessons, projects, or classes will aid the child as well as the adults in maintaining control.

Transitioning between activities is a difficult period for many children, especially those with learning disabilities. There should be a balance of teacher-directed activities with student-guided activities during the day and warnings prior to these changes. Students with attention problems and processing difficulties need time to think about changes and wrap up their work. It may be helpful to summarize the goals of each lesson or concepts learned and then take time to introduce the next activity or lesson. Give students a chance to clean up their areas and place materials in the proper locations. Provide reinforcement for their attention to the work and for task completion. Monitoring progress and providing feedback may be the lead in to the next lesson.

Students with learning disabilities should become active participants in their own learning and be able to generalize skills and their acquired knowledge to future life situations. They should learn to self-regulate their behaviors, be more responsible for their learning, and use effective educational tools to become better organized. Providing positive transitions between activities will be one more tool that is useful to them in focusing on the academic work at school.

Professional Responsibilities

Under federal law, it is mandatory for the general education teacher to be a member of the student's IEP team if the student is placed in her classroom. The roles of teachers have changed in special education, and in recent years the general education teacher plays a more involved role.

Both the general education teacher and the special education teacher must be responsible for the education of students with disabilities and provide the appropriate instruction. The general education teacher is responsible for all the students in his classroom, while the special education teacher is responsible for the inclusion of students with learning disabilities and the instruction of the academic areas indicated on the IEP. The general education teacher must provide accommodations to students with learning disabilities and the special education teacher facilitates those accommodations. They both participate in the development and implementation of the IEP goals and the evaluation of student performance.

Classroom Personnel

Students with learning disabilities most often receive their instruction in the general education classroom. Occasionally, a special education teacher may assist or co-teach, which is especially effective if there are high numbers of students with learning problems in a particular classroom. Sometimes students with learning disabilities receive service from other professionals, such as the speech language pathologist, the occupational therapist, the social worker, a behavior interventionist, or a psychologist. These services may be offered in the general education classroom or on an individual basis outside of the classroom. Sometimes a paraprofessional or aide is needed in the classroom to help the regular education teacher meet the needs of all children or to work with specifically assigned students.

Teacher Advocacy

Advocacy is the collection of beliefs that may promote a condition or the rights of individuals. Educators have an important role regarding advocacy for individuals with learning disabilities. These students have difficulties with any variety of academic areas, daily tasks, and behaviors. It is because of the multiplicity of characteristics that these individuals display that they are so misunderstood by the general public, other teachers, parents, and community members.

Teachers of students with learning disabilities have the responsibility to support these students by making others more aware of the problems these students may face on a regular basis. They may practice advocacy by participating in professional organizations, and they may address public issues within their communities to support these individuals. These practices may relate to policies, definitions, support services, work situations, and funding. Educators may also share awareness with community members to alleviate discrimination and clarify perceptions.

Educators are better able to understand the fluctuating needs of these students, what they may be capable of, and the resources available in the community as students and as adults. As an advocate for students with learning disabilities, teachers should help these individuals learn to express their views and preferences, assist them by selecting community services, and support them in school, work, and the community.

It is critical that educators who dedicate themselves to the education of students with learning disabilities know the methods of advocacy that they may use while training students to be self-advocates. It is so important for students to understand and practice self-advocacy both during their school years and when they become adults.

Abuse and Neglect

Because of the issues surrounding the patterns of learning disabilities, parenting these children can often be very frustrating. The children are misunderstood; the families feel an emotional toll; and unfortunately, the children may be mistreated because of it. Parents must be informed about these disabilities and work with the school personnel to enhance the child's education and advocate for the child's future in the community.

A child with a learning disability affects all other members in the family. Family members may experience guilt, embarrassment, anger, and failure. To avoid problems of abuse or neglect, educators and other professionals should remain in close contact with family members and help them better understand the child's abilities, while accessing necessary community resources and support.

As with all children, any signs or suspicions of abuse or neglect must be reported. Each state mandates reporting procedures, so educators should check state laws and school policies.

Expectations of Student Achievement and Behaviors

Students with learning disabilities may have attitudes about their learning that are not accurate. Many of these students believe that they cannot learn and that they may be stupid. It is important for educators to build upon realistic goals and give adequate, consistent feedback for tasks completed. Students may need help in understanding their abilities and, therefore, realizing that they are intellectually on target for their age, but may just need changes in the delivery of the instruction and accommodations to complete work. Teachers must promote student independence to encourage positive self-esteem, and they must communicate proper, consistent feedback and set expectations for individual students that are clear and attainable.

Expectations do influence student outcomes in learning and regarding their behaviors. These expectations can be the student's own set of expectations, a teacher's preset expectations, or those imposed by parents or peers. If a student perceives expectations of success or those of failure, the student's motivation may also be influenced. Educators should consider placing high expectations on students with learning disabilities, just as they would other students, so they may reach positive achievement levels.

Several valuable tools are available for students with learning disabilities to help manage expectations. Using advance organizers will aid in behavior organization and remind students of rules and routines. Teachers may describe behavior expectations or model the appropriate behaviors as a method toward understanding the expectations. Conducting guided practice or independent practice, both with constructive feedback, also alleviates any misconceptions about the expectations for behaviors. Strategy training is another method toward improving academic performance and the probability of success in the general education classroom.

Professional Research and Literature

Professionals in any area of education should be constantly updated about the changing laws and new practices that affect the education of children. Educators should join professional organizations and subscribe to professional journals that are appropriate for the specific group and age of the children with whom they work. Educators and parents are the most likely groups who may influence additional studies and impact the changes that need to be made on behalf of students with learning disabilities.

Research in this period of history is plentiful. Those that would be most valuable for educators in the field of learning disabilities focuses on brain development and its relationship to learning, medical progress and neurological information, technology in education, policy issues, genetic influences, instructional strategies, and transition practices. The empirical research, uses data drawn from observation or experiences of actual students with learning disabilities, and provides a most beneficial look at students with disabilities in schools. Using the recommendations based on empirical research, such as classroom practices, learning strategies, or assessment, often proves to be very reliable.

Involvement in professional development programs also promotes high-quality classroom practices and knowledge about how to better assist students. Attending workshops and taking additional classes that focus on learning disabilities helps educators understand the individual differences and diverse needs of all students with these types of disabilities.

Teaching Students with Mental Retardation (0321)

Introduction

Working with students who are identified with **mental retardation** may be a challenge as each individual presents with a different set of characteristics and a different personality, and each has different expectations for success. Students with mental retardation cover a wide range of abilities and learn skills at differing rates.

You have probably studied the various aspects of mental retardation, its causes, definitions, complications, and teaching strategies as you prepared for your teaching career. Your coursework may have included information about special education since the category of mental retardation is covered under IDEIA.

Whether you are a recent college graduate or you have just moved into a state where the Praxis II is required for certification, you should find the following study information helpful prior to taking the examination. Although you may have studied a good amount of information, gained knowledge about the educational practices, and analyzed the legal and classroom applications about mental retardation, the following summaries should help you with identifying the areas in which you need the most review. If you believe that you need additional information not found in this study guide, refer to texts on those topics, search the Internet, and speak with practitioners. Websites are provided in the "Resources" section at the end of this book.

As you prepare for this exam, study the background facts about mental retardation as well as the information about services, IEPs, ITPs, and classroom strategies used. You should know about family involvement and complications, assessments, professional roles, curriculum, instruction, and program issues in school environments. Having certain expectations about what is on the Praxis II exam will guide you toward the topics you should cover in your studies.

The Praxis II exam (0321) is a knowledge-based exam and is intended for those individuals who have prepared and now plan to teach students with mental retardation in grades preschool though 12. This Special Education exam is constructed of 50 multiple-choice questions, some of which are related to a presented case study, and examinees are provided with one hour to complete the test. Two content categories are identified in this exam: Factors Other than Direct Instruction that Influence the Education of Students with Mental Retardation, which is focused on 11 questions (22 percent), and Delivery of Services to Students with Mental Retardation with about 39 questions (78 percent).

Content Clusters

Prior to reading the study guide information for teaching students with mental retardation, review the following and form an answer that covers the embedded topic. These questions should help you assess your knowledge pertaining to the subject of mental retardation and should help you focus on the pertinent areas of study. These questions are not written in the multiple-choice format found on the Praxis II (0321) exam, but they do represent the content categories found on the test.

1. Explain the various ways that a family may be impacted by a child with mental retardation and identify how the family's needs may be met.

2. What are the specific eligibility criteria for a child to qualify for special education services under the category of mental retardation, and what ranges of mental retardation exist?

3. Define mental retardation, describe the major types, and the characteristics of individuals identified with the various forms of mental retardation.

4. Summarize the need and use of informal and formal types of assessments for students with mental retardation, how to interpret the results, and how to use that information for individual student program planning.

5. Describe the importance of early intervention services and early childhood services for a child with mental retardation and her family.

6. What are the more important instructional strategies to implement when teaching students with mental retardation?

7. Discuss the importance of behavior interventions for students with mental retardation and identify the different behavioral strategies that may be effectively implemented.

8. What are the future issues and concerns that people with intellectual disabilities will face after they leave the school setting, and how can these problems be addressed?

9. Define the term **adaptive behavior** and explain how it may be assessed and what strategies should be used to improve these skills.

10. Identify the various supports, services, and strategies available in a community for an adult with mental retardation through a transition plan and explain how the team should meet the needs of a student with mental retardation as she prepares to transition from the school setting.

Preview Questions

In this section you are provided with five multiple-choice questions and one case study with three multiple-choice questions so you may test yourself and preview the types of questions that will be included in the Praxis II exam. If you are unsure of the answers to these questions, you can find the information in the study section that follows or look it up on the Internet as part of your further study.

1. According to the U.S. Department of Education, since 1977, the number of children identified with mental retardation has

    A. increased.
    B. decreased.
    C. not been recorded.
    D. remained the same.

2. A major issue for individuals with mental retardation is

    A. parents.
    B. health care.
    C. friendships.
    D. custodial care.

3. It is believed that intelligence is based on two main factors, which are _____ and _____.

    A. biological, mental
    B. mental, behavioral
    C. biological, environmental
    D. environmental, behavioral

4. The assessment of students with disabilities has been studied, and it has been determined that intelligence testing has inappropriately placed students _____ into special education.

   A. of various minorities
   B. of low economic status
   C. with mental retardation
   D. with hearing impairments

5. In developing a transition plan for a high school student with mental retardation, a significant participant at the meeting is the

   A. parent.
   B. student.
   C. employer.
   D. counselor.

The answers are

1. **B.** The numbers may have decreased due to the addition of other types of disabilities and the changes in the definitions.

2. **B.** Health care can be a problem for persons with mental retardation as they may have numerous health issues and may not fully recognize a need or understand the problems.

3. **C.** Research studies indicate that both biological and environmental factors impact intelligence.

4. **A.** Particular minority groups appear to be inappropriately placed in special education due to the assessments used, which may be biased for a certain cultural group.

5. **B.** Students in high school who are in need of transition plans should be participants in the development of the plan, as much as possible.

Read the case study and answer the questions that follow.

A 16-year-old high school freshman diagnosed with mild to moderate mental retardation has received various special education services since kindergarten. The student performs in most academic areas at the fourth-grade level. The student has articulation errors that make conversation difficult unless the listener knows the student. The student also has fluency problems when nervous or upset and has been taught how to alleviate those feelings to become less aggravated. The language issues are on-going, and the student receives services weekly from the speech and language therapist to encourage proper sentence structure and to work on pragmatics. The student also demonstrates motor domain delays with gait and balance problems, which are addressed daily by classroom staff and weekly with the physical therapist. The adaptive behavior concerns are in the area of self-sufficiency. Using cooking utensils and regular home-making appliances are still difficult, and the occupational therapist works on those areas weekly. The special education services and instruction have been provided primarily in inclusive settings until high school, except for occasional pull-out therapy, a behavior intervention, or specific concept development. At the high school level, the student has participated in a self-contained setting for academic instruction in reading and math, and general education classes for science, art, and vocational training. For the most part, this student uses appropriate social behaviors, tries to maintain positive interactions, and is well-liked by the other students. This individual has a part-time job at the local grocery store, two days per week, bagging groceries. The student also has a part-time job at the community multiplex movie theatre cleaning the various theatre rooms. The parents have been supportive of the student throughout the school years. The parents are eager to improve self-advocacy and independent care for future living. The team is developing a transition plan that will help move the student toward more independence as an adult once school is completed. The team needs input from the student and the family regarding preferences for work situations, living arrangements, recreation activities, and community involvement. The professionals have provided a summary of the past performance, the present levels of performance, current goals, and student preferences from doing a class activity. The professionals have asked the family, and student, to write down ideas about the student's future and to identify some areas that need further support.

1. During the meeting, the student states that one preference is to buy a car and learn to drive. The parents are supportive, because they work long hours, and they know their child will need transportation to get to work sites and for future living arrangements. Other members of the team have serious concerns about this goal for the student. However, knowing how this student accesses information and learns by doing, they also think that learning realistic lessons by actual participation is best for this student. The team should

    A. suggest the parents sign the student up for driver's education school and find an inexpensive used car to try out.

    B. encourage the parents to obtain the rules of the road instruction manual, guide the student to study, and permit the student to take the test.

    C. contact the department of motor vehicles to make special arrangements for student accommodations and modifications on the test.

    D. assign a peer student to teach this student how to drive, show the student how to care for the car, and give an oral pretest on the common concepts.

2. The student is interested in working more hours and attending school less. The student is not interested in art class any more and really enjoys working in the vocational department with the cars and other machines. What can the team do to assist the student in meeting this request?

    A. Let the student change the course schedule, take more vocational machine operating classes, and find a job at a gas station.

    B. Tell the student to wait for another year to see whether art is of any further interest while working at a car dealership.

    C. Ask the student to remain in art class until a natural break and investigate options together for work with cars and machines.

    D. Allow the student to visit art galleries and talk with artists to peak interest and work on art projects related to cars and machines.

3. Since this student exhibits difficulty in the area of pragmatics, what strategy would BEST work to help this student feel more comfortable while on the jobs at the grocery store and the theatre?

    A. Model a set of words, phrases, and sentences that are particular to each job and have the student practice certain scenarios.

    B. Request that the parents make a set of cards with vocabulary words that can be practiced each day before going to work.

    C. Incorporate the vocabulary from the job sites into the morning language arts lesson and have students practice saying the words to one another.

    D. Ask a peer partner to work with the student one time per week at each job and help the student by answering questions and talking with the people at the work site.

The correct answers are

1. **B.** For this student, realistic learning is important, so the team should recommend that the parents assist the student to study for the exam and take the test.

2. **C.** The student's preferences should be honored when possible and when they are appropriate to the school program. Changing classes is best done during a natural break and investigating options is important prior to making changes.

3. **A.** Modeling and practicing are both techniques for learning that are effective with students who are mentally retarded. To model a set of phrases and then let the student practice them will help the student to generalize their use.

Study Information

The information found in this section is focused on the broad area of mental retardation. Since it is one component of special education, it is wise to review general principles, theories, and guidelines of the Knowledge-Based Core Principles (0381) Praxis II exam. The categories and services necessary for students with mental retardation are mandated under IDEIA. In addition, early intervention services and early childhood services also play a part in the education of individuals with mental retardation, and therefore, the examinee may desire to review that exam section as well.

Issues about individuals with mental retardation have been evident for many years. As far back as the early 1700s, individuals with mental retardation were noticed in the community, and practices have evolved tremendously since that time. The research and public attitudes about this condition have greatly changed public perspectives and practices. Students with the more mild cases of mental retardation are offered an educational program much like other general education students, and even those with severe to profound mental retardation are being served in school settings rather than institutions. Parent involvement and advocacy has made a huge difference in the public attitudes and perspectives. And school programs have increased and improved across the country, while more early intervention is also provided. Families with a child who has mental retardation should be encouraged by the information available and the programs offered to give these individuals the jump start they need for success in learning.

Several cases of litigation in the field of special education have prompted changes, and those that pertain mostly to mental retardation are presented here for your review. (Others can be found in the Knowledge-Based Core Principles (0381) section of this book.) The early 1970s began a revolutionary change in the attitudes toward individuals with mental retardation and the services provided to them.

1971   *Pennsylvania Association for Retarded Children (PARC) v. Commonwealth of Pennsylvania.* A class action suit that provided the right of an education to individuals with mental retardation.

1972   *Wyatt v. Stuckney.* A case that gave individuals with mental retardation who are institutionalized the entitlement to special education services.

1972   *Mills v. Board of Education of DC.* This case indicated that all individuals with mental retardation can benefit from education or training, and financial resources are not a sufficient reason to exclude students from receiving an appropriate education.

1973   *New York Association for Retarded Children v. Rockefeller.* A case about the institutions for the mentally retarded and the lack of community programs available, as well as the issues of understaffing and terrible living conditions.

1974   *O'Connor v. Donaldson.* This case established the illegal act of involuntary institutionalization of a person who is not dangerous and who is capable of functioning, even though the individual may be diagnosed with mental retardation.

1974–77 *Halderman v. Pennhurst State School and Hospital.* A case that pertained to individuals with mental retardation living in institutions and the need to deinstitutionalize the residents in these segregated facilities.

1982   *Youngberg v. Romeo.* A case that resulted in the constitutional right to habilitative services for those with severe retardation in state facilities and that professionals need to consider different models of treatment and therapy to meet individual needs.

1990   *Parents in Action on Special Education v. Hannon.* A case that ruled that intelligence testing is valid when additional measures are used to determine placement. This case was based on minority students who were identified with mild retardation based solely on an intelligence test with no consideration as to the environment.

These are just a few of the court cases that have shaped special education and its laws, including those services and practices granted to students with mental retardation. As a result of these and other court cases, the federal law that supports special education has changed several times. In all, the current IDEIA has been written, amended, or reauthorized six times (1975, 1983, 1986, 1990, 1997, and 2004).

This section of the study guide is divided into two categories according to the Special Education: Teaching Students with Mental Retardation Praxis II exam. The information provided is only a summary of the content about individuals with mental retardation, but it will give you an idea of the kind of subject matter to study.

Factors that Influence Education

Mental retardation is the third largest category in special education, with learning disabilities being the first and speech and language problems second. About 1–3 percent of the general population have mental retardation, and in the school-age population, it is about 1 percent. The majority of those identified have a mild form of mental retardation, and many also have physical disabilities.

Zigler has identified five personality characteristics of individuals with mental retardation:

- They have low expectations of success.
- They exhibit a fear of failure.
- They have a need for social reinforcements.
- They display outer-directedness.
- They exude overdependency.

Individuals with forms of mental retardation often exhibit **learned helplessness,** which is considered a problem resulting from the low expectations of success and a fear of failure. Most individuals with mental retardation are affected throughout their lifetimes with deficits in intellectual functioning and adaptive behavior deficits. However, many lead independent lives as they learn skills that provide them with functional independence.

The primary characteristic of mental retardation is a deficit in cognitive functioning, most evident with poor memory, attention problems, difficulty understanding new concepts, inability to generalize skills, and little motivation. Researchers suggest that although students with mental retardation may have difficulties with short-term memory, after information is committed to long term memory, individuals with mental retardation will remember it and use it. Although the rate at which a student with mental retardation learns is below the typical child, and at times, the instruction is provided at a slower rate, research shows that individuals with mental retardation can often learn just as well when the learning rate is a regular pace.

A secondary characteristic, but as important in the diagnosis, is the lack of age-appropriate adaptive behaviors. Delays in this area can cross all domains and include self-care skills, social interactions, and behaviors. Adaptive behaviors relate to how a person takes care of herself and how she responds to others. These skills can include communication, self-care, social skills, daily living skills, community use, safety, leisure activities, and work situations. With delays in this area, individuals seem to have problems generalizing skills. When an individual exhibits poor language skills, cognitive delays, a lack of social skills, and inappropriate behaviors, he will find it difficult to sustain personal relationships. Many individuals with mental retardation also show a lack of motivation, which when given a difficult task, will wait for someone to help them. Maturation, personal independence, and social responsiveness are signs of improved adaptive behavior function.

Individuals with **mild** mental retardation can often master academic skills on about a sixth-grade level and learn vocational skills to be self-supportive. They often demonstrate social and communication skills that are appropriate and allow them to function in their community and within society. They may blend in with typical peers and not be identified in school until about the second or third grade when the academic portion of the program becomes more difficult and challenging, and they begin to fall behind.

Individuals with **moderate** mental retardation exhibit delays in academic and adaptive behavior functioning, and their performance is more noticeable due to this lack of abilities. They are often afflicted with more health issues and demonstrate more inappropriate behaviors than those with mild mental retardation. These individuals are often identified in the preschool years.

Individuals with **severe or profound** mental retardation usually have significant central nervous system damage and generally are identified with additional disabilities or medical conditions. They are most often diagnosed at birth or very shortly afterward due to the evidence of a syndrome or symptoms of a medical condition.

Individuals with mental retardation have many positive attributes, and educators should identify the special traits in each student. Many are curious about their environment, friendly with others, have a positive outlook, and will try something new. Most are teachable, functional, hardworking, and capable in their classrooms and in the community. Special strategies and instruction will greatly benefit this population.

Affective Behaviors

Individuals with mental retardation can exhibit inappropriate and challenging behaviors. Some individuals reveal self-injurious behaviors, obsessive-compulsive behaviors, aggressive behaviors, and self-controlling behaviors. Sometimes these behaviors are newly formed and unusual to the student's typical behaviors. Further assessments are then needed to determine the cause and decide the interventions. A functional behavior assessment can be a great asset to the team prior to creating a functional behavior plan for the student to follow.

Individuals with mental retardation are known to be at increased risk for psychiatric disorders. These problems require assistance from professionals who specialize in these disorders. The three categories include **internalizing disorders** (mood, anxiety, panic, depression), **thought disorders** (schizophrenia and dementia), and **conduct disorders** (aberrant behaviors).

Three types of treatment are useful in treating individuals with mental retardation who exhibit these affective behavior disorders.

- **Applied Behavioral Analysis** (ABA), in which the individual's behavior is analyzed during environmental events and reinforcers are used to change the specific behavior
- **Cognitive Behavior Therapy,** which is a combination of behavior techniques with thought restructuring
- **Psychopharmacology**, which is the use of medications to treat psychiatric disorders

Physical and Language Development

Students with mental retardation often require both motor and speech and language services. It is also very important to screen for sensory deficits as many individuals with mental retardation also have vision and hearing problems.

The motor delays occur even with those who have mild mental retardation. Individuals can exhibit problems with balance, gait, and manual dexterity. Research states that when the severity of the retardation increases, the motor problems also increase.

Because cognitive abilities are closely linked to language development, many individuals with mental retardation have speech and language issues. Speech disorders are very common. In general, individuals with intellectual delays exhibit difficulties with articulation, semantics, voice, and stuttering. They have delayed vocabulary acquisition and learn the rules of language much later than typical children. Children with mental retardation have fewer models of language and may not be encouraged to use language enough. Some of the children have hearing problems so development of the language area is difficult and slow. Some forms of mental retardation cause deformity of the oral-motor structures, which increases the difficulty of learning to speak.

General health issues are widespread among individuals with mental retardation. They display such problems as nutritional deficits, lack of exercise, susceptibility to illnesses and diseases, and a higher accident rate. They need physical activity to minimize the effects and improve their further motor development, making gains in physical strength and coordination.

Physical activities, including sports, provide an opportunity for achievement and social interaction with peers. Those with mild mental retardation are capable and enjoy structured physical activities. Individuals with more severe forms of mental retardation may need well-planned activities and programs of exercise that might include adaptive physical education and recreation opportunities.

Family and Personal Living Skills

Families are affected in many different ways when they bring a child who has mental retardation into the family unit and they often need support. They should seek and have access to community resources to obtain wraparound services. The family's culture affects their attitudes about mental retardation, and most families pass through the various stages of grief. Some of the affects are identified here:

- **Social-Emotional**
  - Concerns about the reactions of others
  - Problems with the restrictions on leisure time
  - Issues with siblings and other family members
- **Medical**
  - Limits on health insurance due to conditions
  - Limits on medical care
  - Increases of medical problems and health care
- **Physical**
  - Increase in care-giving needs
  - Lack of sleep and meeting caretaker needs
- **Finance**
  - Increase in child care needs
  - Need for home and vehicle modifications
  - Need for equipment and materials
  - Concerns about insurance issues

The majority of adult individuals with mental retardation live in regular homes instead of residential or custodial care. Sometimes the families assist the individuals if they are more dependent, and some individuals live independently as they may have their own families. These individuals may need the support of community resources and services, such as respite, personal care assistants, nursing services, behavior interventions, and home assistance in order to continue to function well in their setting.

Many adult individuals need financial assistance for living expenses as they do not generally have high-paying jobs, and some may marry and have children, an added expense, difficult to handle. Community and state resources are available to these individuals.

Classifications

Over the years, there have been changes in the terminology used that is related to mental retardation, just as the definitions have changed. Professionals try to classify individuals with mental retardation as it offers educators and service providers additional information about the possible characteristics of the individual, the various interventions that may be implemented, and the instructional strategies that could be utilized. In making these classifications, some professionals still refer to two general labels for mental retardation: Educable Mental Retardation (EMR), and Trainable Mental Retardation (TMR). Some states label students using a tri-level subcategory system: Mild Mental Retardation (MIMR), Moderate Mental Retardation (MOMR) and Severe Mental Retardation (SMR).

Professionals still debate the use of IQ scores to determine the subaverage intellectual functioning of students, yet many still consider the range below 70–75 as the level to determine mental retardation as long as adaptive behavior deficits are also present. This follows the theory that mental retardation is the demonstration of significant intellectual deficits, scoring at least 2 standard deviations below the mean. Since IQ tests are norm-referenced tests, if the norm is 100 points, then a 2 standard deviation score would be about 70 points. Professionals who use this guideline also refer to the following to determine the sub-categories of mental retardation:

50–55 to 70–75	Mild
35–40 to 50–55	Moderate
20–25 to 35–40	Severe
Below 20	Profound

Specific types of mental retardation include disorders and syndromes that may affect individuals in the intellectual and adaptive behavior functions. Some of these include Down Syndrome, William's Syndrome, Fragile-X Syndrome, Prader-Willi Syndrome, Tay-Sachs Disorder, and Lesch-Nyhan Syndrome.

Causation and Prevention

There is a high number of known causes for mental retardation, but in many instances, the cause is unknown. Problems that can cause mental retardation can occur during three different stages: prenatal, perinatal, and postnatal. It is typical to divide the causes into two main groups: **biological** and **environmental.**

Biological conditions include those that are caused by genetic disorders, chromosomal differences, congenital factors, diseases, teratogens, and syndromes. The use of medical technology can aid in the identification of these causes and in some cases limit the impact.

Environmental disadvantages include situations of alcohol use, abuse, neglect, accidents, injuries, toxins, nutritional deficits, lead poisoning, and trauma. Some of these causes are reflective of the choices that parents, particularly the pregnant mother, make in their lives. How they treat the unborn child can affect the intellectual outcome.

Individuals with mild mental retardation typically do not have specific physical or medical causes for the limitations in intellectual function and adaptive behavior function. Most often these cases are caused by heredity, early environment, or some combination of both. In general, the more severe the mental retardation, the more likely it has an identifiable medical or physical cause.

Prevention is possible. It is estimated that about 50 percent of the cases of mental retardation are preventable. It is important to promote public awareness of the causes and the outcomes for individuals with mental retardation. Education and access to health care and prenatal care will greatly reduce the incidences in birth. Advances in medical techniques and procedures provide another option for reducing the number of babies born with mental retardation and the impact of disease, accidents, and trauma to the brain. If the government would increase resources to prevent poverty, many children could escape the difficulties of mental retardation due to environmental factors related to low socio-economic status.

When mental retardation is present, however, educators can still do much to minimize the effects. Conducting child find to provide for early identification and developing programs for early intervention are two ways that young children can be found, supported, and served. See the "Preschool/Early Childhood" section for explanation of **child find.**

Definitions and Terminology

The term mental retardation has been defined over the years to be consistent with the changes in society and the knowledge gained from research. No single definition is accepted by all states. Some states do not even use the term mental retardation, even though it is in the federal law. These states may use one of the following terms: **developmental disability, mental disability, developmental handicap, mental impairment, intellectually impaired, educationally disabled,** or **developmental delay.**

Under IDEA-2004, mental retardation is defined as below average performance in general intellectual functioning with deficits in adaptive behaviors, which manifest during the developmental period and affect educational performance. The American Association of Mental Retardation (AAMR) follows the definition that is not based on an intellectual quotient score, but rather that of an individual's need for support as a function of the different adaptive behavior skill areas. In 2002, the AAMR used the following:

> "Mental retardation is a disability characterized by significant limitations both in intellectual functioning and in adaptive behavior as expressed in conceptual, social, and practical adaptive skills. This disability originates before age 18."

Another organization, Council for Exceptional Children (CEC) embraces the definition suggested by the AAMR. And finally, the American Psychological Association (APA) defines mental retardation as significant limitations in general intellectual functioning and adaptive behaviors with the onset of these limitations before the age of 22 years.

Basically, prior to diagnosing an individual with mental retardation, there are three components to consider with information gathered through assessment of the person. They are an IQ score of about 70 points or below on a standard intelligence assessment, a confirmation of deficits in adaptive behaviors, and the onset of the disability before the age of 18 years.

Delivery of Services

In 1976–1977, the United States Department of Education began recording the number of students identified and placed in school programs with mental retardation. Currently, the numbers have decreased from about 25 percent of the school population to about 12 percent of the school population. The need continues to be great, however, in how to address these students in today's schools. The implementation of No Child Left Behind (NCLB), the addition of technology, and the pursuit toward inclusion for all children causes educators to assess their programs and the students needing services in a much different way. It creates different expectations for the students and the educators (including the service providers). In this section, the perimeters of service delivery, programs, curriculum, and assessment will be investigated.

Current trends in service delivery are to focus on inclusion models and to provide emphasis on self-advocacy, which will empower students as well as instill self-determination in individuals with mental retardation. Public laws may change and trends may revolutionize, but what remains constant is that individuals with mental retardation need the support of schools and communities to reach their full potential.

Conceptual Approaches

There are several theories about development and intelligence, and depending on which one or what combination of theories a school or educator believes, it will be reflected in the programs for students with mental retardation. In this section, you are provided with some of the theories and some of the approaches used in serving individuals with identified intellectual disabilities.

The theories on intelligence include the following:

- **Nature versus Nurture:** Is intelligence acquired or innate?
- **Psychometric:** Intelligence is measured by a single trait or combination of traits.
- **Information-Processing:** Intelligence is measured by an individual's response to internal and external influences and life experiences.
- **Multiple Intelligence:** Intelligence is measured in specific but nontraditional ways.

Professionals can approach their services to individuals with mental retardation by assuming these theories and by considering the **medical, psychodynamic, behavioral, cognitive,** and **sociological** factors that influence a person's development and their responses to their environment.

Medical causes have an affect on the individual that may continue throughout her lifetime, so instructional interventions need to be considerate of how the condition relates to the student's abilities. Advances in medicine (brain research, genetic research, medical treatments, and technology) may have a strong impact on not only those with medical conditions, but for all individuals with mental retardation. Medical providers may need training to better understand and more adequately serve individuals with mental retardation. They should be aware of the variables of intellectual disabilities and the services, resources, and support systems available through referrals.

In the **psychosocial** realm, sociologists have studied separately the relationship of cultural deprivation and poverty on intelligence. From this research, the creation of infant stimulation programs, early identification, early interventions, and early childhood programs have flourished. The emphasis gained, through this knowledge about relieving the impact of cultural deprivation and poverty, is to provide integrated settings with proper supports to aid in learning and functioning independently.

The **behavioral** approach is related to the environment. This idea contends that children may learn new skills when their behaviors are reinforced in their environment. If infants or young children are continually rewarded for positive actions, they will learn that those are the actions to use, thus lessening the poor choices of behavior.

The **cognitive** approach is related to the theories of Piaget, who believed that children go through stages of development related to their age. It is further believed that children with mental retardation go through the same stages, but at different ages than typical children.

Some educators choose to utilize one particular approach while others select a more eclectic style, picking and choosing from each to build an appropriate program for students.

Professional Roles/Issues

The roles of professionals are varied. The teacher shares responsibility of program delivery with the related service personnel, administrators, and parents. The teacher, who shall be trained in mental retardation, also must guide the student's program, monitor student progress, act as liaison to general education personnel, work with parents, access community resources, implement interventions for each student, maintain a safe environment, utilize appropriate curriculum and activities, and administer tests, as well as many other duties. The educator must understand and follow federal, state, and district laws, and deliver a best practices approach in the classroom. Teachers are responsible decision makers in program implementation for students with mental retardation.

Attitudes

During the past four centuries (18th–21st), the societal perspectives on mental retardation have changed. There has been great variety in the attitudes toward people who demonstrate abilities and behaviors that differ from the norm. During the early centuries, most typical people did not understand those with intellectual differences nor did they know how to treat or interact with them.

Those individuals who had mild mental disabilities may not have been identified in society, blending in with people in the 1800s who could not read or write. Since many people did not complete high school or even go through the middle school level, people with mild mental retardation performed as well academically as people with literacy issues.

In the 1900s, mild forms of mental retardation were identified, and family members most often accepted the major responsibility for the education and care of the individual. People with more severe forms of mental impairments were often institutionalized, with society viewing custodial care and protection of others as a priority.

Advocacy

Advocacy for students with mental retardation is the elimination of barriers that will allow inclusion in the educational program and involve the individual in the community (that is, independent living and work situations). Several types of advocacy support individuals with disabilities: **systems advocacy, legal advocacy, self-advocacy,** and **citizen advocacy.**

Systems advocacy involves individuals who have similar disabilities or similar needs who may form a group to represent their rights and interests. **Legal advocacy** is promoted through attorneys who may represent individuals with disabilities or groups of people in litigation. **Self-advocacy** allows individuals to speak about or represent one's own interests and is often taught in the school system to prepare a student for the future. **Citizen advocacy** includes community members who may volunteer to represent or guide an individual with a disability.

Educators play a key role in the advances on advocacy for individuals with disabilities, particularly those with mental retardation. They are tuned in to individual needs, the progress these individuals are capable of, and the resources available in the community during and after transition. It is important for educators to instruct students with mental retardation in advocacy, which will help them after they leave the school setting.

Individuals with mental retardation are often represented by local, state, and national organizations that provide and support advocacy. Advocates may

- Help individuals express their views, preferences, and concerns.
- Assist individuals by evaluating community services.
- Support individuals in school, work, and community programs and events.
- Provide companionship to an individual or respite to a family.

Issues/Trends

On-going issues for individuals with mental retardation in school settings are related to placement and inclusion. These are both much debated issues and should be evaluated based on an individual's abilities and needs.

Certain trends that affect students with mental retardation are evident in schools. Providing early intervention services in a natural setting is a concern for children with mental retardation as they need the interaction and modeling of peers to better acquire skills. The use of technology and access to supported employment are two other trends that individuals with mental retardation face today.

Professional Literature/Research/Organizations

For individuals with mental retardation, there is continued and on-going research that pertains to medical aspects, technology advances, policy issues, and instructional strategies. These are all valuable topics, as is the information. Educators are one group who can pursue and request additional studies and aid in the changes that are needed to better support these individuals.

Through professional literature, educators can search for new knowledge by accessing the journals and publications that are available. The research findings are often shared with educators in the hopes that they will make use of the facts to change strategies and educational processes for these individuals.

It is valuable for educators to join professional groups in order to gain new information and insight into the changes in the field of mental retardation. With the ease of gathering information via electronic devices, educators can stay in touch with organizations that provide assistance to professionals in regards to such areas as classroom strategies, parents as partners, research, and legislation. Some of the organizations available are listed here, and the websites are found in the "Resources" section.

A number of organizations support individuals with intellectual deficits, and many help professionals access information and gain ideas about working with these individuals. Some of the more well-known organizations follow.

- The Council for Exceptional Children (CEC)
- The Association for Persons with Severe Handicaps (TASH)
- The Association for Retarded Citizens (ARC)

Expectations of Student Achievement and Behaviors

Research shows that individuals with mental retardation have high expectations of failure due to their past experiences and the fact that they do not believe in their own abilities. Their feelings and perspectives can be discouraging and create a debilitating attitude that reduces their motivation to perform and learn. They need situations that promote success and encourage efforts.

Students with mental retardation must learn to observe and respond appropriately to the environment and to the people in it. It can be a challenging endeavor. Teachers must plan programs and use strategies that help these students learn the cues and responses that are necessary to function well outside of the classroom. This structured learning should promote self-management skills, encourage success, and provide reinforcements.

Unfortunately, there are professionals who have low expectations for students with mental retardation. This makes reaching goals and achieving success for the student difficult. Teachers with this perspective generally teach with less enthusiasm and provide the student with tasks that are much more simple than they are capable of and add to the feelings of failure that some of the students already have. The students then become less motivated and less interested in learning, achieving fewer goals and developing self-esteem issues.

Teacher expectations can influence academic outcomes for students. Teachers who have effective classroom management, set realistic goals and expectations, provide instructional support, and demonstrate a fondness for learning deliver a message to students with mental retardation that they can achieve and there are supports available to help them. It leaves students with a can-do attitude that permeates their daily attempts at new tasks and their participation in activities.

Many individuals with mental retardation exhibit a variety of behaviors that impact their learning and their involvement with typical peers. They may be disruptive and distractible, or overactive, and have low self-esteem. In addition, many have behavior issues that may be related to social interactions, emotional and behavioral disorders, or difficult, learned behaviors such as aggression or self-stimulation. Research suggests that these challenging behaviors are related to the environment and can be eliminated when effective adaptive behaviors have been learned.

Collaboration with Related Health and Social Service Providers

Utilizing some form of collaboration among professionals is essential to the success of students with mental retardation in the school settings and individuals with intellectual deficits in the community settings. Collaboration is a process in which educators and other professionals can share their areas of expertise and work toward resolving issues for students, providing services and education in appropriate settings, and assisting with accessing and living in their communities as they become adults.

One level of collaboration is a **consultation model** in which the special education teacher works with the general education teacher to promote inclusion for the student. The special education teacher may offer suggestions and materials or demonstrate the use of techniques and activities. Together, they may assess a student's needs and develop the instructional program. Both should work toward supporting the accommodations, modifications, and adaptations that are suitable to each student.

Another level of collaboration is co-teaching (**cooperative teaching**) in which the two teachers (special and general) work in the same classroom with students, some of whom have disabilities. Together, they share the workload and adapt to the individual programs, helping students who need the most support, while others are able to work independently.

Another level of collaboration is the **peer support system,** in which professionals who work with students can request assistance from another professional. They may help one another with assessment techniques, curricula questions, and behavior interventions among other topics. They would not need to be working with the same students, but are available to one another to help.

Service providers who work in the classrooms of special education teachers, such as speech-language therapists and occupational therapists need to develop a strong positive rapport so they may collaborate regularly on students. The special education teacher becomes the primary contact for parents and other providers on an individual case, so communication is an important ingredient to successful programs for students.

Assessments

Assessment is the process of collecting information about the needs and abilities of individuals to help with decision making related to program planning. For students with intellectual disabilities, the process of assessment is no different than that of students with other types of disabilities, and a comprehensive assessment is mandated under federal law prior to placement in special education. However, it is the type of assessment and the tools used that make the difference for individuals with mental retardation.

Two assessment areas are required in most states for a diagnosis of mental retardation: an intelligence evaluation and an adaptive behavior assessment. In addition, a recommendation for a transition assessment to aid in the development of a transition plan also falls under federal law.

Examiners should select the best instrument for each individual tested. They must also understand that an IQ score should not be the only factor that determines a person's intelligence as there are others to consider. Providing only an IQ score to conclude special education needs may very well cause students of certain minority groups (specifically African-Americans) to be misidentified as mentally retarded and misplaced in special education.

Intelligence Testing

The assessment of intelligence is necessary to place a child in special education under the category of mental retardation, and it helps to develop individual goals and to devise the instructional strategies that will be needed. Intelligence assessments measure *maximal performance*, in a controlled setting under particular conditions. These tests assess higher order thinking skills and higher order reasoning abilities. Currently, professionals no longer use the term intelligence quotient to reflect the range of mental skills and abilities. The term used now is **deviation IQ**, which means taking the subtest raw score and converting it into a standard score of participants in the same age group. This creates a standard deviation that is the same for every age level.

Although a dated term, **mental age,** is still used by some school personnel. It describes intellectual functioning as the developmental level. It is the level of acquired ability or knowledge compared to the age of the individual.

Some of the tools used to measure intelligence include:

- Kaufman Assessment Battery for Children (KABC-II)
- Stanford-Binet Intelligence Scale (SBS)
- Wechsler Intelligence Scale for Children (WISC-IV)
- Woodcock-Johnson Tests of Cognitive Abilities (WJ-III-COG)

Adaptive Behaviors Assessments

Adaptive behavior measures focus on everyday living areas or the student's usual actions. These tests are based on interviews and observations. Through observations of social interaction during play and problem solving through daily peer participation activities, adaptive behaviors can be assessed. The severity and type of adaptive behavior delays determine the interventions and the services that will be needed to improve the student's abilities.

Areas to be evaluated to determine a student's level with regard to adaptive behavior functioning include the following:

- Self-help (feeding, toileting, grooming)
- Social skills (interactions, emotions, responsibility)
- Domestic skills
- Community participation
- Communication

Generally adaptive behaviors are assessed by gathering information from family members, teachers, and caretakers familiar with the student through a rating scale or questionnaire, as well as an observation of the student in a daily living situation. Some of the instruments utilized to measure adaptive behaviors are as follows:

- Vineland Adaptive Behavior Scales-II
- Adaptive Behavior Assessment System (ABAS-II)
- AAMR Adaptive Behavior Scale-School (ABS-S:2)
- Scales of Independent Behavior-Revised (SIB-R)

Transition Assessment

A comprehensive transition assessment is essential for students with mental retardation. It should be based on their interests, their preferences, and their abilities with the goal to identify and enhance their vocational needs.

Informal

Informal assessments are often considered ecological evaluations because they reflect how a student interacts with the environment. Informal assessments can provide professionals with critical information about a student, as they are most often an observation of the child in the natural environment, performing in the manner for which she is capable. Sometimes multiple information measures may be needed and could include a combination of such types as checklists, rating scales, play assessments, authentic assessments, and family assessments, to name a few. The observations provide a practitioner with enormous amounts of information about the student and can be done through anecdotal records, event sampling, running records, and other types of informal assessments.

Formal

Formal assessments are more of a clinical basis for evaluating students on standardized instruments. This is most often conducted in a structured setting with restrictive requirements for the examiner and examinee. Some formal assessments include norm-referenced tests, curriculum-based assessments, and criterion-referenced assessments. This form of assessment does provide a team with good information but should include informal assessment information in order for the development of a student's program to be within the appropriate levels for the individual.

Interpretation of Results

A requirement under IDEIA is for the person who conducted the evaluation or a person qualified to interpret the results of the evaluation to be present at the team meeting when results are shared with other team members, including the parents. If careful selection was made about the evaluation tools, consideration of any evidence of bias on the assessment was made prior to the testing, and it is believed that the student comprehended the evaluation process, in spite of any intellectual delays, then the team should feel comfortable that the results are valid.

Information about the student's testing abilities should be reviewed, which include any need for extended time, the repeat of directions, time to think about answers, and how the student tackled tasks. Any of these difficulties may cause the student to tire easily and need additional testing sessions to complete an assessment. Knowing this about a student gives the team members additional information about a student's learning style to consider for the development of a student's program.

There is a need for the continued monitoring of a student's programs through data-based measures so goals can be developed and progress noted. This is done by using formal and informal testing tools and methods.

Use of Results in Program Development

It is critical for a team to obtain comprehensive, efficient, and effective assessment information in order to develop an appropriate program for each individual student. The results will aid the team in identifying the student's needs to create proper goals and link them to interventions and related services.

Development of Reports and Communication of Findings

The communication of findings should be conducted at a team meeting with a review of the scores and data gathered. The written report should reflect the statement of disability, the type of mental retardation, how the disability, mental retardation, affects the student's ability to learn, the best methods for the student to benefit from an education, the kind of interventions that would support the student, the types of assessments conducted, and the related scores. Also needed in the report is a comprehensive look at the student's past performance, developmental milestones, medical information, and a description of the family.

Placement and Program Issues

Many types of services are available to students with mental retardation and many options for programming may be created in schools. However, states differ on their requirements for students with mental retardation, and schools and districts differ in their approaches for these individuals.

Most students with mental retardation are served in special education settings outside of the general education environment, in spite of the recommendations in IDEIA. There are not many still placed in residential facilities as that practice has changed, but has not completely disappeared.

Students with mental retardation should receive their special education services in the general education programs so they can learn from and with typical age appropriate peers. Although students with mental retardation need an instructional emphasis on functional academic skills, they should still be able to access the general education curriculum with accommodations and modifications. When they are in high school, they should also be offered programs that prepare them to develop job and life skills.

Continuum of Services

The **continuum of educational placement** for students with mental retardation is the same as those for all disabilities. They include general education classrooms (inclusive model), resource rooms, self-contained programs (separate, segregated model), separate school (private setting), a residential facility, homebound placement, and hospital settings.

Inclusion has been a trend since the early 1990s. Its purpose was to reduce the number of placements in segregated settings and increase those in the general education and resource placements for students with mental retardation. Inclusion is a recommended practice for servicing students with mental retardation. These students are capable of academic achievement and developing strong functional skills with proper focus on their strengths and abilities. When they participate in their education with typical peers, they can learn much through observation and interaction. Inclusion offers an opportunity to view positive aspects of living and allows them to participate in the quality of life that most would prefer.

A model of **supported education** maintains that students with mental retardation should be placed in inclusive settings to the maximum extent possible. With the added supports such as personal supports, natural supports (parents, siblings), support services (related service personnel), and technical supports, it will ensure that the student is successful. By using these supports, the student is not merely "placed" in an inclusive setting doomed for failure. Adding a functional focus to the curriculum, allowing adaptations to the environment, and using assistive technology are all critical to a supported inclusion model.

Related Services

Related services enable students with mental retardation to benefit from their educational program. Many students with mental retardation have secondary problems that require additional services such as speech disorders, motor problems, or sensory impairments. The related services necessary to ensure a successful program for students with mental retardation should be considered carefully and be specialized for each student's program.

Early Intervention

The benefits of early intervention for children with mental retardation are clear. Studies have shown that children with mild mental retardation perform extremely well, almost at par with their peers, if they receive early programming that is developmentally appropriate and meets with their needs. The problem for children with mild forms is that they are often not identified until early elementary school and, therefore, miss out on the early intervention programs. The value of early intervention for children with moderate and severe to profound mental retardation is also tremendous. Both the children and the families receive the help they need to further the child's education and lessen the impact of mental retardation. The key to the progress and achievement through early identification and early intervention is that the children with mental retardation are offered programs with typical peers. This allows the children with the intellectual disabilities to learn from modeled spontaneous language, imitation of proper behaviors, and practice with adaptive behavior skills. All of this contributes to supporting the child with mental retardation in becoming a natural contributing and functioning member of society.

Family Participation and Support Services

Families have strong influences on children, especially those with disabilities. The family has an important role in the development of a child and the interactions, culture, and values of a family unit are elements that impact a child, especially those with mental retardation. Family participation in school programs is preferred, and it enhances the student's success. In fact, parent participation and parent rights are key features under IDEIA. Families must learn to collaborate with professionals and advocate for their child. Professionals should build upon family strengths while meeting their needs.

Siblings play a huge part in the development of another sibling. They can form critical relationships, and siblings of a child with mental retardation develop very complex challenges. For many, having a sibling with mental retardation adds a layer of responsibility, as it is the sibling who will act as a future caregiver when the parents are no longer able.

For families, support services are helpful in all aspects of family life. Supportive care such as respite services and support groups or counseling can assist the entire family. Wraparound services are an organized and integrated approach to obtaining access service delivery.

Community and Cultural Influences

The community is important for children with mental retardation as it is the goal of their educational program to allow them access to the community so they may become more independent as adults in the community. These individuals must be taught how to use the community resources and how to function within their home community. Many will live and work in a community of typical peers, so educating them with nondisabled peers gives them the opportunity to experience a realistic life situation.

Culture is another influence in the development of a child with mental retardation. The family's culture reflects their views and attitudes toward their child, as well as their support toward the child and his education.

Research has determined that culturally deprived early environments cause a child to be at-risk for developmental disabilities. Children in these environments may demonstrate certain characteristics or symptoms of mental retardation. Their background and environment should be carefully considered prior to making a final diagnosis.

Assistive Technology

Two federal laws enhance the influence and support the use of **assistive technology** (AT) for students with disabilities: IDEIA-2004 and the Assistive Technology Act of 2004. Under IDEIA, the definition of AT states, "equipment or product used to increase, maintain, or improve function capabilities of children with disabilities." The purpose of these laws is to encourage the use of assistive technology to help an individual with disabilities overcome barriers and gain independence. It has beneficial use in school and at work.

AT can be low- or high-tech devices. A **low-tech device** is one that has a reduced cost and is relatively easy to use, such as a pencil grip, keyguard, touch screen, or a tape recorder. A **high-tech device** is more complicated and more costly and includes such devices as a voice-activated computer, or a switch pad for equipment and toys.

Some of the more commonly used AT devices for students with mental retardation include the following:

- Mobility devices
- Computer applications
- Adaptive toys and games
- Positioning equipment
- Augmentative communication aids

Computers and computer programs allow individuals with mental retardation to have some control over their own environment and to facilitate the communication of those with language problems. It can also assist with academic tasks. For example, a word processor can help students learn writing skills while a PDA can aid in self-monitoring behaviors, listing assignments, or using a calculator.

AT does require an assessment of the individual to determine the need and the type of the equipment for the individual and training for the education team, the student, and the family.

There is value in the use of assistive technology, but it is difficult for many school programs to access even though federal law requires its consideration and use. The many ways it can aid students include: allows adaptations, provides access to the environment, fosters peer interactions, decreases dependence, advances copmmunication, supports academic needs, augments strengths, and enhances inclusion.

Classroom Personnel

Personnel support is a fundamental asset in classrooms and programs that serve children with mental retardation. They help to maximize the benefits of the students' individual plans. There are therapists and other service providers, as well as educators and paraeducators who can support these students in inclusive school settings and community environments and during other non-academic activities.

The professionals and school staff who are available are not unlike those for students with other disabilities. These may include an educator (who specializes in mental retardation), a speech-language pathologist, an occupational therapist, a physical therapist, a vision or hearing specialist, a social worker, a job coach, a psychologist, and a paraeducator.

Of all of the personnel available, it is the paraeducator who may provide the most value to a student with mental retardation in terms of daily contact. Because individuals with intellectual disabilities need constant input, reminders and cues, repetitive tasks to build upon skills, and the application of the therapy techniques and academic concepts, it is the paraeducator who can accommodate those requirements. Paraeducators fill many roles, and with proper and continued training, can meet a very high level of intervention needs. They may assist students on the job in the community, support students in general education classrooms, teach adaptive behaviors, help students generalize skills, and accompany them on field trips and school activities.

Curriculum and Instruction

Students with mental retardation require intensive instructional input and often quite specialized instruction. Determining what and how to teach a child with mental retardation is the most important decision a teacher will make when faced with a choice about the curriculum. Each student is an individual with unique needs and those particular needs must be accommodated in order to meet the requirements of the academics in the general education curriculum. Students with mental retardation should be provided with access to a functional/life skills curriculum and vocational skill development. The older students would benefit from competitive employment as a complement to the functional curriculum.

Curriculum is a primary need for a student with mental retardation, and in order to address this need, a teacher must know the child's background, past experiences, family situation, cultural factors, disability characteristics, age, future goals, and specific needs. Students in a classroom have varied needs and come from diverse backgrounds, and those with mental retardation span all levels of skill development and instructional needs. When determining the curriculum needs, teachers must think in terms of adult outcomes for all children with this disability. If a teacher is planning to use a special education curriculum, then it must be aligned with state content and standards, while including the functional aspects.

The three major curricular options for students with mental retardation are

1. General education curriculum with supports and accommodations
2. Special education curriculum with focus on academic and social skills development with remediation
3. Special education curriculum with focus on adult outcomes

The general education curriculum may be appropriate for many students who have mental retardation; however, accommodations and modifications may be necessary for them to receive the full benefit. They may need added supports, and the general education teacher may need some training and consultation services to better serve the student with intellectual delays.

Students can be supported in the general education classroom in several ways:

1. Tutorial assistance in which the student is provided added instruction based on the content that was discussed in class.
2. Learning strategies approach in which students are taught how to learn and not just what to learn. Students learn to become active participants in their learning process.
3. Cooperative teaching is the collaboration between special education teacher and general education teacher. Both support one another and collaborate using their expert knowledge.

Several different curriculum types are recommended for students with mental retardation.

- **Developmentally appropriate practices** (DAP) curriculum, which is an integrated curriculum to allow students to grow in all domains through interactive child-directed activities.
- **Ecological/functional** curriculum, which is based on the importance of interacting in the environment and recognizing diversity.

- **Behavioral-based** curriculum, which demonstrates that as students interact with environment, it must be carefully structured and managed, and events must be changed. The purpose is to instruct students in functional and age-appropriate skill building.

- **Cognitive developmental** curriculum, which is based on Piaget's theory that the child learns by proceeding through various developmental stages. This is especially important to students with intellectual deficits. This type of curriculum provides relevant activities that are age appropriate, discovery-based, and interactive for the child to experience and learn from. It includes consistent reinforcement for attempts and successes, as well as encourages support.

- **Life skills** curriculum, in which students learn functional skills that aid in the transition to the community, covering six domains of adult functioning.

- **Functional** curriculum, which covers an area of major priority for students with mental retardation. It helps to develop skills toward maximizing independence and employment.

Development of Instructional Program

An instructional program for students with disabilities should be based on the assessment and the resulting IEP. It is important for students with mental retardation to be provided functional academic skills development and adaptive behavior skills development.

Community-based instruction (CBI) is a popularly used model that delivers instruction in various community environments to promote the generalization of academic and adaptive behavior skills.

Effective Data Collection

Tracking information on students can be to support evaluations, identify skills acquisition and goal attainment, trace behavior management, and confirm progress reports. Educators have different methods for collecting data on students and determining what type of data may be important to each child's program. The data can be used to adjust strategies in the classroom, adapt an environmental item, or support the student in a community activity. It provides accurate and ongoing information that aids the service providers in addressing an appropriate program for the student.

For students with mental retardation, anecdotal records are an effective method as they are written to be pertinent to each individual and can be developed daily or dated for specific activities and placed in the student's file for later reference.

Preparation of the IEP and the ITP

The purpose of an individualized education program (IEP) is very much the same for all disability categories. It is a guide to a specialized education program for every student with a disability and provides a method of evaluation directed toward the student's progress. An IEP includes an ITP for students who are 16 years of age and older.

An IEP must be based on the student's needs as assessed by a team of professionals. It is mandated under federal law and requires the team to address the present levels of academic performance, identify the supports, decide on the related service providers, design involvement with typical peers, explain how the student will access the general education curriculum, describe progress, and include a transition program.

Transition services are also required under IDEIA. An individual transition plan (ITP) is required for all students with disabilities, but for individuals with mental retardation, it is a critical component of their school program. Professionals and team members should begin the discussion and planning of this outcome-based process very early for students with mental retardation, even as early as elementary school.

The goal for every student with mental retardation is to be at some level of independence by the time they leave school. Successful adult living, work placements, and community involvement are all related to the effective transition plans that formally begin at age 16.

A student's needs should be assessed and a plan developed that includes the coordination and collaboration of community resources, as well as student needs, interests, and preferences. All transition plans require that instructional needs, community experiences, employment plans, post-secondary school programs, adult plans, and a vocational evaluation be included. Students with mental retardation are capable of success in work and community settings with the proper supports and special services.

Instructional Materials and Activities

Materials should be selected in order to promote the acquisition of targeted skills and match a student's abilities and age. These can be games, audios, books, or devices and should be a motivational learning tool for each student.

The activities should be planned based on the targeted goals, skills, and behaviors to be developed. These should be stimulating, and varied, while being adapted to individual, small, or large group active participation.

Teaching Strategies and Instructional Methods

When teaching students with intellectual disabilities, it is not only the content that is important, but the actual process of learning, the delivery of information. Students need to acquire and retain skills. They must master set goals and apply the learning to other situations. It is so important to enhance the cognitive skills with concrete learning experiences and provide remediation such as rehearsal, classification, and visual imagery. The strategies must support the learner and encourage independence.

Some of the recommended instructional strategies include:

- **Task analysis:** Reducing complex skills into smaller sequential tasks
- **Mediated scaffolding:** Providing cues and gradually removing them so students can perform and respond independently
- **Active student response:** Engagement of the learner in tasks and activities
- **Modeling tasks:** Acting out sequences while students observe and then having students imitate the task to learn it. This helps make connections between the material to be learned and the process to learn it
- **Systematic feedback:** Providing positive reinforcement and confirmation to improve learning
- **Transfer of stimulus control:** Providing instructional prompts to aid in correct responses
- **Repetition:** Helps build rote memory skills
- **Generalization:** Using skills learned across various settings
- **Direct measurement:** Frequently checking on student performance

A general, but primary strategy for schools with inclusion programs is for the school to offer a sense of community, where everyone belongs, and abilities are celebrated and adaptations addressed. A specific strategy used in inclusion models is called the **circle of friends.** It is a peer group education model that allows caring relationships and nurturing actions toward persons with disabilities as they help one another to learn.

Instructional methods are an outcome of empirical research. Students with mental retardation need systematic and explicit instruction to perform well. Instructional strategies must be particular to each student and focus on the generalization of skills to other settings.

The methods used for students with mental retardation should be based on the IEP goals and objectives. The teacher should review the targeted skills and choose the methods that will effectively enhance learning for each individual.

The following are some of the best practices suggested for students with mental retardation:

1. Expose them to adaptive behaviors in a variety of settings, especially those that are natural as the need arises.
2. Instruct response to environmental cues and the use of appropriate skills.
3. Teach to generalize adaptive behaviors to other settings.
4. Ensure new skills are maintained and monitored.
5. Address appropriate functional skills.

Modifying Instruction

When educators modify instruction, they make changes in procedures, the curriculum, classroom management, materials, and the environment to facilitate learning. For students with mental retardation, it is important to evaluate this process regularly and make the appropriate changes regularly.

Areas of Instruction

Students with mental retardation require instruction in functional skills, adaptive behaviors, daily living skills, and vocational training. This can be provided in any type of setting as the professionals incorporate these areas into the curriculum and the student's IEP.

Management of the Learning Environment

A positive, safe, and enriching environment is very important to children. But even more important is how well the educator manages it. Classroom management can be a difficult task, especially with the wide range of abilities in children with mental retardation. Accommodating every child's needs and addressing each individual behavior takes time and patience.

Behavior needs greatly vary with individuals who have cognitive deficits and with the high likelihood of mental health disorders, it becomes a challenge for professionals to develop interventions and manage these behaviors. The goal is for individuals to be self-managing and responsible for their own behaviors, so they may integrate into the community as adults and lead productive lives.

Many techniques are available regarding interventions and management of behaviors, but it is not a "one size fits all" for individuals with mental retardation. The team must make a careful analysis of the behavior to determine which technique would work best. Some students need constant interventions and tracking of behaviors while others are working on becoming more self-reliant to manage their own. Educators can use charting and timed interval recordings to manage the improvements.

One particular intervention that has proven to be effective with students who are categorized as mentally retarded is **reinforcement.** The praise or rewards when a student is doing what is expected reduces the difficult behaviors and increases the more desirable behavior.

Functional Behavior Assessments and Functional Behavior Plans are required under IDEIA for student with behaviors that interfere with their daily abilities.

The classroom environment has been found to have a major impact on the learning for students with mental retardation. It should enlighten their desire to learn through stimulation of the auditory, visual, and tactile senses. A positive environment will increase the appropriate and desired behaviors, as well as reinforce the learning programs. It should offer availability of a variety of interactive and age-appropriate activities with easy access to materials. Focusing on the functional curriculum will also help to shape the student's learning.

PART II

PRACTICE TESTS WITH ANSWER EXPLANATIONS

Knowledge-Based Core Principles (0351)

Application of Core Principles Across Categories of Disability (0352)

Preschool/Early Childhood (0690)

Teaching Students with Behavioral Disorders/Emotional Disturbance (0371)

Teaching Students with Learning Disabilities (0381)

Teaching Students with Mental Retardation (0321)

Answer Grid for Knowledge-Based Core Principles (0351) Practice Exam

1 (A) (B) (C) (D)	31 (A) (B) (C) (D)
2 (A) (B) (C) (D)	32 (A) (B) (C) (D)
3 (A) (B) (C) (D)	33 (A) (B) (C) (D)
4 (A) (B) (C) (D)	34 (A) (B) (C) (D)
5 (A) (B) (C) (D)	35 (A) (B) (C) (D)
6 (A) (B) (C) (D)	36 (A) (B) (C) (D)
7 (A) (B) (C) (D)	37 (A) (B) (C) (D)
8 (A) (B) (C) (D)	38 (A) (B) (C) (D)
9 (A) (B) (C) (D)	39 (A) (B) (C) (D)
10 (A) (B) (C) (D)	40 (A) (B) (C) (D)
11 (A) (B) (C) (D)	41 (A) (B) (C) (D)
12 (A) (B) (C) (D)	42 (A) (B) (C) (D)
13 (A) (B) (C) (D)	43 (A) (B) (C) (D)
14 (A) (B) (C) (D)	44 (A) (B) (C) (D)
15 (A) (B) (C) (D)	45 (A) (B) (C) (D)
16 (A) (B) (C) (D)	46 (A) (B) (C) (D)
17 (A) (B) (C) (D)	47 (A) (B) (C) (D)
18 (A) (B) (C) (D)	48 (A) (B) (C) (D)
19 (A) (B) (C) (D)	49 (A) (B) (C) (D)
20 (A) (B) (C) (D)	50 (A) (B) (C) (D)
21 (A) (B) (C) (D)	51 (A) (B) (C) (D)
22 (A) (B) (C) (D)	52 (A) (B) (C) (D)
23 (A) (B) (C) (D)	53 (A) (B) (C) (D)
24 (A) (B) (C) (D)	54 (A) (B) (C) (D)
25 (A) (B) (C) (D)	55 (A) (B) (C) (D)
26 (A) (B) (C) (D)	56 (A) (B) (C) (D)
27 (A) (B) (C) (D)	57 (A) (B) (C) (D)
28 (A) (B) (C) (D)	58 (A) (B) (C) (D)
29 (A) (B) (C) (D)	59 (A) (B) (C) (D)
30 (A) (B) (C) (D)	60 (A) (B) (C) (D)

Knowledge-Based Core Principles (0351) Practice Exam

Read each of the following multiple-choice questions and select the BEST answer. Fill in your choice by using the answer bubble sheet provided.

1. There are six major provisions of IDEIA (IDEA-2004) mandated to schools. Identify one of those provisions from the options given.

   A. implementation of early intervention programs
   B. rehabilitative and transition counseling services
   C. segregated programs for students with severe disabilities
   D. nondiscriminatory identification and evaluation processes

2. The evaluation process can be complicated, and it has been suggested that some groups of children are over identified in special education programs. To ensure that students are receiving appropriate evaluations conducive to their backgrounds, an evaluator should

   A. ask an adult familiar to the child to sit in the room.
   B. conduct two evaluations in two different settings.
   C. administer non-biased tests in the primary language.
   D. request the psychologist administer the evaluations.

3. One of the MOST influential factors in the development of a child's social-emotional domain is the

   A. family.
   B. gender.
   C. siblings.
   D. environment.

4. Educators should demonstrate professional _____ to the students, their peers, families, and their communities.

   A. awards
   B. interest
   C. instruction
   D. competence

5. FERPA provides rights to parents of public school students, and these rights are important for students in special education. Two primary rights for parents that are outlined under FERPA are 1) the right to inspect and review their child's educational records and 2) the right to

   A. prevent unauthorized people from seeing the records.
   B. provide unconditional access to the records for all professionals.
   C. allow review of records by an educator interested in helping the child.
   D. exclude named parties from obtaining the records, such as juvenile authorities.

6. When successful collaboration occurs between a general education teacher and a special education teacher, it is due to the

   A. time available to plan.
   B. amount of resources available.
   C. background and education of each teacher.
   D. disability conditions represented in the class.

GO ON TO THE NEXT PAGE

7. Which of the following examples includes the required components for the development of IEP goals and would be an appropriate annual goal on an IEP?

    A. By December, the student will remember the capital cities of one region of the United States for history class and select one state for a written report with a project.

    B. The student will recognize four mathematical formulas and solve two word problems with 65 percent accuracy as assessed by teacher observation.

    C. The student will participate in all assemblies and programs to enhance social skills and increase the inclusion portion of the program.

    D. By April, the student will increase visual recognition of third-grade vocabulary words by adding 10 additional words from the present level of 30 words with 80 percent accuracy as assessed by The Peabody Picture Vocabulary Test.

8. If a student with a disability requires special services, in order to access and benefit from an education, even though those services are expensive, which of the following legal cases supports this student's right to obtain these services?

    A. *Mills v. Board of Education*

    B. *Zobrest v. Catalina School District*

    C. *Irving Independent School District v. Tatro*

    D. *Rowley v. Hendrick Hudson School District*

9. There are several primary areas for which speech and language therapists place students in a special education program for speech-language therapy. Which of the following three are possible reasons to place a student?

    A. voice, fluency, decoding

    B. articulation, voice, fluency

    C. listening, articulation, voice

    D. fluency, articulation, reading

10. A strategy based on research that provides classroom performance expectations and behavior requirements in consistent and clear terms is known to increase

    A. teacher interest.

    B. student motivation.

    C. student relationships.

    D. teacher accomplishments.

11. After the IEP process has been started, which of the following steps allows the team to determine whether the student is meeting the goals set forth?

    A. placement

    B. development

    C. annual review

    D. implementation

12. The name most associated with the cognitive development theory is

    A. Carl Jung.

    B. Jean Piaget.

    C. Sigmund Freud.

    D. Marie Montessori.

13. Progress on improving attitudes toward people with disabilities has been spurred by the movement of using "people first" language, which is demonstrated in which example?

    A. a deaf student

    B. a learning-disabled boy

    C. a preschool girl with autism

    D. the special education classroom

14. A middle school student with an emotional disability demonstrates disruptive behaviors in the general education setting but is placed in this inclusive setting the majority of the day. According to research, a key factor in controlling this student's behavior is

    A. modeling.

    B. extinction.

    C. discipline.

    D. responsibility.

15. There are several required components for an IEP. Which of the following is necessary when writing goals for a student?

    A. short-term objectives

    B. related service providers

    C. least restrictive environment

    D. present levels of performance

16. Prior to being identified with a learning disability, students exhibit certain problems that alert a teacher of a possible need. Which of the following is the main reason that elementary students are being referred for possible special education services?

A. math deficits
B. reading delays
C. behavior issues
D. listening problems

17. Identify which of the following court cases focused on the school's responsibility to provide medical services to students with disabilities if the situation does not require a physician's care?

A. *Tatro*
B. *Honig*
C. *Brown*
D. *Rowley*

18. A middle school student has been suspended for 14 days for getting into a fight on school grounds. The team is now required to

A. provide the IEP information to local authorities and terminate the student's special education services.
B. conduct a functional behavior assessment and develop a behavior intervention plan.
C. provide training to all staff members on behavior interventions before the student returns to school.
D. conduct special education services in the home until an alternate placement may be established for the rest of the year.

19. A 17-year-old high school student with mental retardation is receiving transition services and the IEP team is revising the plan. The team wants to implement an instructional program to help prepare the student for the future. Which of the following curricula is the best choice for this student?

A. functional curriculum
B. social skills curriculum
C. developmental curriculum
D. behavior-based curriculum

20. A set of characteristics that need to be addressed in a student's IEP if the disability is Emotional Disturbance are the _____ behaviors.

A. abstract
B. affective
C. adaptive
D. acquired

21. Which of the following is a recommended method for teaching students with disabilities about employment and life skills in the area of vocational skills training?

A. peer tutoring
B. independent practice
C. life strategies education
D. community-based instruction

22. A federal law that was passed in 1988, called The Technology Assistance Act for Individuals with Disabilities, supports programs for assistive technology for individuals with disabilities of

A. all ages.
B. low incidence.
C. high incidence.
D. secondary ages.

23. A common descriptor of a student with an emotional disturbance according to the law is

A. motor delays.
B. language deficits.
C. atypical emotions.
D. low adaptive behaviors.

24. The ultimate goal of teaching self-care skills for a student with a disability is to become independent in her own care. To perform at this level, students must learn the necessary skills and then _____ across settings.

A. practice
B. schedule
C. organize
D. generalize

25. Federal law requires a transition plan as a component of a student's program in special education. It is appropriate for the school district to request that the _____ assist with the development of the plan and the services to the student.

A. interagencies
B. parent association
C. community adult center
D. special education director

GO ON TO THE NEXT PAGE

26. A(n) _____ is a method used to check student achievement and teacher instruction.

   A. achievement test
   B. portfolio
   C. norm-reference test
   D. summative evaluation

27. A kindergarten student, being evaluated for special education services, has just been identified with a delay in pragmatics. This means the child lacks the ability to

   A. match speech sounds to written symbols.
   B. understand the functional use of language.
   C. comprehend words represented in written language.
   D. recognize letters and sounds to form words and phrases.

28. In research conducted on effective reading outcomes it has been found that a significant factor related to success was the

   A. book selections.
   B. grouping of students.
   C. independent practice.
   D. seating arrangements.

29. Four primary domains must be addressed and included when an IEP-ITP team begins to develop the transition program for a student with disabilities. Which of the lists suggests the proper items to focus on in the plan?

   A. leisure, assessments, domestic, academic
   B. domestic, community, leisure, vocational
   C. vocational, assessments, community, family
   D. academic, community, vocational, recreation

30. In 2001, the U.S. Department of Education statistics showed that the category with the highest incidence in the population served under special education was

   A. learning disability.
   B. mental retardation.
   C. other health impaired.
   D. emotional disturbance.

31. In which of the following disability categories would a student have difficulty developing the proper social skills due to the isolation created by the communication barrier and the lack of personal relationships?

   A. Autism (A)
   B. Mental Retardation (MR)
   C. Learning Disabilities (LD)
   D. Emotional Disturbance (ED)

32. Which of the following is the most common related service added to student IEPs?

   A. transportation
   B. behavior interventions
   C. speech-language therapy
   D. paraprofessional services

33. Which of the following categories of special education is characterized by limited strength, vitality, or alertness?

   A. Emotional Disturbance
   B. Other Health Impaired
   C. Orthopedic Impairment
   D. Traumatic Brain Injury

34. An example of a study skill that is necessary for all students with disabilities is

   A. reading.
   B. test taking.
   C. oral presentation.
   D. behavior self-management.

35. A 16 year old high school student with mild mental retardation is interested in learning how to fix cars and wants to work at a gas station upon graduation from school. As the team prepares to create a transition plan, which of the following demonstrates a program that includes the consideration for the least restrictive environment?

   A. Obtain a job at a local gas station.
   B. Ask parents to purchase books on the topic.
   C. Place in high school auto shop class with a peer tutor.
   D. Enroll in a community college mechanics class.

36. Although the medical community has not determined a single cause for the rising conditions of autism, they have not found any link to (the)

   A. genetics.
   B. neurology.
   C. environment.
   D. immunizations.

37. Students with _____ are most likely to have academic gaps between their achievement and abilities in the areas of reading, writing, and math.

    A. Mental Retardation
    B. Learning Disabilities
    C. Hearing Impairments
    D. Emotional Disturbance

38. Parents of an elementary student whose physician diagnosed the child with severe asthma have requested that the child be allowed alternatives to recess and physical education class, as well as additional time to complete work when the child experiences fatigue or has a breathing episode. Which law protects the rights of this child and requires the teacher to develop accommodations for this child based on the medical needs?

    A. 504
    B. ADA
    C. IDEIA
    D. NCLB

39. The concept of inclusive programs for students with disabilities began in the early

    A. 1960s.
    B. 1970s.
    C. 1980s.
    D. 1990s.

40. An Orthopedic Impairment can be considered a temporary placement in special education and is most often the result of

    A. genetic conditions.
    B. diseases or accidents.
    C. biochemical imbalances.
    D. environmental influences.

41. Two very distinct methods of instruction that may be used with students who have disabilities are _____ instruction and _____ instruction.

    A. explicit and implicit
    B. adapted and modified
    C. precision and strategic
    D. diagnostic and generalized

42. For students in special education, the IEP team must consider the most appropriate option for delivery of educational services such as a general education class, or a resource room. These options are called

A. supplementary aids and services.
B. scale of assessments and therapies.
C. continuum of educational placements.
D. special education instructional settings.

43. When a team of professionals share roles and cross disciplines to complete student assessments and plan a program, this team is referred to as the _____ team.

    A. multidisciplinary
    B. interdisciplinary
    C. transdisciplinary
    D. intradisciplinary

44. A primary factor in the prevention of many different types of disabilities in children is the access to

    A. family therapy.
    B. crisis management.
    C. proper and early prenatal care.
    D. appropriate community resources.

45. Identify which of the following is an essential element of instruction.

    A. present exam
    B. grading project
    C. modeling of task
    D. evaluating concepts

46. A speech-language therapist works with an elementary student twice a week in the general education program. In the classroom, the therapist helps the student with speech and pragmatic language in the natural setting while participating in the activities. What model is this an example of?

    A. pull-out model
    B. inclusive model
    C. segregated model
    D. consultative model

47. Research conducted on positive behavior supports has shown that the MOST effective method of increasing appropriate behaviors in students with disabilities is

    A. creating a crisis management plan.
    B. utilizing a school-wide prevention.
    C. instructing targeted small groups.
    D. implementing individual interventions.

GO ON TO THE NEXT PAGE

48. Two existing federal laws that mandate that schools and IEP teams ensure LRE and FAPE for students with disabilities are

    A. 504 and IDEIA.
    B. ADA and IDEIA.
    C. NCLB and IDEIA.
    D. FERPA and IDEIA.

49. One of the organizations that covers the majority of disabilities and is recommended for professional membership is the

    A. CEC.
    B. APA.
    C. LDA.
    D. NAA.

50. The IEP process involves a comprehensive look at a student with a disability in order to properly develop a program to receive special education services. An important issue in responding to the needs of students is to be aware of the family's

    A. education level.
    B. economic status.
    C. cultural diversity.
    D. generational structure.

51. Collaboration is an effective model for general education teachers and special education teachers in addressing individual student needs and programs. Which of the following are tasks that require collaboration between these two disciplines?

    A. observations and therapeutic progress reports
    B. pre-referral interventions and IEP development
    C. related service plans and behavior interventions
    D. child study team meetings and special education testing

52. According to IDEIA, when the IEP team begins to develop goals for the student's educational program, the goals must be written for

    A. all of the areas listed in the present levels of performance.
    B. all of the subject areas in which the student is taking a class.
    C. only the areas that the student demonstrates a delay or deficit.
    D. only the areas that the parents request specific work be addressed.

53. One of the most effective methods of encouraging students to use appropriate and socially acceptable behaviors is the use of

    A. extinction.
    B. random consequences.
    C. rewards and acknowledgement.
    D. unexpected natural reinforcements.

54. A middle school student with mental retardation was placed by the principal in a self-contained program because the general education teachers were concerned and unsure of how to manage the student's language delays during academic instruction. The parents filed a complaint that serious procedural violations had been committed, which may cause harm to their child. If the case were to move forward, the courts would likely consider this action

    A. a denial of FAPE.
    B. a lack of related services.
    C. unlawful and impose employee fines.
    D. a mistake that may be corrected with parent instruction.

55. A child with seizures, who is deaf and confined to a wheelchair, receives services through special education under the category of Multiple Disabilities. This student requires specialized transportation to attend school and access services. In which section of the IEP should this service be included?

    A. objectives
    B. present levels
    C. modifications
    D. related services

56. An example of which type of measurement is the student's ability to present an oral report?

    A. behavior evaluation
    B. portfolio assessment
    C. summative evaluation
    D. performance assessment

57. Accountability in the schools is the primary purpose for the passage of the No Child Left Behind (NCLB) Act. What is the academic provision in this law that is so highly questioned for students with disabilities?

A. All students will be proficient in reading, writing, and math.

B. Students with disabilities are exempt from state standards testing.

C. Students with disabilities must receive services in inclusive classrooms.

D. All students are allowed some exceptions in reading and writing programs.

58. Teamwork is encouraged when working with students who have special needs to promote academic success. Identify the various types of teams that are prevalent in public school settings.

A. multidisciplinary, consultation, and coordination

B. intradisciplinary, interdisciplinary, and consultation

C. coordination, intradisciplinary, and transdisciplinary

D. multidisciplinary, interdisciplinary, and transdisciplinary

59. A widely utilized process for determining problematic behaviors and the environmental variables that may contribute to these behaviors is the use of the "ABC" technique, which represents

A. after, before, correct.

B. action, build, condition.

C. analyze, behave, categorize.

D. antecedent, behavior, consequence.

60. When a team is examining the relationship between special variables in the environment and the problem behaviors of a student with disabilities, the process of _____ is being conducted.

A. a behavior intervention plan

B. gathering standard testing data

C. a functional behavior assessment

D. an observable intervention strategy

Knowledge-Based Core Principles (0351) Practice Exam Answer Key

1.	D	31.	A
2.	C	32.	C
3.	D	33.	B
4.	D	34.	D
5.	A	35.	C
6.	A	36.	D
7.	D	37.	B
8.	A	38.	A
9.	B	39.	D
10.	B	40.	B
11.	C	41.	A
12.	B	42.	C
13.	C	43.	C
14.	A	44.	C
15.	D	45.	C
16.	B	46.	B
17.	A	47.	B
18.	B	48.	A
19.	A	49.	A
20.	B	50.	C
21.	D	51.	B
22.	A	52.	C
23.	C	53.	C
24.	D	54.	A
25.	A	55.	D
26.	D	56.	D
27.	B	57.	A
28.	B	58.	D
29.	B	59.	D
30.	A	60.	C

Answer Explanations for Knowledge-Based Core Principles (0351) Practice Exam

1. **D.** Only D is a **primary provision** of the six major provisions listed under IDEIA.

2. **C.** Evaluations that are nonbiased and conducted in the primary language are requirements under federal law and should reflect high reliability and validity. If evaluators follow the guidelines, students should not be unnecessarily placed in special education.

3. **D.** Although all are factors in a child's development of the social-emotional domain, the one that has the most impact is the environment. Family, gender, and siblings are all components of the environment.

4. **D.** Professional competence is an important aspect of being an educator. Staying involved in professional organizations, reading journals, attending conferences, and using research-based practices all lead to professional competence.

5. **A.** FERPA (Family Education Rights and Privacy Act) is a federal statute that pertains to the privacy rights of students and their parents. One of the most basic rights is to prevent unauthorized people from seeing the records. Only those professionals who have direct involvement with the student may have access. Juvenile authorities and auditors may inspect the records without parent permission. An education record includes files, documents, and other materials that contain information about a student and are maintained by the education agency.

6. **A.** Successful teacher collaboration is dependent on the amount of time that is available to both teachers for planning and developing the program.

7. **D.** It is an appropriate goal as it contains the required components. The goal is presented in measurable terms (increase visual recognition), and it can be assessed by the teacher using a specific measurement tool (Peabody Picture Vocabulary Test). It also includes the specific skill to be targeted (10 additional words added to current 30), the appropriate mastery of projected achievement (80 percent accuracy), the date for completion (by April), and specifically using a formal assessment (PPVT-standardized test).

8. **A.** In the *Mills v. Board of Education* case, the courts ruled that all children with disabilities have the right to receive appropriate and beneficial services in order to access their education regardless of the district's ability to pay. The Irving-Tatro case was about related service provisions involving medical care; the Zobrest case concerned a ruling for related services; and the Rowley case focused on the need for a sign language interpreter.

9. **B.** Services provided in speech therapy must fall under specific types of speech or language problems, which may include delays in expressive or receptive language, articulation, voice, and fluency.

10. **B.** Research has been conducted on student motivation for students with disabilities. The Skinner and Belmont study (1991) showed that an effective way to increase students' motivation to learn was to ensure that they understand the criteria for class assignments and the expectations for acceptable classroom behaviors.

11. **C.** Each of the options is a step in the IEP process. The annual review step is the point at which the IEP team will assess the progress of the student on the goals that were written.

12. **B.** Jean Piaget is considered the founder of this theory, which focuses on mental skill development and affects all other domains of learning.

13. **C.** People first language is the most appropriate manner in which to address or refer to an individual with a disability. People first language suggests the gender or the name of the person first and then the name of the disability.

14. **A.** Modeling is a successful intervention for students with behavior issues. This involves the demonstration of the appropriate behavior by another individual or a group so the student will pattern her behavior after the model. The best place to implement this strategy is in a natural setting.

15. **D.** The present levels of educational performance (PLEP) is a requirement for IEP development and necessary to develop goals. This is a description of the student's strengths and needs based on the assessments and pertinent information gathered.

16. **B.** When students begin reading instruction, the student who demonstrates delays in gaining reading skills alerts a teacher as to a potential learning disability.

17. A. In 1984 the case *Irving Independent School District v. Tatro* established an interpretation of the federal special education law regarding medical services. The results of this case forced the school to provide non-physician required medical services to allow a physically impaired student to attend school.

18. B. Under IDEIA, an FBA (Functional Behavior Assessment) is required once a student violates a code of conduct in school, and it results in the development of a BIP (Behavior Intervention Plan). If the student has a BIP in place, then the team must reassess the plan using the FBA model and make the appropriate changes.

19. A. The functional curriculum is an excellent choice for students with mental retardation. It helps students develop the knowledge and skills to support their independence in school settings, community environments, work situations, personal times, social situations, and daily living situations.

20. B. Students with emotional disturbances generally have problems with affective behaviors and need interventions and therapy to learn to self-manage them. Affective behaviors are the outward manifestation of the student's emotional state.

21. D. Community-based instruction is a highly recommended research-based method that includes hands-on, interactive opportunities in vocational and life skills training. It is wise to begin this instruction around the age of 10 or 12, especially for students with severe disabilities. As the students age, using this instruction for extended periods and more often during the high school years offers the direct instruction and guidance needed to generalize the skills.

22. A. The Technology Assistance Act provides support to statewide programs across the country for individuals with disabilities of all ages in the area of assistive technology.

23. C. Students identified with Behavioral Disorder/Emotional Disturbance exhibit inappropriate internalizing and externalizing behaviors, atypical emotions to common situations, and a lack of skills necessary to develop positive relationships.

24. D. Students with disabilities who become independent and function appropriately in the community as adults have learned to generalize the skills learned without prompts.

25. A. Transition plans should include a statement that describes the responsibility of community interagencies who may not only support the student while in school, but also implement and provide continued services when the student graduates.

26. D. The summative evaluation is used to determine how well a student is achieving and to also make decisions about the teacher's instruction; whereas the other three choices make determinations about the student's abilities only.

27. B. A child with a delay in pragmatics is having difficulty with the functional use of language, such as that used to engage in conversation. The child may demonstrate problems making eye contact, using nonverbal behaviors, and taking turns speaking with others. Children with problems in pragmatics are often also served in categories such as autism, mental retardation, learning disabilities, and language delayed.

28. B. In a study by Vaughn (2003), it was determined that effective reading outcomes are critically impacted by the grouping of students.

29. B. An ITP (Individual Transition Plan) is mandated for students (16 and older) who have disabilities and are receiving services in the special education program. The ITP team must follow specific guidelines for its structure and implementation. The areas that must be addressed include, but are not limited to: domestic, community, leisure, and vocational skills.

30. A. The category of learning disabilities accounted for more than 50 percent of all students served in special education programs in 2001. It accounted for more than twice the number of students receiving speech and language services and more than all the other categories combined.

31. A. Most students diagnosed with Autism appear to be isolated due to the communication issues and lack of social competence. They often avoid people and are generally not able to express or understand emotions.

32. C. There is a high incidence of students with disabilities receiving speech and language services in addition to the services for the primary disability. Students identified according to these categories may receive related services for speech and language therapy: learning disability, hearing impairment, mental retardation, vision impairment, autism, and traumatic brain injury.

33. **B.** The category of Other Health Impaired is defined as an individual who exhibits limited strength, vitality, or alertness, and adversely affects the student's educational performance, such as diabetes and epilepsy.

34. **D.** Behavior self-management is a critical skill for all students with disabilities. Even the students with the most severe disabilities are capable of managing some of their own behaviors. The other options are considered study skills, but not every student with a disability needs these particular skills.

35. **C.** At this time, the student's plan "to fix cars and work at a gas station" is only an area of interest. Obtaining a job at a gas station would not be the first step, as it could set the student up for failure. The community college mechanics class may be too difficult at this time, unless accompanied by an adult and tutored through the course. The ideal would be to place the student in the high school course with a peer to see whether the interest continues and to observe the skill development. Since this is a student with mild mental retardation, an inclusive setting would most likely be a good first step.

36. **D.** The medical research has determined that there are no links that show a connection of the emerging autism cases to immunizations or vaccinations. They have found links to the other items listed: genetics, neurology, and the environment, as well as stating that the condition is based on abnormal brain development and multiple biological causes.

37. **B.** Students who are being evaluated for possible learning disabilities are assessed in the areas of reading, written expression, and mathematics as they are most likely to demonstrate a gap between achievement and ability in one or more of these three areas. The other categories mentioned demonstrate delays in these areas, but not a gap in achievement levels.

38. **A.** This student's diagnosis falls into the area of support for persons with disabilities under Section 504 of the Rehabilitation Act. According to this scenario, the student does not appear to be having academic problems, so the accommodations would only be necessary with regard to the medical condition.

39. **D.** The concept of inclusion evolved in the early 1990s as a result of the federal law, IDEA. The concept was described in the law, but it took a couple of years for the idea to be clearly understood and even palpable to many educators. It is still a highly debated issue even today.

40. **B.** Most Orthopedic Impairments are related to illnesses, diseases, accidents, injuries, or traumas to the body, and some are considered temporary, but students with an orthopedic impairment may still need the services of special education due to the impact on their educational performance.

41. **A.** Explicit instruction and implicit instruction are used with students who have disabilities. It depends on the student's functioning level and the subject area or the task to be completed on which of these two are used. In explicit instruction, the teacher provides the knowledge and supports the learning process. In implicit instruction, the focus is on the student being an active and involved learner who constructs knowledge by using previously learned knowledge.

42. **C.** Under federal law, **the continuum of educational placements** is a critical piece of the educational program development. The team must determine the student's needs, write a plan for the types of services, and then decide where the services will occur. The list of options moves from least restrictive to most restrictive.

43. **C.** The transdisciplinary team approach is considered to be a very effective method in addressing student programming, yet the most difficult to implement. A transdisciplinary team shares roles and cross disciplines on all aspects of a student's program.

44. **C.** A key factor in the prevention of disabilities is the early proper prenatal care for mothers-to-be. If pregnant mothers follow a regime of guided medical care, receive proper nutrition, and are not exposed to toxins during pregnancy, many types of disabilities could be prevented.

45. **C.** One of the essential elements of instruction is the modeling of the task to be completed by the students.

46. **B.** When therapy is provided in the general education classroom during typically scheduled activities in the natural setting, this is a form of inclusion. It is recommended under federal law to provide services with non-disabled children and is a sample of therapeutic best practices.

47. **B.** The one method found through research to be most successful in helping students learn self-discipline is the utilization of a school-wide prevention approach. For students, it is a consistent and understandable way to learn behaviors in a natural setting as they are modeled by peers and reinforced by staff.

48. A. All the acronyms represent current federal laws that have mandates affecting individuals with disabilities. The two that require IEP teams to address LRE (least restrictive environment) and FAPE (free and appropriate public education) for children with disabilities are IDEIA (IDEA-2004) and Section 504. ADA (Americans with Disabilities Act) refers to accommodations for employment opportunities and public access while FERPA (Family Education Rights and Privacy Act) focuses on privacy rights.

49. A. The CEC (Council for Exceptional Children) is a highly rated professional organization with divisions for many of the separate categories of disabilities. Many special education professionals are members of this national organization.

50. C. Students enter schools coming from very diverse backgrounds, and students with disabilities are accepted in different ways by their families depending on the culture. Educators must be culturally aware of all students they work with, but cultural diversity is a powerful aspect in the development of an IEP and the implementation of interventions. Some of the factors related to a student's disability may not be embraced by some cultures, so educators should carefully address the cultural diversity of the family when working with students with disabilities.

51. B. When working with students who have disabilities, a best practice is the use of collaborative efforts between the general education teacher and the special education teacher. Two specific areas in which collaborating is effective is during the pre-referral intervention stage when the special education teacher can support and help suggest interventions that may work for the child and during IEP development if the child proceeds with special education testing and placement.

52. C. Under IDEIA, an IEP team is required to write goals for the student's deficit areas. A present level of performance statement is mandated as a component of an IEP, and it will drive the areas for the target skills included in the goals.

53. C. Delivering immediate responses and acknowledgement (rewards) for acting appropriately and socially acceptably is very effective in supporting positive behavior management with students identified with disabilities.

54. A. Under the federal special education law, students with disabilities are entitled to a **free and appropriate public education** (FAPE), which means that all of the provisions of the law and the procedural guidelines must be followed. Placement requires the consensus of the student's IEP team, which includes the parents. The decision is based on the student's present levels of performance and least restrictive environment. Parents may file complaints that could proceed to the judicial system when procedural violations occur.

55. D. Special transportation is considered a related service under federal law on an IEP. If this student requires transportation to access the special education services outlined in the individual education program, it must be added to the IEP as a related service.

56. D. A performance assessment is an informal measure used by teachers to assess a student's ability to complete a task specific to a topic or subject area

57. A. The provisions included in the No Child Left Behind Act of 2001 are established for compliance of ALL children, whether they are identified with a disability or not. This law requires that all children across the country will be proficient, at their grade level, in reading, writing, and mathematics.

58. D. Professionals in special education utilize three models of teams: multidisciplinary, interdisciplinary, and transdisciplinary. The most recommended is the interdisciplinary, as it is the most effective when planning and implementing student programs.

59. D. The ABC Analysis technique stands for *antecedent*, *behavior*, and *consequence* and is a widely known method for creating a student's behavior management plan.

60. C. The FBA (functional behavior assessment) is mandated under federal special education law. It is a process whereby the team may assess a student's behaviors in the environment and determine how events and factors contribute to the inappropriate behavior.

Answer Grid Application of Core Principles across Categories of Disabilities (0352) Practice Exam

1 Ⓐ Ⓑ Ⓒ Ⓓ	26 Ⓐ Ⓑ Ⓒ Ⓓ
2 Ⓐ Ⓑ Ⓒ Ⓓ	27 Ⓐ Ⓑ Ⓒ Ⓓ
3 Ⓐ Ⓑ Ⓒ Ⓓ	28 Ⓐ Ⓑ Ⓒ Ⓓ
4 Ⓐ Ⓑ Ⓒ Ⓓ	29 Ⓐ Ⓑ Ⓒ Ⓓ
5 Ⓐ Ⓑ Ⓒ Ⓓ	30 Ⓐ Ⓑ Ⓒ Ⓓ
6 Ⓐ Ⓑ Ⓒ Ⓓ	31 Ⓐ Ⓑ Ⓒ Ⓓ
7 Ⓐ Ⓑ Ⓒ Ⓓ	32 Ⓐ Ⓑ Ⓒ Ⓓ
8 Ⓐ Ⓑ Ⓒ Ⓓ	33 Ⓐ Ⓑ Ⓒ Ⓓ
9 Ⓐ Ⓑ Ⓒ Ⓓ	34 Ⓐ Ⓑ Ⓒ Ⓓ
10 Ⓐ Ⓑ Ⓒ Ⓓ	35 Ⓐ Ⓑ Ⓒ Ⓓ
11 Ⓐ Ⓑ Ⓒ Ⓓ	36 Ⓐ Ⓑ Ⓒ Ⓓ
12 Ⓐ Ⓑ Ⓒ Ⓓ	37 Ⓐ Ⓑ Ⓒ Ⓓ
13 Ⓐ Ⓑ Ⓒ Ⓓ	38 Ⓐ Ⓑ Ⓒ Ⓓ
14 Ⓐ Ⓑ Ⓒ Ⓓ	39 Ⓐ Ⓑ Ⓒ Ⓓ
15 Ⓐ Ⓑ Ⓒ Ⓓ	40 Ⓐ Ⓑ Ⓒ Ⓓ
16 Ⓐ Ⓑ Ⓒ Ⓓ	41 Ⓐ Ⓑ Ⓒ Ⓓ
17 Ⓐ Ⓑ Ⓒ Ⓓ	42 Ⓐ Ⓑ Ⓒ Ⓓ
18 Ⓐ Ⓑ Ⓒ Ⓓ	43 Ⓐ Ⓑ Ⓒ Ⓓ
19 Ⓐ Ⓑ Ⓒ Ⓓ	44 Ⓐ Ⓑ Ⓒ Ⓓ
20 Ⓐ Ⓑ Ⓒ Ⓓ	45 Ⓐ Ⓑ Ⓒ Ⓓ
21 Ⓐ Ⓑ Ⓒ Ⓓ	46 Ⓐ Ⓑ Ⓒ Ⓓ
22 Ⓐ Ⓑ Ⓒ Ⓓ	47 Ⓐ Ⓑ Ⓒ Ⓓ
23 Ⓐ Ⓑ Ⓒ Ⓓ	48 Ⓐ Ⓑ Ⓒ Ⓓ
24 Ⓐ Ⓑ Ⓒ Ⓓ	49 Ⓐ Ⓑ Ⓒ Ⓓ
25 Ⓐ Ⓑ Ⓒ Ⓓ	50 Ⓐ Ⓑ Ⓒ Ⓓ

Read each of the following questions and select the BEST answer. Fill in your choice on the answer bubble sheet provided.

1. A valuable source for providing information about a student's behaviors is

   A. peer opinions.
   B. office records.
   C. parent observations.
   D. a principal's contacts.

2. When the special education teacher at the middle school meets weekly with the general education language arts teacher to discuss specific strategies and the accommodations for a student with a learning disability, they are participating in a _____ model.

   A. resource
   B. itinerant
   C. co-teaching
   D. consultation

3. A speech/language pathologist may use certain assessment methods on a student with possible deficits. Which of the following might be included in this evaluation process?

   A. examining class test scores and interviewing peers
   B. reviewing course grades and speaking with family members
   C. completing a behavior rating scale and conducting observations
   D. gathering language samples and administering standardized tests

4. Reading skill development for students with disabilities can be enhanced by the use of visual cues as these promote

   A. word recognition.
   B. word comprehension.
   C. proper word spellings.
   D. knowledge of word order.

5. When a general education teacher and a special education teacher work together to plan lessons, gather materials, and instruct in the same room, this is an example of

   A. mentorship.
   B. co-teaching.
   C. alternative teaching.
   D. consultative programming.

6. Which of the following is an example of an accommodation that may be used for a student with disabilities during the implementation of the educational program?

   A. study skills training
   B. exemption from certain tasks
   C. limited number of math problems
   D. provide different task, but same concept

7. At an IEP meeting on an elementary student with mental retardation, the general education classroom teacher is concerned that this student should not have to take the state standard high stakes test with the rest of the students. The special education teacher should

   A. ask the parents to sign an exempt form.
   B. eliminate the student from the assessment process.
   C. provide a paraprofessional to help in taking the test.
   D. explain that this student needs to take the test with accommodations.

GO ON TO THE NEXT PAGE

8. Research has created a list of competencies believed to be appropriate for paraprofessionals to be successful in school settings. One of the first tasks that a supervisor should do with paraprofessionals is to

   A. explain their role.
   B. establish a training module.
   C. observe them with students.
   D. evaluate their work in the classroom.

9. Educators rely on the research conducted on individuals with disabilities. Which type is the most reliable and informational for classroom use?

   A. transitional studies
   B. empirical-based research
   C. studies of basic principles
   D. knowledge-based research

10. An effective method to use in developing classroom rules and expectations is to

    A. involve the students.
    B. use a standardized set.
    C. establish common guidelines.
    D. base them on core knowledge.

11. Which of the following is a step in direct instruction?

    A. no homework
    B. teacher lecture
    C. guided practice
    D. student grouping

12. A high school teacher is in the first year of teaching and is having a difficult time managing students in the science lab. The students tend to get into things they should not, are disruptive during the lesson, and are not focusing on the activities. The teacher is frustrated and asked a mentor to observe a couple of the science lab classes to determine the problem that may exist. What was the first thing the mentor asked the teacher?

    A. Did you create an alphabetic seating chart?
    B. Do you have classroom procedures established?
    C. Do you have too many students enrolled in class?
    D. Did you purchase the better materials in the catalog?

13. A paraprofessional who works in an elementary inclusive model with students who are identified with moderate mental retardation may have several duties and multiple tasks to complete daily. Select one of the following to BEST describe a task to be handled by this paraprofessional.

    A. Supervise a student teacher.
    B. Assist students with grooming care.
    C. Select the reading materials for students.
    D. Help parents choose an after school program.

14. A general education teacher is concerned about a child in the fourth-grade class who is having problems in reading. The teacher has referred the student for evaluation for special education services. During this process, what information should the teacher gather to share with the team?

    A. grades in all subjects and scores on all classroom tests
    B. behavior records that demonstrate social skill level
    C. performance levels in class and any interventions provided
    D. previous year's grade level work samples and parent comments

15. Read the following items and select the one that best describes a type of modification used with students who have disabilities.

    A. different task
    B. time extension
    C. preferential seating
    D. amplification system

16. Select three of the BEST traits that paraprofessionals should have in order to work with students who have disabilities in a school setting.

   A. happy, smart, concerned
   B. flexible, motivated, patient
   C. wise, independent, groomed
   D. sympathetic, clever, relaxed

17. For a student with a disability, which of the following types of assessment measurements would provide the BEST information about the student's independent living skills?

   A. a standardized test
   B. a functional assessment
   C. an alternative assessment
   D. a curriculum-based assessment

18. A special education teacher has been asked by a supervisor to observe a student in a general education classroom who is struggling with behavior problems. What tool(s) would be useful as this teacher assesses the student in this situation?

   A. functional behavior assessment
   B. response generalization ratings
   C. behavior checklist and observation
   D. cumulative folder information and test scores

19. Before a student turns 16, the IEP team should discuss options for the student's future and develop a plan that guides the student from school to adult life. This is called an Individualized

   A. Education Plan.
   B. Transition Plan.
   C. Graduation Plan.
   D. Family Service Plan.

20. As the implementation of a student's program begins, who is responsible for providing specific information about the goals, along with the accommodations and modifications to the student's teachers?

   A. the education team leader
   B. the special education teacher
   C. the special education secretary
   D. the speech and language therapist

21. A fifth-grade teacher is preparing for parent-teacher conferences and has created a system in which student work, such as reports, art projects, and math worksheets, could be placed in a small decorated box for each child to share with parents. What type of assessment is used to deliver concrete examples of the student's performance?

   A. checklist assessment
   B. portfolio assessment
   C. task-based assessment
   D. standardized assessment

22. A high school student with severe multiple disabilities is three years from aging out of school and special education programming. Which of the following will be of major concern for the parents after the student no longer can access school support?

   A. post-high school education
   B. placement in a group home setting
   C. structured employment opportunities
   D. involvement in the community recreation activities

23. A term used in special education that is related to behavior modification and behavior management and means *to decrease the probability of a response by withholding a previously reinforcing stimulus* is called

   A. satiation.
   B. feedback.
   C. extinction.
   D. punishment.

GO ON TO THE NEXT PAGE

24. A student with mild cerebral palsy needs assistance in order to get outside to the bus at the end of each school day. The bus stops just outside the door of the classroom, but the student has problems with opening and closing the doors in the school. Which of the following is the most natural accommodation that the team could use?

A. Ask a peer to walk with the student.
B. Request that the parents pick up the child.
C. Hire a paraprofessional to guide the student.
D. Have the teacher take the child early to the bus.

25. Since feedback is an important aspect of learning, which of the following types of feedback is MOST critical to students?

A. one that is accompanied by rewards
B. the type that compares students to peers
C. the kind that delivers corrective criticism
D. one that helps students notice their own progress

26. Teachers often utilize informal assessments in the classroom to track student progress in order to change instructional delivery and content to suit learner needs. Which of the following is the BEST selection for an age-appropriate, second-grade activity to check spontaneous writing skills?

A. an essay test
B. a daily journal
C. a short answer quiz
D. a sentence building worksheet

27. According to studies on classroom management, an essential component of instruction time is during the transition from one lesson or activity to the next. The transition period is a time when

A. academic levels soar.
B. attention spans improve.
C. disruptive behaviors occur.
D. students can rest and relax.

28. An effective instructional strategy used with students who have second language needs is

A. chained responses.
B. contingent teaching.
C. cooperative learning.
D. adult to child tutoring.

29. Use of standardized achievement tests is common practice in schools across the country. However, many professionals are concerned about the scores that students get and how those are interpreted. What is the primary reason that teachers do not like to use these tests?

A. It is too thorough and detailed for elementary students.
B. Students may be evaluated on content they have not been taught.
C. The test shows only the progress of content areas for high school students.
D. Students are not allowed modifications and accommodations on these tests.

30. A fourth-grade general education classroom teacher has five students with learning disabilities and four students who are at-risk for learning problems. The teacher began using advance organizers and concept maps for some lessons and found this to be helpful to these students. This strategy is used in

A. goal setting.
B. pre-teaching.
C. lesson review.
D. word retrieval.

31. The delivery rate of teachers has been studied for effectiveness, and it has been determined that the method that reduces behavior issues in the classroom is when information is presented

A. at a brisk pace.
B. in large amounts.
C. in limited amounts.
D. at a slow repetitive pace.

32. Under the law, assessments for student placement in special education must be non-discriminatory. What is the best practice for an evaluator to ensure that all students have the most valid and reliable testing situation?

A. Use multiple measures.
B. Explain directions twice.
C. Allow parent observation.
D. Administer a primary exam.

33. When a teacher begins to work with a culturally diverse population, what should this teacher do to provide these students with a successful learning environment?

    A. promote cultural awareness
    B. request a change of placement
    C. work with an ethnic co-teacher
    D. de-emphasize the cultural differences

34. After a student is identified with a disability and an IEP is about to be developed, what is the area that teachers should focus on from the assessment to prepare for future learning?

    A. the characteristics of the disability
    B. the impact of environmental factors
    C. the discrepancies found in each evaluation
    D. the interpretation of the instructional implications

35. Inclusion is a _____ in which students with disabilities are educated with typical peers to the maximum extent possible.

    A. setting
    B. program
    C. philosophy
    D. general class

36. When a team reviews evaluation results, discusses the implications, and develops goals and plans for programming and services, they are practicing

    A. reliability focus.
    B. proficient associations.
    C. integrative management.
    D. positive decision-making.

37. The special education teacher at the elementary school is preparing to write progress reports for all of the students with disabilities to be sent home with the first report card. What should the teacher remember MOST when writing these reports for parents?

    A. the parents' education
    B. the type of disability
    C. the language of the home
    D. the characteristics of the child

38. Which of the following types of curriculum would be the MOST appropriate for the instruction of students with moderate to severe mental retardation?

    A. social skills
    B. career skills
    C. pre-academic skills
    D. functional life skills

39. A high school student identified with a physical disability, and placed in the general education classroom, receives special education services from the occupational therapist and the speech therapist. Due to the motor problems and communication issues, this student uses computer programs to support instruction. This use of assistive technology is considered

    A. a related service.
    B. physical therapy.
    C. an inclusion service.
    D. an alternative service.

40. A middle school student with moderate mental retardation has a severe speech impairment that makes about 80 percent of the student's speech unintelligible to a new listener. To help the student communicate more effectively in the regular classroom, the special education teacher may suggest the use of

    A. a pad of paper.
    B. some sign language.
    C. an interpreter or translator.
    D. an assistive technology device.

41. A science teacher who has students with disabilities in the classroom considers the needs of students when presenting a lesson. This teacher includes some strategies that are helpful to struggling students, such as giving hints and providing suggestions or ideas to students. This strategy is called

    A. coaching.
    B. modeling.
    C. pre-teaching.
    D. scaffolding.

GO ON TO THE NEXT PAGE

42. Students who have deficits in utilizing written expression, such as those identified as learning disabled or with autism, may need the support of

   A. a notetaker.

   B. an interpreter.

   C. a tape recorder.

   D. a word processor.

43. Assistive technology devices and equipment are described in two categories:

   A. high- and low-tech

   B. small and large tools

   C. fast and slow apparatus

   D. strong and slight systems

44. The philosophy of _____ in an educational setting establishes an environment of respect and allows teachers to be responsive to all learners.

   A. peer tutoring

   B. universal design

   C. direct instruction

   D. authentic learning

45. Under federal law, the relationship between special variables in the environment and the problem behaviors must be observed and documented. This is the process of conducting a(n)

   A. annual review of placement.

   B. state standards academic exam.

   C. functional behavior assessment.

   D. therapeutic intervention strategy.

46. A sixth-grade student with mental retardation demonstrates difficulty performing daily skills necessary for independence. Those skills include brushing teeth, toileting, general grooming, and ordering a drink at a fast food restaurant. These skills are referred to as

   A. learned behavior skills.

   B. adaptive behavior skills.

   C. cognitive behavior skills.

   D. independent behavior skills.

Read the following case study and then answer the multiple choice questions that follow. Select your answer and fill in the bubble sheet provided.

Case Study

A 16-year-old student with specific learning disabilities wants to attend school after graduating high school. The student has demonstrated difficulty with the academic program since the learning disabilities are significant in the areas of reading, written expression, and mathematics. The student works hard to overcome the issues with academics, and the IEP team established a schedule for assistance with peer tutors and the use of a resource center in the library to get help with assignments. The student is very proficient on computers and is interested in watching the computer math competitions in the math club. In spite of the severe learning disability, this student has done well with supports and accommodations.

The student has performed well in the vocational training programs and shows an interest in art and music. This student's drawings have been placed in the local art shows and been awarded placement awards several times. The student has also joined the after school auto club to learn more about general auto maintenance.

The parents have been consistently involved in the child's educational program, and this student is well supported in the home. Parents agree that the student should go on to a post-graduate educational facility and would like for their child to study landscaping since he works part time at the local nursery.

During the transition team meeting, the parents suggest that they could call some of the local community colleges to get information about attending school. The counselor suggested that he could go online and research any special supports that would be helpful to this student for academic remediation. The community agency representative decided that she could gather information about other colleges in the state.

47. Based on the information, what is an area that the team should include on this transition plan to aid the student with the post high school transition?

    A. Improve self-advocacy skills.

    B. Seek community adult agencies.

    C. Read a book on college placement.

    D. Prepare the student for a technology school.

48. Which of the following would be the most logical programming for this student in a post high school setting?

    A. art and computers

    B. math and music

    C. landscaping

    D. mechanics

49. What should the community agency do to assist this student with choosing an area of study which would be supportive of a future career?

    A. Find the student a job in a field of choice.

    B. Conduct a vocational assessment.

    C. Send the student to a job fair.

    D. Provide work training.

50. What should the goals and activities for the individual transition plan be based upon?

    A. a vocational assessment

    B. progress report information

    C. student's standardized scores

    D. student's interests and preferences

Application of Core Principles across Categories of Disabilities (0352) Practice Exam Answer Key

1. C		26. B	
2. D		27. C	
3. D		28. C	
4. A		29. B	
5. B		30. B	
6. A		31. A	
7. D		32. A	
8. A		33. A	
9. B		34. D	
10. A		35. C	
11. C		36. D	
12. B		37. C	
13. B		38. D	
14. C		39. A	
15. A		40. D	
16. B		41. A	
17. B		42. D	
18. C		43. A	
19. B		44. B	
20. B		45. C	
21. B		46. B	
22. B		47. A	
23. C		48. A	
24. A		49. B	
25. D		50. D	

Answer Explanations for Application of Core Principles across Categories of Disabilities (0352) Practice Exam

1. **C.** Parents make strong observations of their children, since they are with them more often in varied and natural settings. Evaluators should be sure to obtain parent observations and inventories when assessing a student in special education.

2. **D.** The consultation model is one of support from special education personnel to general education personnel who work with students with disabilities. They meet often to discuss specific students, the strategies that work, and the accommodations that are needed.

3. **D.** A speech-language pathologist who is evaluating a student for possible deficits and placement in special education would use standardized assessment tools and may gather a language sample from the student during a typical school activity in a natural environment.

4. **A.** For students who are having problems learning to read and remember words, a visual cue, which is a shape or visual configuration, will allow the reader to recognize a word or group of words automatically.

5. **B.** Teachers who work together from different disciplines in the planning, preparation, and delivery of lessons are practicing co-teaching. In a co-teaching model, the special education teacher who works with the general education teacher in the same classroom helps all students and not just those placed in special education.

6. **A.** Only study skills training is considered an accommodation, or a support, while all others are examples of modifications, which are changes to the program or content of curriculum.

7. **D.** According to special education law, a student with disabilities MUST participate in the same state and district testing as nondisabled students, unless the IEP team decides the child is exempt or should take an alternate test. However, this only occurs for the most severe students, an average of 1 percent of the population. Students with disabilities are allowed to have the same accommodations for test taking as for classroom work.

8. **A.** To develop a positive work environment for paraprofessionals, the supervisory teacher, and the students it is important to identify and explain their role and duties as related to the position of paraprofessional. The paraprofessional should clearly understand the expectations, daily duties, and responsibilities for students in order to perform appropriately.

9. **B.** When educators need to find research on areas of interest they should search for empirical-based studies, as these provide the most realistic view and outcomes of students with disabilities.

10. **A.** Rules need a positive format that is easy for students to understand and remember. No more than five major rules should be established in a classroom. When students are involved in the decisions about the rules, they become more active and involved.

11. **C.** The method of direct instruction incorporates three key components: sequential instruction through teacher demonstration; guided practice check understanding; and feedback for work effort and completion.

12. **B.** The first important step in the establishment of teacher control and management in a classroom is to establish clear, concise, and easy to remember classroom procedures and rules. If those are not developed and posted, the students will use the behaviors they choose.

13. **B.** A paraprofessional is a staff member who, under a teacher's supervision, provides services in various school settings. A paraprofessional should be directed by a teacher and not supervise others, work directly with parents, or select academic materials.

14. **C.** To help the team through the referral and assessment processes, the teacher should share information pertinent to the abilities related to the student's academic performance. Providing the team with performance levels, through work samples, tests, and grades, as well as implemented interventions and how those worked for the student would help the team proceed with possible identification and placement for services.

15. A. Assigning a task that is different than the task for non-disabled students is a type of modification, as it changes the instruction. The other options are all types of accommodations that do not change the instruction, but support it.

16. B. These are all positive characteristics; however, flexibility, motivation, and patience will aid students with disabilities and support the classroom programs more than the others listed.

17. B. Using a functional assessment, especially for those students with more severe disabilities, aids the team in examining the student's independent living skills levels across various typical settings.

18. C. Using a checklist will allow the teacher to also observe the situation while using a simple recording method to establish behavior criteria, such as frequency, severity, rate, and so on. The checklist will guide the observation while the teacher watches the student and takes notes to later write a narrative description of the situation.

19. B. An Individualized Transition Plan is mandated as a component of the IEP for all students receiving special education services by age 16.

20. B. It is the role of most special education teachers to act as the case manager for students with disabilities. The special education teacher should provide copies of the IEP, a list of accommodations and modifications, and answer any questions for all of the student's general education teachers.

21. B. A portfolio assessment is an excellent way for a teacher to share information with parents about a student's performance in class. This is a collection of student work samples during a specific period of time.

22. B. The most concerning issue for parents of children with severe disabilities is the placement of their child outside of the home. However, parents know that they will not always be available to care for their child as they get older and it is the parents who are responsible for making the arrangements and following through as it is a personal family decision. The other items listed are important to a transition plan, but services are available, and the team can make decisions and arrangements for these services.

23. C. Extinction is a behavior technique used with students to eliminate the inappropriate behavior by taking away the influencing stimulus.

24. A. The most natural accommodation is for a peer to walk with the child to assist with opening and closing doors. The peer would need some training and not be expected to perform any tasks or provide physical support. The other options are possible but would not be the first considerations.

25. D. Feedback that aids students in noticing their own progress, delivered in a positive way, can help them develop self-esteem and encourage them to remain active and motivated toward learning.

26. B. All of these answers could be used in second grade to check writing skills, but the best selection for an informal assessment to determine the level of natural and spontaneous writing skills is through a daily task such as journal writing.

27. C. Techniques implemented to address activity and lesson transitions are very important. Smooth transitions help the learners remain engaged, but disorganized transitions increase disruptive behaviors.

28. C. Research shows that when students work together, they improve their own skills and those of their peers. A cooperative learning situation is especially beneficial for second language learners, as the instruction is structured, and students all gain academic knowledge and improve social skills.

29. B. Standardized achievement tests are written by companies with a focus on general subjects and only a limited number of questions related to content. It is a concern of many teachers that the evaluation would examine material not covered and, therefore, not show a realistic picture of student achievement.

30. B. Pre-teaching assists students with learning new concepts and vocabulary. The strategy of using advance organizers and concept maps is part of the pre-teaching process and is particularly helpful to students with learning disabilities.

31. A. Research shows that instruction provided at a brisk pace gains more attention from students and, therefore, minimizes behavior problems, and students gain more from the instruction.

32. **A.** Using multiple measures is a recommended best practice in order to obtain valid data from the initial evaluation. It is a good practice for special education professionals to administer multiple tests through different evaluators in different settings.

33. **A.** There are many ways that a teacher can promote cultural awareness to enhance the instruction in the classroom and enrich the learning environment. Bringing in speakers, asking for family members to share information, and setting up activities that emphasize various cultures all add to the education of the students and help them in embracing differences.

34. **D.** Federal law requires the interpretation of assessment results by a qualified person. It should include how the results of the evaluation impact the student's education. From this information, a team can create goals and develop the IEP.

35. **C.** Inclusion is a philosophy encouraged by the federal law for students with disabilities. The idea is to educate students with disabilities as much as possible with non-disabled students in the general education setting.

36. **D.** Regarding decision-making in IEP teams, certain guidelines ensure this happens in a positive and student-oriented manner. The purpose of a team is to collaboratively focus on the student's needs through evaluations and create an appropriate educational plan that will offer benefit to the student.

37. **C.** The teacher should be very conscious of the diversity of the students on the caseload and make every effort to prepare progress reports respectful of the language and the culture of the family. Some reports may need translation into another language.

38. **D.** Students with moderate to severe mental retardation generally need instruction in the functional life skills, which focus on independence, everyday activities, employment skills, self-direction, and recreation.

39. **A.** To improve the instructional program for this student, assistive technology is necessary to compensate for motor and communication deficits. A student is generally assessed for assistive technology and the results shared in the present levels of educational performance, while the service is added to the related service section of the IEP.

40. **D.** Assistive technology devices (augmentative communication devices and alternative devices) are essential for students with severe speech impairments as it promotes communication so the student becomes more independent.

41. **A.** Several effective strategies support the acquisition of knowledge for students with special needs. Coaching guides students into thinking about what they are learning and helping them become more involved.

42. **D.** Word processing software is available for use in classrooms on personal computers for students with disabilities. It provides the added support to the learning process and for completing assignments when the disability is a barrier.

43. **A.** The devices considered as assistive technology are described as being high-tech or low-tech. The high-tech are more complicated and usually have the need for power, such as a computer. The low-tech are more simple, such as a pencil grip or a grabber for picking up items.

44. **B.** The concept of *universal design* is in the creation of an educational environment designed so students with diverse needs will have meaningful access to curriculum. Teachers are more flexible with instructional strategies, methods, and materials.

45. **C.** An FBA (functional behavior assessment) mandated under federal law is used to assess student behaviors based on an observation of performance in the environment and by determining how the environmental factors contribute to the behavior.

46. **B.** Adaptive behavior skills are those that focus on daily living skills required to function independently. These may include self-care skills and social skills, as well as functional academics and leisure-time activities.

47. **A.** It appears that the parents, the agency representative, and the counselor are performing the tasks that this seemingly bright and capable student can do. The student should learn self-advocacy skills, so the student may perform at a more independent level. Instruction in self-advocacy would be a valuable addition to this plan.

48. **A.** The student appears to be most competent and highly interested in the areas of art and computers, so these would be the best selections as there is a pattern of success. The student does not do well in math, and his interest is more directed at the computer aspect. Mechanics is only a basic interest and landscaping is the parents' choice.

49. **B.** Vocational assessments provide information about an individual's skills and preferences which help to determine the most suitable career choices.

50. **D.** An essential part of a transition plan is to figure out what the student wants for the future. This can be done by asking for interest areas and preferences or conducting a vocational assessment in which results would suggest these areas.

Answer Grid for Preschool/Early Childhood (0690) Practice Exam

1 Ⓐ Ⓑ Ⓒ Ⓓ	41 Ⓐ Ⓑ Ⓒ Ⓓ	81 Ⓐ Ⓑ Ⓒ Ⓓ
2 Ⓐ Ⓑ Ⓒ Ⓓ	42 Ⓐ Ⓑ Ⓒ Ⓓ	82 Ⓐ Ⓑ Ⓒ Ⓓ
3 Ⓐ Ⓑ Ⓒ Ⓓ	43 Ⓐ Ⓑ Ⓒ Ⓓ	83 Ⓐ Ⓑ Ⓒ Ⓓ
4 Ⓐ Ⓑ Ⓒ Ⓓ	44 Ⓐ Ⓑ Ⓒ Ⓓ	84 Ⓐ Ⓑ Ⓒ Ⓓ
5 Ⓐ Ⓑ Ⓒ Ⓓ	45 Ⓐ Ⓑ Ⓒ Ⓓ	85 Ⓐ Ⓑ Ⓒ Ⓓ
6 Ⓐ Ⓑ Ⓒ Ⓓ	46 Ⓐ Ⓑ Ⓒ Ⓓ	86 Ⓐ Ⓑ Ⓒ Ⓓ
7 Ⓐ Ⓑ Ⓒ Ⓓ	47 Ⓐ Ⓑ Ⓒ Ⓓ	87 Ⓐ Ⓑ Ⓒ Ⓓ
8 Ⓐ Ⓑ Ⓒ Ⓓ	48 Ⓐ Ⓑ Ⓒ Ⓓ	88 Ⓐ Ⓑ Ⓒ Ⓓ
9 Ⓐ Ⓑ Ⓒ Ⓓ	49 Ⓐ Ⓑ Ⓒ Ⓓ	89 Ⓐ Ⓑ Ⓒ Ⓓ
10 Ⓐ Ⓑ Ⓒ Ⓓ	50 Ⓐ Ⓑ Ⓒ Ⓓ	90 Ⓐ Ⓑ Ⓒ Ⓓ
11 Ⓐ Ⓑ Ⓒ Ⓓ	51 Ⓐ Ⓑ Ⓒ Ⓓ	91 Ⓐ Ⓑ Ⓒ Ⓓ
12 Ⓐ Ⓑ Ⓒ Ⓓ	52 Ⓐ Ⓑ Ⓒ Ⓓ	92 Ⓐ Ⓑ Ⓒ Ⓓ
13 Ⓐ Ⓑ Ⓒ Ⓓ	53 Ⓐ Ⓑ Ⓒ Ⓓ	93 Ⓐ Ⓑ Ⓒ Ⓓ
14 Ⓐ Ⓑ Ⓒ Ⓓ	54 Ⓐ Ⓑ Ⓒ Ⓓ	94 Ⓐ Ⓑ Ⓒ Ⓓ
15 Ⓐ Ⓑ Ⓒ Ⓓ	55 Ⓐ Ⓑ Ⓒ Ⓓ	95 Ⓐ Ⓑ Ⓒ Ⓓ
16 Ⓐ Ⓑ Ⓒ Ⓓ	56 Ⓐ Ⓑ Ⓒ Ⓓ	96 Ⓐ Ⓑ Ⓒ Ⓓ
17 Ⓐ Ⓑ Ⓒ Ⓓ	57 Ⓐ Ⓑ Ⓒ Ⓓ	97 Ⓐ Ⓑ Ⓒ Ⓓ
18 Ⓐ Ⓑ Ⓒ Ⓓ	58 Ⓐ Ⓑ Ⓒ Ⓓ	98 Ⓐ Ⓑ Ⓒ Ⓓ
19 Ⓐ Ⓑ Ⓒ Ⓓ	59 Ⓐ Ⓑ Ⓒ Ⓓ	99 Ⓐ Ⓑ Ⓒ Ⓓ
20 Ⓐ Ⓑ Ⓒ Ⓓ	60 Ⓐ Ⓑ Ⓒ Ⓓ	100 Ⓐ Ⓑ Ⓒ Ⓓ
21 Ⓐ Ⓑ Ⓒ Ⓓ	61 Ⓐ Ⓑ Ⓒ Ⓓ	
22 Ⓐ Ⓑ Ⓒ Ⓓ	62 Ⓐ Ⓑ Ⓒ Ⓓ	
23 Ⓐ Ⓑ Ⓒ Ⓓ	63 Ⓐ Ⓑ Ⓒ Ⓓ	
24 Ⓐ Ⓑ Ⓒ Ⓓ	64 Ⓐ Ⓑ Ⓒ Ⓓ	
25 Ⓐ Ⓑ Ⓒ Ⓓ	65 Ⓐ Ⓑ Ⓒ Ⓓ	
26 Ⓐ Ⓑ Ⓒ Ⓓ	66 Ⓐ Ⓑ Ⓒ Ⓓ	
27 Ⓐ Ⓑ Ⓒ Ⓓ	67 Ⓐ Ⓑ Ⓒ Ⓓ	
28 Ⓐ Ⓑ Ⓒ Ⓓ	68 Ⓐ Ⓑ Ⓒ Ⓓ	
29 Ⓐ Ⓑ Ⓒ Ⓓ	69 Ⓐ Ⓑ Ⓒ Ⓓ	
30 Ⓐ Ⓑ Ⓒ Ⓓ	70 Ⓐ Ⓑ Ⓒ Ⓓ	
31 Ⓐ Ⓑ Ⓒ Ⓓ	71 Ⓐ Ⓑ Ⓒ Ⓓ	
32 Ⓐ Ⓑ Ⓒ Ⓓ	72 Ⓐ Ⓑ Ⓒ Ⓓ	
33 Ⓐ Ⓑ Ⓒ Ⓓ	73 Ⓐ Ⓑ Ⓒ Ⓓ	
34 Ⓐ Ⓑ Ⓒ Ⓓ	74 Ⓐ Ⓑ Ⓒ Ⓓ	
35 Ⓐ Ⓑ Ⓒ Ⓓ	75 Ⓐ Ⓑ Ⓒ Ⓓ	
36 Ⓐ Ⓑ Ⓒ Ⓓ	76 Ⓐ Ⓑ Ⓒ Ⓓ	
37 Ⓐ Ⓑ Ⓒ Ⓓ	77 Ⓐ Ⓑ Ⓒ Ⓓ	
38 Ⓐ Ⓑ Ⓒ Ⓓ	78 Ⓐ Ⓑ Ⓒ Ⓓ	
39 Ⓐ Ⓑ Ⓒ Ⓓ	79 Ⓐ Ⓑ Ⓒ Ⓓ	
40 Ⓐ Ⓑ Ⓒ Ⓓ	80 Ⓐ Ⓑ Ⓒ Ⓓ	

CUT HERE

Preschool/Early Childhood (0690) Practice Exam

Read each of the following questions and select the BEST answer. Fill in your choice on the answer bubble sheet provided.

1. Under IDEIA, the delivery of educational services for young children with special needs is mandated to be provided in which of the following settings?

   A. full inclusion sites
   B. therapeutic settings
   C. natural environments
   D. special school programs

2. What should an early childhood director of a public preschool program do if the parents of a two-year-old child with language and cognitive delays request immediate enrollment in the public school preschool program for the current school year?

   A. Coordinate an emergency IEP team meeting to create specific goals.
   B. Ask the parents to consider waiting another year for preschool services.
   C. Place the child instantly in school to ensure access to all early intervention services.
   D. Assist the parents in contacting the agency handling early intervention services.

3. A focus has been placed on the subject of *diversity* in education. In order for an early childhood teacher to begin teaching the concept of cultural awareness and the acceptance of others for the purpose of learning *diversity*, this teacher should

   A. read stories about a few of the obvious cultures represented in the school.
   B. allow each child to share information about his family with the entire class.
   C. identify for the children the different cultures from around the world.
   D. teach terms from several different languages to the children throughout the year.

4. When the federal government passed a mandate in the late 1980s to the then existing special education legislation, it required states to include the _____ for young children ages 3 to 5 years.

   A. conditions for isolated therapeutic sessions
   B. establishment of parent-infant support systems
   C. provision of public education and related services
   D. training of early childhood educators and personnel

5. A child who was enrolled in a preschool program at the age of 3 with a speech and language delay has just turned 5. Since the child will attend kindergarten at the beginning of the school year, the IEP team is preparing to transition the child. What step must the team comply with in order to provide this child with an appropriate kindergarten placement and program?

   A. Observe the child in the kindergarten program for at least three weeks before setting final goals.
   B. Write a comprehensive IEP with the kindergarten teacher to include goals that meet the standards for the new class.
   C. Conduct a review of records, and if necessary, an evaluation to determine the need for continued speech and language services.
   D. Request that the parents sign the written statement of acceptance that the child has successfully completed preschool language services and may attend kindergarten.

GO ON TO THE NEXT PAGE

6. Children engage in several levels of play as they progress in the area of play development. The most basic level is called

   A. parallel play.
   B. solitary play.
   C. associative play.
   D. cooperative play.

7. When a young child consistently fails to utilize the expected developmental speech sounds and repeatedly demonstrates problems with pronunciation, this child MOST probably has

   A. a fluency syndrome.
   B. a cognitive problem.
   C. a vestibular disability.
   D. an articulation disorder.

8. As society changes, greater emphasis is placed on early childhood education, and more focus is drawn to how these programs evolve. Two of the MOST important trends in the area of early childhood education are

   A. transition services and evaluations.
   B. staff training and open classroom spaces.
   C. direct teaching and child-directed activities.
   D. natural environments and parent involvement.

9. Children with special needs require attention and care to support their education and growth. One of the essential ingredients in providing an appropriate program for children with special needs is for the school to emphasize

   A. specialized curriculum.
   B. interagency collaboration.
   C. transdisciplinary activities.
   D. multidisciplinary programs.

10. When the parents of a young child with disabilities inquired about their child enrolling in the preschool program at the local elementary school, the principal explained that one step in the placement process would be for the professionals to conduct a comprehensive evaluation of their child for the purpose of

   A. meeting the requirements of the No Child Left Behind Act.
   B. identifying the materials necessary to educate the child appropriately.
   C. helping them (the parents) face the various stages of the grieving process.
   D. gathering information to make critical decisions about the child's program.

11. Young children can get chronic illnesses, diseases, and infections that affect their development. If a child has developed *chronic otitis media* between the ages of birth and 5 years, the area of development most likely affected is the _____ domain.

   A. motor
   B. self-help
   C. cognitive
   D. speech/language

12. A special education early childhood teacher must maintain several roles in relation to addressing the needs of children, family, and related service staff in a preschool setting. The primary role in preparing a child and her family for the transition from preschool to kindergarten is to

   A. organize the data from the various providers, interpret the findings for the team, and identify the services that meet the child's needs.
   B. describe the child's needs to the team, prepare the parents for the change of placement, and provide records to the new teacher or school.
   C. explain the child's disability to the new class of students, train the teacher, and choose the materials that best suit the child's strengths and needs.
   D. talk with the child and parents about the standards for kindergarten, write an IEP for the new kindergarten teacher, and purge the preschool records.

13. An early childhood teacher who gathers information about a family's structure and seeks information about how this family perceives a disability is establishing a relationship to become more _____

  A. empathetic.
  B. culturally aware.
  C. resourcefully productive.
  D. effectively communicative.

14. The use of *developmentally appropriate practices* is an area of early childhood education that is often reviewed in order to determine the efficacy of a preschool program. The theory behind these practices is that children

  A. learn through active engagement of their environment.
  B. develop relationships when the focus is on their basic needs.
  C. develop thinking skills only by direct experience and activity.
  D. learn to adapt and change behaviors when events are shaped and modeled.

15. A child with _____ is demonstrating difficulty during child-directed play periods with peer interactions characterized by grabbing toys, hitting others, and stuttering.

  A. a motor-linguistic delay
  B. a cultural-linguistic delay
  C. a receptive language delay
  D. an expressive language delay

16. It is a recommendation from most states that early childhood programs receive accreditation from a national organization to let parents, community, and other educators know about the high quality of services that are offered. Which of the following organizations is BEST known for organizing materials for accreditations and supporting early childhood programs through the accreditation process?

  A. CEC
  B. ACEI
  C. PACE
  D. NAEYC

17. Based on research, _____ are one of the most critical foundations that a young child must have in the early stages, as it has positive effects on a child's intellectual growth.

  A. cultural identities
  B. appropriate behaviors
  C. nurturing relationships
  D. academic opportunities

18. Young children must be screened and if a problem is noticed, then evaluated. These are steps in the overall special education process. When professionals screen or evaluate a young child, the assessment instruments must be considered

  A. parent friendly.
  B. easily administered.
  C. academically skewed.
  D. culturally non-discriminatory.

19. Through many studies on young children, researchers have determined that the first domain of learning that develops in a child is the _____ domain that provides the child his first learning experiences.

  A. motor
  B. language
  C. cognitive
  D. emotional

20. Early childhood educators must meet the needs of a variety of children while addressing an array of standards required by many states. When they review the available curriculum programs, they should seek one that

  A. clearly identifies goals, objectives, and outcomes.
  B. defines the special needs child in a natural environment.
  C. provides motivating activities and stimulating literacy tasks.
  D. addresses a language rich environment through art and music.

GO ON TO THE NEXT PAGE

21. Parents, upset with a recent diagnosis of mental retardation of their four-year-old child, are seeking information from the local school to help them determine what to do about their child's future. The parents believe their child has a very limited future and will be continually placed in classes with other retarded children. What is the first step that the preschool director/teacher should do?

 A. Suggest that they get a second opinion from a specialist in the field and accompany them to the appointment to ease the tension and take notes.

 B. Gather information and conduct assessments so the information and results may be shared with the service providers in order to identify the present levels of performance.

 C. Provide comfort and guidance to the parents, by explaining the stages of grief and giving them the names and phone numbers of other parents, which will encourage them to develop a support network.

 D. Confirm their concerns and have them meet with the special education director who will describe the various self-contained classes that their child will be enrolled in for the remainder of her educational program.

22. Children diagnosed with autism exhibit an array of delays when looking at the autism spectrum, and they require support to reach certain goals. Most often, each child identified with autism demonstrates delays in these areas:

 A. language and motor
 B. behaviors and self-help
 C. cognitive and emotional
 D. social and communication

23. A genetic defect evident by both persistence and stability, with rare neurological regression and that affects a child's development, is a medical condition known as a(an)

 A. illness.
 B. disability.
 C. teratogen.
 D. syndrome.

24. Under the public law for children with disabilities, IDEIA, it is required that a transition conference be held _____ before the child reaches the age of 3.

 A. 15 days
 B. 30 days
 C. 60 days
 D. 90 days

25. According to Part C of IDEIA, when the focus of the interventions is on the family unit, which of the following is being implemented?

 A. IEP
 B. LRE
 C. FAPE
 D. IFSP

26. Under IDEIA, there is a provision for young children with disabilities that requires the preschool program to ensure that each child receives services and accommodations in the LRE. What does this mandate mean?

 A. An advocate will be secured by the parents to determine the placement of the child with a disability.

 B. When a child requires therapy services due to an identified disability, those services will be provided at no cost to the parents.

 C. For any child who needs additional help for maintaining appropriate behaviors, a paraprofessional will be assigned to that child.

 D. A child who is identified with a disability and is eligible for special education services must be placed in the most typical setting possible.

27. The initial phase in the special education assessment process in which professionals from local agencies screen and locate young children who might not be developing at typical rates and may need specific interventions or certain educational services is called

 A. Child Find
 B. Early Referral
 C. Primary Reviews
 D. Comprehensive Assessment

28. The theory of multiple intelligences was developed by

   A. Dewey.
   B. Froebel.
   C. Gardner.
   D. Montessori.

29. Data shows that there is a powerful link between family _____ and disabling conditions.

   A. values
   B. culture
   C. poverty
   D. education

30. During the middle childhood years (ages 6, 7, and 8), children's _____ is/are becoming more stable if they have been properly influenced and supported by healthy relationships with adults and peers.

   A. self-concept
   B. reading skills
   C. memory process
   D. coordination skills

31. Lev Vygotsky had a powerful impact on educators' understanding of language development, and he believed that his _____ significantly influenced the learning process.

   A. cognitive theory
   B. behavioral theory
   C. psychosocial theory
   D. socio-cultural theory

32. An inexperienced early childhood teacher is concerned about meeting with various families at parent conference time. He has gathered pertinent academic performance information about each of the students, supported by individual student portfolios and assessment information. He feels prepared to speak about the children in his class but is unsure how the parents will react when he shares information. What should he do to prepare for these meetings?

   A. Consider the parents partners in the child's education and remember to share the responsibility for the child's successes and failures with parents, listen to parents, and work collaboratively on behalf of the child.
   B. Listen to the parents' concerns first, chat about their lives to find out more about the family, and then provide a standardized written outline of all the gathered information and data that the parents may take home and read.
   C. Present a survey to the parents prior to the conference to ask questions about the family and how they would like the conference to proceed. Then determine with which families to meet and which to schedule phone conferences.
   D. Conduct a family phone interview and proceed with a pre-conference update on the format of the conference. If families are not receptive, schedule an administrator or peer educator to sit in on the meetings.

33. Which of the following methods of setting up a learning environment for young children BEST reflects how early childhood teachers should address children's various needs while preparing the children from diverse cultural and educational backgrounds to succeed in this world?

   A. reduce program enrollments
   B. improve the availability of technology
   C. use developmentally appropriate practices
   D. require regular training for parents and teachers

34. The _____ to Assessment is often utilized in early childhood programs for young children ages 3–5 years. The information gathered for this play-based evaluation is primarily done by a team of professionals who are working simultaneously together, by observing and playing with the child.

   A. Linder Approach
   B. Vygotsky Ratings
   C. Montessori Method
   D. Piaget Observations

GO ON TO THE NEXT PAGE

35. Studies involving diverse families suggest there are strong variations in their _____, which must be observed and addressed by educators.

A. work ethics
B. economic status
C. parenting attitudes
D. education backgrounds

36. A 7-year-old student with mild mental retardation and moderate multi-sensory impairments is attending first grade. The student was in a full inclusion setting during preschool and kindergarten, being successful according to an IEP. The parents are now concerned about the child's ability to maintain adequate academic performance as the child enters second grade. What is the best way to handle the child's situation and address the parents' concerns?

A. Place the child in a self-contained program for multi-disabilities during all academic periods, monitor progress, and reassess each nine weeks, involving the parents.
B. Review the parents' concerns and ask what setting and materials they would like to see in place for the child to be most successful over the next two years.
C. Continue the child in the first grade with a one-to-one aide, provide an after school tutor, and identify other supports needed to help satisfy the parents' concerns.
D. Identify with the parents the child's present levels of performance, the specific types of sensory impairments, and how they affect the child in the classroom, and then assess set goals and benchmark progress on the IEP.

37. Since strong language development is important for young children to enhance literacy skills, which activity identifies one of the BEST methods used to promote language and literacy development?

A. singing to children
B. dramatizing a story
C. modeling play with toys
D. writing stories for children

38. The theory that expresses a series of developmental stages is called the Cognitive Theory. This approach to addressing the needs of young children in the field of education was created and defined by

A. Piaget.
B. Skinner.
C. Gardner.
D. Vygotsky.

39. It is evident that sibling relationships endure and the siblings of children with disabilities often

A. experience the stages of grief.
B. worry more about the family situation.
C. are able to ignore the problems at home.
D. excel in school because of increased attention.

40. In early childhood programs, *play* becomes a very important aspect of the curriculum and the BEST method to use when planning for play is to

A. integrate it throughout the day.
B. schedule it after an academic block.
C. use it at the beginning and end of the day.
D. establish rules to control the environment.

41. A type of assessment that is conducted in a variety of environments with an observation component to identify how the child's performance is influenced in various settings is called _____ assessment.

A. a dynamic
B. a portfolio
C. an authentic
D. an ecological

42. Under IDEIA, _____, states are assisted in developing a plan to address the needs of children with developmental delays, ages birth to 2 years.

A. Part C
B. Part H
C. Part F
D. Part B

43. Cognitive delays can be the result of several different factors. One of the more common types of cognitive delays is Down Syndrome, which is caused by

   A. a metabolic disorder.
   B. a teratogen exposure.
   C. an environmental condition.
   D. a chromosomal abnormality.

44. The foundation of cognition includes perceptual skills. During the early years of development, these skills are most evident in which area?

   A. visual
   B. tactile
   C. auditory
   D. olfactory

45. A parental right that is mandated within the procedural safeguards of special education law is to ensure

   A. efficacy.
   B. diversity.
   C. standards.
   D. confidentiality.

46. When assessment information is gathered by the process of an observation on a child, this is referred to as a _____ assessment.

   A. standards-based
   B. norm-referenced
   C. performance-based
   D. criterion-referenced

47. The role of the father with a young child who has special needs has a powerful effect on the child's development because he spends more time

   A. engaged in play activities with the child.
   B. supporting the mother with school affairs.
   C. caring for the other children in the family.
   D. working to support the child's economic needs.

48. Which of the following curriculum types requires frequent assessment and collection of data to evaluate a child's skill acquisition?

   A. ecological curriculum
   B. behavioral curriculum
   C. constructivist curriculum
   D. developmental curriculum

49. A common condition for which a child may obtain special education services under the category of orthopedic impairments is

   A. asthma.
   B. cerebral palsy.
   C. attention deficit.
   D. cortical deficiency.

50. To promote language acquisition, children should developmentally have an acquired vocabulary of about 1,000 words between the ages of

   A. 2 to 3 years.
   B. 3 to 4 years.
   C. 4 to 5 years.
   D. 5 to 6 years.

51. A first-grade child with a hearing impairment and his family moved from one state to another in mid-October. The child was provided special education services under an IEP, but the new school had not received permanent records when the parent attempted to enroll the child. The parents presented a copy of the IEP with the health records and expected the same services to commence. What should be done at the school for the child?

   A. Conduct a comprehensive assessment and write a new IEP.
   B. Place the child in regular education classes until records arrive.
   C. Place the child in special education classes until the records arrive.
   D. Conduct a review of the existing records and make an interim placement.

GO ON TO THE NEXT PAGE

52. When a three-year-old child and his family needed services, several state and local community agencies worked together to obtain educational program services, health assistance, respite care, and mental health support. This effort is an example of

    A. services coordination.

    B. local disability network.

    C. interagency collaboration.

    D. community services systems.

53. When identifying a young child for intervention services, it must be determined whether the child is at-risk or has a disability. If a child was found to have low birth weight with complications, the evaluator should recognize this is a condition related to which of the following?

    A. unknown risk

    B. biological risk

    C. established risk

    D. environmental risk

54. Physical disabilities may be caused from different factors and include sensory and motor delays. When a physical impairment is the direct result of an illness, an accident, or child abuse, it is considered

    A. a static disability.

    B. an acquired disability.

    C. a congenital disability.

    D. a developmental disability.

55. The three major components to developing a curriculum are

    A. goals, theories, and activities.

    B. guidelines, lessons, and strategies.

    C. objectives, subjects, and evaluation.

    D. content, skill development, and methods.

56. When young children do not acquire or do not develop skills as quickly as other children in the same age range, the child is considered to be developmentally delayed. The developmental delay most often identified in infancy is a

    A. social delay.

    B. motor delay.

    C. language delay.

    D. cognitive delay.

57. The _____ system is one of the MOST essential components to consider with parents to promote a successful transition for a child.

    A. placement

    B. assessment

    C. communication

    D. service delivery

58. A philosophy of early childhood education that emphasizes the importance of play and the support for social-emotional development of a child was developed by _____, who is considered the *father of kindergarten*.

    A. Jean Piaget

    B. Reggio Emilia

    C. Frederich Froebel

    D. Maria Montessori

59. When the multidisciplinary team was preparing the child and family for the transition into kindergarten, the team reviewed the child's language development skills, the child's overall language acquisition, and the child's delays that were exhibited throughout preschool. The team discussed the interventions that were utilized and developed goals for the new IEP. The speech/language pathologist reminded the team that the child's language delays have an affect on the child's _____ and that goals for this area should also be addressed.

    A. hearing abilities

    B. concept acquisition

    C. social development

    D. constructive memory

60. Children with language and social problems will most likely demonstrate delays in which of the following areas?

    A. semantics

    B. phonology

    C. pragmatics

    D. morphology

61. For children to acquire language, they need environments that

    A. are free from distractions and noise.

    B. offer motivating cognitive instruction.

    C. provide intellectual and verbal stimulation.

    D. imitate positive speech production and sounds.

62. On a _____ team, members equally share roles and cross all disciplines as they assess a child, plan a program for a child, and provide services to the child. The members include families and professionals.

  A. interdisciplinary
  B. intradisciplinary
  C. transdisciplinary
  D. multidisciplinary

63. The greatest risk for acquiring a severe developmental disability occurs during the period

  A. of the last trimester.
  B. of the first trimester.
  C. between conception and birth.
  D. between the first 6 and 9 months after birth.

64. When an early childhood educator reviews the scoring tables on a standardized test to compare the performance of one child to a group of other children in the same age group, he is using a _____ assessment.

  A. authentic-based
  B. norm-referenced
  C. ecological-based
  D. criterion-referenced

65. Fluency issues are fairly common in young children. When a child exhibits difficulty with fluency, what strategy is known to be MOST effective in addressing this area?

  A. Allow the child ample time to speak.
  B. Interrupt the child and ask the child to begin again.
  C. Ask adults to use isolated words when talking to the child.
  D. Stop the child from talking and give them the proper words.

66. When a transdisciplinary team prepares to deliver related services, they do so using which of the following approaches?

  A. integrated therapy
  B. segregated therapy
  C. mainstream classes
  D. self-contained classes

67. The theory that was created by Maslow supports the idea that children's basic needs must be met so his primary focus for children was on

  A. attending.
  B. belonging.
  C. supporting.
  D. comprehending.

68. The most primitive of the senses at birth is

  A. taste.
  B. sight.
  C. smell.
  D. hearing.

69. Which of the following types of hearing loss has the greater negative effect on language development?

  A. prelingual
  B. congenital
  C. postlingual
  D. adventitious

70. Early childhood educators can save time when documenting goal attainment and reviewing children's individual programs if they are efficient in

  A. calling parents.
  B. writing reports.
  C. records management.
  D. classroom organization.

71. The primary purpose of a developmental screening is to decide whether a child needs

  A. early intervention.
  B. a paraprofessional.
  C. a formal evaluation.
  D. special education services.

72. Most home-based programs are

  A. child oriented.
  B. parent oriented.
  C. sibling oriented.
  D. therapy oriented.

GO ON TO THE NEXT PAGE

73. One of the main goals of providing therapy to young children is for them to _____ in other areas.

    A. generalize skills

    B. stabilize movement

    C. accommodate needs

    D. facilitate knowledge

74. Empirical research has proven to be a valuable tool in developing early childhood programs because it most

    A. closely reflects the naturalistic focus on children.

    B. clearly defines the controlled aspects of child behaviors.

    C. carefully identifies the subjects and evaluators of children.

    D. cautiously approaches the sensitive topics about young children.

75. When analyzing language acquisition, children developmentally begin to attach meanings to words at about _____ of age.

    A. 1 year

    B. 2 years

    C. 8 months

    D. 18 months

76. There are three major types of hearing impairments: mixed, sensori-neural, and

    A. genetic.

    B. cochlear.

    C. profound.

    D. conductive.

77. Early childhood educators face issues with significant impact on programs for young children. Which of the following is an example of a barrier that will greatly affect the education of young children in the future?

    A. lack of technology tools and resources

    B. required accreditations and certifications

    C. increase of bilingual, single parent homes

    D. lack of monetary and administrative support

78. When a child is suspected of a physical delay, she may require services through an occupational therapist (OT). An assessment of the child's level of performance is made by an OT whose primary course of information is

    A. parent reports.

    B. teacher checklists.

    C. clinical observations.

    D. developmental records.

79. When an interventionist provides information to parents/family about their child with disabilities and instructs the family on how to work with their child, the BEST choice is to conduct the services in

    A. separate classes.

    B. integrated settings.

    C. home-based services.

    D. center-based programs.

80. Recent brain research has discovered that intelligence _____ at birth.

    A. begins

    B. is fixed

    C. is not fixed

    D. does not begin

81. There are many philosophies on the types of programs in which children with special needs should be placed to access their appropriate education. Research has shown that the inclusion model should be considered for

    A. all children who have multiple disabilities.

    B. all children with any condition or disability.

    C. the children with the more severe disabilities.

    D. the children with the least amount of special needs.

82. The first step in identifying a family's need for community resources is to

    A. conduct a family assessment.

    B. send the family to a community fair.

    C. meet with the interdisciplinary team.

    D. survey the extended family members.

83. When an educator utilizes _____ testing, the information may show that although a child has certain knowledge of and mastered particular skills, he is not using them regularly.

    A. formal
    B. informal
    C. task analysis
    D. behavior analysis

84. The period of the day in an early childhood program that most likely will increase negative behaviors in children is the time during

    A. recess.
    B. language.
    C. grooming.
    D. transitions.

85. A key component to selecting a quality curriculum is the

    A. scope and sequence.
    B. activity information.
    C. chaining of assignments.
    D. developmental assessments.

86. We know much about the synapses that occur in the brain, stimulating learning. At which age is a child's brain 2 1/2 times more active than an adult's?

    A. age 5
    B. age 3
    C. age 12
    D. age 15

87. Training parents through an early childhood program often

    A. has the affect of empowerment.
    B. makes little difference in the child's program.
    C. takes a tremendous amount of time for the teacher.
    D. changes the structure and design of a child's goals.

88. An early childhood educator sets up an art activity using clay that includes a variety of clay tools. She watches the children access the center and keeps track of the skills they use. She writes a brief summary about each child to keep on file. What method of assessment is she using?

    A. Rating Scale
    B. Anecdotal Record
    C. Diagnostic Screening
    D. Developmental Checklist

89. A _____ team works closely together for each individual child they serve. This team often evaluates children together.

    A. intradisciplinary
    B. transdisciplinary
    C. interdisciplinary
    D. multidisciplinary

90. Music in an early childhood curriculum strongly supports which of the following standard areas?

    A. physical
    B. emotional
    C. language/literacy
    D. science/mathematics

91. By indirectly accessing the various processes of _____ children most often learn about the social function of their behaviors.

    A. play
    B. therapy
    C. language
    D. academics

92. A support system for parents that seems to be most effective is

    A. the parent program at the local school.
    B. a group of parents with similar children.
    C. a hospital-managed group of parents and children.
    D. the extended family members on both sides of the family.

GO ON TO THE NEXT PAGE

93. The method found to be the MOST effective in educating young children is called

    A. PDE.

    B. PAR.

    C. APR.

    D. DAP.

94. Both an IEP and an IFSP are part of the requirements under IDEIA for young children under the age of 5 years. Which of the following is a similarity of these two documents?

    A. They must have specific goals set for the child.

    B. They have an annual review period for all goals set.

    C. They must be written within 45 days of the child's referral.

    D. The present levels statement pertains only to the specific disability.

95. Social-emotional development is an important domain but one that takes time to develop. When a child enters elementary school, one social preference that changes is that the child may choose _____ over dependence on parents.

    A. sports

    B. siblings

    C. friendships

    D. play activities

96. The provision for education services and special services for children ages 3–5 years is mandated under which of the following federal laws?

    A. IDEIA, Part B

    B. IDEIA, Part C

    C. FERPA, Part D

    D. FERPA, Part H

97. The main reason that an early childhood program should seek accreditation is to

    A. obtain additional funding.

    B. manage parent programming.

    C. develop policies and procedures.

    D. confirm accountability and efficacy.

98. When an early childhood educator seeks to obtain a curriculum program for use in the classroom, an important component to evaluate when selecting the curriculum for children with special needs is the

    A. content of the literacy lessons.

    B. number of classroom activities.

    C. intervention strategies provided.

    D. amount of time required to prepare.

99. The approach that stresses instruction for a child's individual goals through child-initiated activities is called

    A. contextual.

    B. psycho-social.

    C. activity-based.

    D. academic-based.

100. Which of the following items was an initiative of President Johnson's "War of Poverty"?

    A. The Technology Act

    B. The Head Start Project

    C. The Perry Preschool Program

    D. The Medicaid Early Screening

Preschool/Early Childhood (0690) Practice Exam Answer Key

1. C	35. C	69. B
2. D	36. D	70. C
3. B	37. A	71. C
4. C	38. A	72. B
5. C	39. A	73. A
6. B	40. A	74. A
7. D	41. D	75. A
8. D	42. A	76. D
9. B	43. D	77. A
10. D	44. A	78. C
11. D	45. D	79. C
12. B	46. C	80. C
13. B	47. A	81. B
14. A	48. B	82. A
15. D	49. B	83. B
16. D	50. B	84. D
17. C	51. D	85. A
18. D	52. B	86. B
19. A	53. B	87. A
20. A	54. B	88. B
21. B	55. D	89. C
22. D	56. B	90. C
23. D	57. C	91. A
24. D	58. C	92. B
25. D	59. C	93. D
26. D	60. C	94. C
27. A	61. C	95. C
28. C	62. C	96. A
29. C	63. C	97. D
30. A	64. B	98. C
31. D	65. A	99. C
32. A	66. A	100. B
33. C	67. B	
34. A	68. B	

Answer Explanations for Preschool/Early Childhood (0690) Practice Exam

1. **C.** A natural environment is a place such as the home, a preschool, or a child care center, where a child might attend whether she had a disability or not. In a natural environment, children experience play and developmentally appropriate activities that enhance learning. It is in these settings that IDEIA mandates the educational services for children with disabilities.

2. **D.** Under Part C of IDEIA, each state must establish a program or an agency to provide early intervention services to children under the age of 3. In this specific situation, the early childhood director should help parents by assisting with a referral to the area agency that handles the early intervention services.

3. **B.** Diversity is an abstract concept that may be very difficult for young children to understand. When a preschool teacher works with young children on the topic of diversity, which includes cultural awareness, languages, abilities, and so on, the teacher needs to provide realistic and meaningful instruction. One of the BEST methods to present this abstract concept in a beneficial and informative way is to allow all the children in the program to share their own culture, customs, and languages with the class, which may include family member assistance.

4. **C.** The federal special education law in effect in the late 1980s was Public Law 94–142 and was referred to as the Education for All Handicapped Children Act (EHA). In 1986, PL 99–457 was created as an amendment to PL 94–142 and required states to lower the age of eligibility for special education services and related services to age 3 years.

5. **C.** The IEP team is required to conduct an annual review of the child's program, especially prior to a move into another program (such as preschool into kindergarten). Early intervention services under Part C and Part B of IDEIA offer assistance to children in their areas of disabilities, and many children begin to perform at typical levels when they reach the kindergarten level. It is critical for the team to review records and possibly conduct another evaluation to determine whether the child needs continued services or whether the child should be dismissed from services.

6. **B.** Solitary play generally occurs between the ages of 2 and 2.5 years as a child plays independently. The child may engage in a variety of activities but does not initiate play with other children, even to the point of ignoring other children who might be playing in the same location or with the same or similar materials.

7. **D.** An articulation disorder, which is also described as phonological dysfunction, must be identified by a speech and language pathologist who uses standardized assessment tools to evaluate the child and determine the typical developmental expectations for the age. An articulation disorder is most often characterized by the inability to produce age-appropriate speech sounds and recurring difficulties when making pronunciations.

8. **D.** The concepts on natural environments and parent involvement are very important for schools to address and comply with, as they are both emphasized in the law. Since these two areas were first included in IDEA under Part C and began to demonstrate effectiveness, they were both added to Part B under IDEIA. A natural environment is a setting in which a child would typically spend her time if there was no disability. These are the settings that are now required for children with disabilities to receive their special education services.

9. **B.** Interagency collaboration is beneficial to a child's program as it increases the performance of children and enhances family and community involvement. Interagency collaboration is a means to meeting children's varying and diverse needs because a variety of agencies can provide comprehensive and coordinated services to young children and their families.

10. **D.** When a child is referred for special education due to a suspected disability, an evaluation must be conducted. The purpose of the evaluation is to determine the child's needs and how the disability affects the child's achievement. Based on the results of the assessment, a child's program may be developed or modified. Therefore, an assessment is conducted in order to gather information to make critical decisions about the child's program.

11. **D.** *Chronic otitis media* is a common, yet serious infection that may affect a child's ears. A young child who has this constant, yet intermittent infection over a period of months, will probably experience delays in speech and language development. This is due to the child's hearing being affected while the infection is present. When a

child has an active infection, a mild to moderate conductive hearing loss may be detected. Since the child is not hearing well during the infected period, he does not develop the appropriate speech sounds and typical language patterns. Should the infection persist for longer periods, the child may also suffer a permanent sensori-neural hearing loss.

12. **B.** In organizing the transition of a preschool student, the early childhood special education teacher should coordinate a meeting with the receiving team that includes the parents. This teacher should then review the child's program, describe the student's progress, and explain how the child accessed the environment. This teacher must also be sure that the parents understand the changes that a transition brings and should watch for how these changes might affect the child and the family in order to assist them with making the adjustment. The teacher must prepare the records to be received by the new team.

13. **B.** Becoming more familiar with each family in a program, and observing their perceptions about their child's disability aids a teacher in understanding the family's values and culture. This may be a beginning step in developing rapport with the family.

14. **A.** Developmentally appropriate practices (DAP) is a theoretical approach to working with young children in the age group of birth to 8 years. It focuses on children's developmental skills and abilities, their individual differences, and their cultural and environmental involvement. It is known through the use of this practice that children learn through active engagement of their environment.

15. **D.** An expressive language delay may affect a child in many ways, as it is a problem for the child to retrieve and utilize words in daily communications. When a child is observed as grabbing items, hitting others, and stuttering, the early childhood educator should be aware of the child's expressive language abilities. It is most likely, that aside from behavior issues, this child is experiencing problems with using language and expressing thoughts.

16. **D.** The National Association for the Education of Young Children (NAEYC) has created a set of standards to assess the quality of early childhood programs. Many programs across the country seek the assistance of the NAEYC to provide guidance and the structured steps that lead them toward the knowledge about the efficacy of their program. Many educators, parents, and community members view accreditation as a method of accountability for the programs that enhances the lives of young children.

17. **C.** Brain research has proven that the relationships a child has in her early years (usually with a parent or primary caregiver) have a significant impact on the child's development, social-emotional state, and future learning.

18. **D.** It is a requirement under federal law, IDEIA, that evaluation tools must be chosen and administered to be culturally and racially nondiscriminatory.

19. **A.** The motor domain has been determined to be the first domain of learning that a child is exposed to, since from very early on, a newborn experiences physical contact and engages in learning. A child can collect enormous amounts of data through the motor domain and store this information in the brain for later use.

20. **A.** Although different types of curricula are available, and various theories are related to these programs, the most important components to review by educators when selecting a program is whether it clearly identifies goals, objectives, and outcomes for children. It is critical that an early childhood curriculum be based on a particular theory of learning (goals), include guidelines for implementing the program (objectives), and have a plan for evaluating the child's performance (outcomes).

21. **B.** It is best to request any records from the parents and obtain permission to get records from the physician when parents offer information about a diagnosis. The school team may then want to proceed with a screening and possibly an assessment, followed by a meeting with the parents and the service providers who conducted the assessments. When the child's present levels of performance are outlined, parents may gain a foundation on which to base more realistic views of their child's current abilities. This meeting begins the process of creating a program and developing an IEP, where the team can set goals.

22. **D.** According to the diagnostic criteria in the DSM-IV, Autism is characterized by impairments in social interactions, verbal and nonverbal communications, along with some behaviors, interests, and activities.

23. **D.** A syndrome is classified as the signs and symptoms of a disorder that affects a child's developmental patterns. Generally, a syndrome is persistent and stable in presentation, with rare regression neurologically. Many syndromes are genetically caused.

24. D. Transition services are important for the child, the family, and the schools, and, therefore, it has been included and mandated by public law, IDEIA, PL108-446 (previously PL105-17, PL99-457, and PL102-119). When a child with disabilities transitions from a Part C intervention program to Part B preschool services, the child is entitled to a transition conference with participants of both teams 90 days before the child's third birthday.

25. D. Under IDEIA, there are two sections that mandate services for young children: Part B and Part C. Part B focuses on children ages 3–5 years in natural environments (typically in school settings) utilizing the format of an IEP for delivery of education services, in which parents and family are partners on a team. Part C focuses on children ages birth through 2 years in the natural environment (most often the home) where the interventions are centered on the family through an IFSP.

26. D. The LRE is the *least restrictive environment*. This mandate means that children with disabilities should be placed in environments with typical children to the greatest or most appropriate extent possible.

27. A. Child Find is a step required under federal law to locate children in a community who may be in need of special education services. The purpose is to find the children who may have disabilities, or who are at-risk and would benefit from early intervention and/or special education services. Agencies and schools are encouraged to speak with families and screen young children to determine their needs.

28. C. The multiple intelligence theory that encompasses nine different intelligences and focuses on allowing children to learn according to their interests and abilities was created by Howard Gardner. He believed that intelligence can be categorized and measured through these different strands, but that these areas do not operate separately from one another.

29. C. Although family economic status alone is not necessarily a factor that results in disabilities, the state of being in a poverty situation impacts those conditions that influence the causes of a disability. Families living in poverty often lack the resources for prenatal services and health care for young children, exhibit poor nutritional choices, are at-risk for more diseases, and exhibit drug and alcohol abuse at higher rates. These are all leading factors in causing disabilities.

30. A. During this age period, a child's self-concept is more stable and can continue to be greatly influenced by the child's perception of what others, adults and peers, may think of him. A child in this age range can be rather critical of self and compare self to others so it is important for the child to have healthy relationships where acceptance, empathy, and understanding are key.

31. D. In the late 1800s, in Russia, Vygotsky worked on studying and analyzing child development with regards to the relationship between culture and knowledge developing the socio-cultural theory. He believed that higher order thinking skills varied from culture to culture due to the uniqueness of each culture, and that language is the key to learning.

32. A. The DEC-CEC (Division for Early Childhood-Council for Exceptional Children) has created four recommended practices to use with families. The first of these is *families and professionals share responsibility and work collaboratively,* which places the focus on the development of a partnership of these two entities: parents/family and professionals. The teacher should not tell the parents information about the child, but ask questions, listen, guide, reflect, and interact, and parents must feel respected and trusted.

33. C. The recommended philosophy for early childhood programs is the use of developmentally appropriate practices (DAP). This acknowledges each child at the present level of performance that she is functioning at and allows the child to reach competency of skills at her own learning rate. The activities provided would be considered appropriate for every child, as they are modified to suit each child's needs.

34. A. Linder developed the Transdisciplinary Play-Based Assessment Model, which is widely used in early childhood programs. The environment is set up for the child to access toys and materials that cross all domains while the team observes and plays with the child.

35. C. According to several research studies, it is evident that families from different cultures possess various parenting attitudes. Educators must be particularly sensitive to following the cultural variations and remember that the parent and family process is quite diverse in this global society.

36. D. When parents share a concern about their child's program and performance with a member of the team, it is important for that staff person to review the child's program and progress, either through a parent conference or at a meeting of the team. In this situation, it is best for this team to identify the child's present levels of performance, review the specific types of moderate sensory impairments in the areas of vision and hearing and how they affect the child in the classroom, and then assess the set goals and benchmark progress on the IEP.

37. A. When adults sing to children, it provides them with skill development opportunities in the following areas: vocabulary, listening, patterns, rhythm, voice pitch, and meaning. Although there are other methods to enhance the develop of literacy and language, this is the best choice of the answers.

38. A. Jean Piaget influenced the field of education when he recognized the stages that children go through in their cognitive development. He found that children's experiences actually influence their concrete thinking processes, and this supports cognitive development.

39. A. Siblings are an important family component for children with disabilities. Whether a positive relationship or not, siblings impact and influence a child with disabilities. Yet, siblings can often be neglected even though they, too, experience the various stages of grief that parents go through. Siblings should be provided information about the disability—how to handle, speak, and play with the child who has the disability—and given language on how to talk with others about their brother's or sister's problems.

40. A. In a developmentally appropriate setting, play would be utilized as a focus for learning. The room would be set up with center activities, and children could access toys and materials as they are interested. Play would be integrated throughout the day so children could practice the skills they learn during the teacher-directed periods.

41. D. An ecological assessment is utilized to gain perspective about a child in her environment and to determine how the environments that the child must function in might influence the child's educational performance. This is conducted by using assessments and observations in a variety of settings in which the child regularly must function.

42. A. Both Part B and Part C are included under IDEIA. Part H recently became Part C. Under Part C, children ages birth through age 2 are served, while under Part B, children ages 3–5 years are served.

43. D. Down Syndrome is a congenital condition due to a chromosomal abnormality where an extra 21st chromosome is present and results in moderate to severe mental retardation. Children with Down Syndrome exhibit physical characteristics that include hearing problems, facial similarities, poor muscle tone, and smaller noses and ears.

44. A. Perceptual skills cover five main categories: visual, auditory, tactile, olfactory, and gustatory. The area that surfaces with the most skills in the developmental process is *visual*. It includes fixing, tracking, depth perception, discrimination, visual memory, and figure ground.

45. D. All information about a child, her program, progress, and performance is required to remain confidential. This confidentiality is mandated under special education law.

46. C. A performance-based assessment is defined as being a method of evaluation that includes an observation of a child, or the creation of a product, in order to identify how the child acts in his own environment. It is also sometimes referred to as an authentic assessment.

47. A. A variety of studies have shown that the role of the father is especially critical in a family unit with a child who has a disability. Although a father seems to think more about the long-range goals of economic security and future issues for the child, it is most often the father who is engaged in play activities of a physical nature that enhances the child's development in several learning domains.

48. B. The theory behind the behavioral curriculum is that the child's environment should be structured and managed. Direct instruction is an element of the behavioral curriculum. Teachers must frequently assess and collect data on children so modifications may be made.

49. B. An orthopedic impairment is the category within special education reserved for children with identified physical disabilities. It covers disabilities that limit a child's mobility and ambulation and adversely affects his educational performance. Conditions that may fall under the category of OI include muscular dystrophy, spina bifida, rheumatoid arthritis, and cerebral palsy.

50. B. According to the developmental charts, children who are in the age range of 3–4 years should have a vocabulary of at least 1,000 words.

51. D. According to federal law, a team may proceed with an interim placement for a child whose complete permanent records have not yet arrived from the transferring school. An interim setting would be considered based on a review of the records the parents provided. After the complete set of records is available, the team should review the placement and programming to determine the appropriate setting and services. It may be necessary for the team to develop a new IEP.

52. B. The primary purpose of interagency collaboration is to obtain and coordinate services needed by a family with a child identified with special needs. The agencies work together to provide the individual services that each agency specializes in to address the needs of the family and the child.

53. B. A component of the assessment process includes obtaining information about a child's medical and developmental history. Having low birth weight and complications can be a factor related to at-risk problems or a developmental disability. Low birth rate is a condition associated under the category of *biological risk*.

54. B. A congenital disability is a condition that a child is born with. A static disability is one that does not change over a period of time. A developmental disability is a general term for disabilities across the learning domains. An acquired disability is one caused by illness, accidents, abuse, and so on.

55. D. The three areas of curriculum development are to establish content, identify skill development, and select methods.

56. B. Young children are physically active in their environment, and they access their environment through physical means. Children learn to touch, grasp, hold, push, and pull at the infancy stage. Should a child fall behind in development, it would be more easily recognized in the motor area, as they would not be physically involved at the same level that other children are.

57. C. Parents and family often need additional support when it comes time to transition their child from one program to another. Not only during the planning stages, but throughout the entire procedure, an organized and effective communication system must be established as it is a valuable factor for success.

58. C. It was Frederich Froebel in the 1800s who realized that young children learn best through play and that social-emotional development contributes to a child's whole being. He established the first kindergarten in Germany during this time period, and in 1856, the first kindergarten was created in America.

59. C. Children who exhibit delays in language often demonstrate delays in the social domain, too. Because a child may have difficulty expressing herself or understanding other children, it would make social situations more complicated and developing peer relationships troublesome. For children with language delays, using conversational skills, and making social interaction attempts can be extremely difficult.

60. C. Pragmatics is the use of language in social settings and includes body language and facial expressions as well as conversational skills. This is a difficult area of language development for children with language and social problems. Semantics involves the meaning of language, including cultural variations. Phonology is the sound system of language, and morphology is the study of the units of oral language.

61. C. An environment that gives a child verbal and intellectual stimulation allows the child to grow in many areas, particularly language. With the added verbal usage and the cognitive renditions, children can participate in skill development that enhances the language domain.

62. C. On a transdisciplinary team, all members are viewed as equals, They rely on one another and collaborate in addressing the best interests of the child. They include the family in an active role and support one another in reaching goals.

63. C. Many factors and events may adversely affect the development of a child in utero (a fetus). If there is a loss or addition of a chromosome, the result may be an addition or deletion of hundreds of genes. Just one gene can affect more than 7,000 disorders. Therefore, the period of greatest risk is between conception and birth.

64. B. A norm-referenced test compares the performance of an individual child to other children in the same age group. A criterion-referenced test defines a child's performance based on an established (a set) criteria. An authentic-based and ecological-based test evaluates how a child performs in her daily environment.

65. A. Fluency problems are also referred to as stuttering or dysfluency as they are caused by a disruption to the flow of speech. Children may repeat words, use prolonged sounds, or experience long pauses in their speech. With young children, it is normal for them to have some fluency issues when they are first learning to put words together and think of the concepts they want to present, but if it begins to hamper their ability to communicate, then it needs interventions. It is recommended that children experiencing fluency issues be allowed ample time to talk so attention is focused on what they are saying, and they can begin to control the problem as it may remedy itself.

66. A. Most members of a transdisciplinary team believe in the provision of integrated services, particularly therapy, into the regular schedule and activities of a preschool program.

67. B. Children have a basic need to feel loved. Children must feel like they "belong," and when this happens, children develop self-esteem and "can do" attitudes. Maslow's theory on *belonging*, demonstrates that children require that their basic needs be met, at a minimum level.

68. B. When comparing the five senses (sight, hearing, smell, taste, and touch), sight or vision is the one least developed at birth. The reason for this is that this sense receives no stimulation in utero. It takes newborns about two months to develop vision, peaking at about 8 1/2 months and becoming relatively complete at age 1 1/2 years.

69. B. A congenital hearing loss has a greater negative effect on language development because it occurs prior to birth. The child does not have the advantage of hearing spoken language and speech, so it is much more difficult to learn and use it.

70. C. Early childhood educators must maintain proper records and abide by federal, state, and school requirements in doing so. The primary purpose for their efficiency is to utilize the records to document goal attainment in the classroom and consistently and constantly review individual student programs so adjustments may be made on a regular basis.

71. C. An initial developmental screening is often conducted by early childhood teachers along with information contributed by parents for the purpose of deciding the need for a more formal and comprehensive evaluation.

72. B. Most home-based programs are parent-oriented, as they provide professionals in the home to train the parent(s) to work with the child. These programs do provide services to the child along with therapy as needed, and at times may include the siblings, but the primary focus is on the direct instruction to the parents on how to manage their child and implement the goals set.

73. A. Therapy in various areas of delay provides a child with additional services and a variety of interventions. It is very important for the child to generalize the skills learned in therapy to other settings as it will allow the child more independence.

74. A. Empirical research is often referred to as *naturalistic* research and is most often conducted in an observation format. There is generally not a control group, as the observation aspect of this research is found to be more beneficial than evaluating a control group. Although it may be harder to interpret the results of this type of research, many scientists and educators believe it offers more valuable information, as it provides a more functional look at children, which helps in developing programs for young children.

75. A. As babies begin to listen to the natural language of their home, they learn rhythm and cadence of the human voice and do not yet attach meanings to words. They may understand what is said and recognize certain words, but not until age 1 do they actually attach meanings to individual words. At around 18 months, babies can acquire one word every two hours, and they begin to combine words into meaningful patterns.

76. D. The third type of hearing loss is called *conductive*. A conductive loss is generally caused by an obstruction in either the middle or outer ear that interferes with sound traveling to the inner ear.

77. A. Society is heavily involved in the Technology Age. Changes occur more rapidly each day, and the progress of technology moves faster and faster by the minute. The schools, especially early childhood programs, will suffer from the lack of equipment, training, and other resources, which would otherwise enhance young children's education and lives. The money that will be required to make adequate changes and additions to the technology needed will just not be available. Children will be behind societal expectations prior to reaching the third grade.

78. C. Clinical observations are an important and often primary source of information for an OT regarding a child's performance in the physical and self-help domains. These observations are conducted in typical settings (home, school, park, and so on) while the child is engaged in daily activities as the observations offer objectivity to the OT.

79. C. Many early childhood programs develop a program that includes home-based services. Home-based services may be provided to families of children with disabilities on a weekly or bi-weekly basis. The services should aid the family in learning to provide services to their child.

80. C. Some parts of the brain are "hard-wired" at birth. These include breathing, heart rate control, sucking, moving, and body temperature. What researchers have determined is that intelligence *is not fixed* at birth. The brain develops throughout the very early years based on a child's experience, background, and relationships.

81. B. The inclusion model should be considered for all children, no matter the type or severity of the disability. Federal law requires that when creating a program for any child in special education that the continuum of placements be fully considered. Inclusion in a typical setting is the first type of setting on the continuum.

82. A. Educators can help parents to access community resources, such as medical providers, health professionals, therapists, mental health centers, respite care, employment centers, and counselors. It is most valuable for a family assessment to be conducted first in order to identify the needs, set family goals, detail the outcomes, and identify the resources that will promote success. Part of the assessment is in knowing what community resources are available and how to obtain them.

83. B. Informal testing is a critical component of the assessment process. It provides insight into the child's actual performance level on a daily basis. This is primarily conducted through observation of the child during play, snack time, grooming, and outdoor activities. It may also be called an authentic or ecological assessment.

84. D. When children are expected to move from one place to another or to change activities, it can result in some active behaviors. Some children have difficulty completing one task and moving on to another, while some have trouble understanding the ending and beginning of a new activity. Some children demonstrate the inability to move from one location to another without exhibiting additional and sometimes inappropriate behaviors. Often language and cognitive delays are the causes of these issues.

85. A. The scope and sequence portion of a curriculum is the most important section when making a determination to select an appropriate program. This provides the educator with an outline of the materials, the goals, and the schedule in which to teach concepts. It should also include explanations for all types of learners and adaptations for the diverse learners.

86. B. As a brain develops in the early years, it has the capabilities to continue to learn and expand those capabilities based on interactions and experiences. When a child turns 2, he has about the same number of synapses as an adult. By age 3, that number more than doubles (2.5 times). Children's brains remain this way until about age 10 when decline (natural pruning) begins.

87. A. Involving family/parents in the training component empowers them. The training allows parents to learn how to guide their child's activities and skill development and instills knowledge in them to be effective advocates in managing their child's care and program.

88. B. An anecdotal record is a type of informal assessment. Observing a child in a daily activity or routine can aid in evaluating skill acquisition and goal attainment. Keeping a simple written record about the behavior allows an evaluator to have additional information.

89. C. An Interdisciplinary Team is a group of professionals with defined roles that includes the parent(s). They often evaluate a child together and utilize ongoing communications, sharing evaluation results, and a child's progress. This team's focus is to develop an integrated plan of services for the child and family, and it is often a very effective team model in early childhood settings.

90. C. Music provides support for the various areas of language and literacy. Through music, children can experience phonological awareness, rhythm, and vocabulary building.

91. A. When children play, they are engaging in interactions with others. This encourages the development of social behaviors that include facial expressions (smiles, frowns), communication (use of gestures, observations of others, and responses), and performing roles and pretending. It is through play that these areas become more refined.

92. B. Sometimes a family of a child with a disability needs an active support system. Research shows that when family needs are met, a child's progress is enhanced. Families often find active, comfortable support from other parents in similar situations. Those with a similar child may help by providing emotional support, explaining disability issues, and sharing life experiences.

93. D. DAP or developmentally appropriate practices have been researched and determined to be the most beneficial in educating young children. This method allows children to be children and to select and access the materials and activities they desire while learning at their own rates.

94. C. Both an IEP and an IFSP are mandated as legal documents to be written within 45 days of the child's referral for special needs services. An IEP is developed for children over the age of 3 years, and the IFSP is for children under the age of 3 years.

95. C. In the early elementary years, children are practicing their newly learned skills in all areas. They are involving themselves more with other adults and other peer relationships and activities in their world. Children are learning to control their emotions and communicate their needs as well as manage their behaviors based on the situation in the environment. Their responsibilities are becoming evident, and at about age 6, children tend to prefer friendships over dependence on parents.

96. A. The federal law that entitles children to special education services is called IDEIA (The Individuals with Disabilities Education and Improvement Act). This provides services to children from birth through age 21. The specific section in the law that provides services to young children ages 3–5 is Part B. The Part C portion of the law relates to the early intervention services for children under the age of 3 years. The federal law titled FERPA (Family Education Rights and Privacy Act) relates to privacy and does not entitle children to the services stated. There is no separate section titled Part D or Part H in FERPA.

97. D. For many reasons, early childhood and preschool programs should consider evaluation and accreditation. Program improvement, research, and accountability are excellent reasons to review practices and services. Educators are advocates for child-friendly and family-focused programs, especially those that demonstrate and practice a high quality of services. Program efficacy is an important attribute to staff, parents, families, and community members.

98. C. The interventions that are contained in an early childhood curriculum are important for a teacher to evaluate when she is planning to purchase a curriculum program. Because the main focus of early childhood programs in public schools is to work with children who have special needs, the strategies provided for these children will be critical to their success.

99. C. An activity-based approach focuses on instruction that addresses a child's individual goals through child-initiated activities, while an academic-based approach has a more traditional focus on pre-academic skills in which children are engaged in teacher-directed activities. The psycho-social approach emphasizes psychological and social development, and the contextual approach takes the role of the environment as the key to enhancing a child's development.

100. B. When Lyndon Johnson was President in 1964, he declared the War on Poverty in order to address the needs of young children living in disadvantaged situations. Congress then enacted Project Head Start, which was an outreach program for economically disadvantaged preschoolers and their families. This program was intended to give young children a head start by taking advantage of the early developmental period in order to prepare the youngsters for school.

Answer Grid for Teaching Students with Behavioral Disorders/Emotional Disturbance (0371) Practice Exam

#	A	B	C	D		#	A	B	C	D
1	Ⓐ	Ⓑ	Ⓒ	Ⓓ		26	Ⓐ	Ⓑ	Ⓒ	Ⓓ
2	Ⓐ	Ⓑ	Ⓒ	Ⓓ		27	Ⓐ	Ⓑ	Ⓒ	Ⓓ
3	Ⓐ	Ⓑ	Ⓒ	Ⓓ		28	Ⓐ	Ⓑ	Ⓒ	Ⓓ
4	Ⓐ	Ⓑ	Ⓒ	Ⓓ		29	Ⓐ	Ⓑ	Ⓒ	Ⓓ
5	Ⓐ	Ⓑ	Ⓒ	Ⓓ		30	Ⓐ	Ⓑ	Ⓒ	Ⓓ
6	Ⓐ	Ⓑ	Ⓒ	Ⓓ		31	Ⓐ	Ⓑ	Ⓒ	Ⓓ
7	Ⓐ	Ⓑ	Ⓒ	Ⓓ		32	Ⓐ	Ⓑ	Ⓒ	Ⓓ
8	Ⓐ	Ⓑ	Ⓒ	Ⓓ		33	Ⓐ	Ⓑ	Ⓒ	Ⓓ
9	Ⓐ	Ⓑ	Ⓒ	Ⓓ		34	Ⓐ	Ⓑ	Ⓒ	Ⓓ
10	Ⓐ	Ⓑ	Ⓒ	Ⓓ		35	Ⓐ	Ⓑ	Ⓒ	Ⓓ
11	Ⓐ	Ⓑ	Ⓒ	Ⓓ		36	Ⓐ	Ⓑ	Ⓒ	Ⓓ
12	Ⓐ	Ⓑ	Ⓒ	Ⓓ		37	Ⓐ	Ⓑ	Ⓒ	Ⓓ
13	Ⓐ	Ⓑ	Ⓒ	Ⓓ		38	Ⓐ	Ⓑ	Ⓒ	Ⓓ
14	Ⓐ	Ⓑ	Ⓒ	Ⓓ		39	Ⓐ	Ⓑ	Ⓒ	Ⓓ
15	Ⓐ	Ⓑ	Ⓒ	Ⓓ		40	Ⓐ	Ⓑ	Ⓒ	Ⓓ
16	Ⓐ	Ⓑ	Ⓒ	Ⓓ		41	Ⓐ	Ⓑ	Ⓒ	Ⓓ
17	Ⓐ	Ⓑ	Ⓒ	Ⓓ		42	Ⓐ	Ⓑ	Ⓒ	Ⓓ
18	Ⓐ	Ⓑ	Ⓒ	Ⓓ		43	Ⓐ	Ⓑ	Ⓒ	Ⓓ
19	Ⓐ	Ⓑ	Ⓒ	Ⓓ		44	Ⓐ	Ⓑ	Ⓒ	Ⓓ
20	Ⓐ	Ⓑ	Ⓒ	Ⓓ		45	Ⓐ	Ⓑ	Ⓒ	Ⓓ
21	Ⓐ	Ⓑ	Ⓒ	Ⓓ		46	Ⓐ	Ⓑ	Ⓒ	Ⓓ
22	Ⓐ	Ⓑ	Ⓒ	Ⓓ		47	Ⓐ	Ⓑ	Ⓒ	Ⓓ
23	Ⓐ	Ⓑ	Ⓒ	Ⓓ		48	Ⓐ	Ⓑ	Ⓒ	Ⓓ
24	Ⓐ	Ⓑ	Ⓒ	Ⓓ		49	Ⓐ	Ⓑ	Ⓒ	Ⓓ
25	Ⓐ	Ⓑ	Ⓒ	Ⓓ		50	Ⓐ	Ⓑ	Ⓒ	Ⓓ

Teaching Students with Behavioral Disorders/Emotional Disturbance (0371) Practice Exam

Read each of the following multiple-choice questions and select the BEST answer. Fill in your choice by using the answer bubble sheet provided.

1. In observing the prevalence of emotional disabilities, gender is a factor in the actual numbers. Evidence shows that boys are more apt to demonstrate _____ behaviors than girls.

   A. exceptional
   B. internalizing
   C. externalizing
   D. non-exceptional

2. Which of the following organizations have challenged the federal definition for BD/ED in hopes that Congress will change the existing definition under IDEIA to make it more specific to the school age population?

   A. NAMI and APA
   B. APA and CCBD
   C. CCBD and NMHSEC
   D. NMHSEC and NAMI

3. The perception of individuals with behavior disorders/emotional disturbances has evolved over the years. The definitions and the policies have also changed. All of these things are influenced by factors that include science, philosophy, politics, laws, and

   A. culture.
   B. society.
   C. religion.
   D. environment.

4. The definition of an *emotional disability* under the federal law, IDEIA, includes several specific components. Which of the following is one of those detailed items?

   A. a tendency to establish friendships only with peers of the same sex
   B. undeveloped speech skills that contribute to withdrawal and anxiety
   C. inability to develop physically as compared to students of the same age
   D. inappropriate types of behavior or feelings under normal circumstances

5. Read the following lists and select the one that identifies the five patterns of emotional and behavioral disorders.

   A. hopelessness, inattention, withdrawal, panic, fear
   B. mania, sadness, hyperactivity, self-injurious, delinquency
   C. frustration, moodiness, distractibility, maladjustment, psychoses
   D. aggression, anxiety, depression, impulsivity, relationship problems

6. IDEIA defines emotional disturbance; however, two principles that are required under this law may impact the implementation of proper interventions and instruction for these students. These are

   A. DSM and OHI.
   B. LRE and FAPE.
   C. IEP and related services.
   D. BD/ED and assessments.

GO ON TO THE NEXT PAGE

209

7. Of the following, which is the category most closely associated with conduct disorder?

   A. anxiety
   B. aggression
   C. depression
   D. impulsivity

8. Which type of emotional and behavioral disorder is most often thought to be under identified?

   A. anxiety
   B. aggression
   C. internalizing
   D. externalizing

9. When describing affective disorders to parents at an eligibility meeting, it might be best to describe them as those problems that impact

   A. memory.
   B. academics.
   C. relationships.
   D. communication.

10. Many professionals believe there are two main categories that influence the development of behavioral and emotional disturbances. Within these categories, _____ are many varieties of specific causes.

    A. cultural and at-risk
    B. medical and familial
    C. developmental and health
    D. environmental and biological

11. The use of positive behavior support systems is appropriate for school-wide or individual programs. One main reason to implement a system of this kind is because it is

    A. more efficient than other programs.
    B. socially valid and usable in natural settings.
    C. easy for students to remember with tangible rewards.
    D. a standardized method supported by university research.

12. The term used for a type of positive reinforcement that should minimize or eliminate a specific, inappropriate behavior is

    A. planned ignoring.
    B. an extinction burst.
    C. a negative reinforcer.
    D. a graduated imitation.

13. The stimulus that occurs prior to a behavior is called the

    A. response.
    B. adaptation.
    C. antecedent.
    D. consequence.

14. Two skills are considered important for students with behavior problems as they move around and change settings. One skill recommended is the use of conflict resolution skills and the other is the use of

    A. listening skills.
    B. verbal responding.
    C. impulse responses.
    D. self-management skills.

15. A student identified with an emotional disability regularly demonstrates anxiety prior to taking a class test. The team determined that the antecedent is the announcement of the upcoming test. Then the student worries for several days and cannot study. The student has done poorly on previous tests, and the team has set this as a goal to overcome. What can the team do to assist this student?

    A. Help the student develop positive studying habits.
    B. Have the teacher change the required test to a project.
    C. Allow a paraprofessional to help by writing the answers.
    D. Ask the parents to keep the student home if the anxiety is too obvious.

16. A high school student's team has identified specific problems during certain times of the day with impulsive behaviors. The team has recorded that the antecedent is any unstructured activity. During these times, the student has verbal outbursts and moves around the room often. What can this team plan to alleviate these problems?

    A. Tell the student to manage the impulsive urges.
    B. Place the student in more structured settings all day.
    C. Suggest a replacement behavior for the student to use.
    D. Provide a paraprofessional who will control the outbursts.

17. Which of the following would aid a general education teacher in working positively with a student who is diagnosed with a behavioral disability?

    A. Allow the teacher to send the student to the resource room when inappropriate.
    B. Give the teacher a copy of the behavior plan and explain how it works in that classroom.
    C. Let the teacher decide the best behavior strategies and work with the parent to implement them.
    D. Provide the teacher with a list of the student's positive characteristics and refrain from discussing the disability.

18. An elementary student with behavior problems is placed in a general education classroom all day. To aid with the behaviors, the team decided that a key to success for this child was the _____ the child would be exposed to in this setting.

    A. diversity
    B. modeling
    C. instruction
    D. responsibility

19. What are the four goals of student misbehavior that should be considered when a team conducts a functional behavior plan? These will help in establishing proper treatments and interventions.

    A. anger, control, response, mastery
    B. assertiveness, logical, strength, retaliation
    C. abusive, corruptive, vengeance, hopelessness
    D. attention seeking, power, revenge, helplessness

20. The purpose of a behavior contract is to promote which of the following components?

    A. contributions by peers
    B. involvement of a parent
    C. responsibilities of the student
    D. reinforcements from the teachers

21. When a student is to be assessed for a possible behavior or emotional problem, it is best to use assessments that are conducted

    A. using several methods in multiple settings.
    B. sharing clinical methods in only two settings.
    C. utilizing one selected method in an integrated setting.
    D. employing specific methods in no more than two settings.

22. A theory that was developed by William Glasser supports a therapy by the same name. It is named _____ theory or therapy.

    A. social
    B. behavior
    C. reality-based
    D. person-centered

23. An intervention that has proven effective with students who have relationship problems is _____ because it helps them realize that other people have feelings and emotions, while showing them how to interact with the people in their lives.

    A. social skills training
    B. values-based education
    C. friendship control training
    D. core-relationships education

24. The person whose theory produced the Psychodynamic Model was

    A. B. F. Skinner.
    B. Chess Thomas.
    C. William Glaser.
    D. Sigmund Freud.

GO ON TO THE NEXT PAGE

25. In developing the most appropriate interventions for a student with BD/ED issues, they should be directly related to the most recent

A. grades.
B. therapies.
C. assessment.
D. observation.

26. Behavior plans are critical for the improvement of students with BD/ED problems. Some professionals use plans with negative consequences and some with positive reinforcement. The importance of using a positive behavior plan is that it

A. respects the student and addresses the specific behaviors.
B. is punitive, which helps to impose strict discipline measures.
C. only needs to be written once after a comprehensive assessment.
D. teaches one replacement behavior so the student can develop others.

27. When a Functional Behavior Assessment must be conducted, information is gathered about the student's behavior in several settings. One source that can provide essential information is the

A. parent.
B. sibling.
C. therapist.
D. principal.

28. Which of the following conceptual models emphasizes the treatment of the child while also addressing changes in the family, school, and community?

A. ecological
B. behavioral
C. social discipline
D. psychoeducational

29. Research on the impact of the school setting for students with BD/ED problems indicates that _____ may be a significant factor that contributes to a student's academic failure.

A. peer pressure
B. ineffective instruction
C. parent non-involvement
D. extracurricular activities

30. When a team includes goals for self-management skills related to inappropriate behaviors on an IEP for a student with an emotional disability, the intent is for the student to learn to control the behaviors in various settings and to gain

A. a circle of friends.
B. a sense of independence.
C. better organizational skills.
D. more time to work on academics.

31. A student from South America who was just evaluated for special education has been in this country for two years. The child has exhibited problems even as an infant, and the parents were concerned then. Now that the student has been identified with BD/ED needs, the team is ready to develop the behavior intervention strategies. What should the team consider doing before writing the plan?

A. Research the relevance of the proposed interventions on this particular culture.
B. Develop the plan based on other students from similar backgrounds and cultures.
C. Engage the student in a discussion of preferences for selecting the language to be used.
D. Check with the parents regarding their views on the cultural influences of existing behaviors.

32. A strategy known to be effective for engaging students with BD/ED in the classroom as active learners is to use

A. peer tutors.
B. response cards.
C. paraprofessionals.
D. assignment notebooks.

33. Behavioral theory is generally based on

A. operant conditioning.
B. operant consequences.
C. adaptive conditioning.
D. adaptive consequences.

34. Behavioral theory and its approach have identified an analysis technique that is dubbed the "ABC" method. This is utilized as professionals develop behavior support plans for students, once the target behaviors have been defined. What do the "A," "B," and "C" stand for?

A. alter, build, construe
B. action, belief, condition
C. analyze, basics, correction
D. antecedent, behavior, consequence

35. One of the most effective methods for supporting positive behavior that is used in school programs is

A. rewards and acknowledgements.
B. natural consequences in typical settings.
C. discipline and correction of inappropriate behaviors.
D. random reinforcements so there are no constant conditions.

36. A teacher in an alternative program for students with emotional and behavioral disabilities maintains a record of the number, interval, and specific situation of all the behavioral issues for each student in the classroom in order to

A. send reports to parents and principal.
B. demonstrate progress on goal attainment.
C. determine the antecedents for each behavior.
D. prove that an additional teacher is necessary.

37. Which of the following describes the methods behind the psychoeducational approach used by teachers in classrooms for students with behavioral and emotional problems?

A. control and regulation
B. cooperation and authority
C. consequences and restraint
D. communication and discipline

38. An area of the federal law that is most difficult for the schools to manage with regard to students with behavioral and emotional disabilities is

A. discipline.
B. equipment.
C. medications.
D. transportation.

39. A middle school student with a behavior disorder under IDEIA is caught with a knife in his pocket and drinking alcohol in the locker room after school. The principal contacts the police who arrest the student. Before the student may return to the school program, the team must follow the rules for the school and those under the law. Which of the following is the next step they must take?

A. Conduct a manifestation determination hearing.
B. Plan a meeting with the parents and social worker.
C. Speak with the student about the inappropriate behaviors.
D. Meet with all of the student's teachers to change the rules.

40. A standard tool of assessment that may be used to evaluate how a student feels, thinks, and behaves in a variety of situations is the

A. health profile.
B. parent interview.
C. achievement scores.
D. personality measurement.

GO ON TO THE NEXT PAGE

Read the following case study and then answer questions 41–44, which follow.

An eight-year-old, second grade, Caucasian child was recently identified for services under the primary category of ED with a secondary focus on LD (Learning Disabilities). The child is on medication for an ADHD diagnosis from a primary care provider. The child lives at home with very young parents (22 and 23), who are not married and frequent drug users. Neither has a regular job, with the father doing odd jobs at a nearby apartment complex, and the mother helping at a local flower shop. The child is often late to school or absent, as the mother regularly oversleeps and either brings the child to school an hour or more after the day begins or does not bring the child at all. On several occasions, the child was found wandering nearby the school, in an attempt to walk to school unaccompanied by an adult. The mother reports that the grandparents live with them sporadically; however, the grandmother is an alcoholic, who sometimes cares for the child, and the grandfather has been in and out of jail for minor acts. Overall, the adults in this child's life provide little attention or guidance.

The child demonstrates great difficulty with academic tasks and functions at about the kindergarten level in most subject areas. Although the child has low academic skills, the child is often very verbal in class, yet inappropriate and disruptive. These inappropriate behaviors are used to make others laugh, and often the child gets over stimulated and extremely silly. This student has difficulty settling down with typical interventions.

The child often moves around the room, out of seat and off task, as well as leaves the classroom without permission. The child also has trouble during unstructured times, such as transitions and recess. The child fights with peers, generally pushing, hitting, and pinching others. Because of these problems, the child was provided an instructional assistant to help with transitions, on the playground, and staying on task, but it has not helped much. The child has been rude to the adults and kicked an aide one day. There is a lack of coping skills when angry or upset, as evidenced by outbursts, tantrums, or offensive language. The child has made extremely racist comments to others who are enrolled in this diverse elementary school setting. And with regularity, this child uses fowl language and is often heard singing inappropriate and vulgar rap songs.

The team does not think that the child is being medicated properly or consistently, even though they have reports that the prescriptions are being filled. The father reports that there is a community agency that has provided a therapist to work with the child, but he does not know much more about it, as a community social worker usually takes the child to the appointment after school. The community agency is investigating the medication issues.

The team recently met to reconsider the child's placement, but neither parent attended the meeting. The team reviewed the overall case and wanted to discuss the option of a change in placement. The child is difficult to manage in a regular classroom, low functioning in all academic areas, verbally abusive to peers and adults, and has had physical altercations with other children and adults. The team will need to reschedule the meeting in hopes that the parents will be able to attend and discuss the child's program.

41. Which of the following LRE options should be the next step proposed for this child's placement?

    A. residential care
    B. resource classroom
    C. homebound placement
    D. self-contained program

42. When the team conducted a functional behavior assessment, they needed to determine the reason(s) for the child's inappropriate behaviors in the classroom in order to determine the proper interventions. Based on this case scenario, what would be the best selection for the reason this child behaves in this way?

    A. to be funny
    B. to seek attention
    C. to make adults angry
    D. to get out of doing work

43. Based on the facts of this case, what strategies or interventions would seem to work best in changing the behaviors of this child?

  A. consistent feedback and positive reinforcement for desired behaviors

  B. consequences for inappropriate behaviors and phone calls to the home

  C. a peer helper to model the proper behaviors with documented progress

  D. a behavior plan that is similarly implemented in the home and at school

44. To understand more completely how the community therapist works with this child and the interventions that are being used, what should the school team do first to collaborate with this therapist?

  A. Send a team member to the facility to observe a therapy session.

  B. Invite the therapist to a team meeting to share the therapeutic information.

  C. Obtain permission from parents to access records and speak to the therapist.

  D. Call the therapist and ask for information and a copy of the therapy reports.

Read the following case study and then answer questions 45–47, which follow.

A fourth grader lives with one parent, a mother, in the home. At times, the child has been placed with various relatives, as the father is not part of the family unit, and sometimes, the mother is not around. She then has an uncle or grandparent stay with the children, but they do not share the same parenting skills. There is another child in the home who is a half-sibling and in the second grade. This younger child was just placed in a residential, psychiatric hospital for uncontrollable maladaptive behaviors. This younger child's father was diagnosed with mental illness when he was 24 years old.

Over the past three years of school, the fourth-grade child has changed schools five times, as the mother has to move around often to find work. Each time the child enrolls in another school, the school records take a long time to arrive or do not arrive at all, as the mother does not always give the proper information about the previous school.

The fourth grader presents with behaviors that are threatening to others, such as fighting, bullying, and intimidating. At one school, the records revealed that this child pushed a teacher, not due to being angry, but because the student felt the teacher was in the way. This child swears at others and uses verbal insults, but is sneaky about doing so. The other children are afraid of this student so no reports of inappropriate behaviors are made by peers. This child makes comments to others when no adult is around or in listening distance. This student enjoys telling stories about people who have been hurt or traumatized as the child thinks they are funny.

The child receives special education services under the category of ED and has related services for speech and language issues and a social worker who aids in behavior counseling. The student often refuses to go with the speech pathologist to work on fluency and articulation issues and once or twice has refused to go to counseling. The child is defiant in class and refuses to do class work. The teacher has reported that the child's expression is frightening, as she noticed that when an adult speaks with the child, the child stares with "wild eyes."

The child has stated that no matter what anyone says, if he wants something, it will be obtained. This student seems to work the system to get what is desired and has no guilt or empathy for others. The child is currently in a resource setting to support the academic and behavior portion of the program. However, the team believes that the program should be readdressed due to recent escalations in inappropriate behaviors.

GO ON TO THE NEXT PAGE

45. The team would like to review the least restrictive options of this child's program. The child will need another functional behavior assessment due to the recent problems, and the team is very concerned about the current resource program. What would be another possibility for this child in order to provide academic services and behavior management in a proper environment?

A. residential care
B. alternative school
C. home-based program
D. general education classroom

46. What type of interventions may work for this student while still in the current setting?

A. reward time with peers as an incentive
B. time out in a quiet area or separate room
C. notes home to parent for positive behavior
D. a behavior chart on the desk for self-management

47. This student has been defiant with the speech therapist and the social worker by not complying with the request to go with them for services. What could these related service providers do to eliminate a power struggle with this student?

A. Cancel the current session if the student is obstinate.
B. Contact the parent to speak with the student about respect.
C. Postpone all related services until the student is more compliant.
D. Provide the related services and interventions in the classroom.

Read the following case study and then answer questions 48–50, which follow.

A fifth-grade Mexican-American student lives at home with mother, father, two brothers, and a sister. The primary language of the home is Spanish, yet the children are becoming bilingual. The mother knows a little English, but the father knows none. The older sister is in high school and performing at an average level but does not spend much time in the home. The older brother who is 16 has been arrested twice, once for a DUI and the second time for gang activities. The younger brother, who is 2, is favored by the parents, especially the mother.

The father works at a local restaurant but is not home in the evenings and is not involved with the children. He has never attended a school function or meeting. The mother works as a seamstress in a local dress shop, but it is not a regular position. She attends most school meetings and tries to help the children when she can. She does not support the fifth grader and will tell people that the child is worthless and cannot do anything. When she is at work, however, the care of the toddler falls to the fifth grader.

The fifth grader is placed under the category of LD (Learning Disabilities), but has inappropriate behaviors that are addressed through related service providers (behavior coach and social worker). The child is placed in a general education monolingual English classroom with pull-out for second language instruction and reading. The student is a non-completer and can sit all day with no responses. The child presents with a flat affect, is listless, and refuses to work. Sometimes, the student falls asleep for long periods of time.

A recent IQ test indicated that the child falls within the range of low average or borderline IQ, and classroom performance is at second- or third-grade level. The team has identified that the function of this child's behavior is task avoidance due to academic difficulties. This student states a fear of failure and, therefore, demonstrates low self-esteem, which seems to be exacerbated by parent comments in the home. However, when working individually with the examiner, the student was able to perform more tasks than the student expected, which was pleasing.

The mother is very strict with this child, perhaps because of the difficulty that has occurred with her older boy. The school team believes they have convinced the mother to obtain outside community counseling under the state assistance program.

This student loves playing soccer at recess with a group of friends who have the same ethnic background. Art and drawing motivate this child during the school day, and the child excels in this area.

48. What school strategy or educational intervention would be appropriate for this student in order for the class work to be completed and for the child to increase self-esteem?

    A. Hire a tutor to help with homework and class work.

    B. Allow the student to join the soccer team and the art club.

    C. Provide an instructional aide and reward on task behaviors.

    D. Work with the parent to establish a sleep schedule and be positive.

49. This student will be attending the middle school for the next school year. Which of the following should the team consider MOST when creating the program and class schedule for this student?

    A. an art class

    B. an ESL class

    C. a speech group

    D. a reading group

50. When the team meets with the parents, to discuss the student's program for the coming year, which of the following school personnel should be present and for what reason?

    A. the art teacher to assess the student's skills and abilities and to write a goal

    B. the principal to talk about the structure of the upcoming discipline program

    C. the soccer coach to explain that an exception to join the team may be accommodated

    D. the school nurse to speak about the sleeping problem and potential medical concerns

Teaching Students with Behavioral Disorders/Emotional Disturbance (0371) Practice Exam Answer Key

1. C		26. A	
2. C		27. A	
3. C		28. A	
4. D		29. B	
5. D		30. B	
6. B		31. D	
7. B		32. B	
8. C		33. A	
9. C		34. D	
10. D		35. A	
11. B		36. C	
12. A		37. D	
13. C		38. A	
14. D		39. A	
15. A		40. D	
16. C		41. D	
17. B		42. B	
18. B		43. A	
19. D		44. C	
20. C		45. B	
21. A		46. B	
22. C		47. D	
23. A		48. C	
24. D		49. A	
25. C		50. D	

Answer Explanations for Teaching Students with Behavioral Disorders/Emotional Disturbance (0371) Practice Exam

1. **C.** Research has shown that boys are more likely to be labeled under the BD/ED category than girls. Boys also seem to be identified with externalizing behaviors such as being antisocial or aggressive more often than girls. Although girls can have aggressive behaviors, they are more highly likely to exhibit internalizing behaviors such as depression and eating disorders.

2. **C.** The Council for Children with Behavior Disorders is a subgroup of CEC (Council for Exceptional Children) and they, along with the NMHSEC (National Mental Health and Special Education Coalition), have rewritten the definition for behavioral disorders/emotional disturbances, which they prefer will be used as the federal definition under IDEIA. CCBD and NMHSEC have jointly submitted a proposed definition to Congress.

3. **C.** Several factors have influence over the perceptions, education, definitions, and policies that affect students with behavioral disorders/emotional disturbances. These include science, philosophy, politics, laws, and religion.

4. **D.** The specific components of the IDEIA definition include

   - an inability to learn that cannot be explained by intellectual, sensory, or health factors.
   - an inability to build or maintain satisfactory interpersonal relationships with peers and teachers.
   - inappropriate types of behavior or feelings under normal circumstances.
   - a general pervasive mood of unhappiness or depression.
   - a tendency to develop physical symptoms or fear associated with personal or school problems.

5. **D.** Although all of the mentioned traits may be exhibited in individuals with emotional and behavioral disorders, the correct answer lists those five that professionals believe to be the main categories.

6. **B.** Students with behavior and emotional disorders can be difficult to treat properly in the school environment. The need for treatment and the effective interventions to directly address the issues for these students are sometimes better provided in more segregated or alternative settings. These students often perform better and make gains when their program is strictly structured and managed by clinical staff. Therefore, addressing the LRE (least restrictive environment) and FAPE (free and appropriate public education) through special education can be very complex.

7. **B.** The pattern of aggression includes conduct that often inflicts injury or harm on others and may include forms of disobedience and disrespect. The behaviors that are related to aggression are threatening behaviors, assault, fighting, and antisocial acts. Students may also have clinically diagnosed mental problems that include conduct disorder and oppositional defiant disorder.

8. **C.** Because internalizing behaviors are not always easily observable, there is some speculation that this type of disorder may be under identified and underserved. These behaviors pertain to mood, anxieties, withdrawal, and depression. A student who is quiet, alone, reserved, and may not act out, could be at-risk, but is not easily recognized by the adults in the student's environment.

9. **C.** The affective behaviors are those that pertain to social-emotional development, interpersonal skills, and relationship problems.

10. **D.** The two main categories of causes for behavioral and emotional disturbances are environmental factors and biological factors. The environmental causes relate to a child's behavior in the family, at school, and in community settings, while the biological causes may include brain disorders, genetic influences, and temperament.

11. **B.** A positive behavior support system is excellent for use in schools as it is a proactive method that teaches students to use and manage appropriate behaviors. It is socially valid, is used in natural contexts, and maintains the pride of individuals it seeks to help.

12. A. Planned ignoring is a strategy that can be used with children who have emotional or behavioral disorders in an attempt to minimize or eliminate the behavior. When the behavior begins, the adult does not respond to the act but ignores the student's behavior. Eventually the student's behavior will be extinguished as the student is not getting any attention for it.

13. C. An antecedent is generally considered the stimulus for an occurring behavior. This is the cause for the behavior and is an important piece for a team to identify when they are working to create a behavior plan and interventions.

14. D. Through research, it has been determined that students with behavior problems often perform better and appear more well adjusted when changing settings if they can use conflict resolution skills and self-management skills to keep their behaviors appropriate.

15. A. The student needs to learn how to take tests, since in the future the student may face a project at work or in the home that causes the same feelings of anxiety. The best solution is to help the student learn how to study by giving the student guidelines to develop study habits and monitor the acquisition of these skills.

16. C. Providing the student with another behavior as an option to learn to control the impulsivity is a good way to help the student understand the feelings and begin to self-manage those periods of difficulty. A replacement behavior can be a simple remedy for the student in these situations.

17. B. General education teachers have not been trained in working with students who have BD/ED problems. However, they should be part of each student's team if the student is placed in their class. Providing the teacher with a copy of the behavior plan will aid in the understanding of the goals and how to carry out the interventions.

18. B. An intervention that often works well for elementary children to promote appropriate behaviors is modeling. When prosocial behaviors are used by peers in a natural setting, children with disabilities will be more likely to imitate them. When a child uses the appropriate behavior, the child is reinforced and continues to be successful.

19. D. According to Dreikurs in the social discipline theory, there are four primary reasons that support the behaviors demonstrated by children: attention seeking, power, revenge, and helplessness.

20. C. A contract is generally an agreement that is mutually established by a teacher and a student, or the educational team and the student, in order to address and replace inappropriate behaviors. The purpose for the contract is to aid in the development of student responsibilities, self-management, and behavior changes.

21. A. Utilizing several methods of assessment across various settings for a student with potential behavioral and emotional disabilities gives the team a better idea of the student's abilities and needs. This is a recommended best practice and involves several professionals and the parents in determining the most appropriate program for the student.

22. C. The reality-based theory, also choice therapy, was begun by Glasser and focused on love, power, pleasure, and freedom.

23. A. Students with BD/ED problems in the area of relationships may not know the issues they have in building and sustaining them. They need social skills almost every day of their lives as they deal with friends, family, and other people in society.

24. D. Sigmund Freud was the originator of the theory of psycho-analysis that supports the psychodynamic model. He thought it was important to work with individuals to uncover the unconscious thoughts that drive personality and behaviors.

25. C. A comprehensive assessment would offer the most information about a student and would give professionals the opportunity to create a plan based on the student's needs. Grades, therapy reports, and observation are all components of a solid assessment.

26. A. The implementation of a positive behavior plan is helpful to students with BD/ED problems, as it separates the behavior from the individual. Students need to be respected in spite of problem behaviors with an emphasis on changing the inappropriate behaviors, not the person.

27. A. The information that parents can offer to a team assessment is very important. They know their child's personality and the skill levels related to behaviors and social interactions. They are able to notice and remember the behaviors that their child has used in various settings in and out of the home. The other people listed in this question do offer information, but most parents have a critical viewpoint.

28. A. The ecological model is one that defines BD/ED problems as individuals who do not adjust well to their own environment and setting (ecosystem). This includes family, school, and community. It stresses treating the child while making changes to the ecosystem to allow the child to function in it.

29. B. Research on how schools impact the success of students with BD/ED conditions determined that ineffective instruction was a major contributor to students who fail in the school system. It was evident that these students may not be receiving their academics using the instructional strategies that are most beneficial for their conditions.

30. B. For students with emotional disabilities, learning appropriate skills for various situations is difficult but very important. How these students adapt to the changing settings in life will mean so much to them. Learning how to self-manage behaviors lets the students be the barometers of their own selves. This, in turn, allows them to gain a sense of independence, which is a positive motivator.

31. D. Although the team may consider all of these options, the one that is the best selection is the answer that includes the parents in the development of the interventions. Involving parents is important for students of diverse backgrounds, since all cultures do not define acceptable behaviors in the same way. Together, the team must select the proper interventions that the family will accept, or the results will not be favorable.

32. B. Response cards are an excellent strategy to use for all students, but especially those with behavior and emotional problems. The use of these cards keeps students on task and provides them with the opportunity to participate in each question by the teacher. Using these reduces inappropriate behaviors and keeps students involved in their learning.

33. A. Behavioral theory is based upon operant conditioning and the belief that behavior is related to environmental stimuli.

34. D. The ABC Analysis technique is a commonly used approach in schools by teams who assess and provide services to students for their behaviors. The letters represent antecedent, behavior, and consequence. When a team takes this approach, they can more easily understand a student's behaviors across settings and create an appropriate plan that targets the function of the behavior.

35. A. Research conducted on strategies that support positive behavior management has determined that one of the best methods to use is that of providing rewards and acknowledgements to students with behavioral and emotional problems who perform socially appropriately. The studies further show that when students receive this positive feedback they are more likely to use those desired behaviors again.

36. C. Although all of the answers have some value related to this question, the best answer is that the teacher will be able to analyze the data collected on each student to determine the antecedents. As the teacher reviews each recorded situation and the documentation, a revision of a student's plan and environment may be made based on the antecedents that are present.

37. D. The psychoeducational approach is commonly used in schools to manage students with behavioral and emotional problems. It emphasizes care, discipline, and communication with students in order to help the student learn internal control (self-management skills).

38. A. The law has established guidelines for schools to follow in order to provide disciplinary action to students with disabilities. Since these students are placed in special education for their behavior problems, it is tricky for the school staff to follow the guidelines and the school policies while providing adequate support to meet the student's needs.

39. A. A manifestation determination hearing must be conducted for any student in special education to determine the reason for the behavior and to decide whether it was related to the disability. The IEP team proceeds with the hearing with teachers, parents, and the student present prior to the student's re-entry into the school.

40. D. A personality measurement is a standard measure and may be conducted using the interview format. This tool may also be used together with other assessments to collect information about the many aspects of a student's condition.

41. D. The student presents with maladaptive behaviors, which may be compounded by the home situation. Without the parental support and appropriate role models, this child is left to do as he pleases. Placing the child in the home for services would not help with goal attainment, and homebound services are generally for children with chronic illnesses. The child may need residential care at some point, but this is not the next step in the LRE continuum. Resource class could be considered, but since the child does not do well in the regular classroom, has difficulty with transitions, and is physical with instructional aides, the movement that this option requires would not meet the child's needs. The best option is for placement in a self-contained classroom, in which the child may be closely monitored, work at the academic level that is appropriate, and in which behaviors will be addressed consistently.

42. B. The team most likely determined that this child is using behaviors to seek attention. Due to the home situation, this child receives very little attention and guidance. Since the child is at such a young age, he requires more attention. The behaviors of using vulgar language, singing rap songs, and making racist comments may be the result of the modeling the child receives in the home. This child will need to be taught to seek attention in more appropriate ways with the help of professionals.

43. A. This child may not understand what proper behaviors are in social settings at this young age, due to the lack of prosocial models in the home. Therefore, the child should be consistently provided with frequent feedback and positive reinforcement when a desired behavior is demonstrated. At this time, it does not appear that answers B or D would work as they involve the family's support, which is not available. Since the child has problems with peers, is verbally and physically abusive, answer C makes for an unsafe situation for other children.

44. C. The first step in securing information about a community service provided to a child and establishing a collaborative effort with an outside agency, is to request permission from the parents to do so. This team should request that parents sign a release of information that the school team may access the records and work with the community therapist in the best interests of this child's development.

45. B. The child would most likely benefit from placement in an alternative school to gain structure and consistency for the difficult behaviors. Residential care may be an option if the alternative does not help, but it is not the next option in the LRE continuum. Home-based services would not appear to aid the student due to the lack of support in the home. A general education class was the first step in the LRE options, but the child is not successful with the more restrictive placement of resource programming.

46. B. This student needs time away from others, especially when exhibiting inappropriate behaviors. While the student remains in the current setting, a time-out area may be set up that is secluded from other children. This will eliminate the audience and will protect other children from frightening or dangerous situations. This student is not able to self-manage behaviors at this time, and rewarding the student with time with peers places others in a difficult situation. Communicating with the parent is important to keep her involved in the process, but at this point it would not do much to improve this student's behaviors.

47. D. This student believes that he is in charge of everything and everyone. The related services may be provided within the classroom setting, and the providers should attempt to do so. This student may be embarrassed or upset that these services are noticed by others, which may show a weakness, so he might prefer to leave with the therapist rather than feel shamed.

48. C. The best solution is to provide an aide to this student so the sleeping can be interrupted and the student can remain on-task. When the student is on-task and using desired behaviors, the student should be positively rewarded. The problem is during class time, so a tutor would not help this problem, and joining the soccer team and art club may be positive moves for the student, but they do not help with the sleeping problem or work completion. The community counselor should help the parent create a sleep schedule and alter his negative communication style.

49. A. Since art is a motivating aspect of the student's day and the student excels in this area, building an art class into the daily schedule may support the student's need for building self-esteem by creating a sense of pride and accomplishment. This might be the class in which task completion could be emphasized, as well, and it may help in minimizing some of the behaviors.

50. D. When a student exhibits a behavior that may have some underlying medical issue, it is important to involve the school nurse who may speak with parents about these possible medical concerns and help the parents obtain the resources to follow through. A student with a sleeping problem may have a health condition that requires treatment. It would be important for the student to have a medical exam to rule out any health problems.

Answer Grid for Teaching Students with Learning Disabilities (0381) Practice Exam

1 Ⓐ Ⓑ Ⓒ Ⓓ	26 Ⓐ Ⓑ Ⓒ Ⓓ
2 Ⓐ Ⓑ Ⓒ Ⓓ	27 Ⓐ Ⓑ Ⓒ Ⓓ
3 Ⓐ Ⓑ Ⓒ Ⓓ	28 Ⓐ Ⓑ Ⓒ Ⓓ
4 Ⓐ Ⓑ Ⓒ Ⓓ	29 Ⓐ Ⓑ Ⓒ Ⓓ
5 Ⓐ Ⓑ Ⓒ Ⓓ	30 Ⓐ Ⓑ Ⓒ Ⓓ
6 Ⓐ Ⓑ Ⓒ Ⓓ	31 Ⓐ Ⓑ Ⓒ Ⓓ
7 Ⓐ Ⓑ Ⓒ Ⓓ	32 Ⓐ Ⓑ Ⓒ Ⓓ
8 Ⓐ Ⓑ Ⓒ Ⓓ	33 Ⓐ Ⓑ Ⓒ Ⓓ
9 Ⓐ Ⓑ Ⓒ Ⓓ	34 Ⓐ Ⓑ Ⓒ Ⓓ
10 Ⓐ Ⓑ Ⓒ Ⓓ	35 Ⓐ Ⓑ Ⓒ Ⓓ
11 Ⓐ Ⓑ Ⓒ Ⓓ	36 Ⓐ Ⓑ Ⓒ Ⓓ
12 Ⓐ Ⓑ Ⓒ Ⓓ	37 Ⓐ Ⓑ Ⓒ Ⓓ
13 Ⓐ Ⓑ Ⓒ Ⓓ	38 Ⓐ Ⓑ Ⓒ Ⓓ
14 Ⓐ Ⓑ Ⓒ Ⓓ	39 Ⓐ Ⓑ Ⓒ Ⓓ
15 Ⓐ Ⓑ Ⓒ Ⓓ	40 Ⓐ Ⓑ Ⓒ Ⓓ
16 Ⓐ Ⓑ Ⓒ Ⓓ	41 Ⓐ Ⓑ Ⓒ Ⓓ
17 Ⓐ Ⓑ Ⓒ Ⓓ	42 Ⓐ Ⓑ Ⓒ Ⓓ
18 Ⓐ Ⓑ Ⓒ Ⓓ	43 Ⓐ Ⓑ Ⓒ Ⓓ
19 Ⓐ Ⓑ Ⓒ Ⓓ	44 Ⓐ Ⓑ Ⓒ Ⓓ
20 Ⓐ Ⓑ Ⓒ Ⓓ	45 Ⓐ Ⓑ Ⓒ Ⓓ
21 Ⓐ Ⓑ Ⓒ Ⓓ	46 Ⓐ Ⓑ Ⓒ Ⓓ
22 Ⓐ Ⓑ Ⓒ Ⓓ	47 Ⓐ Ⓑ Ⓒ Ⓓ
23 Ⓐ Ⓑ Ⓒ Ⓓ	48 Ⓐ Ⓑ Ⓒ Ⓓ
24 Ⓐ Ⓑ Ⓒ Ⓓ	49 Ⓐ Ⓑ Ⓒ Ⓓ
25 Ⓐ Ⓑ Ⓒ Ⓓ	50 Ⓐ Ⓑ Ⓒ Ⓓ

CUT HERE

Teaching Students with Learning Disabilities (0381) Practice Exam

Read each of the following multiple-choice questions and select the BEST answer. Fill in your choice by using the answer bubble sheet provided.

1. A teacher must establish the *classroom tone* as she organizes the learning environment for the purpose of

   A. stating the rules.
   B. conducting guided practice.
   C. accommodating all students.
   D. setting the stage for learning.

2. In order for professionals to meet the varying needs and learning styles of individuals with learning disabilities, they should select instructional techniques that ensure student success. The recommended practice in choosing these is to

   A. choose educator favorites.
   B. ask for parent preference.
   C. use research-based methods.
   D. select teacher-made materials.

3. For students with learning disabilities, accessing the general curriculum is critical to their ability to be responsible for their learning and become more independent. The use of _____ is a positive way to support students.

   A. electronic text
   B. a word processor
   C. an electronic calculator
   D. a digital speech recorder

4. A primary characteristic that is most typical of students identified with learning disabilities is

   A. math deficits.
   B. cognitive delays.
   C. speech problems.
   D. reading difficulties.

5. A process that works well with students who have learning disabilities to promote positive performance and improve achievement is to

   A. remove the students when off-task.
   B. isolate the instruction for these students.
   C. conduct independent practice with feedback.
   D. promote group instruction and written assignments.

6. A particular strategy, which is based on research to increase student motivation, is one that

   A. delivers compliments on a daily basis.
   B. builds relationships for at-risk students.
   C. allows extrinsic rewards for every completed task.
   D. provides expectations in consistent and clear terms.

7. The key instructional practices of _____ are indicative of the behavioral theory.

   A. implicit teaching and direct instruction
   B. explicit teaching and direct instruction
   C. explicit teaching and indirect instruction
   D. implicit teaching and indirect instruction

8. One theory of positive behavior supports that increases or changes a target behavior by providing a reward system is best identified as

   A. attribution.
   B. attainment.
   C. recognition.
   D. reinforcement.

GO ON TO THE NEXT PAGE

9. Which of the following set of descriptors suggests the primary characteristics of a child with ADD or ADHD?

   A. inattentive, impulsive, and hyperactive
   B. impulsive, unmotivated, and disorganized
   C. helplessness, social deficit, and hyperactive
   D. poor behaviors, underachiever, and inattentive

10. There are debates about the methods in which students with learning disabilities may receive their grades. One example of an alternative grading system is

   A. contract grading.
   B. strategic grading.
   C. report card grading.
   D. assessment grading.

11. Piaget's theory promotes the stages of learning and a child's maturational level that are key to which of the following psychology theories?

   A. conduct
   B. behavioral
   C. processing
   D. developmental

12. For a student with a learning disability who demonstrates inappropriate behaviors, the IEP team should create a _____ according to the federal special education law.

   A. functional behavior plan
   B. behavior skills curriculum
   C. behavior intervention strategy
   D. classroom management technique

13. A precursor that may be evident in a young child and that may indicate the potential for a learning disability is a

   A. speech delay.
   B. reading deficit.
   C. motor problem.
   D. hearing difficulty.

14. Significant gains in academics and social skill development have been documented when the following method is used in a general education setting for students with learning disabilities.

   A. peer tutoring
   B. alternative grading
   C. behavior checklists
   D. reading volunteers

15. A method utilized during the assessment process by parents and teachers to rank a student's behaviors is called the

   A. case history.
   B. rating scales.
   C. anecdotal record.
   D. informed consent.

16. Which of the following is an example of an assistive technology tool helpful to a student with a learning disability who has difficulty writing?

   A. eraser
   B. calculator
   C. headphones
   D. spell checker

17. One form of technology programming that has had a major impact on students with learning disabilities is the

   A. Internet.
   B. calculator.
   C. cell phone.
   D. digital recorder.

18. A technique that will promote student engagement in learning activities, support a positive environment, and foster teacher-student relationships is for the teacher to

   A. clarify and establish rules and directions in written form.
   B. videotape the learning environment and share it with students.
   C. contact each student's parents and provide written progress reports.
   D. circulate throughout the classroom to check student work and progress.

19. Language skills are often troublesome for students with learning disabilities. Which of the following indicate the more commonly identified areas of specific language problems for students with learning disabilities?

- A. verbal prompts and expressive phrases
- B. phonological awareness and pragmatics
- C. oral expression and listening comprehension
- D. auditory perception and receptive vocabulary

20. A student's social skills and emotional status are best evaluated through the use of the _____ technique.

- A. observation
- B. rating scale
- C. criterion referenced
- D. portfolio assessment

21. When comparing gender, research has determined that there appear to be _____ who are identified with learning disabilities.

- A. more boys than girls
- B. fewer boys than girls
- C. just as many boys as girls
- D. unknown numbers of boys or girls

22. A general education teacher is mandated to be a member of a student's IEP team under which of the following laws?

- A. LRE
- B. FAPE
- C. IDEIA
- D. FERPA

23. Which of the following is a significant indicator for children with emerging learning disabilities?

- A. reading and speaking problems
- B. social and emotional disturbances
- C. behavior and motivation concerns
- D. discrepancy between ability and achievement

24. A formal mathematics test that is utilized to assess a student's individual mathematics ability is considered

- A. an achievement test.
- B. a portfolio assessment.
- C. an authentic assessment.
- D. a norm-referenced test.

25. The primary goal of *learning strategies instruction* is to assist students with learning disabilities in

- A. controlling their own learning.
- B. managing their daily schedule.
- C. transitioning into the community.
- D. developing functional behavior skills.

26. When students gain the awareness of their own learning styles and thinking processes, we refer to this as

- A. metacognition.
- B. sensory awareness.
- C. neurological impact.
- D. strategy development.

27. An effective method of instruction for use in general education classrooms when there are high numbers of students with learning disabilities enrolled is the application of

- A. co-teaching.
- B. aide instruction.
- C. resource support.
- D. transition services.

28. At a parent-teacher conference, a teacher may provide an evaluation that consists of concrete examples of what the student has learned and what the student is capable of doing. This type of assessment tool is called a

- A. task inventory.
- B. checklist inventory.
- C. portfolio assessment.
- D. standardized assessment.

GO ON TO THE NEXT PAGE

29. To assist a student with a learning disability in the areas of *memorization* and *retrieval of information,* teachers should impose the use of _____ strategies, which are widely used as accommodations in the general education program.

    A. phonics

    B. cue card

    C. modeling

    D. mnemonic

30. During the development of a transition plan for a student with a learning disability, the team should enlist the _____ to assist with services needed for the student.

    A. physician

    B. parent's insurance

    C. community agencies

    D. special education director

31. Educators should practice advocacy by

    A. selecting resources for parents.

    B. reading current research studies.

    C. participating in school workshops.

    D. joining professional organizations.

32. Scientists believe that neurological damage that causes learning disabilities most likely occurs during

    A. the prenatal stage.

    B. the birth stage.

    C. the postnatal stage.

    D. all three stages.

33. The research on learning has led experts to determine that in the general education classrooms where content-area teachers are providing services to students with learning disabilities, an important strategy to use is *content enhancements.* One such example that aids a student in orienting and preparing for the lesson is

    A. a notetaker.

    B. a mnemonic device.

    C. an advanced organizer.

    D. a description of the exam.

34. Educators are in a position to recognize signs of abuse and neglect in students. Children with learning disabilities may be difficult for families to manage as each member affects other members in different ways. This theory is called the

    A. developmental theory.

    B. family systems theory.

    C. affective behavior theory.

    D. individual contact theory.

35. Which of the following has proven to be an effective method in the prevention of learning problems?

    A. proper medications

    B. regular genetic testing

    C. early intervention programs

    D. improving family economics

36. When a teacher works with students who have learning disabilities in the area of written language, the teacher may use a technique that prompts the students to think about their spelling and spelling errors. This technique is called

    A. reflective spelling.

    B. evaluative spelling.

    C. receptive spelling.

    D. phonological spelling.

37. A primary component for the successful inclusion of a student with a learning disability in the general education program is

    A. curriculum.

    B. counseling.

    C. consultation.

    D. collaboration.

38. Teachers must reinforce students' attitudes about themselves and their abilities, as students with learning disabilities often believe they are not as capable as their counterparts. Which of the following is an effective way of promoting a more positive attitude about a student's individual abilities?

    A. enlist a peer tutor

    B. promote independence

    C. encourage segregation

    D. provide a paraprofessional

39. According to the federal law, *exclusionary factors* must be addressed when a student is being considered for placement as a student with a learning disability. Which of the following is an example of one of those factors?

    A. math problems

    B. school placement

    C. sensory impairment

    D. reading disadvantage

40. If a teacher, using a picture, asks a student with a learning disability "Can you tell me what you think might happen next?," what method of instruction does this utilize?

    A. practicing word recognition fluency

    B. decoding specific constructed syllables

    C. scaffolding oral language skill development

    D. constructing phonological awareness responses

41. The most common environment for service delivery to students with learning disabilities aside from the general education classroom is the

    A. resource room.

    B. alternative setting.

    C. itinerant placement.

    D. self-contained class.

42. Several organizations have developed definitions for the special education category of *learning disability*. The definitions of these groups may differ but one, The National Joint Committee on Learning Disabilities, presumes that the disorder is intrinsic to the

    A. economic background.

    B. central nervous system.

    C. emotional disturbances.

    D. minimal brain dysfunction.

43. When a student with a learning disability needs services from a speech-language pathologist for a language delay, the team should review the section on the IEP called

    A. related services.

    B. compulsory services.

    C. continuum of services.

    D. supplementary services.

44. There are two language-related teaching strategies that are frequently used with students who have learning disabilities to promote language skill development. These are imitation and

    A. practice.

    B. modeling.

    C. repetition.

    D. modification.

45. Under IDEIA, the rights afforded to parents or guardians on behalf of their child with a learning disability are called

    A. procedural safeguards.

    B. student oriented liberties.

    C. rights and responsibilities.

    D. parent and family privileges.

46. One advantage of large group instruction for students with learning disabilities is that it

    A. is time efficient.

    B. has minimal distractibility.

    C. addresses diverse learners.

    D. improves pacing of instruction.

47. The research studies that offer data drawn from observation or experience provide educators with more realistic information about students, their performance, and the effective methods that may be adapted into the classroom settings. This is called

    A. cogent research.

    B. rational research.

    C. empirical research.

    D. pragmatic research.

GO ON TO THE NEXT PAGE

A high school student, who was identified with a learning disability in written language and mathematics and received a medical diagnosis of attention deficit hyperactivity disorder in third grade, is exhibiting difficulties in his junior year art class. Although the student has done well throughout his school career, receiving adequate grades and good reports for behavior, this year is more difficult than other years. The team is concerned about the student because of the problems in the advanced art class, that may cause the student to not pass the course, not be ready to graduate, and may drop out of school.

The transition team was exploring opportunities at the local community college for the student to take some art classes over the summer, as the student not only has an interest in art, but appears to have impressive talent. The student worked with the community college advisor during the first nine weeks to enroll in the courses. During this time, the special education teacher worked with the student on an English report that pertained to an art topic, and together they contacted artists in the area so the student could observe and interview them. This was a boost to the self esteem of this student, and all seemed to be going well until the second nine week period.

In the advanced art class, the student began demonstrating erratic behaviors and refuses to remain seated during the instructional component. The student prefers to work on the art project that was assigned at the beginning of the course and does not feel the technical portion of the course is valuable to those who already have a talent for art. The other students are working on learning perspectives and analyzing angles through the use of protractors and rulers. They have studied various artists who use these techniques and have been assigned daily to read short vignettes and comment on them in their art journal.

This student has not completed any of these assignments during this nine week period, and the art teacher has called a meeting.

48. Which of the following individuals will add the most critical information to the discussion of this student's progress in the art class?

   A. general education teacher, parent, principal
   B. art teacher, student, special education teacher
   C. school counselor, psychologist, transition specialist
   D. community college advisor, social worker, behavior coach

49. Art class seems to be a course in which this student would participate as an active learner and demonstrate positive progress. The team must now determine what issues are causing these changes in attitude, behavior, and grades. What areas of this course seem to be causing problems for this student?

   A. lack of interest in technical information and reading vignettes
   B. incomplete daily work and trying to complete another assignment
   C. being seated for a class discussion and not working on an art project
   D. use of math tools to figure angles and the written journal assignment

50. Identify the one strategy that would be MOST effective in supporting this student in this art class.

   A. structured notes
   B. graphic organizer
   C. peer learning/tutoring
   D. paraprofessional support

Teaching Students with Learning Disabilities (0381) Practice Exam Answer Key

1.	D	26.	A
2.	C	27.	A
3.	A	28.	C
4.	D	29.	D
5.	C	30.	C
6.	D	31.	D
7.	B	32.	D
8.	D	33.	C
9.	A	34.	B
10.	A	35.	C
11.	D	36.	A
12.	A	37.	D
13.	C	38.	B
14.	A	39.	C
15.	B	40.	C
16.	D	41.	A
17.	A	42.	B
18.	D	43.	A
19.	C	44.	B
20.	A	45.	A
21.	C	46.	A
22.	C	47.	C
23.	D	48.	B
24.	A	49.	D
25.	A	50.	C

Answer Explanations for Teaching Students with Learning Disabilities (0381) Practice Exam

1. **D.** The classroom tone includes the teacher's attitude toward learning, the environmental setting, and the students, as well as the teacher's ability to support and identify expectations. Because the classroom tone influences student learning, it should include these proper and positive components.

2. **C.** The research on learning and learning disabilities has produced information about the methods and materials most effective with students who are learning disabled. Utilizing scientifically research-based interventions seems to be directly related to outcomes of successful student achievement.

3. **A.** Electronic text is designed to aid students with learning disabilities to obtain information from texts that are used in the general education program in a digital format. This text may be converted into other forms such as large print or audio books.

4. **D.** Reading difficulties are often the first sign of a potential learning disability and one of the most common areas of implemented services for those students who are placed in special education for a learning disability.

5. **C.** When students can perform a task or behavior without a model, a cue, or a prompt, and the teachers can give positive or constructive feedback, students with learning disabilities become more engaged and motivated.

6. **D.** In 1991, Skinner and Belmont conducted research related to the various aspects of motivation in a learning environment. Their findings pointed out that one of the preferred methods of increasing student motivation for learning was to ensure that each student fully understood the criteria for assignments and the expectations for acceptable behaviors.

7. **B.** The theory of Behavioral Psychology promotes acknowledging a students' stage of learning in planning the instruction. The key components of this approach, which have been found to be effective with students who have learning disabilities, are *direct instruction* and *explicit teaching*.

8. **D.** Reinforcement is a recognized method of a positive behavior support system. Providing a reinforcement most often guarantees that the target behavior will be repeated if it is a desired behavior or will decrease if it is an undesirable behavior.

9. **A.** Although all of the characteristics listed may be found in students with learning disabilities, the three that are primary indicators of a condition of either ADD or ADHD are when a student is inattentive, impulsive, and hyperactive.

10. **A.** The debate centered around grading for students with learning disabilities is founded in the question of equity. Many educators have favored alternative methods of grading, which reflect the student's abilities and consider the disability factors. Some of these grading systems include contract grading, shared grading, IEP-based grading, and multiple grading.

11. **D.** Piaget, a noted psychologist, believed that children must pass through maturational stages of development. He alleged that children's abilities to learn are based on the specific developmental stage they are in at the time of instruction as well as their readiness level to receive the particular information. He promoted the Developmental Psychology Theory.

12. **A.** Federal law requires the use of a functional behavior intervention plan for students who demonstrate inappropriate behaviors that interrupt the educational process. This plan is created by the IEP team and based on a functional behavior assessment.

13. **C.** Young children who exhibit problems in the motor domain may have the potential for a learning disability. Problems with the motor domain may be a developmental indicator of learning difficulties because of the relationship between the two. The motor domain includes the areas of perception and sensory integration, which impact the cognitive domain, and is a key area of early learning.

14. **A.** Peer tutoring has been studied and found to be of benefit to both the student with the disability and the student who is acting as the tutor. Students with learning disabilities often demonstrate gains in academics and social skills due to the peer interaction and one-on-one instructional time.

15. B. Rating scales are one type of assessment tool that provides valuable information to the examinee about a student's performance in her natural environment. Separately, a parent, teacher, or other adult rates a student according to a checklist group of questions. These rating scales are then scored and compared to determine the student's consistency and problem areas across various settings.

16. D. A spell checker program can assist a student with written language problems by making the appropriate changes to the student's work. The student would be able to self-correct and, therefore, learn the proper spellings of words being used.

17. A. Although all of the suggested answers have had an impact on students with learning disabilities and provide a function in their lives, the one with the most positive and versatile impact has been the Internet. It provides many students with learning disabilities with access to educational information, the ability to communicate, and a method to help them in their daily activities in the community.

18. D. When the teacher is visible to all students and provides supports and assistance throughout the lesson, students become more engaged in their learning and are motivated to try difficult tasks. This is especially helpful to students with learning disabilities who are placed in general education classrooms.

19. C. Language problems most often identified in students with learning disabilities are in the areas of oral expression and listening comprehension. They may also have problems with directions, vocabulary, and language structures.

20. A. Since a student's social skills change depending on the situation and the environment, it is best to observe the student's use of the skills in different settings. For the best information on an evaluation for emotional and social skills, an observation should be conducted.

21. C. There seems to be an equal number of girls and boys with learning disabilities, although research finds that the girls often go unnoticed and are not always identified. Due to the differences in the genders there may be variations in the characteristics of the types of disabilities, so girls often do not exhibit the outward signs that lead to referrals in special education.

22. C. Under the federal law, IDEIA, the Individuals with Disabilities Education Improvement Act, 2004, a general education teacher is required to be a participating member of each student's IEP team, when the student is enrolled in his classroom. FERPA is a federal law that pertains to privacy, while LRE and FAPE are components of IDEIA.

23. D. Although students with emerging learning disabilities may academically have problems in reading, written language, and mathematics, the most noticeable evidence of a possible learning disability is the discrepancy between ability and achievement in all areas.

24. A. An achievement test is used to measure mastery of content in a particular subject area.

25. A. The learning strategies instruction approach is a proven method of teaching students with learning disabilities how to learn rather than gaining the actual information in a lesson or curriculum. They can use these strategies across the curriculum subject areas and into adulthood as these effective strategies allow them to be in control of their learning and be successful with academic tasks.

26. A. Metacognition is defined as the ability of a student to become more aware of her own thinking processes and to use these in order to achieve academic success. When a student has metacognitive skills, she is conscious of her own cognitive abilities and learning style and uses them to regulate achievement and facilitate successful learning situations.

27. A. Co-teaching is an effective method of supporting students and teachers in the general education classroom. This allows the regular education teacher to provide the instruction according to the general education curriculum, while the special education teacher assists with the instruction and implements the accommodations for all students who require them.

28. C. A portfolio assessment is a collection of work samples from a certain period of time about a particular student. This may include projects, written assignments, or art, depending on what is to be assessed. This is a recommended method of assessment for parents to view the actual student work and verify progress.

29. D. Mnemonic strategies are used in many subject areas and should be considered a powerful accommodation for students with learning disabilities. Students will benefit from the use of these strategies, as they memorize the acronym and retrieve the representational information.

30. C. A statement that describes the responsibility of community agencies during and after a student's transition from high school to adult life is required under federal law.

31. D. Educators may contribute to the field of education, specifically that of learning disabilities, by practicing advocacy on behalf of these individuals. They may join professional organizations to address issues such as state policies, definitions, support services, work situations, and funding.

32. D. It is thought that brain injuries may occur in any of the three stages of the birth process: the prenatal stage, during the birth, or in the postnatal stage. The impact of the damage may span a variety of problems and will affect development and learning.

33. C. An advanced organizer is an example of a *content enhancement* that is a valuable tool for use by students with learning disabilities in the general education classroom. An advanced organizer should be provided to students before the beginning of a lesson as it may include information about the topic, introduce concepts, or outline tasks.

34. B. The *family systems theory* is a fundamental concept when dealing with children who are identified with disabilities. This theory promotes that any member of a family unit can affect any other member in the unit. A child with a disability has a powerful effect on each member and a child with a learning disability can cause stress for all members in various ways.

35. C. On-going studies have shown that when the needs of young children are addressed early (birth to 6 years) the probability of developing a learning problem or disability is greatly reduced. Schools should focus on the development and learning of young children through early intervention programs and not wait for a child to fail in school before being identified and school-age interventions implemented.

36. A. Many students with learning disabilities are identified with problems in written language and most have difficulty with spelling. It is best to use a systematic strategy to aid in correctly spelling new words. The approach of reflective spelling will help students understand the errors they make and encourage them to be more strategic when approaching spelling on written assignments.

37. D. Successful and effective inclusion is based on the practice of collaboration between the general education teacher and the special education teacher. These professionals must use their respective expertise to work together in providing direct services to students.

38. B. Students with disabilities may consider themselves unable to complete the same tasks as their peers and, therefore, develop poor attitudes about themselves or their education, have low self-esteem, and may lack independence. When teachers help students understand their own intellectual abilities, set clear expectations, and promote independence, students with disabilities improve their attitudes.

39. C. In the federal law, IDEIA, the definition for learning disabilities is clear that a student may not be identified as such if the learning problem is the result of a visual, hearing, or motor disability; mental retardation or emotional disturbance; or environmental, cultural, or economic disadvantage. Therefore, sensory impairment is one of the exclusionary factors to be considered.

40. C. To assist students in the acquisition of knowledge and skills, the method of scaffolding is often used. When a teacher asks a question about a picture that allows an expanded response, that encourages the use of problem-solving skills and promotes the student's use of oral language skills this teacher is using scaffolding.

41. A. Most students with learning disabilities are placed the majority of their school day in a general education classroom. They receive services from the regular education teacher and from the special education teacher through the collaborative model, the consultation model, or the co-teaching model. For some students with learning disabilities, another common educational placement is the resource room where they may receive additional services directly from a special education teacher and related service providers.

42. B. The definition of the NJCLD reflects their stand on the disorders of learning being due to central nervous system dysfunction.

43. A. Related services are determined by the IEP team if the student with a learning disability exhibits deficits in areas that require the services of other professionals besides the classroom teachers. This may include services from a speech-language pathologist, an occupational therapist, a physical therapist, or a psychologist.

44. B. Modeling is a commonly used language skill strategy effective with students who have learning disabilities. In modeling, a student observes the teacher performing a task or using a rule before the student is required to answer, perform, or use the information.

45. A. Procedural safeguards are a set of requirements by which parents may participate in the development and on-going implementation of an educational program for their child with a disability. This includes making decisions, participating in assessments, reviewing an IEP, and being informed of other needs related to the child's program.

46. A. Large group instruction is less time consuming for the educators, as one lesson may be prepared and the presentation uses a shorter period of time than providing instruction for several individuals. The other suggested responses are all considered disadvantages.

47. C. Empirical research about students with learning disabilities is conducted with genuine subjects who have these conditions and generally in natural and realistic environments. The researchers gather their information based on practical observations of the individuals performing specified tasks or using particular materials. These studies provide educators with more realistic findings.

48. B. There are many members of a student's team and all individuals have information to share which aids in the support and education of a student. In this situation, the student is the critical individual who can add information that will allow others to problem solve the situation and get the student back on track to pass the course and graduate. The student is old enough to be involved in the education process, to participate in meetings, and to join in the decision making efforts.

49. D. The student's learning disability has been determined to be in written language and mathematics. If this student is having problems writing in the daily journal, and trying to understand perspectives using math tools, it will make the time in the course very difficult. To compound the problem, since the student is already having difficulty with grasping the information, being asked to sit and listen impacts the attention deficit previously diagnosed.

50. C. For this student to be successful in this course, the assignments must be completed to a satisfactory level. Since the student has problems with mathematics and written language, an appropriate strategy to use with this student is peer learning/tutoring. A peer partner may be assigned to this student to work together to review the concepts of perspective and angles and to practice the measurements. In regards to the written assignment, the peer can assist by discussing the artist and then composing a response together that the peer will write down.

Answer Grid for Teaching Students with Mental Retardation (0321) Practice Exam

1 Ⓐ Ⓑ Ⓒ Ⓓ	26 Ⓐ Ⓑ Ⓒ Ⓓ
2 Ⓐ Ⓑ Ⓒ Ⓓ	27 Ⓐ Ⓑ Ⓒ Ⓓ
3 Ⓐ Ⓑ Ⓒ Ⓓ	28 Ⓐ Ⓑ Ⓒ Ⓓ
4 Ⓐ Ⓑ Ⓒ Ⓓ	29 Ⓐ Ⓑ Ⓒ Ⓓ
5 Ⓐ Ⓑ Ⓒ Ⓓ	30 Ⓐ Ⓑ Ⓒ Ⓓ
6 Ⓐ Ⓑ Ⓒ Ⓓ	31 Ⓐ Ⓑ Ⓒ Ⓓ
7 Ⓐ Ⓑ Ⓒ Ⓓ	32 Ⓐ Ⓑ Ⓒ Ⓓ
8 Ⓐ Ⓑ Ⓒ Ⓓ	33 Ⓐ Ⓑ Ⓒ Ⓓ
9 Ⓐ Ⓑ Ⓒ Ⓓ	34 Ⓐ Ⓑ Ⓒ Ⓓ
10 Ⓐ Ⓑ Ⓒ Ⓓ	35 Ⓐ Ⓑ Ⓒ Ⓓ
11 Ⓐ Ⓑ Ⓒ Ⓓ	36 Ⓐ Ⓑ Ⓒ Ⓓ
12 Ⓐ Ⓑ Ⓒ Ⓓ	37 Ⓐ Ⓑ Ⓒ Ⓓ
13 Ⓐ Ⓑ Ⓒ Ⓓ	38 Ⓐ Ⓑ Ⓒ Ⓓ
14 Ⓐ Ⓑ Ⓒ Ⓓ	39 Ⓐ Ⓑ Ⓒ Ⓓ
15 Ⓐ Ⓑ Ⓒ Ⓓ	40 Ⓐ Ⓑ Ⓒ Ⓓ
16 Ⓐ Ⓑ Ⓒ Ⓓ	41 Ⓐ Ⓑ Ⓒ Ⓓ
17 Ⓐ Ⓑ Ⓒ Ⓓ	42 Ⓐ Ⓑ Ⓒ Ⓓ
18 Ⓐ Ⓑ Ⓒ Ⓓ	43 Ⓐ Ⓑ Ⓒ Ⓓ
19 Ⓐ Ⓑ Ⓒ Ⓓ	44 Ⓐ Ⓑ Ⓒ Ⓓ
20 Ⓐ Ⓑ Ⓒ Ⓓ	45 Ⓐ Ⓑ Ⓒ Ⓓ
21 Ⓐ Ⓑ Ⓒ Ⓓ	46 Ⓐ Ⓑ Ⓒ Ⓓ
22 Ⓐ Ⓑ Ⓒ Ⓓ	47 Ⓐ Ⓑ Ⓒ Ⓓ
23 Ⓐ Ⓑ Ⓒ Ⓓ	48 Ⓐ Ⓑ Ⓒ Ⓓ
24 Ⓐ Ⓑ Ⓒ Ⓓ	49 Ⓐ Ⓑ Ⓒ Ⓓ
25 Ⓐ Ⓑ Ⓒ Ⓓ	50 Ⓐ Ⓑ Ⓒ Ⓓ

CUT HERE

Read each of the following multiple-choice questions and select the BEST answer. Fill in your choice by using the answer bubble sheet provided.

1. The main concern regarding *intelligence assessments* by professionals who evaluate individuals for mental ability disorders is that the assessments

   A. are often too difficult and cause frustration.
   B. take more time than the individual can handle.
   C. do not identify a person's total capabilities and abilities.
   D. scores reflect the particular thinking skill, but not the type.

2. The most prevalent type of mental retardation is called

   A. Down Syndrome.
   B. Fragile X Syndrome.
   C. William's Syndrome.
   D. Prader-Willi Syndrome.

3. The prevalence numbers for students who are identified with mental retardation in schools has decreased over the years due to changes in professional attitudes, the affects of early intervention programs, and the

   A. changes in the MR definition.
   B. improved teaching strategies.
   C. advances in medical treatment.
   D. progress on behavior interventions.

4. When a family has a child with mental retardation, the family unit may be impacted in a variety of ways. These may include

   A. medical, financial, and legal.
   B. academic, legal, and personal.
   C. financial, medical, and emotional.
   D. personal, academic, and emotional.

5. Studies conducted on students with mild mental retardation show that they generally perform best when placed in _____ settings.

   A. itinerant
   B. resource
   C. inclusive
   D. self-contained

6. For students with mental retardation to achieve greater independence, they must be able to make significant gains in the area of adaptive behaviors. Most programs find that it is most beneficial to teach these skills

   A. in cooperative learning groups.
   B. in natural settings as they are needed.
   C. in small groups or an individual basis.
   D. by setting aside instruction time each day.

7. The team for a preschool student identified with mild mental retardation is meeting to discuss the placement for kindergarten and to prepare for the transition from preschool. Since the beginning of preschool, the student has been placed in an inclusive setting, as documented in the IEP. The student's performance and IEP goal attainment has been very positive in the current setting, but the parents are concerned that with the academic focus of the kindergarten program their child may not continue to be successful. What should the IEP team recommend at the transition meeting?

   A. Place the child in an inclusive kindergarten class with identified supports to meet the newly established goals.
   B. Identify a part-time resource, part-time self-contained setting with kindergarten placement for the special classes (art and PE).
   C. Place the child in the self-contained program for the academic subjects and reconvene the team to review progress in 3–6 months.
   D. Identify continued placement in the preschool as the least restrictive environment for an additional year so the student maintains success before moving on to kindergarten.

GO ON TO THE NEXT PAGE

8. The APA, the American Psychological Association, defines *mental retardation* as significant limitations in general intellectual functioning and _____, with the onset of both limitations prior to the age of 22 years.

   A. attention span
   B. spoken language
   C. social interactions
   D. adaptive behaviors

9. A high school student identified with severe mental retardation has been placed in a self-contained setting as the student's academic abilities and skill performance levels are in the second-grade range. The student works in the custodial department after school and has a part-time position on the weekends at a local hotel in housekeeping with a job coach. The student's IEP team plans to meet regarding the student's transition from high school into a community program for adults. Which of the following seems to be the BEST program to meet this student's needs and skill levels?

   A. Work Study Program
   B. Technical Preparation Center
   C. Vocational Education Program
   D. Community Rehabilitation Center

10. A student's skills in *adaptive behavior* areas can be measured by using the _____ assessment.

   A. WISC-IV
   B. Vineland II-ABS
   C. Stanford Binet-5
   D. Kaufmann Battery-II

11. School psychologists who evaluate students' mental skills and abilities by identifying an *Intelligence Quotient* often use which of the following assessments to measure those areas?

   A. Scales of IB-R
   B. Edgar Doll Scales
   C. Vineland AB-II Scales
   D. Woodcock-Johnson III

12. When an IEP team focuses on improving functional skills for a student and develops goals in that area, one consideration to make is that the skills need to be

   A. easily measured.
   B. remediated weekly.

   C. conducive to transitions.
   D. age and socially appropriate.

13. A student who is diagnosed with mental retardation in the severe range most likely has an IQ score in the range of _____ points.

   A. 30–50
   B. 20–40
   C. 50–70
   D. 40–60

14. There is a primary difference between an adaptive behavior assessment and an intelligence test. An adaptive behavior assessment evaluates a student's typical actions, but the intelligence test determines information on

   A. social skills.
   B. affective behaviors.
   C. academic activities.
   D. maximal performance.

15. Community-Based Instruction (CBI) is a major component in programs that provide services to students with moderate to severe and profound disabilities. A critical step for an educator in expanding the classroom to include a CBI program is to

   A. verify the school district's policies regarding liability.
   B. speak with each parent for students who require these services.
   C. rewrite student IEP goals, transition plans, and behavior programs.
   D. partner with all the community agencies who service this category.

16. Students who are identified with mild mental retardation often have reading problems that are exacerbated in decoding errors. What should educators do to assist a child with this issue?

   A. Focus only on those errors that change the meaning of a given sentence.
   B. Ignore each error so the student will gain more confidence and increase skills.
   C. Correct every error with an explanation and have the student reread the passage.
   D. Identify about the first 50 percent of the errors and monitor the student's improvement.

17. According to the definitions under federal law and through the various professional organizations, the primary indicator of mental retardation is when a child demonstrates a delay in the area of

    A. language.
    B. social skills.
    C. adaptive behaviors.
    D. physical development.

18. An elementary aged child identified as moderately mentally retarded and who has a functional behavior plan recently began to use inappropriate behaviors on the playground. The student has become aggressive with other children and has bitten and hit several children. Over the past two days, the student has also started fights and kicked a peer. What should the educator do to resolve this situation and manage the student's behaviors?

    A. Assign a peer to guide the child and teach more positive behaviors.
    B. Convene a team meeting to assess the behaviors and address the plan.
    C. Contact the parents to request they keep the child home for several days.
    D. Ask the principal to discipline the child and withdraw the recess privilege.

19. A student with Down Syndrome works in the school bookstore. The student helps customers with orders, checks inventory with the owner, stocks shelves, counts change, and sometimes works at the register. This work situation provides an opportunity for the educator to conduct an observation as a part of an informal assessment. What skill areas would the educator be able to assess for meaningful information?

    A. reading, writing, and mathematics
    B. time management, communication, and writing
    C. computer skills, reading, and time management
    D. mathematics, communication, and interpersonal skills

20. A student with mental retardation and other multiple disabilities demonstrates difficulty in the developmental domains of language, cognition, motor, and self-help/adaptive. The student participates in therapy sessions with a speech pathologist to address the language skills and a

physical therapist to meet the motor needs, but the educator is troubled about the student's acquisition of skills in the adaptive behavior area. The skills the student has the most trouble with include toileting and dressing. What is the BEST method for this teacher to use in order for the student to make progress in the self-help/adaptive domain?

    A. peer modeling
    B. hand over hand
    C. direct instruction
    D. chained response

21. Through studies on mental retardation, it has been determined that individuals with intellectual deficits are at an increased risk for

    A. eating disorders.
    B. physical symptoms.
    C. psychiatric disorders.
    D. psychological symptoms.

22. When the school team works with a high school student to make a phone call to the community work force system to ask about the jobs that are available, this is a form of

    A. self-advocacy.
    B. citizen advocacy.
    C. system advocacy.
    D. community advocacy.

23. Prior to 1975, many individuals with intellectual disabilities were institutionalized and provided with _____ until litigation changed this perspective of people with mental retardation.

    A. custodial care
    B. direct instruction
    C. informal services
    D. personal assistants

24. Advocacy for individuals with disabilities, especially mental retardation, is critical to their overall development and their future involvement in the community. There are four types of advocacy: legal advocacy, self-advocacy, citizen advocacy, and

    A. parent advocacy.
    B. systems advocacy.
    C. educator advocacy.
    D. personal advocacy.

GO ON TO THE NEXT PAGE

25. When a child with mental retardation enters a family unit, there is great impact on the group. One particular area is the _____ area.

    A. cognitive
    B. language
    C. social-emotional
    D. self-help/adaptive

26. When a student with moderate mental retardation is placed in a general education class, accommodations and modifications are often necessary for the student to achieve success. Read the following outcome that is intended for a science class at the fourth-grade level and determine which would be the best example of a modification to meet that student's needs.

    Write two 3-page reports: one about an animal that lives in the desert and one about an animal that lives in the ocean.

    A. Read a book about each animal and talk to the teacher about the animal facts.
    B. Write a 2-page report about each animal and include pictures on the third page.
    C. Develop a 1-page outline of the most important information about each animal.
    D. Draw a picture of each animal in its environment and write a sentence about each animal.

27. Students with difficult behaviors who are identified with mental retardation need behavior supports to learn to manage their behaviors. The one thing that a behavior support should focus on is

    A. when the behavior will cease.
    B. who will manage the behavior.
    C. where the intervention will occur.
    D. the reason for the problem behavior.

28. A student identified with moderate mental retardation has a behavior plan that focuses on improving on-task behaviors. The teacher has provided a compliment to the student each time the student begins a grooming activity independently. If the student starts to increase this on-task behavior independently, the compliment serves as a specific example of a

    A. stimulus.
    B. modeling tool.
    C. positive reinforcer.
    D. guided auditory cue.

29. Zigler has identified five personality characteristics that are specific to individuals with mental retardation. Which of the following is one of the five characteristics?

    A. fear of others
    B. interdirectedness
    C. social appropriateness
    D. low expectations of success

30. Which of the following is an example of a low-tech device?

    A. a toy switch
    B. a pencil grip
    C. a hearing aid
    D. a laptop computer

31. Some teachers have low expectations for students with mental retardation. This has an effect on the overall education system for these students. Which of the following demonstrates what most teachers do when they lower the expectations?

    A. They teach less fervently and provide simple tasks.
    B. They lower the grading scale to accommodate these students.
    C. They use more visual aids and eliminate the need for assessments.
    D. They create a functional curriculum and eliminate progress reports.

32. When working with students who have mental retardation, educators must use specialized instruction that includes activities that are varied, age appropriate, and

    A. aim toward transition goals.
    B. include behavioral objectives.
    C. incorporate reading and writing.
    D. allow students to actively respond.

33. A student with mild to moderate mental retardation works for a local coffee shop cleaning tables and performing tasks in the kitchen. The student is a very hard worker, but the employer is having some problems with the student and plans to inform the parents that the student is at risk of losing the job. The student has been an excellent candidate for community placement due to the ethics and responsibility shown in school and at home. However, since the student walks to this job, the student has been chronically late. This student has been known to lack memory skills when distracted and apparently the walk to work is enough to get the student off track. The supervisor has discussed the problem with the student several times and is now seeking the support of the special education teacher before contacting the parents and dismissing the student employee. The teacher should

A. hire a tutor who will teach the student how to tell time.

B. suggest that the parents or student buy a watch with an alarm.

C. ask the parents or a sibling to drive the student to work each day.

D. make a daily schedule the student can look at as a reminder to go to work.

34. A primary component for a student with mental retardation in an inclusive setting is to be provided with

A. activities.

B. equipment.

C. paraeducator.

D. accommodations.

35. Teaching students with mental retardation new skills in the classroom and in real-life situations and environments helps them to

A. generalize skills.

B. remember tasks.

C. maintain behaviors.

D. receive reinforcement.

36. The main goal for individuals with mental retardation is to live and work independently as adults. This requires that individuals learn to make decisions, follow schedules, be responsible, and interact socially. When these individuals are young, it would be very important to provide them with many opportunities to

A. organize self.

B. make choices.

C. read and write.

D. manage behaviors.

37. Next to Down Syndrome, *Fragile X Syndrome* is one of the more common forms of mental retardation, and it is the most common _____ cause of the intellectual disability.

A. trauma

B. disease

C. hereditary

D. teratogen

38. A student with mild mental retardation works part time at a local bakery. The supervisor participated on the team during the transition planning period to ensure that all aspects of the position were covered. The team was satisfied with the work the student had completed in school while working in the kitchen and felt the student would make a smooth transition. The supervisor has recently noticed that the student works better when another employee is present, but when left to work alone has not been able to handle the machines. What should the transition team plan to do to support this student in working toward independence on the job at the local bakery?

A. Discuss the provision of a job coach.

B. Reassign the student to another position.

C. Give written directions on how to use the machines.

D. Tutor the student at school on how to use the machines.

GO ON TO THE NEXT PAGE

39. The form of collaboration that is most helpful in inclusion settings is

    A. advisement.

    B. consultation.

    C. independent.

    D. informational

40. An elementary student diagnosed with mild mental retardation in second grade is demonstrating difficulty with the pronunciation of word endings. Which of the following strategies should the educator use to BEST help this second grader improve in this area?

    A. Review the alphabetic letters and sounds used each day.

    B. Reteach each individual vowel sound and sample words.

    C. Focus on the larger word parts and identify word families.

    D. Require the student practice new word pronunciation daily.

41. An organization that has been well-established over the years to support individuals with mental retardation is the ARC. What does ARC stand for?

    A. Agency of Retarded Citizens

    B. Academy of Retarded Children

    C. Alliance for Retarded Children

    D. Association for Retarded Citizens

Read the following case study and then answer questions 42–44, which follow.

A third-grade elementary student with mild-moderate mental retardation exhibits multiple disabilities in motor, language, and hearing. The child has had health issues for the past 2 years and sometimes must be out of school for treatments for long periods of time. The school works with the parents to provide services as the child can handle the interventions. When the child is well, the majority of the program is delivered in an inclusive setting with some time during the day in the resource room for remediation of academic skills. The child also works with a hearing specialist three times per week in a one-to-one situation to enhance auditory training and vocabulary building. The child has had previous intermittent episodes with inappropriate behaviors and has a functional behavior plan for the staff and family to follow. The additional disabilities are managed through therapy and daily interventions in the classroom. The student has demonstrated problems when transitioning between activities or lessons, and either the teacher or therapist is generally prepared to support the student and ease into the next activity.

The IEP Team is planning ahead for the fourth grade, as the school has a unique program for that grade level. The teachers at that level focus on one area of instruction, and the classes move between four classrooms to receive instruction in language arts, math, science, and history. For the rest of the day, students remain with their assigned teacher. In the third grade, the student has performed well overall and maintains a first-grade level in reading and a second-grade level in math. The third-grade teacher has worked very hard to provide appropriate adaptations to the curriculum and the environment, which allows the student to participate and have a sense of belonging. The student enjoys school and has made some friends from class who live in the same neighborhood. A couple of days each week, they all walk to school together and often eat lunch at the same table. The parents are pleased with the inclusive program, even though the child is not performing at grade level.

42. When this student moves on to the fourth grade, what is the most critical consideration that the IEP team should make to enhance this student's program?

    A. Change the functional behavior plan.

    B. Increase the academic remediation time.

    C. Enroll the friends in the same classroom.

    D. Provide a paraeducator to assist with transitions.

43. What type of supportive materials would be best suited to this student's needs when the teacher is delivering concept information in class?

    A. visual

    B. outline

    C. auditory

    D. notetaking

44. The third-grade teacher assigns 10 spelling words to the class each week. The students are responsible for learning to spell each word and using two different words each day in a written sentence. By the end of the week, they are expected to have 10 sentences using the 10 words written in their journals. Which of the following represents an appropriate adaptation for this student with mental retardation?

A. The student should learn the same 10 words and write as many sentences as possible.

B. The student must learn 10 words from the four main subjects each week and write 10 sentences.

C. The student must learn five words that are personally meaningful, with two or more sentences each week.

D. The student should learn the vocabulary from the third-grade reader and write simple sentences for each word.

Read the following case study and then answer questions 45–46, which follow.

A student with mild to moderate mental retardation has been in inclusive settings since the first grade. The student has done well overall and has become a positive member of the class each year. Now that the student is in the middle school, the student is exhibiting difficulty with memory and attention skills. The problems are most evident as the student does not remember daily routines and does not maintain appropriate behaviors in the various settings at school (PE class, lunch room, outdoor time, bus stop). The team has conducted an observation of the student during all class periods and all other times of the day. They noticed that the student appears nervous and alone.

45. What is the first intervention that the team might try to help the student during the non-class periods?

A. Shorten the attendance day for the student.

B. Obtain a paraprofessional to be with the student all day.

C. Assign a peer to guide the student to the proper locations.

D. Change the student's schedule and place in a self-contained setting.

46. Which of the following strategies would BEST promote more positive behaviors and ensure consistency across all settings?

A. Contact parents to discuss the need for daily routines.

B. Remind the student for each pending schedule change.

C. Provide a daily picture/word schedule and conduct chart.

D. Reteach daily routines and ignore inappropriate behaviors.

GO ON TO THE NEXT PAGE

Read the following case study and then answer questions 47–50, which follow.

A junior in high school who has received special education services all through school is interested in becoming more involved in the IEP and ITP process. This student's placement in special education began early in the school career. Since there was no preschool program available in the community, this child did not enroll in school until age 5 for kindergarten. Exhibiting language problems and behavior outbursts, the child was evaluated and determined to need speech and language services and considered speech and language impaired with the need for a functional behavior plan.

As the child moved into first and then second grade, there were concerns by the school professionals that academic progress was slow and other areas were affected. Staff treated this child as an at-risk individual due to the difficult home situation. With father working odd jobs and abusing alcohol and mother in and out of treatment and jail facilities, this youngster did not have a consistent and nurturing home life. When the family refused to work with the school team to investigate the child's needs, a referral was made to the social worker, who then contacted a local agency for a report of neglect. The agency placed the child in a foster care center until a full investigation could occur. The child demonstrated independence and a will to learn, but academic tasks were a challenging area. During the second semester of the second grade, a recommendation by the speech–language pathologist and the second-grade teacher for case review to the school child study team resulted in a referral for a comprehensive evaluation. Once permission from the surrogate parent was received, and the child was assessed, it was found that the child was delayed in cognition, language, motor, social-emotional, and self-help-adaptive domains. A diagnosis by the school psychologist resulted in the child being identified for additional special education services under the category of mental retardation.

This student began to progress quickly with the added supports, related services, and direct instruction via placement in a general education classroom. As the years moved on, the child appeared to be well-adjusted and capable of the academic tasks presented with adaptations and accommodations. The special education program continued to support this student and once the student entered high school, additional supports were available as the academic program changed. The area of motor was on target with peers and the areas of social skills and language delays greatly improved, with dismissal from language therapy prior to the completion of the IEP for this year.

In high school, the IEP team focused on academic enrichment, and functional skills to prepare the student for community living. The student was on the track team and participated in the art club. The student enjoyed attending music events and went to many of the sporting events with friends. The student's academic areas are at about the fourth-grade level in reading, writing, and mathematics.

The student is anxious to realize the dream of independent living and is a solid contributor to the IEP team. The student wants to take the lead on the development of the transition plan now that graduation is very near.

47. With the changes in this student's educational program and the student's involvement in the development of this IEP and ITP, which of the following related services should remain as a benefit to this student?

    A. social worker

    B. behavior coach

    C. occupational therapist

    D. speech/language pathologist

48. What type of community involvement would help this individual with accessing living arrangements, a work situation, and future technical training, if desired?

    A. vocational resources

    B. assisted living center

    C. agency collaboration

    D. rehabilitation services

49. In developing a transition plan that follows the student's preferences, which of the following would seem to be the first perfect job for this individual after leaving high school?

    A. cashier at the local music shop

    B. library assistant stocking shelves

    C. sales person for art supply company

    D. usher at the community event center

50. After the student completes high school and increases self-care at home or is living independently in the community, what type of assistive technology devices would appear to best support this individual's continued needs?

    A. cell phone and calculator

    B. PDA and laptop computer

    C. GPS system and cell phone

    D. calculator and a laptop computer

Teaching Students with Mental Retardation (0321) Practice Exam Answer Key

1. C	18. B	35. A
2. A	19. D	36. B
3. A	20. D	37. C
4. C	21. C	38. A
5. C	22. A	39. B
6. B	23. A	40. C
7. A	24. B	41. D
8. D	25. C	42. D
9. D	26. D	43. A
10. B	27. D	44. C
11. D	28. C	45. C
12. D	29. D	46. C
13. B	30. B	47. A
14. D	31. A	48. C
15. A	32. D	49. D
16. A	33. B	50. B
17. C	34. D	

Answer Explanations for Teaching Students with Mental Retardation (0321) Practice Exam

1. C. The primary use of an intelligence test is to determine the possible success for individuals in academic settings. Although an intelligence quotient may reflect a person's abilities and potential, it is not the only determining factor in assessing a person's capabilities. Other avenues must be investigated to make a more thorough determination of a person's total capabilities and abilities.

2. A. Down Syndrome is the most prevalent genetic condition with about 1.3 infants born in each 1,000 births. The other forms of mental retardation do not occur as frequently with only 0.06 to 0.6 per 1,000 births.

3. A. The definitions for mental retardation have changed over the years. In the very early years, for example, in the 1950s the definitions were broad, and more children were identified than probably existed. Then between 1970 and 1985, the AAMR changed the cut-off scores for mental retardation from 1 standard deviation to 2 standard deviations. As the definitions were refined and developed with more detail, the incidence of documented mental retardation decreased.

4. C. Research shows that families are affected in many ways when they have a child with mental retardation. Although for most families, culture affects their attitudes toward mental retardation, many families follow the various stages of grief. It has been determined that almost all families are affected in the financial, medical, and emotional aspects. In the financial area, families have increased expenses for child care, vehicle modifications, added equipment, and insurance. The medical area includes additional health issues and limits on care. For the emotional aspect of the family unit, more time is necessary to care for a child with a disability, and there are issues with other children and sometimes the marriage.

5. C. Research on the success of various placement options for students with mild mental retardation have determined that the majority of students with this condition demonstrate increased benefits in inclusive general education settings. These students have proven that they achieve at higher rates when they are surrounded by their typical peers in a more natural environment rather than in a resource class or a self-contained program with children who exhibit the same or more severe disabilities.

6. B. It has been found that students with mental retardation most often learn adaptive behavior skills and retain those skills when taught in the natural environments. Learning and using the skills naturally helps a student develop them appropriately, practice them, and then apply the skills to other settings.

7. A. The expectations by the team for this child's success and placement should remain high. Since the child has demonstrated success in the inclusive preschool setting and on all IEP goals, the student should have access to a very similar model as the transition to kindergarten occurs. The federal law requires that the least restrictive environment be considered, and an inclusive model is the first on the continuum. The IEP team may address the child's needs as the year proceeds, but this student should be placed in the most natural setting provided the appropriate supports are in place to maintain a positive experience.

8. D. The following is the actual definition from the APA:

"Mental Retardation (MR) refers to (a) significant limitations in general intellectual functions, (b) significant limitations in adaptive functioning, which exist concurrently, and (c) onset of intellectual and adaptive limitations before the age of 22 years."

9. D. The best program from these choices is the Community Rehabilitation Center, as it provides adult interactions in an employment model that is designed for individuals with more severe disabilities. The Vocational Education Program is a school program where students take courses to develop skills prior to graduating. The Work Study Program, also a school program, teaches functional skills in an inclusive model and includes on and off campus jobs. The Technical Preparation Center provides a course of study that may lead to an AA degree or certificate from a vocational school.

10. B. The Vineland II-ABS is a common tool used to measure five domains of an individual's adaptive behavior function. It is comprised of a rating form for both parents (caregivers) and teachers to provide information about the individual being assessed. Many professionals believe this scale is one of the best for evaluating adaptive behavior. The WISC-II, the Stanford Binet-5, and the Kaufmann Assessment Battery II are all individually administered intelligence tests.

11. D. The Vineland AB-II (created by Edgar Doll), the Scales of Independent Behavior, and the Edgar Doll Scales are tests used to assess the adaptive behavior domain. The Woodcock-Johnson III Test of Cognitive Abilities is a tool used to evaluate intelligence.

12. D. When writing goals for a student in any area, even though the student's skills may be at a low level, a consideration for improvement in a particular area needs to be made based on the child's age and the social appropriateness of the skill to be developed.

13. B. A student identified with severe mental retardation would demonstrate an Intelligence Quotient score between 20 and 40 points on a 100-point scale. It is possible that a student who scores in this range can gain independent self-help skills; however, academic achievement may be difficult and limited.

14. D. An intelligence test assesses an individual's abilities and potential for success in an academic environment. Therefore, it is estimated that a test of intelligence determines a person's maximal performance on the given tasks.

15. A. In developing a CBI program in a school, educators must be familiar with the insurance liability coverage provided under their district's policy. Since students and staff members would be traveling off campus for community events, activities, and work, an educator must know what is allowed while students and staff are en route to a location or while on that other property. It may also be a requirement for an educator to acquire signed releases from a student's parents, which gives permission for their child to be off campus.

16. A. An educator should decide to correct those errors that are most valuable, as not every reading error is a major problem. Students with mild mental retardation should not be expected to read every word correctly. An educator should identify those errors that change the meaning of a sentence, allowing a student enough time to analyze the situation and decode the information. This will help the student improve, as a student can learn from a mistake that has applied meaning.

17. C. As definitions changed for mental retardation, adaptive behavior functioning became one of the primary factors in determining whether a child had mental retardation or not. There were many children, especially those in families of low socio-economic status, particularly African-Americans, who were being identified with mental retardation based solely on an IQ test. When reviewed further, it was found that these children simply had a lack of experience and could not perform well on an IQ exam, while the adaptive behaviors were in the normal range. Adaptive behaviors are considered the individual's ability to function in his environment. Currently an IQ test is not the sole factor in determining mental retardation. An assessment of adaptive behavior functioning is required prior to making the diagnosis.

18. B. To assist this student in appropriately interacting with other students during recess, the team should convene to further discuss the student's current behavior needs, a possible assessment of the behaviors, and the behavior plan. Sometimes students with mental retardation demonstrate behaviors that have not been present before and may not have a known reason. When a student has an episode of inappropriate behaviors that emerge, it is important for the team to review the student's program.

19. D. This situation offers an opportunity for the student to learn many skills that will be helpful in future employment opportunities and allows the educator an occasion to observe and informally assess some of the student's learned skills. As the student counts change and works at the register, mathematics skills are needed. Helping with orders and checking inventory utilizes interpersonal and communication skills.

20. D. Skills in the adaptive behavior area are best taught through chained response. By using this method, the individual tasks can be identified through simple steps and then linked together to form a more complex task.

21. **C.** Various studies and samples of the population have proven that the incidence for mental health issues is higher in individuals with mental retardation than the general population by almost three times more. Conditions associated with psychiatric disorders (affective behaviors) increase with the severity of the disability and include extreme behavior disorders, depression, mania, schizophrenia, and obsessive-compulsive-disorder.

22. **A.** Self-advocacy allows individuals to speak about or represent one's own interests and is often taught in the school system to prepare a student for the future. Activities that reinforce self-advocacy may include having a student make a phone call to a local community agency for information or to visit with a community center to express interests.

23. **A.** Prior to 1975, the definitions for mental retardation were very broad, and services for these individuals in schools was rare, except for those with the more mild forms. In the 1900s, the mild form of mental retardation was identified, and in general, the family accepted the responsibility for the education and care of the individual. Those individuals with more severe forms of intellectual impairments were most often institutionalized. Society viewed them as needing custodial care and thought that others should be protected from their behaviors.

24. **B.** Systems advocacy is the fourth type that is recognized, and it involves individuals who form together because they have similar disabilities or similar needs. They may form a group to represent their ideas, their rights, and their interests to community members, school personnel, or the legal system to make changes on their behalf.

25. **C.** The social-emotional area is affected in a family when a member is diagnosed with mental retardation. Most specifically, the family must address concerns about the reactions of other people in their community, their extended family, and their place of work. The family members may have restrictions on leisure time as the needs and care of the member with special needs will take time and money. There are also issues that develop with siblings and other family members who need attention and needs met. It is not an easy situation for the family, and resources should be sought out to assist them.

26. **D.** A modification is a change to the curriculum or an assignment. In this case, it allows the student with mental retardation the opportunity to participate in the general education program. Educators must expect that all students should be exposed to the state and district standards, as well as the outcomes of the curriculum. Each of the examples may be considered a type of modification or accommodation, but for a student with moderate mental retardation, the best option is to draw a picture and write a sentence about each animal.

27. **D.** When working toward resolution of a behavior, it is important to know the reason it exists. The use of a functional behavior assessment will help to identify the cause or the antecedent of the behavior. The goal is to reduce the challenging behaviors and increase the preferred behaviors, but knowing the reasons behind the behavior is the first priority.

28. **C.** Teachers can use a positive reinforcer to address behaviors in the classroom. A positive reinforcer increases the appropriate behavior that is being sought while decreasing the inappropriate behavior. In this instance, a compliment is an example of a reinforcer that positively motivates the student's on-task behavior.

29. **D.** In the studies that Zigler conducted, he found that the majority of individuals with mental retardation exhibited the same five characteristics: low expectations of success, a fear of failure, a need for social reinforcements, outer-directedness, and overdependency.

30. **B.** Low-tech devices under the category of assistive technology refer to those items that are inexpensive and easy to use for the individual with the disability. Out of the list, the pencil grip is considered a low-tech device. It helps students who have motor problems learn to use a pencil properly and eases the task of writing. The laptop computer, a toy switch, and a hearing aid are all more difficult to use and more costly to obtain and, therefore, are considered high-tech devices.

31. **A.** Teachers who have low expectations for students, especially those with mental retardation, tend to put less effort into their teaching. They offer students simple tasks as they do not expect the students will be able to accomplish very much. As a result, students become uninterested in learning, perform with less independence, develop fewer skills, and often acquire self-esteem issues.

32. D. The instruction for students with mental retardation must first target their present levels of performance, be age appropriate, and include aspects of the general curriculum. The activities must keep the attention of the learners and help them be motivated to learn more. Allowing the students to actively respond will keep them interested and on task.

33. B. The best option to promote continued independence and behavior self-monitoring is to suggest that the parents or the student buy a watch with an alarm so a time for a reminder may be set and perhaps a second reminder to be set a few minutes later. Since the student has a strong work ethic, but lacks memory skills, a tangible object such as a watch will help in the application of the learned skill. If the student is being distracted on the way to work, clearly a reminder to go to work should help. The other suggestions listed do offer options, but the watch would be the best based on the needs of this student.

34. D. When a student with mental retardation is placed in an inclusive settings supports are often needed. The primary need is to modify the instruction so the student is working at her ability level. This requires an accurate assessment of the present levels of academic performance, as well as adaptive behavior functioning. Then the team can establish the accommodations, modifications, or adaptations that may be required to support the individual.

35. A. A key element in the instruction of students with mental retardation is training them to generalize skills. When important life skills are taught in a classroom, they also need to be taught and observed in real-life settings and situations. Community-based instruction is one way to manage the instruction in authentic environments.

36. B. Individuals with mental retardation need to learn how to make decisions, as it is an important life skill. To do this, they need many opportunities to make choices. They should begin this skill training when very young by selecting clothing, toys, and food options. Making choices leads to decision making, which is a complicated process. These skills take time to learn and can become more generalized.

37. C. Fragile X is caused by an abnormality in a sex-linked chromosome. The most common form of transmission is from the mother to the son. It is believed that a severe deficiency of a protein that helps the brain function is present in children with this condition.

38. A. Providing a job coach for support temporarily would be a benefit to the student and the best possible situation. Since the student has shown that working the bakery machines is feasible when working alongside another employee, it is probable that the student will be able to perform the task independently with some additional training and support. A job coach would teach the skills while the student is on the job, allowing the student to practice the techniques with coach observation. This will permit the student extra support while developing the skill, time to generalize the task and to work towards mastery of the skill.

39. B. When aiming for the success of students with mental retardation in an inclusive general education setting, it is extremely important for the team members to provide support to one another through collaboration. The best method for assisting the general education teacher is for the special education teacher to provide consultation on a regular basis. The special education teacher can help the general education teacher to understand the disability, to identify the individual's strengths, to review the types of accommodations or modifications to make, and to determine the use of particular learning strategies.

40. C. When young students make errors on pronunciation, especially at the ends of the words, it is fairly common. It is an especially difficult task for students with mental retardation as it is a more detailed task. The teacher and speech language pathologist should focus on the larger word parts and identify word families. For example, the teacher could present the following words both visually and auditorily and the ask the student to say each one: cat, cab, can. The teacher can also present the word families so the student can hear the same sound in each word: fan, can, ban, man.

41. D. The ARC, which stands for the Association for Retarded Citizens, is a national organization that also establishes separate local and state units. It provides information to professionals and parents regarding mental retardation and supports advocacy efforts for individuals with mental retardation.

42. D. Although all of the options should be considered, the one that is most critical is the paraeducator who can assist with the transitions, which are a difficult task for this student. The teacher and therapist could share the management in the third grade, but since the student will be changing classrooms at least four times per day, it will increase the anxiety and may cause additional inappropriate behaviors to emerge. The paraeducator can closely follow the functional behavior plan, and if the student begins to show independence, the paraeducator may be weaned from the program.

43. A. Since the student has a hearing problem, an increased use of visual materials would greatly reinforce the information given by the teacher during concept lessons. Vocabulary word development would also be best supported if provided with visual cues.

44. C. The student would benefit from having words that are personally meaningful to the student, and five would be a new word each day. That may be a challenge, but with the proper selection of words, the student should be able to learn them. Writing sentences could be a difficult, so only two would be required for the week. The other options are certainly possible, but based on the student's needs this would be the best choice to begin with.

45. C. Students with mental retardation who have been successful in inclusive settings often respond well to peers and creating a peer assistant to guide the student in moving to the proper locations will be a simple and less threatening solution.

46. C. Using a daily picture or word schedule provides students who have difficulty remembering the opportunity to learn the routine by recognizing each step, and students should begin to internalize the routine, leading to greater independence. When a conduct chart is available to the student who is exhibiting inappropriate behaviors, the student has a constant reminder that aids in minimizing the inappropriate behaviors. Encouraging the student to carry the schedule from setting to setting and keeping the conduct chart close at hand will greatly improve the situation.

47. A. With the major changes in this student's program over the years, it seems that the speech-language pathologist, the occupational therapist, and the behavior coach are no longer needed to provide related services to this person. The individual has performed well and achieved age appropriate skills in the social, language, and motor areas. Since the student is still in a foster care system, the social worker would be the best selection for a continued service as the individual moves along the community systems. The social worker could assist the student with accessing community resources and being a liaison with the foster care agency.

48. C. When an individual needs a variety of resources, such as those for living, working, and going to school, the best option is to gain access to a group of agencies. Through agency collaboration, where they combine their efforts on behalf of the individual, a person can obtain all of the necessary supports to have a more successful adult experience.

49. D. All of these positions have possibilities for this student, although the best selection for the very first job out of high school is the usher position at the community event center. The other three jobs will have more reading and mathematics requirements than this position. The student enjoys art, music, and sports and has improved in social skills. A community event center offers art shows, concerts, and sporting events, so the student would seem to enjoy being at this location. With the social skill improvement and on target language skills, it would seem that the student would enjoy working with people in a less stressful manner than making change, or expecting a customer to buy art supplies.

50. B. Although all of the technology devices would be beneficial to this student in some manner, the best choice is the PDA and the laptop computer. The PDA would allow the individual to manage schedules and keep valuable information on person at all times. This individual could make lists, maintain an address book, use a calculator, find directions, and make personal contacts via email when out in the community by using a PDA. The laptop computer would offer home and away access to information and to maintain personal contacts.

Resources

At the writing of this book, the Internet sites provided were current, active, and accurate. However, over time, due to the constant changes in the information provided on the Internet, addresses may change. The sites given may change or become obsolete.

Abuse/Neglect

www.thechildabusehotline.com; National Child Abuse Hotline 800-422-4453

www.childabuseprevention.org; Child Abuse Prevention Network

Assistive Technology

www.atnet.org; AT Network

www.resna.org; Rehabilitation Engineering & Assistive Technology Society of North America

www.tash.org; TASH

Development

www.modimes.org; March of Dimes Birth Defects Foundation

www.zerotothree.org; Zero To Three

www.nichd.nih.gov; National Institute of Children's Health and Human Development

Disabilities

www.ericdigests.org; Educational Resources Information Center

http://nichcy.org; National Information Center for Children and Youth with Disabilities

www.ldinfo.com; Learning Disability Information

www.chadd.org; Children and Adults with Attention Deficit Disorders

www.ldresources.com; Learning Disability Resources

Autism

www.NationalAutismAssociation.org; National Autism Association

www.autism-society.org; ASA–Autism Society of America

Behavioral Disorders and Emotional Disturbance

www.nami.org; National Alliance for the Mentally Ill

www.nasoline.org; National Association of School Psychologists

www.nmha.org/children; National Mental Health Association

Learning Disabilities

www.ldonline.org; Learning Disabilities Online

www.ldaamerica.org; Learning Disabilities Association America

www.dldcec.org; Division for Learning Disabilities of the Council for Exceptional Children

www.ncld.org; National Center for Learning Disabilities

Mental Retardation

www.arc.org; Association of Retarded Citizens

www.councilonmr.org; Council on Mental Retardation

www.aamr.org; American Association on Mental Retardation

www.ideapractices.org; Council for Exceptional Children

Early Childhood Information

www.naeyc.org; National Association for the Education of Young Children

www.nieer.org; National Institute for Early Education Research

www.dec-sped.org/; The Division for Early Childhood

Research

http://ies.ed.gov/ncser/; NCSER: National Center for Special Education Research

www.ed.gov/about/offices/list/osers/nidrr/index.html; OSERS: National Institute on Disabilities and Rehabilitation Research

Transition

www.nyec.org/; National Youth Employment Coalition

http://education.umn.edu/nceo/; National Center on Educational Outcomes (NCEO)

www.ncil.org/; National Council on Independent Living (NCIL)